MILLENARIAN DREAMS
××××× *AND* ×××××
RACIAL NIGHTMARES

CONFLICTING WORLDS

New Dimensions of the American Civil War

T. Michael Parrish, Series Editor

MILLENARIAN DREAMS

××××××× *AND* ×××××××

RACIAL NIGHTMARES

THE AMERICAN CIVIL WAR AS
AN APOCALYPTIC CONFLICT

John H. Matsui

LOUISIANA STATE UNIVERSITY PRESS

BATON ROUGE

Published by Louisiana State University Press
www.lsupress.org

Designer: Michelle A. Neustrom
Typeface: Chaparral Pro

Cover illustration: Detail of Civil War-era envelope showing Columbia holding sword and American flag. Library of Congress.

Cataloging-in-Publication Data are available from the Library of Congress.

ISBN 978-0-8071-7482-1 (cloth: alk. paper) — ISBN 978-0-8071-7531-6 (pdf) — ISBN 978-0-8071-7532-3 (epub)

For Chris, Brennan, and Taylor
Honors Cadets, Students of Life

Contents

Acknowledgments

POPULIST POLITICS AND PROVIDENTIAL palavers led me to this topic and carried me through to the finished product. Although I discovered the seeds of this project while a graduate student, the seedling appeared in Lexington, so it is no surprise that the nineteenth-century faculty and families of Virginia Military Institute and Washington College feature heavily in these pages. Crucially, the Brexit referendum and US election of 2016 convinced me that religion and race are still politically relevant.

Happy weeks were spent on the road and in archives to assemble this tome. I am particularly grateful to the archivists of Bowdoin College's George J. Mitchell Department of Special Collections and Archives, the Virginia Museum of History and Culture, the University of North Carolina's Louis Round Wilson Special Collections Library, the University of Virginia's Albert and Shirley Small Special Collections Library, and Washington & Lee University's Special Collections in Leyburn Library.

The Elephant House café in Edinburgh and London's Shepherd's Bush borough provided congenial writing spaces as I composed the final pages. Many thanks go to Gary Gallagher, Steve Longenecker, Nicholas Picerno, and David Silkenat for enabling me to present elements of this work at Bridgewater College, the University of Edinburgh, and the University of Virginia. Mikki Brock of Washington & Lee University generously shared her office and ideas about the history of religion. The pathbreaking conference on the Crusades and the Civil War organized by Matthew Gabriele and Virginia Tech's Religion and Culture Department encouraged me to think across centuries and continents. The Society of Civil War Historians conference in Pittsburgh helped me sharpen my concept of how Virginia and Virginians foregrounded this project; thanks to this meeting I fortuitously met my publisher.

I am grateful to T. Michael Parrish for inviting me to contribute to the Louisiana State University Press series he edits. Ben Platt, then at Basic Books, demonstrated early interest, blowing a "Protestant Wind" into the sails of this project, for which I remain thankful. I met Taylor while drafting this manuscript. May we have many future adventures to share.

××××× PROLOGUE ×××××

The Civil War as an Eschatological Crisis

UNNAMED DEMOCRATS AND REPUBLICANS in Union blue collaborated to compose the most apocalyptic and lasting song of the American Civil War, though Republicans predominated in the final version. The "Battle Hymn of the Republic" had grassroots origins among Union soldiers who sang various versions of "John Brown's Body" as a marching song during the first year of the war.[1] Yet a company of the Sixth Wisconsin Volunteer Infantry led by Rufus Dawes, the great-grandson of Paul Revere's Revolutionary colleague William Dawes, provided the abolitionist Julia Ward Howe with the inspiration for elevated lyrics to replace the soldiers' references to the moldering body of John Brown. Howe attended a review of the Union Army of the Potomac in November 1861. Reports of advancing Confederate forces broke up the review. According to Dawes, while his company marched back to its camp near Arlington at the head of Irvin McDowell's division, one of his sergeants began singing "John Brown's Body" as Howe passed by.[2] One of her companions, abolitionist pastor James Freeman Clarke, turned to her and recommended that she write "some good words for that stirring tune," to which she replied, "I had often wished to do this, but had not as yet found in my mind any leading toward it." Early the next morning Howe woke from a sound sleep in a Washington hotel inspired with just the right words, scrawling "the verses almost without looking at the paper," verses published in the *Atlantic Monthly* the following February.[3] Building upon earthy lyrics set to the tune of a religious revival camp song, Howe emphasized "the glory of the coming of the Lord." The final stanza linked the death of Jesus to contemporary defenders of the Union, inviting them to "die to make men free" just as Christ "died to make men holy," for "God is marching on."[4] For readers familiar with a version of "John Brown's Body," she linked

1

Brown's death with Christ's, positioning his execution at the center of the Christian mission to free enslaved people.

The term "millenarian" appears throughout this text, and I divide American Protestants of the Civil War era into "premillenarian" and "postmillenarian" camps. Those familiar with the Bible may immediately think of the final book of the New Testament. Revelation is a good text to keep in mind as you read this study, for it is also known as the Apocalypse of John or The Apocalypse. For those unfamiliar, Revelation deals with prophecies as to the second coming of Jesus Christ, the divine judgment of humanity, and the end of the world.[5] "Millennium" and "apocalypse" are interchangeable terms for the purpose of my work. I argue that Protestants' wartime political ideology and racial views were closely tied to their religious optimism or pessimism regarding human nature, perfectibility, and end-times (or eschatological) views.

Northern Democrats desired to restore the Union to the status quo antebellum, while Republicans—all northerners in 1861—sought to transform the United States, and especially the southern states, into a free-labor, industrialized nation. So runs the old tale. This text argues that a new twist on the story of fratricidal politics may be found by adding the religious dimension of millenarian eschatology to the well-studied ideological flashpoints between northern politicians, voters, generals, and citizen-soldiers. Most crucially, enslaved African Americans sought freedom, a national change requiring nothing less than a major revolution and the reconstruction of southern society. Southern Democrats pressed for or acquiesced to the secession of slaveholding states to preserve the white man's republic they believed to be threatened by the victory of a Republican presidential candidate elected solely by northern electoral votes.

Religion emerged as a crucial element in the cost, prosecution, and causes of the Civil War in the scholarship of the past two decades. The war's unprecedented death toll presented a crisis of faith for many Protestant Americans, who assumed that a "good death" occurred at home, surrounded by family and involving a confession of faith and hope of heaven, as historian Drew Faust noted.[6] The violent demise far from home of tens of thousands of men, whose bodies often could not be returned home or even identified—lonely deaths without friendly witness of peaceful composure and expressions of familial love—was deeply disturbing. If some took comfort in the civil-religious hope that mortal sacrifice in the service of the nation merited entrance into heaven, many others disagreed with this new dispensation. As Kathryn Lum argued, "disappointed ex-slaves" and "conservative white Christians" continued "to deploy the threat of damnation to solidify group identity and condemn . . . adverse behaviors."[7]

In 2006 historian of religion Harry Stout published a scathing review of the military policies of each belligerent side. While crediting the Union with attaining the moral high ground for (eventually) ending slavery, Stout castigated it for pursuing immoral policies throughout, for failing to abide by the (Christian) just-war tradition. The "right side," in other words, "won *in spite of itself.*"[8] Contemporaneously, Mark Noll argued that the deadly four-year military conflagration resulted not least from a sectional theological crisis that overlapped with economic and political divides. Yet to refer to a "theological crisis" is to limit study to the learned perspectives of seminary-educated pastors and theologians. My concern is with the majority of Americans who—black or white, female or male—were members of Protestant churches or at least regularly attended them. In other words, I emphasize "lived religion," or how ordinary Americans practiced their religious beliefs, instead of the sophisticated theological views of pastors. In an era when the average American listened to three times as many sermons as the six pieces of mail they received, Protestantism had a strong influence on everyday citizens, so that delving into the lived religion of Protestant Americans provides us with an intellectual history of the masses.[9]

If both postmillenarian and premillenarian Christians agreed that the return of Christ was imminent and that their savior's return inaugurated the arrival of heaven on earth, their disagreement over its timing was key to their disparate political stances. Literalist postmillenarians held that one thousand years—the millennium—of peace and harmony must precede the Second Coming. Their premillennial siblings believed this paradise could exist only after Christ's return. Postmillenarians cherished great hope concerning the perfectibility of mankind and their nation prior to their savior's return, while premillenarians held grave doubts about the moral improvement of men or nations via human effort.[10] Pious Protestants hold no monopoly on millenarian politics; the blending of millenarian belief with political ideology can be found in secular movements, such as the thousand years of world dominance the German Third Reich was to enjoy in Nazi cosmology.[11] Setting aside a literal millennium, the French Revolution and Communism emerge as other secular examples. The purpose here is to postulate that, in the context of the Civil War, millenarianism was by definition religious, and Protestant at that. Two distinct millenarian cosmologies were crucial in dividing the major political parties' ideologies, for evangelical Protestants dominated the culture of the Democratic and Republican Parties. Populist religion dominated the nation in the antebellum and Civil War years to an extent not seen again until the Cold War, when apocalyptic fears again drove Americans to church and end-times speculation of a distinctly premillenarian flavor.

Following the eighteenth-century Great Awakening, the majority of American evangelicals subscribed to postmillenarian eschatology, at least in the northern states. There this dominance translated into a duty "to reform the world according to the norms of godliness in order to usher in the millennium and prepare for the return of Christ."[12] These reforms included campaigns to prohibit prostitution and the sale of alcohol, implementation of public schooling inclusive of the King James Bible, and—for the most radical—the abolition of slavery. Political and theological postmillenarianism merged as particularly attractive to pious Republicans and enslaved southerners. Democrats (pro-Union northerners and pro-Confederate southerners) in contrast held to a premillenarian desire to avoid a revolution purporting to bring about God's kingdom on earth by human (Republican) means. This eschatological difference reinforced the partisan divide between northern Republicans and Democrats and exacerbated the existing racial divisions in the Confederate states, with major implications for the war.

Disagreement over human agency was crucial to this eschatological divide. Postmillenarians argued that God expected good Christians to actively perfect the world via moral reform—of self and society—and free-labor ideology. Premillenarians defended hierarchy or racial mastery (or both), leaving some room for earthly improvement via the "slow unplanned operation of social trends," to use Jack Maddex's words.[13] From the 1830s, following the success of the Second Great Awakening revivals in converting the middle classes, northern Protestants increasingly emphasized self-control as the heart of lived religion. As Paul Johnson argued, evangelical men in the free states regularly voted, abstained from alcohol, treated their wives and children with affection, and "spent [their] spare time convincing others that if they organized their lives in similar ways, the world would be perfect."[14] Southern evangelicals—the yeomanry first, then later many but not all elite planters—emphasized mastery, wrote Stephanie McCurry. Evangelical yeomen were hardly egalitarian in their worldview, constructing their identity based on superiority to women and the enslaved. While paternalistic toward family and enslaved people, they could turn quickly violent if their headship was challenged; the same was true for wealthy planters who joined the evangelical ranks.[15] Evangelical religion was "a critical weapon in the sectional propaganda battle," used most particularly to mobilize proslavery sentiment among southern yeomen.[16] David Goldfield held that southern evangelicals embraced "a millennial view similar to the North's" in their use of apocalyptic language to assail enemies.[17]

My thesis dissents from earlier scholarship on antebellum eschatology. In concert with Maddex, Robert Calhoon argued proslavery southerners were postmillenarian, and they "proclaimed without a trace of irony that slavery's infinite capacity for improvement and moral enhancement" made it ideal for observing "the onset of the millennium" within an institution.[18] Proslavery clergy saw "master-slave relationships as intimate and continuous conduits of [applied] Christian spirituality. . . . Optimistic, persuaded of the systemic nature of change in a middle-class culture," Calhoon noted, "yet driven by the specter of what slavery might become . . . , these churchmen equated the moral regulation of slavery with the march of progress."[19] Yet they could not envision a moral world without slavery or at least racial hierarchy, disqualifying them as postmillenarian for this study. It was important to take "mankind as they are, and not as we may desire them to be," wrote one southern theologian. "That there will always be" a propertyless or laboring class, "at least till the millennium," he thought natural.[20] When theology clashed with southern culture, theology changed, while theology changed northern culture.[21] Kenneth Startup noted that the antebellum political and economic crises ultimately reinforced southern clergymen's sense that "theirs was a greedy, unrighteous era," leading to pessimism and anticipation of "final judgment" on the horizon.[22] They presided over secession and justified the Confederate war effort. As a Richmond newspaper noted following disasters at Vicksburg and Gettysburg in the summer of 1863, had the clergy "pronounced . . . against us . . . we never could have carried on the war."[23]

Conflict over public education reinforces my position. Postmillenarian identity in this conceptualization requires faith in education as a crucial ally to the perfection of society, in addition to the traditional Protestant view that basic literacy was necessary for reading the Bible. Although premillenarians could support education for themselves and their allies, it was clear that southern Democrats were willing to keep millions of enslaved people from reading the scriptures for themselves if it also kept them from plotting revolution.[24] Denial of education also prevented poor yeomen from recognizing the oppressive economic system that planters dominated, as Keri Merritt has argued.[25] Postmillenarians raised in impoverished—or enslaved—circumstances, such as Frederick Douglass and Oliver Otis Howard's mother, looked to education as a crucial foundation for advancement for themselves, or at least for their children.[26] Many immigrants also looked to it as part of their rise in American society.

A majority of immigrants to the free states in the two decades before the war began were Roman Catholic, whether German or Irish. Nineteenth-century Catholics in the United States—including native-born Americans like William Tecumseh Sherman's adoptive family—were by and large amillennial. In other words, they did not spend time speculating on the Second Coming, seeing Christ's earthly reign as a present reality rather than a future event. Protestant millenarian belief often hinged upon depicting the Catholic Church and its leaders as demonic antichrists working against Christ's kingdom on earth.[27] Protestant theologians feared the spread of Catholicism on the American frontier by the 1830s as an apocalyptic danger to the survival of the nation.[28] The Catholic hierarchy was comfortable in its status as serving as a conduit between the "church militant" on earth and the "church triumphant" in the afterlife. Irish Catholic immigrants found a congenial home in the Democratic Party, while the numbers of anti-Catholic former "Know Nothing" Protestants who joined the fledgling Republican Party in the mid-1850s reinforced their sense that the new party was a nativist force that augured no good for them.[29] Considering Republicans' millenarian efforts to impose temperance and turn Catholic children into "good" Protestants by teaching them to read the King James Bible in Sunday schools and urban public schools, Irish Catholics in the free states gained an increasingly premillenarian outlook as a form of cultural resistance to a Republican-Protestant revolution.[30] This was exacerbated by Catholics' perception of the economic threat that the abolition of slavery posed. They feared the mass exodus of four million newly freed African Americans to northern cities would exacerbate competition for menial jobs and depress wages.[31]

I argue that postmillenarian ideology came to dominate the northern states during the war years and the nation as a whole following the Union victory in 1865. James Moorhead crafted some of this thesis decades ago with an emphasis on four Protestant denominations.[32] Postmillenarian optimism pervaded the proimperial tendencies of the 1890s, made its peace with the scientific theory of evolution, and ceded its place in American evangelicalism to the dispensational premillenarianism imported by John Nelson Darby during the war.[33]

Most of the Protestants introduced in the pages below belonged to one of five denominations. Baptists, Episcopalians, Methodists, and Presbyterians lived in both slave and free states, while Congregationalists lived almost exclusively in free states, particularly those in New England. The Congregationalists' New England preponderance is not surprising, given that they were the theological descendants of the seventeenth-century Puritans.[34] Of the four national denominations, all but the Episcopalians—the preserve of elite planters and merchants and overrepresented in the antebellum US Army's officer corps—divided over slavery before 1860.[35] If the Episcopal Church had "high" and "low" church divisions, the Baptists and Methodists were decidedly low church, not requiring that all pastors attend seminary. Presbyterians and Episcopalians valued educated ministers, accordingly mandating seminary training for their clergy. Fulfilling their value of an educated ministry, Presbyterians established colleges—Virginia's Washington College, the College of New Jersey in Princeton, Lafayette College in Pennsylvania, and Miami University of Ohio among them—out of all proportion to their share of the national population.[36] One of our postmillenarian northerners was raised a Quaker, a member of the Society of Friends. Unlike most denominations, Quakers rejected an established clergy, emphasizing the spiritual equality of all women and men. They also rejected slaveholding, banishing any members who persisted in claiming other human beings as property.[37]

I selected twelve individuals to represent American Protestant Christianity in its various forms and extremes during the sectional crisis over the "peculiar institution" of southern slavery. Christian readers will no doubt notice the potential for symbolism in this sample size, reminiscent of the twelve apostles, the chief followers of Jesus in the New Testament. I selected them to represent the regions, denominations, and ethnic groups of the antebellum United States. As I endeavor to cover battlefields, (church) benches, boardrooms, boudoirs, and (government) bureaucracies, most of the dozen were not serving soldiers. In this I subscribe to John Adams's view that just as the Revolution was a struggle in the minds of the people and not just on the battlefields, so the Civil War involved a religious conflict fought in the minds and hearts of the nation's evangelical Protestant majority. As with the biblical apostles, these twelve often divided against one another and over how to serve their savior. While five of the major characters were proponents of the Confederacy, they hailed from Border and Upper South states, not just the Deep South. The populous mid-Atlantic states of Pennsylvania and New York were host to three of the seven Unionists, including one partisan of the Democratic Party. Unlike most books about the American Civil War era, half of our dramatis personae are women, including one who took part in combat operations along with black and white Union soldiers.

In addition to these, I selected two peripheral men as prophets. They represent the John the Baptist or Moses of each millenarian impulse, fated to ignite but not direct this war. Moses, for instance, led the chosen people for decades yet never set foot in the promised land, while John Brown did not live to see emancipation. Brown heralded postmillenarian efforts to reconstruct the nation into a brave new world. In contrast, Edmund Ruffin trumpeted premillenarian fears. Brown of course died before the war began, yet his utopian attempt to foment a slave rebellion was a postmillenarian application of Protestant faith that inspired many northerners and the enslaved during the conflict. Ruffin pulled the lanyard on a cannon in Charleston to inaugurate a war started by premillenarian Protestants who feared the results of a democratic election that threatened to destroy their world.

The selection of these women and men overturns the traditional narrative of the Civil War as a military conflict between "North and South." It also shows that political eschatology was not determined by the free will–Calvinist divide in Protestantism; Calvinist Daniel Harvey Hill was premillenarian, while Calvinist Oliver Otis Howard was postmillenarian. Only five of the Protestants were officially involved in the Union or Confederate war efforts. Two (Robert L. Dabney and Leonidas Polk) were clergymen who also served as Confederate officers. Of 31.5 million Americans tabulated in the 1860 census, only one-tenth served in the warring armies of 1861–65 (roughly 900,000 in the Confederate forces and just over 2 million in the Union armies), so it seems appropriate that a majority of the twelve were civilians.[38] By focusing on the eschatological divide between pre- and postmillenarian Protestants, it is clear there were northern premillenarians (Democratic voters) and southern postmillenarians (African Americans). West Point–graduate George Brinton McClellan and fellow northern Democrats shared more in common with opposing general and fellow West Pointer Leonidas Polk than with fellow Union general Howard—another West Point graduate but an antislavery officer with Republican proclivities—on an eschatological level. It is then appropriate to introduce the major characters not by sectional origin, but by eschatological adherence, and to discuss them briefly, two by two:

POSTMILLENNIALS	PREMILLENNIALS	AMILLENNIAL
Anna E. Dickinson	Robert L. Dabney	Charles Hodge
Oliver O. Howard	Daniel H. Hill	
Julia W. Howe	Emma F. LeConte	
Sojourner Truth	George B. McClellan	
Harriet Tubman	Leonidas Polk	
	Margaret J. Preston	

Let us begin with our two prophets. John Brown (1800–59) was born in Connecticut, the direct descendant of Puritans, but spent most of his dramatic life in Ohio, upstate New York, and Kansas. He was a Congregationalist, befitting his Puritan roots, until the 1840s. While other white abolitionists demonstrated interracial solidarity in public but shunned friendship with African Americans in private, Brown consistently lived out his faith. He hired and worked alongside African Americans, invited the self-emancipated to the same (meager) dinner table as his family, and sat beside them in church when other white Protestants shunned their company.[39] Brown's near-contemporary Edmund Ruffin (1794–1865) was his diametric opposite in nearly all things racial and religious. Along with Thomas J. Jackson (the future "Stonewall") and dozens of Virginia Military Institute (VMI) cadets, Ruffin witnessed how bravely Brown faced his execution. Born in Virginia, Ruffin largely evaded the evangelical influence of the Second Great Awakening that made the slave states bastions of Baptist and Methodist Protestantism. Surrounded by death from an early age, he sought to reform Virginia's agriculture but, unlike northern reformers, could not extend his reform mindset to race relations.[40] While Brown's insurrection exacerbated tensions between the free and slave states in 1859, Ruffin fired the first (and arguably the last) shot of the American Civil War. While Brown could not live in a nation where slavery was a positive good, Ruffin could not live in a nation where slavery was rendered an eradicated evil.

Charles Hodge (1797–1878) was the leading Presbyterian theologian in the northern states. Principal of Princeton Theological Seminary, Hodge objected to postmillenarians' social conscience as excessively perfectionistic and tending toward Arminianism (free will doctrine) or outright heresy. Uninterested in eschatology, he serves as our sole "amillennial," or undecided, at least in 1861. He sided with the "old school" in the 1837 denominational divide, rejecting attempts to involve his church in the debates over slavery. Historians credit Hodge's doctrinal conservatism with keeping Kentucky in the Union.[41] Robert Lewis Dabney (1820–98) was born in Virginia and became a Presbyterian pastor in his home state after seminary training in Richmond; by 1853 he was also a professor of theology. A Unionist until his seceded, Dabney served as a regimental chaplain and then as Stonewall Jackson's chief of staff, merging pastoral and martial duties. After 1865 he continued to defend the rightness of the Confederacy's cause by speech and pen, joining Jubal Early, J. William Jones, and William Nelson Pendleton (all fellow Virginians) in crafting the "Lost Cause" narrative, which still influences white southerners' views of the war today.[42] Hodge and Dabney were leading Calvinist theologians with similar theological convictions if different sectional allegiances from 1861.

Daniel Harvey Hill (1821–89) was born in South Carolina but was an influential Calvinist in North Carolina by 1861. He graduated from West Point in 1842, four years before George McClellan and his future brother-in-law Jackson. Following gallant service in Mexico, Hill joined the faculty of Washington College in Virginia for five years before moving to North Carolina, first for a professorship at Davidson College, then later superintendence of the North Carolina Military Institute.[43] The devout Presbyterian saw service in both Virginia and (from September 1863) Tennessee, thanks in part to his difficulties with accepting a subordinate role to anyone he deemed his inferior.[44] Philadelphia native George Brinton McClellan (1826–85) was a member of the West Point Class of 1846 (along with Jackson and George Pickett) and, like Hill, a premillenarian Protestant. His elite upbringing—he began studying at the University of Pennsylvania at age thirteen before his West Point cadetship—and political ambitions linked him to the northern Democratic leadership, the "doughfaces," with predictable consequences as rebellion turned to revolution. This premillenarian class was "so wedded to the status quo of a Southern-dominated Democracy and Union, both politically and philosophically, that they were willing, to openly defy their con-

MILLENARIAN DREAMS AND RACIAL NIGHTMARES

stituencies, actively pursue proslavery policies, and rend their own party" to maintain their ties to premillenarian planters.[45] McClellan could not countenance the possibility that slavery might be abolished in the course of the war. While the senior Union general in Virginia during the first half of 1862, McClellan lectured President Lincoln that the war should be fought according to "Christian" limited-war principles, which meant that slavery should not be abolished in favor of the status quo antebellum, despite the prayers of the enslaved.[46] Ironically, McClellan's sluggishness directly contributed to the postmillenarian revolution and emancipation both he and Hill abhorred.

Harriet Tubman (1822–1913) was born enslaved on Maryland's Eastern Shore. After freeing herself in 1849, Tubman risked several other trips back into slave states to free relatives during the 1850s. Once the Lincoln administration formally made emancipation a Union policy, Tubman joined Union forces in South Carolina to help black and white soldiers liberate thousands of enslaved southerners.[47] Born Isabella Baumfree in upstate New York, Sojourner Truth (1797–1883) was raised in slavery and, like Tubman, remained illiterate throughout her life. Yet by the late 1820s, she found freedom and evangelical faith. Along with several other abolitionists, Truth was a Millerite Adventist in 1843, temporarily turning to premillenarian pessimism. Moving to Massachusetts, Truth (her name from 1843) engaged in antislavery public-speaking tours. She allegedly confronted a despairing Frederick Douglass in 1852. The ambivalently religious if not outright skeptic Douglass argued that the only way for the enslaved to gain freedom was to take up arms "and redeem themselves." Truth replied in front of an abolitionist audience, "Frederick, *is God dead?*"[48] Truth owned property in Michigan and resided there with a group of Adventists from upstate New York by 1861. She helped recruit black soldiers for the army—a grandson served in the Fifty-Fourth Massachusetts Infantry—and continued speaking against slavery, facing antiwar opposition in Indiana. Truth's most dramatic public-speaking moment had occurred in that state in 1858. A mob interrupted her speech. Accused of being a man in women's clothing, she was challenged to allow white women to examine her breasts to prove her sex. She replied that many a white child had nursed from her and opened her dress, inviting the proslavery men to take nourishment as other white men had while infants. If there was any shame here, Truth maintained, it was that of those who attacked her public character.[49] If she could not read a book, Truth declared, "I can read the people," recognizing the importance of supporting an electable political moderate like Lincoln over more authentically postmillenarian politicians.[50] Tubman and Truth represent black postmillenarianism on either side of the Mason-Dixon Line.

Anna Elizabeth Dickinson (1842–1932) of Philadelphia was a Quaker convert to Methodism. If she never saw combat, Dickinson was nevertheless dubbed "America's Joan of Arc" by stumping for the Republican Party and emancipation, thereby persuading thousands of men to exercise the democratic rights denied her to craft a postmillenarian postwar world.[51] Her rhetoric helps represent the lasting frustration of radical black and white abolitionists like William Lloyd Garrison and Wendell Phillips at the reluctance of President Lincoln to act decisively against slavery. Emma Florence LeConte (1847–32) of South Carolina was, like Dickinson, a teenager at war's outbreak. In 1864 and 1865 she recorded in her diary an account of the apocalyptic swathe that Sherman's Union army burned through her home state. Her voice represents the hundreds of thousands of premillenarian women and men who felt helpless at the hands of "Yankee barbarians" despite their fervent prayers in the final year of the war.[52]

Oliver Otis Howard (1830–1909) was a New Englander, a West Point graduate, and a Republican. By 1856 he was a young lieutenant and a supporter of the Republican Party, which made him unpopular with southernborn officers and conservative northerners alike.[53] Maine was the first state to craft a law prohibiting the sale of alcohol, a crusade dear to northern evangelicals, in the early 1850s. Howard's support of this law while a cadet marked him as sympathetic to the antislavery and protemperance Free Soil Party.[54] New England Democrats opposed prohibition. Leonidas Polk (1806–64) was a premillenarian counterpart to Howard. A full generation older than him, Polk was known as a devil-may-care lark during his cadetship until his dramatic conversion at the hands of the academy's Episcopal chaplain opened the floodgates of revival and induced him to choose the ministry over the military.[55] By 1861 Polk was the Episcopalian bishop of Louisiana, founder of the University of the South, and until recently a sugar planter, owning as many as 134 human beings at one time.[56]

Margaret Junkin Preston (1820–97) earned the name "Poet of the Confederacy." Born in Pennsylvania, where her father was a pastor and later president of a Presbyterian college, Preston moved to Ohio and then Virginia as her father successively took up the presidency of two other Presbyterian colleges. It was in Lexington that her younger sister met and married the eccentric war veteran, VMI professor, and devout Presbyterian Jackson. Preston herself eventually married a recently widowed colleague of Jackson's, yet another Presbyterian.[57] Julia Ward Howe (1819–1910) won more-lasting fame than Preston by her pen. Neither a minister nor a college president, Howe's father was a devout Episcopalian banker who funded frontier churches and helped found New York University. Surrounded by literati and reformers from an early age, she dabbled in many of the perfectionistic reform efforts that drew antebellum northern evangelicals, although she rejected her father's Calvinism in favor of Unitarianism.[58]

While these dozen apostles and two prophets are the main focus of this work, dozens of other participants—civilians and soldiers—appear periodically. My veterans—Tubman excepted—achieved high rank early in the war, discounting the experience of most combatants, the common soldiers and volunteer officers. I endeavor by these voices to reply to Walt Whitman's postwar claim that "the real war will never get in the books."[59]

A final note on the chapter titles. Although throughout this text I refer to "apocalypse" and "millennium" interchangeably, the titles imply that an apostle is postmillenarian if referred to alongside the word "millennium," but premillenarian if paired with "apocalypse." This also indicates that those experiencing an apocalypse were experiencing the defeat of their eschatological position in that year, while those facing their millennium were realizing their desired outcome. The name in the title does not mean that the apostle is the focus of that chapter but rather an indicator of its theme.

××××× INTRODUCTION ×××××

Harriet Tubman's (Pre)Millennium, 1850–1859, and the Fugitive Slave Act

HAVING STOLEN HERSELF in the fall of 1849, Harriet Tubman returned to the Eastern Shore of Maryland several times in the 1850s to free her family. By 1859 she was known as a latter-day Moses among abolitionists. Tubman was not waiting passively for a white Moses to lead her people to freedom. As a postmillenarian Protestant, she was bringing about an exodus from Maryland, however small in scale.

A year before Tubman freed herself, the Junkin family moved from Easton, Pennsylvania, to Lexington, Virginia. George Junkin answered a call to leave the presidency of Lafayette College to take on that of Washington College in southwestern Virginia. While living in their native Pennsylvania in 1831, the Junkins hosted a young missionary and his wife who were soon to depart for the South Pacific islands. "It requires strong faith to leave country and kindred," Julia Junkin wrote her sister, "to seek a home among savages, cannibals as they are on the island to which they expect to go."[1] Eleven-year-old Margaret Junkin was impressed with the visitors, and their sojourn with her family sparked a lifelong interest in missions. She later founded the first missionary society in Lexington, though not until after the American Civil War; foreign missions had limited appeal in the southern states, certainly compared with northern Protestant interest in proselytizing the world.[2]

The year 1850 was crucial in the march to an apocalyptic civil war, although Tubman discerned this fact rather sooner than young Junkin. After months of debate, aside from accepting admission of California to the Union as a free state while setting Texas's borders and ending the slave trade in the nation's capital, Congress approved a new fugitive slave law as part of the five bills known today as the Compromise of 1850. Now planters

14

or their deputized agents were empowered to compel white northerners to aid them in the recapture of their mobile property whenever loose in northern states.[3] This crisis point arrived thanks to the agency of enslaved people—African Americans whose premillenarian masters variously argued were too content, Christian, or contemptible to desire freedom—who by the thousands decided with their feet, leaving southern plantations in hope of a better life. Their postmillenarian flights for freedom "came to be seen as a threat to the survival of the slave system," noted R. J. M. Blackett, for their actions "raised questions both about [the legitimacy of fugitive slave laws] and the economic and political system [the 1850 Fugitive Slave Law] was meant to protect."[4]

In 1856, while Charles Sumner's freedom of speech was bludgeoned on the floor of the Senate chamber and antislavery settlers were shot at in Kansas Territory, New England Universalist educator Elizabeth Peabody published a school textbook for children. Known as America's first woman lecturer for her 1827 talks on the "Historical School," Peabody published *Chronological History of the United States* to combine her faith and her vision of history. She possessed a strong sense of the sacred nature of human history, by which one could see "God's conversation with man upon his nature, duties, and destiny."[5] Peabody "read history a different way" from contemporary Christian providentialists like the postmillenarian abolitionist Charles G. Finney, seeing history as "the gradual improvement of the political and religious climate in which the perfected individual self, of which Christ was the avatar, emerges in radiant wholeness." For her, "American exceptionalism, Romantic perfectionism, and Christian language . . . blend[ed] in a unique vision of past and future."[6] Once humanity grasped the mind of God through a proper understanding of history, Americans could make "new [postmillenarian] experiments in the light of truth."[7] They could progress, in other words, and antebellum societal progress was often the domain of Protestant-dominated colleges.

Let us now turn to the ways that several institutions of higher learning—military academies included—educated several of our disciples (including Oliver O. Howard) at the hands of professors such as D. H. Hill, Charles Hodge, and Emma LeConte's father. They also contributed to the mounting crisis over slavery in the 1850s. Only about 1 percent of antebellum Americans—and virtually no African Americans outside of abolitionist Oberlin College—enjoyed even a year at one of these colleges. Yet these hallowed halls—their students, professors, alumni, and intellectual influence on the wider society—were disproportionately Protestant in their ideology and similarly crucial to the ignition and outcome of the war.

Prewar Prophecies

Eighty years after the Continental Congress declared independence from Great Britain, South Carolina politician Laurence M. Keitt accompanied Virginia governor Henry A. Wise to Lexington for the dedication of a bronze statue of George Washington and commencement at the Virginia Military Institute (VMI). On July 4, 1856, Keitt addressed a packed audience in Lexington Presbyterian Church—where church member and VMI professor Thomas Jackson illegally taught enslaved Lexingtonians to read the Bible—about the triple foundations (material, intellectual, and moral) of enduring civilization. While ancient Greece rested on material and intellectual foundations and ancient Israel enjoyed only a moral foundation—and so each perished—the southern United States was based on all three and so endured as a uniquely stable society.[8] Anticipating by two years the argument of fellow South Carolinian James H. Hammond that any viable society required a "mudsill" class of ignorant and unskilled laborers to perform work that educated men disdained, Keitt argued that the southern states' enslaved people enabled planters to enjoy life. He also warned VMI cadets in the audience that life was constant warfare, warfare now threatened against Virginia and her sister states by northern fanatics. Now cadets must be prepared to join the "noble band of saints, martyrs and confessors" who fought for Virginia and against England in the Revolution in a struggle to create yet another new nation.[9] Less than two months before his visit to Lexington, Keitt accompanied fellow South Carolinian representative Preston Brooks into the Senate chamber of the US Capitol to prevent interference as Brooks beat Senator Sumner for attacking slavery.[10]

According to historian Jennifer Green, southern military colleges played a significant role in promoting the growth of a nonagricultural middle class in the future Confederate states, though that class was to remain miniscule compared to its northern counterpart. "Many of the traits that cadets promoted mirrored those of northern evangelical reformers," wrote Green. Yet this southern middle class valued the "northern" emphasis on both education and religion with the added "southern" values of honor and rugged manhood.[11] However much they inculcated "northern" values into their cadets, however, VMI and other southern military colleges mirrored other regional institutions of higher learning in reinforcing white supremacy linked to a determined defense of slavery up to and including secession. A loyal Virginian and Union officer encouraged his commander to destroy the institute in 1864, dubbing it "a most dangerous establishment where treason was systematically taught." This colonel ranked VMI and the University of Virginia as the two most notorious schools imparting "monstrous doctrines" among all "the educated men in the South."[12]

West Point

When one considers that graduates of the US Military Academy at West Point played a disproportionate role in leading the Union and Confederate armies, a word is apposite upon the men who attended the academy and the culture it fostered in them. Well before 1850, West Point banned cadet debates on nullification, yet sectional tensions within the corps grew nonetheless, and by 1860 the cadet battalion was organized into companies according to section.[13] George Brinton McClellan, arguably one of the two most famous members of the Class of 1846, testified to the social influence—if not outright dominance—of southern cadets. The Philadelphia native arrived following studies at the University of Pennsylvania and quickly fell in with his southern peers, including his Virginian roommate Ambrose Powell (A. P.) Hill. "Some how or other I take to the Southerners," he confessed, for "almost all my associates—indeed all of them—are Southerners; I am sorry to say that the manners, feelings, and opinions of the Southerners are far, far preferable to those of the majority of the Northerners at this place."[14]

Oliver Otis Howard arrived at the cliffs above the Hudson River that provide West Point its imposing geographical location in 1850. Howard was already a college graduate, having completed his studies at Maine's Bowdoin College earlier that year. Graduating fourth of forty-six cadets in 1854, the lieutenant soon enough was transferred to the quagmire of the Third Seminole War. If he did not find a foe to fight in Florida, Howard found evangelical Christianity, which he brought along with him when he returned to West Point as an instructor.[15]

Sectional tensions only increased following Howard's graduation from the academy. Emory Upton of upstate New York attended the antislavery and evangelical Oberlin College—the first American college to admit women and African Americans on an equal footing with white men—for two years before transferring to West Point, where Lieutenant Howard taught mathematics. Upton wrote home in 1858 that it was a "hard place to practice religion; though few scoff at it, yet a great majority totally disregard it."[16] A cadet from Virginia noted that North Carolina Presbyterian Stephen Dodson Ramseur—one year ahead of Upton—was the "one professing Christian in the class."[17] Ironically, Ramseur's roommate Wade Hampton Gibbes of South Carolina accused Upton of having black girlfriends at Oberlin, then fought a duel with the junior cadet; the "national significance of the affair was interpreted at once" by the cadets who watched.[18] The duel took place in December 1859 in the wake of Brown's raid and increased sectional tensions.

Harvard

If VMI and West Point were bastions of social conservatism, Harvard College during the antebellum decades was a place for bold young men to declare independence from tradition, starting with Ralph Waldo Emerson's Divinity School Address in 1838. Boston Brahmins like Francis Channing Barlow, Charles Russell Lowell, and Robert Gould Shaw attended the college in the 1850s. Lowell—who was to marry Shaw's younger sister during the war—became the voice of his generation of antislavery elitists when he delivered his class's graduation address in July 1854. "The Reverence Due from Old Age to Youth" reversed the social contract of deference due to wise elders by callow youths from its title forward. Including references to Islam and Hinduism in his discourse, Lowell argued that youth had the requisite intellectual and physical energy to transform society to how it *should* be. The world "always advanced by impossibilities achieved," and if youthful ideas were fragile, they needed nurturing to protect the creative process to produce quality results rather than the quantity that Americans emphasized.[19] Shaw's parents seemed more committed to abolitionism than their son, a generational trend that seemed to bear out between northern antislavery reformers who came of age in the 1830s and their children who entered adulthood shortly before the war. As Shaw complained to his mother, "Because I don't talk and think Slavery all the time, and because I get tired . . . of hearing nothing else, you say I don't feel with you, when I do."[20]

The Prophets

After fleeting views of several colleges that prepared elite youth for careers in military service, teaching, the law, business, and theology, it is time to turn to two men whose school days were long behind them. If already in their late fifties, the radical racial and political views of John Brown and Edmund Ruffin helped inspire younger men and women to take up arms—and Julia Ward Howe to take up a pen—to defend or crusade against slavery. Although these men were well past any societal expectation of military service, they both took up arms to further the causes they otherwise espoused by voice and pen.

If the sectional crisis found them in very different economic circumstances, each man began with similar, agrarian roots—Brown on a farm in Connecticut and Ruffin on a plantation—and they were otherwise recognizable as patriarchs in an Old Testament sense; they each fathered at least eleven children. Several of their adult children perished fighting for the cause so adamantly espoused by their prophetic patriarch.

The year 1859 brought the ideologies of our two prophets to a head. Ruffin, the owner of almost one hundred fellow human beings as of the 1840 census, had spent several decades and much of his own fortune attempting to reeducate his fellow planters to use marl and other agricultural reforms to rejuvenate Virginia's depleted soil. Now he warned against the depletion of the Union's value to southern planters in the face of abolitionist attacks on the "peculiar institution." In January 1859 Ruffin recorded that at last his warnings were receiving their due. "I have had more notice taken on my late pamphlet than on anything I ever wrote before."[21] His proslavery prophecies received far more credence nine months later following the actions of his fellow prophet.

Brown began 1859 a fugitive from justice. Three years before he had risked his life—losing one of his sons in the process—to defend Kansas from proslavery forces seeking to turn the territory into a slave state. The nighttime murder by broadsword of several proslavery settlers led to infamy; his name and face were slapped onto federal wanted advertisements, forcing Brown to seek refuge in Canada while planning the next step in his divine war against slavery. If he secured funding from six prominent white abolitionists—including Howe's husband, Samuel—to mount a raid in a slave state and provoke an armed rebellion, Brown nevertheless failed to recruit Harriet Tubman or Frederick Douglass to his cause.[22] Supposing his mission succeeded—at least initially—these prominent African Americans and others could provide crucial leadership to recruiting and expanding an army of the self-emancipated.

Samuel Gridley Howe was a logical supporter of Brown's venture, for in his youth he was a revolutionary. Three months after he heard the Marquis de Lafayette extol the Greek struggle for independence at the 1824 Harvard Medical School commencement, Howe had sailed for Greece.[23] Although disillusioned that the republican experiment in Greece ended with the intervention of the Great Powers to plant a monarchy, Howe turned to humanitarian reforms closer to home, including educational reforms for the deaf and blind.[24] Howe was nevertheless an active participant in romantic revolutions aiming at postmillenarian progress that his wife, Julia, could only dream and write about.

Brown selected Harpers Ferry, on the border between western Virginia and Maryland, for his raid. The town hosted a poorly guarded US arsenal—good for securing firearms and ammunition for his army—however its location boded ill for raising that army; few enslaved people resided in mountainous western Virginia and Maryland. Brown and his army of twenty-odd men successfully took the arsenal and several hostages, but an escaping Baltimore and Ohio Railroad train brought word to the nation's capital of the insurrection. A company of marines led by Robert E. Lee and J. E. B. Stuart arrived while Brown fatally—or fatalistically—dithered.[25] The arsenal was stormed and Brown captured. Put on trial for treason against the Commonwealth of Virginia, Brown had weeks to transmit his postmillenarian word out to the world through the clamorous press corps, which may well have been the point of his insurrection in the first place. Premillenarian Democrats—whether northern or southern—quickly denounced postmillenarian Republicans for not condemning the raid vociferously enough, possible proof that many of them sympathized with or even had clandestinely supported the insurrection.[26] Ruffin took up on these allegations when he weighed in with his own prophetic publication. Following the unsurprising conviction, Virginia's governor feared that abolitionists might mount a second raid to liberate the incarcerated prophet, ordering several militia companies as well as the VMI cadet corps to guard the execution site.

Ruffin traveled to the execution and reportedly borrowed an overcoat from a VMI cadet to stave off the December chill. Regardless of the reality of rescue efforts, Brown was content to die a martyr rather than live as a fugitive. Although no record exists that our prophets exchanged any words, Ruffin noted that Brown met his end with his convictions intact. Regardless of whether he saw Ruffin in the crowd, Brown as he approached the scaffold warned the world via a note handed to a guard that he was "now quite certain that the crimes of this guilty land will never be purged away but with blood."[27] He knew how to speak truth to power to the very end.

Eloquence was not power, however. Premillenarian fear and thirst for order was in the ascendancy following the raid and Brown's execution, postmillenarian dreams of progress in flight, sometimes literally. Raid financier Howe fled to Canada, fearful of arrest should his role be discovered. While Julia remained "free" in New York, Samuel temporarily joined Douglass and the exodus of other self-emancipated people fleeing the Fugitive Slave Law and the long arm of the "Slave Power" by entering the British Empire.[28]

Inspired and fired by what he saw at Brown's scaffold as well as northern reluctance to condemn his fellow prophet while also anticipating a Republican victory the following November, Ruffin published the novel *Anticipations of the Future, to Serve as Lessons for the Present Time*. He prophesied therein that the 1868 reelection of Republican president William H. Seward resulted in civil war. He chose South Carolina's Fort Sumter as the spot where this fratricidal conflict began, with an attack instigated by southern forces.[29] Ominously, Ruffin chose a quote from Patrick Henry to garnish the title page, though not "Give me liberty, or give me death." No, Ruffin selected "If this be treason, make the most of it" from 1765 to commence his fictional set of letters to the *London Times* from an Englishman residing in the United States. If his fellow prophet was dead, Ruffin perceived that *his* truth—meaning the postmillennial vision that guided Brown to Harpers Ferry—was still marching on in 1860, a crucial election year. Ruffin saw the abortive insurrection as only part of "a widespread conspiracy of northern men," for in death Brown "found general sympathy among the Republican party and throughout the northern section."[30]

In their devotion—or in enemies' eyes, fanaticism—to their divergent causes, Brown and Ruffin resembled nothing so much as latter-day Puritans. Although Ruffin cast off his Episcopal upbringing before the actual outbreak of civil war, his steely determination to defend the hierarchical plantation society he grew up in rivaled the more traditional Calvinism of D. H. Hill and the future "Stonewall" Jackson. As for Brown, he was a direct descendant of Puritans.

Neo-Cavaliers and Neo-Puritans: Legacies of the English Civil War

The English Civil War of the 1640s presents unforgettable—at times tragic—previews to the American version, not least because both sides in both civil wars featured the "hotter sort of Protestants" who valorized their holy crusade while demonizing the other side with their political theology.[31] As David Goldfield argued, the fact that a plurality of white citizens in both sections were devoted evangelical Protestants led to a longer and bloodier civil war than might have otherwise ensued, for both sides were convinced that God was on *their* side.[32] When one looks for latter-day portrayals—or caricatures—of the Puritan of the old country or New England, one need look no further than George Santayana's *The Last Puritan*. Historian Thomas Buell certainly did so as he sought to depict Harvard graduate Francis Barlow to his readers. Like his ancestors in seventeenth-century New England, Barlow "sought perfection. He found shades of gray in people and institutions intolerable, and corruption—especially in government—had to be swept away and society purified."[33] If his mentors at Harvard and in the vicinity of Boston such as Emerson tended to Unitarianism, Barlow was a secular representative of the Yankee heirs of Puritanism that southern Protestants loved to loathe.

The southern cavaliers of the mid-nineteenth century, by contrast, represented to go-ahead Yankees the worst form of luxurious laziness mixed with a temper that could blaze into sudden violence should they deem their property or honor besmirched. Indeed, they represented nothing so much as latter-day supporters of Charles I during the English Civil War to their democratic (Republican) opponents. Although the majority on neither side anticipated this, the Confederacy's alleged martial nature and superior cavalry mirrored the Royalists' dominance during the *initial* phase of the English conflict.

Southerners could hardly resist romanticizing their generals as latter-day cavaliers in the mold of Prince Rupert, if not an even more storied knightliness akin to King Arthur's Camelot. One of Leonidas Polk's relatives viewed the bishop-general as an exemplar of "the spirit of ancient chivalry as handed down to us in the Morte d'Arthur."[34] Polk himself could relate to this romanticism, having in his twenties traveled to the north of England specifically to visit Sir Walter Scott's house.[35] His superior Albert Sidney Johnston was to the Confederacy "as royal Arthur [was] to England's brave romance"—not bad for a descendant of Puritans.[36]

The highest-ranking Confederate field commander to die on the battlefield acknowledged the peculiarities of his Puritan ancestors to his son. "Notwithstanding their follies, their fantastic & ludicrous mental constitution, we no doubt owe" the Puritans "nearly all that is valuable in our glorious form of government," Johnston wrote in 1851. Despite this laudable legacy of representative democracy, he found little "in them to love, but a good deal to laugh at & pity & much to admire."[37] Almost named after the Puritan martyr Algernon Sydney by his parents, Johnston was born in Kentucky, fought for Texas independence, and in 1861 rejected the New England of his forebears in favor of the Deep South of his wife's family.[38] Ironically, there were a few prominent—and notably Calvinist—Confederate leaders like Jackson and D. H. Hill who appeared to have stepped out of the dour mold of Oliver Cromwell. They had few rivals as latter-day Covenanters and heirs to the pious generalship of Cromwell and Philip Skippon among their Union counterparts, except perhaps Howard, Upton, or (in a secular sense) Barlow. Ulysses S. Grant was certainly unprepossessing but not particularly pious or otherwise severe. Yet few rebel officers wanted to be like them; their protégés were outnumbered by the host of young peacocks who emulated J. E. B. Stuart, Wade Hampton III, and John B. Gordon. And of course George Armstrong Custer followed in the wake of the stylish southern cavaliers more than the example of Cromwell's "Ironside" cavalry in his romantic pursuit of glory. Even so, Custer's embrace of new weapons technology, such as Spencer repeating carbines, and the technological innovations afforded by the industrializing northern states—breechloading rifles, ironclad warships, and others—testified to the Union neo-Puritans' love of progress.

A Virginian loyal to the Union lambasted his home state's aversion to progress, believing "the Old Virginia people as a decadent race" who exhibited marked declines in "manners, morals, and mental capacity." It was now "high time that war had come to wipe out this effete race and give this splendid country to a more active and progressive generation."[39] Not all white southern Protestants rejected progress, however.

In his study of "the last generation" of antebellum Virginians, historian

Peter Carmichael argued that elite Virginia men who studied at the University of Virginia or otherwise came of age in the 1850s believed that their state "could pursue progressive economic, political, and educational reforms without sacrificing Christianity and slavery." Yet they were all too well aware that they must avoid the northern states' slide "into spiritual experimentation, racial egalitarianism, and an obsession with materialist values."[40] William R. Aylett told a home-county audience, "The mighty winds which sweep by us on their way to distant lands tell us . . . their moving principle is progress." The 1854 University of Virginia graduate continued: "And shall not we be governed by progress also [and] the law of nature and of God? Yes . . . it *must* be so."[41] Southern intellectuals and their students, Carmichael claimed, portrayed "the South as a religious civilization struggling against an otherwise hostile, godless world. Their defense was not a pathological response to guilt over slavery or a feeling that the world had turned against them."[42] Rather, it was a premillenarian project to defend the Protestant South against the excesses of the polyglot society of Catholic immigrants and Republican perfectionists up north. If many northerners considered themselves Christians, they lacked the slave states' Protestant unity of belief and purpose and so disqualified themselves as belonging to a truly civilized society. A "nation without Religion," wrote David Watson in 1855, cannot "have civilization."[43] Watson's fellow undergraduates at the University of Virginia provided further evidence for this invidious view of northern religion in 1856. Pious students argued that a chapter of the Young Men's Christian Association was necessary in Charlottesville due to the "religious destitution and comparative spiritual, as well as mental, darkness prevailing in an adjoining section of the country."[44]

Young Virginians could embrace progress "with few reservations because they subscribed to an optimistic reading of world history," observed Carmichael. Yet that road to progress was paved with the corpses of those who failed to learn history's lessons. They could therefore interpret "dark periods of world history as moments of purification."[45] Carmichael pointed to the example of Robert Rives's 1859 master's thesis on the Crusades as an instance of faith in the future by hard-won lessons from the past. Rives judged the slaughter of Crusaders at Muslim hands a necessary stage in human progress. "When we consider the character of the majority of those that fell in this war, and reflect that they formed for the most part the very scum of society, it was surely at least a step towards a better state of things."[46] The question remained whether a sustained conflict between free and slave states required the sacrifice of the First Families of Virginia as well as the yeoman "scum," and if such sacrifice would avail their cause.

WHILE IT IS IMPORTANT to consider the large majority of Americans who took no part in combat during the Civil War, it is also helpful to consider the major armies for the macrolevel demographic and religious perspective it adds to our emphasis on fourteen individual Protestants. In considering at least two armies in each war year from 1861 to 1864 (inclusive), particular attention will be paid to their geographic origins, with related demographic, religious, and political ramifications fleshed out where possible. For Union armies, four geographic regions will be held in tension: New England, mid-Atlantic, Midwest, and Border South.[47] Wherever possible, I will further distinguish the urban or rural origins of each regiment. This has ethnocultural implications; regiments of immigrants from Boston, New York, or Philadelphia are likely to be made up of Roman Catholic supporters of the Democratic Party and therefore, for our purposes, qualify as premillenarian. New Jersey was a heavily urban state that split its electoral vote in 1860 and was one of only three states to give its electoral votes to Democratic candidate McClellan in 1864; regiments from that state will be categorized as premillenarian and Democratic.[48] Regiments from upstate New York hailed from a "burned-over" district containing many antislavery evangelical Protestants and so will be categorized as postmillenarian and Republican.[49] The Confederate armies will similarly be disaggregated according to regional origins. Their regiments separate neatly into three regional groupings: Deep South, Upper South, and Border South.[50]

1

JOHN BROWN'S APOCALYPSE
x x x x x 1859–1860 x x x x x

ON THE FOURTH OF JULY, 1859, Massachusetts abolitionist Thomas Wentworth Higginson introduced Harriet Tubman to the annual Massachusetts Anti-Slavery Meeting as "a conductor on the Underground Railroad." He noted that Tubman was known in the South as "Moses," for "that ancient leader, who took men and women into the Promised Land"; she then spoke to great applause from the assembled abolitionists.[1] Harvard alumnus Higginson had already proven his willingness to shed blood—his own or others'—when he participated in the violent attempted rescue of self-emancipated slave Anthony Burns from a Boston jail in 1854. A deputy US marshal was mortally wounded in the melee.[2] Tubman would next meet Higginson in South Carolina under very different circumstances in the summer of 1863.

Tubman spent the day of John Brown's execution in the company of other friends of the revolutionary prophet. Her host noted that Tubman commented that she had given great thought to Brown's public death at the hands of the Commonwealth of Virginia, "and it's cl[e]ar to me, it wasn't John Brown that died on that gallows. When I think how he gave up his life for our people, and how he never flinched, but was so brave to the end; its clar to me it wasn't mortal man, it was God in him." Tubman related Brown's Christ-like death to the Calvary-like sufferings of the enslaved: "the groans and tears and prayers I've heard on the plantations, and [I] remember that God is a prayer-hearing God, [and] I feel that his time is drawing near."[3]

PROPHETS ARE FAMOUSLY INTOLERANT of unrepentant moral backsliders. Even as he awaited execution, Brown allegedly grumbled against Frederick Douglass for backing out of his mission. An admittedly unfriendly witness claimed hearing Brown express this frustration from his cell, at any rate.[4] Brown also attacked the most famous brother of the most famous woman in America. Harriet Beecher Stowe, a daughter of famed Calvinist theologian and slavery moderate Lyman Beecher, was the 1851 author of *the* great American novel of the nineteenth century, *Uncle Tom's Cabin*. Henry Ward, one of Lyman's many children and Harriet's younger brother, was by 1859 the most famous preacher in the northern states. From his New York pulpit, Henry attacked slavery and helped send cutting-edge Sharps rifles in crates labeled "Bibles" to Brown's antislavery allies in Kansas in 1856.[5]

One of Beecher's beneficiaries out west was the "Jayhawker" James Henry Lane. A native of Indiana and a colonel of Indiana regiments during the war in Mexico, Lane arrived in Kansas in 1855. He was both a Democrat and an antislavery advocate, at least insofar as he wanted to preserve the territory for hardworking white men. He accordingly served as the president of the convention that drafted the antislavery Topeka Constitution for Kansas even as proslavery settlers wrote the Lecompton Constitution. He subsequently served as commander of the Free State Army. Lane traveled the western states on a lecture tour that castigated his party's compromises over the future of Kansas and Nebraska. "The failure of popular sovereignty, and, even more important in Lane's mind, the abandonment of the free-state cause" by President Franklin Pierce and Senator Stephen Douglas, led to his secession from the Democratic Party. "Reports of his speeches in Cleveland and elsewhere generate the image of an evangelical revival, where Lane's political conversion seems to mimic a religious one. Lane seemed a sinner admitting his faults and preaching his path to redemption." Yet he "did not denounce traditional Democratic Party principles—he claimed to be a *true* Democrat still—but blasted the current Democratic leadership. To him, *they* were the sinners, *they* had strayed and consequently pulled Kansas Territory—and the nation—down with them." Lane told the crowd that he was educated to find his "democratic principles in the letters of Washington, Jefferson, and Madison, but, he continued, 'were Jefferson now in Kansas, the Administration party would hang him.'"[6]

Following Brown's failed raid, Pastor Beecher backslid, falling into the slaveholders' argument that "so long as a man remains a servant, he must obey his masters," a view to which Lane still subscribed.[7] Brown closely read Beecher's sermon condemning his actions thanks to a newspaper smuggled into his jail cell by a journalist, recording his thoughts on the newsprint. "Why don't Beecher come South to preach?" Brown scrawled sarcastically in response to the claim that religious education was the solution to slavery. "Come on, Beecher."[8]

Another John Brown spent the last week of November guarding the similarly named prophet. A native of Petersburg, this Brown could trace his ancestors to the First Families of Virginia, to brothers "John and Henry Brown," who arrived in the seventeenth century.[9] Artillerist John Thompson Brown expected to face danger or death at the hands of Yankee invaders bound and determined to rescue the insurrectionist. Yet his anxiety did not prevent him from attending "a most excellent and appropriate sermon from a Presbyterian" one morning; that evening he "went to a prayer meeting." If anything happened to him, the militiaman asked his wife—intriguingly named Mary like the revolutionary prophet's second wife—to tell his mother "that I died with the same devotion to her which I have always had, and that I hope I died a true Christian."[10]

WHATEVER TUBMAN AND SOJOURNER TRUTH and thousands of other postmillenarian black Protestants thought of Brown, Edmund Ruffin and millions of premillenarian Democrats begged to differ. If Ruffin no longer said prayers, those of devout white premillenarians ascended to God during the secession crisis to save the Union *and* slavery—or in the case of many southern premillenarians, to save the South with slavery and without the Union should northern postmillenarians be victorious at the November polls. Diehard, or "fire-eater," southern Democrats agreed with their premillenarian prophet that there could no longer be any room for compromise over the safety of slaveholding in the wake of the postmillennial prophet's raid on Harpers Ferry.

Indeed, the sectional compromises over slavery that began in 1819 (if not in 1787)—Missouri, 1850, Kansas-Nebraska—came to an abrupt end with Brown's apocalyptic raid. White southerners abhorred the incendiary egalitarian rhetoric of northern abolitionists yet could console themselves in private that their enemies were pacifist men with long hair or feminist ("unsexed") women with short hair. But Brown was no pacifist. He brought fire and sword to Virginia and promised more violence by his example, antislavery violence previously confined to northern cities as Higginson and other activists sought to free self-emancipated persons recaptured by agents of the "Slave Power." The periodic efforts of prophetic black revolutionaries such as Nat Turner and (possibly) Denmark Vesey too were discounted by southern white premillenarians who presumed African American passivity once a suitably large number of alleged conspirators were executed.[11] Even sympathetic abolitionists like William Lloyd Garrison downplayed the efficacy of political violence while acknowledging that slave rebels had the same justification for armed resistance as the American revolutionaries of 1776.[12]

The fruit of Deep South unwillingness to compromise any further was plucked at the Democratic national convention in April 1860, when sufficient southern delegates refused to nominate the Illinoisan frontrunner and champion of compromise Senator Douglas. Not only did they refuse to bow to further compromise; they sat through fifty-seven ballots and denied Douglas the two-thirds supermajority required for nomination even as he consistently won a majority of delegates.[13] Dozens of these men walked out of the follow-up convention held in Baltimore in June, formed their own southern convention, and nominated a southerner to oppose Douglas and whomever the Republicans chose.

As for the Republicans, the secession of southern Democrats from their own party that summer meant that this was their upstart party's election to lose. Yet Republicans needed to choose a candidate who was not so controversial on the issue of slavery as to lose crucial votes in the western and mid-Atlantic states. The problem remained that both of the frontrunners—William H. Seward of New York and Salmon P. Chase of Ohio—were now notorious on the issue. Seward staked his claim with an 1850 speech in which he declared that there was a "higher law" than the Constitution that justified the admission of California as a free state and could be invoked by others to support armed opposition to the Fugitive Slave Law.[14] Chase was known for defending accused fugitives from slavery in court *pro bono* and for his firm faith.[15] An obscure, one-term congressman from Illinois had calculated back in 1856 that the party needed only to win certain battleground northern states to claim victory regardless of the southern states in 1860. This could be done by winning over nativist voters without adopting a platform that alienated northerners who abhorred nativism.[16] His name was Abraham Lincoln. Unlike Seward and Chase, both former governors, Lincoln lacked a college education. Yet what he lacked in scholastic or elected experience, the western lawyer more than made up for in political acumen.

Lincoln was no evangelical in 1860, let alone an abolitionist. As a child he endured the fundamentalist Baptist faith of his parents, letting off steam by standing on a stump after church on Sundays and delivering mock sermons to his peers that cast the preacher he caricatured in a poor light while offending his father.[17] Considering himself a slave to his father until the age of eighteen—his wages subject to his parents' will until he reached adulthood—Lincoln rejected their hardscrabble, agrarian existence. Years later, on hearing that his father lay on his deathbed, the estranged young man counseled relatives that his sire could find more comfort in his God than the company of his absent son.[18] An autodidact, Lincoln left the farm to gain a legal education and then opened a law practice in Illinois. As his law partner William Herndon noted, Lincoln's ambition was "a little engine that knew no rest."[19] Yet by 1860 he was married, with four sons, to a devout Presbyterian from Kentucky. Mary Todd hailed from a planter family and embodied for Lincoln the upward mobility he strove for. As with the spouse of future Union general George McClellan, Lincoln's wife encouraged her husband to attend church, even if he never formally joined one.[20]

Now in 1860, Lincoln benefited from the fact that the Republican convention was held in Chicago. After numerous ballots, several northern states shifted their delegates to the black-horse candidate from Illinois.[21] If many young Virginians mobilized to defend progress in their languishing home state by protecting slavery, young westerners and northerners marched through their towns and cities as members of "Wide Awake" brigades to champion Lincoln in the first election they were old enough to participate in.[22]

At least as important as the party's choice of candidate was the Republican platform. The crucial leg of their 1860 national foundation was that the presidential candidate must refuse to countenance any further expansion of slavery into new states or territories. This doomed the party's chances with undecided moderates living below the Mason-Dixon Line, particularly former Whigs in the southern states. Moderates who could not accept the southern Democrats' position that slavery must be accepted anywhere and everywhere nor vote for Douglas's northern party of popular sovereignty to determine future slave states thus chose to form a fourth party.[23] They clung to the masts of Constitution and Union.

Even as white Americans looked with hope and anxiety toward the election of 1860, black postmillenarians abroad still awaited any real sign of substantive change through electoral politics alone. If our female apostles Tubman and Truth never traveled outside North America, black male post-millenarians like Douglass traveled to the British Isles, continental Europe, and sometimes even to Africa. Those moving to the western coast of Africa from the 1840s either settled in Liberia—with the questionable support of the American Colonization Society—or worked as missionaries under the auspices of Anglo-American missionary societies. Among those laboring with British ecclesiastical support were Alexander Crummell in Liberia, Edward Jones in Sierra Leone, and Martin Delany in modern Nigeria. Crummell and Jones were principals of colleges intended to educate a creolized African elite and who brought "civilization and Christianity and commerce" to a benighted continent—a most postmillenarian, Anglo-American project. Delany, overcome by premillenarian pessimism in the United States, sought land on which to colonize African Americans and bring Western agricultural reform to Africa, hoping that postmillenarian black nationalism could spring forth from African soil.

Crummell was born in New York to free parents, although one of his grandfathers was kidnapped into American slavery from Sierra Leone. Pastoring an Episcopal church in his native city, Crummell traveled to Britain to raise funds for his poor congregation. While there, British benefactors convinced him to apply for admission to Cambridge University, where he successfully completed his studies to become the first African American Oxbridge graduate. He arrived in Liberia before 1859 as a missionary of the American Episcopal Church, eventually helping found a college.[24] "Indeed," Crummell argued in a tract to combat the hoary assumption that the Old Testament curse placed by Noah upon Ham passed on to his rebellious son's African descendants, "it is an almost foregone conclusion, that the negro race is an accursed race, weighed down, even to the present, beneath" Noah's "malediction. The prejudice against this race seems as wide, as absolute, and as decided, as that entertained by the Jews against the Samaritans" at the time of Christ.[25] Even well-meaning white postmillenarian abolitionists in Britain and New England burdened Crummell with such assumptions of lingering racial curses stemming from biblical events.

A native of Charleston, South Carolina, Jones's father was a self-emancipated tailor whose financial success enabled his son to attend and graduate from Amherst College. By 1841 Jones was in charge of Fourah Bay College in Sierra Leone. From this post in a coastal city, he noted that many of the sea captains who called at the port were "as lawless and violent as any brutal planter in America."[26] A few days after John Brown's raid, Jones wrote his British employers of his wish to take his six half-American children to Germany following the death of his second wife in order to save them from the same illnesses that carried away his wives. It remains telling that he did not consider sending his offspring to the republican United States but to the undemocratic German-speaking kingdoms. Cost might have weighed here, though his first wife was the daughter of a self-emancipated refugee from the American Revolution by way of Nova Scotia and a German missionary; perhaps his in-laws still resided in Europe.[27]

Born in western Virginia as the United States prepared for a second war with Great Britain, Martin Robison Delany devoted the eighteen months preceding South Carolina's secession to travels in western Africa and England. Years before Turner's revolt impelled Virginia to outlaw the teaching of enslaved people to read and write, Delany's freeborn mother moved her children to Pennsylvania due to local disapproval of her efforts to educate them.[28] He entered Harvard Medical School with support from the Massachusetts branch of the American Colonization Society—an antislavery group that problematically wished to send the enslaved "back" to Africa—yet was expelled a year later after white students protested his presence.[29] After four months in Liberia, Delany traveled to Yorubaland in modern Nigeria, spending seven months there and signing a treaty in Abeokuta for a tract of land for their colony. He intended this cotton-cultivating colony as the first station of a "transcontinental railway line, which, when linked with a black transatlantic shipping line, would ignite a commercial revolution throughout Africa and its diaspora."[30] Arriving in England shortly after Douglass departed from a successful speaking tour, Delany found philanthropic hosts who formed an African aid society to fundraise for his Niger Valley project. Chairing the society was Lord Alfred Churchill, also leader of an organization seeking new sources of cotton beyond the slave-grown staple of the southern United States.[31] The highlight of Delany's life occurred in July 1860, when he addressed the International Statistical Congress in London, with Prince Albert in the audience, during which several southerners from the American delegation walked out in protest.[32]

Ironically, civil war in Yorubaland created a four-year period of chaos and renewed slave raiding around the site of the proposed colony—hardly an enticing advertisement for American colonists seeking a refuge from white prejudice. Returning to North America, Delany struggled to find recruits in Canada or the United States.[33] He clung to the colonization mast as long as he could, even as civil war at home excited prospects for emancipation under the American flag. "My destiny is fixed in Africa, where my family and myself, by God's providence, will soon be happily situated," Delany declared as late as September 1861.[34]

In Princeton, New Jersey, theologian Charles Hodge fought for the Union, at least within his already sundered Presbyterian denomination. He devoted more than forty years to editing the *Biblical Repertory and Princeton Review* and, when civil war broke out, was working on a three-volume *Systematic Theology* intended to be the definitive work of scholastic Calvinism, finally published in 1872–73.[35] Indifferent to the timing of the Second Coming—and therefore above the postmillenarian-versus-premillenarian debate—Hodge concerned himself rather with keeping American Presbyterians together.[36] During the 1830s, he held that Christianity unambiguously taught "that slaveholding is not in itself a crime, that it is a mere waste of time to attempt to prove it," and so "it is plain that the church has no responsibility and no right to interfere with respect to the slave laws of the South."[37] Since at least 1849 Hodge, as editor of the *Princeton Review,* publicly espoused gradualism with regards to any reform of slavery, writing in support of a book authored by Kentucky Presbyterian Robert J. Breckenridge—uncle of future US vice president and Confederate general—that argued for gradual emancipation.[38] "A Presbyterian in the Far South"—probably a South Carolinian—attacked both Breckenridge and Hodge for failing to recognize that the "WHOLE SOUTH [IS] WANTING SLAVE LABOR," or at least the Deep South. Besides, "God has doomed the African race to slavery, for ages past, and so far as we can see, for ages to come."[39]

What emerges from the anonymous Presbyterian's condemnation of even such a gradual plan for emancipation as this was the increasing divide between the Border and Deep South. If slavery seemed less and less profitable in Border states like Virginia, Maryland, Tennessee, and Kentucky—as noted with alarm by our prophet Ruffin—it was more and more essential to the economies of states that cultivated cotton such as South Carolina, Louisiana, Mississippi, and Alabama. Virginia and its Border state neighbors were now societies with slaves, while the states of the Deep South were slave societies, several of whose politicians now openly debated reopening a slave trade with Africa.[40] Protestants in the Deep South, including Bishop Polk, dared not criticize this dispensation even if they wanted to.

James Henley Thornwell, a Presbyterian theologian from South Carolina, may well have penned the 1849 attack on Breckenridge and Hodge. He joined more moderate southern theologians such as Virginia's Robert Dabney in assuming that the theological debate over slavery had been won handily by their side. Slavery, they held, "was allowed in both the Old and New Testaments. Paul specifically urges those in bondage to remain in bondage, and in Philemon and elsewhere, he emphasizes servants' duty to obey their masters." Although challenged by black postmillenarians, these men subscribed to the widely held notion that Ham was cursed along with his descendants to slavery, descendants who included Africans and therefore African Americans.[41] Thornwell would consider the democratic election of a Republican in 1860 to be unacceptable, worthy of a sundering of the Union akin to the Old Testament division between Israel and Judah into northern and southern kingdoms lest southern premillenarians prove unfaithful to God. His personal response to secession was to secede editorially from Hodge's *Princeton Review* and establish the *Southern Presbyterian Review*. "The parties in the conflict are not merely abolitionists and slaveholders," Thornwell editorialized during the war. "They are atheists, socialists, communists, red republicans, Jacobins on the one side, and friends of order and regulated freedom on the other. In one word, the world is the battleground—Christianity and Atheism the combatants; and the progress of humanity at stake."[42] In Thornwell's blinkered view, the civil contest was a struggle not between rival eschatologies, but rather a Manichaean conflict between good and evil, and the cause of human progress was decidedly a southern one.

Should southern states secede from the Union in response to the Harpers Ferry raid or a postmillenarian outcome to the 1860 election, it would be up to moderate amillennials like Hodge to try to keep the Border South in the Union. Yet in defending union in Christ over union (or disunion) due to slavery, Hodge was challenged to join one eschatological side or the other. His voice and moderate example was valued to Unionist Calvinists in Kentucky, Tennessee, and Virginia. In the last state Hodge's fellow Presbyterian theologian Robert Dabney taught at a seminary in Richmond while Margaret Preston's father presided over Washington College in Lexington.

If a Unionist, Dabney was sorely vexed by northern abolitionists. Less than two weeks after Brown's execution, he wrote to the secretary of the "so called" American Tract Society in Boston to complain of the unsolicited publications sent him by the society that, while containing "a number of articles of evangelical and wholesome tendency," he discerned were "inserted merely to gild the pill of abolitionism." He objected to the "use of precious gospel truth, to hoodwink simple good people" with "pernicious error."[43] His correspondent closed their heated epistolary exchanges with an observation of his own regarding "a most painful sense of the infatuation that has come upon our brethren at the South especially of the once noble state of Washington, and Jefferson, and Patrick Henry" to shout down any opposition to slavery.[44] Dabney echoed his less restrained colleague Thornwell when it came to the Bible, slavery, and abolitionists. Southerners "must go before the nation with the Bible as the text, and 'Thus saith the Lord' as the answer . . . , we know that on the Bible argument the abolition party will be driven to unveil their true infidel tendencies. The Bible being bound to stand on our side, they have to come out and array themselves against the Bible."[45]

Pennsylvania native and Presbyterian president of Lexington's Washington College George Junkin criticized his young students' increasingly secessionist sentiments and felt besieged, a gloom that grew to despondency following the Deep South's secession from the Union. A devout Unionist, Junkin wrote a Presbyterian minister living near Staunton, Virginia, of his apprehensions. "We are in fearful times," he confessed, "but the Lord reigneth and I have no serious fears for the issue." Junkin referred to Andrew Jackson's resolute determination to preserve the Union during the Nullification Crisis and hoped that no one would be hanged for what he deemed South Carolina's "treason," though "a few deserve it. I have no confidence in man's wisdom; but as" he said at the 1860 Washington College graduation, "God made this government and He will not let man destroy it."[46] Junkin did not anticipate it, but his grown offspring decided to support rebellion, daughter Margaret putting pen to paper to compose poetry to transform secession into a southern sublime.

The recipient of Junkin's Unionist letter, Reverend Francis McFarland, was a cousin to the first northern general to lead an invading army into the Shenandoah Valley in 1861, underscoring the fratricidal nature of this war between Protestants. Philadelphia's Robert Patterson was a descendant of Scotch-Irish Presbyterian immigrants to North America and already a militia general. "I hope Virginia will elect Union men to her [secession] Convention and not follow the lead of Mad Cap South Carolina," Patterson wrote. Echoing Dabney's sentiments, Patterson declared, "We of the North are as much annoyed by the fanaticism and Abolitionism of Massachusetts as you of the South are by . . . the disloyalty of South Carolina."[47]

Margaret Junkin still mourned the death of her beloved sister Elinor, previously married to Thomas J. Jackson. Stiff in public, the VMI professor demonstrated the depth of his love and loss in response to his sister-in-law several months after the loss of their beloved relation. "You and I were certainly the dearest objects which she [Elinor] left on Earth. And if her emancipated spirit comes back to Earth, and sees how we are bound together, and how we have a mutual bond[?] of strong affection for Her," Jackson wrote, "do you not suppose that it thrills her with delight?" He recounted recently standing at her grave and that of his mother-in-law, "both covered with snow: though their bodies rested beneath the cold covering; yet was it not in color emblematic of their spiritual robes of white?"[48]

Junkin may well have been in love with the man who had married her younger sister. Margaret's 1853 letter to her engaged sibling betrayed sentiments that strike modern readers as the outpourings of a teenaged romantic, not someone firmly in her thirties. "However I may be of the opinion that you will not need me so much, if you become a wife, I will not state one jot of my need of you and my clinging to you," she wrote Elinor. "I will endeavor to keep in check my selfishness, and find a pure pleasure in your new happiness and prospects—and instead of not liking the Major because he does the same thing I do . . . [and] believes you necessary to his happiness, I will try and make that a very reason for liking him better." If their mother suspected that Margaret had "a decided dislike of him," it was perhaps due to ambivalence stemming from her older daughter's own attraction for the pious professor, for she admitted to "have vexed you and mother so much in this matter."[49] Regardless, the apparent spinster Junkin married the same year that Jackson remarried, this time to the daughter of the Presbyterian president of Davidson College. Although now two years married to one of the professor's colleagues—with stepchildren and children of her own—she was keen to keep up her writing. A year before her marriage at age thirty-seven, Junkin published her first novel, *Silverwood*. This achievement covered the same socioeconomic changes of upholding traditional notions of honor while adapting to the market economy faced by the final antebellum generation of young Virginians.[50]

Southwest of Lexington, another Unionist fulminated against secessionists. Born in western Virginia, this man gave up his carpentry training when born again at a Methodist camp meeting. Unlike most of the white men discussed so far, he was an Arminian, a Methodist circuit-riding preacher turned newspaper editor, and Whig politician, not a Calvinist. Yet like Dabney and Junkin, William G. Brownlow of eastern Tennessee saw no contradiction in defending the Union *and* slavery. As the election approached, Brownlow allowed that if Lincoln were elected and then attempted to interfere with the interstate slave trade, Congress passed hostile legislation, and the Supreme Court upheld such measures, then he "would take the ground that *the time for Revolution has come.*" He could then advocate "*that all the Southern states should go into it;* AND I WOULD GO WITH THEM."[51] Brownlow had little inkling of his—and George Junkin's—impending (figurative) martyrdom for their Unionism.

Bishop Polk devoted the years immediately preceding the sectional crisis engaged in the mission of promoting southern institutions of higher education—an effort shared by Dabney, D. H. Hill, Junkin, and LeConte—as he looked for a fitting site for an Episcopal university. The sale of his Leighton plantation in April 1854 enabled Polk to turn to a family concern; his father served as a member of the University of North Carolina's board of trustees for over forty years. Father and son corresponded about curriculum development, faculty, and the woeful preparation offered by the southern educational system, which resulted in ill-prepared first-year college students compared to their northern counterparts.[52] A bishop of the still-united American Episcopal Church, Polk partnered with the bishop of Georgia in arguing for southeastern Tennessee, the joint of the Deep and Border Souths, as the best location for the school. Yet this educational union of the southern regions was to be effected in order to shelter impressionable young gentlemen from the radical ideas that abounded in northern colleges.[53] Finished shortly before the presidential election, the University of the South was dedicated by Polk on October 10, 1860, with three trinitarian taps on the cornerstone with a mason's hammer. The bishop intoned the college's purpose: "the cultivation of true Religion, learning and virtue, that thereby God may be glorified, and the happiness of man advanced."[54] Arsonists burned Polk's house near the campus while he was ministering in New Orleans on the night of April 12, 1861, at the same time that cannon fired on Fort Sumter as Edmund Ruffin looked on. Polk's wife, focused on saving possessions, had to be carried out of the structure by an enslaved person, bidding "Farewell, old friends" to their books as she was carried through the library.[55] Although some claimed that abolitionists were to blame, the bishop suspected one or more of his own enslaved people.[56]

His home a smoldering ruin, Polk spent part of the day after Christmas giving unsolicited advice to James Buchanan on the state of the smoldering nation. The bishop advised the lame-duck president that the federal government should allow the Deep South to break away peacefully. He gave no hope for the restoration of the United States, not even "the remotest prospect for the reunion of the two sections as long as slave labor shall prove advantageously applicable to the agricultural wants of the Southern Confederacy."[57] The Republican president-elect might have benefited from reading Polk's bold claim.

Bishop Polk had nearly become the subject of a transatlantic Episcopal brouhaha in the 1840s for his slaveholding at the hands of another bishop, no less than the son of the English abolitionist William Wilberforce. Samuel "Soapy Sam" Wilberforce was composing a history of American Episcopalians and heard on "good authority" that Polk "had taken his old slaves on a visitation, and sold them so profitably that he paid all the expenses of his visitation."[58] Wilberforce intended to include this account in his history until another English divine persuaded him of its untruth. Nevertheless, the book condemned his American cousins for their moral compromises rendering the church "a mighty buttress" of slavery and "certain of its Bishops [as] its reckless and unblushing champions."[59] Slavery also divided Polk's own family. The bishop parted ways with his eccentric brother-in-law Kenneth Rayner, a Whig and afterward a Know Nothing planter-politician, in 1858. In light of the civil war in Kansas and increasing Irish Catholic immigration, Rayner held that voter fraud and machine politics were worse than slavery as threats to the Union, while "the bishop deemed abolitionist agitation as the greatest threat" to the nation.[60]

Presbyterian Daniel Harvey (D. H.) Hill was another worthy champion of southern education and, like Polk, a graduate of West Point. He was also the son-in-law of Davidson College president Robert Morrison, a fellow Presbyterian. In 1859 Hill became the first superintendent of the North Carolina Military Institute. Prior to the college presidency, he was a professor at Davidson College and before that taught at Washington College in Lexington, Virginia, where he met the future "Stonewall" Jackson. From 1857 to 1859

Hill wrote three books: a textbook of college algebra and two religious studies, one on the Sermon on the Mount and the other on the Crucifixion. At least two betrayed concerns about sectional conflict and a strong pro-southern bent. The mathematics text included invidious statements about northerners and abolitionists, while *A Consideration of the Sermon on the Mount* included speculation about a future civil war.[61] On July 16, 1857, Hill became Jackson's brother-in-law when the widowed professor married another daughter of Robert Morrison, sister of Hill's wife. In 1860 he went on a speaking tour around North Carolina, his theme the American Revolution. A Kentucky theologian later alleged that Hill "complained bitterly of the injustice which had been done to the South by the northern historians of the Revolutionary War; and in which he asserted, in substance, that all the battles gained in the Revolution by Northern troops were a series of 'Yankee tricks,' and that the real, hard, open fighting" was endured by southern patriots.[62]

Near Philadelphia, the teenaged Anna Dickinson—a recent convert to Methodism from her Quaker upbringing—began her career as a schoolteacher in Berks County. She was already a published author, at age thirteen winning the approving editorial eye of abolitionist William Lloyd Garrison with her essay condemning the abuse of an abolitionist schoolteacher in Kentucky. Garrison published her piece in the *Liberator* in February 1856.[63] If not yet able to earn a living as a public speaker advocating emancipation, Dickinson auditioned her voice in defense of women in January 1860, when she rebutted a man who scorned women's abilities at a meeting of progressive Friends. Having read about this forthcoming debate on "Woman's Rights and Wrongs," Dickinson attended without parental permission. A "bristling dictatorial man" announced that, while his daughters were the equal of any, they anticipated a traditional, domestic life and were unsuited to a professional career. If Dickinson intended to be a passive audience member, she now sprang to her feet, shook her "slim finger in his face," and exclaimed to the speaker, "in Heaven's name, sir, what else is to be expected of such a father?" She continued in a similar vein until the man fled the hall.[64]

Many miles south of Philadelphia, the almost-teenaged Emma LeConte was minding her diary in Columbia, South Carolina. If her reflections do not reach us until the last hours of 1864, it is appropriate to note her circumstances as secession and internecine war loomed. LeConte's father, Joseph, was a graduate student of natural sciences under Louis Agassiz at Harvard following collegiate studies in his native Georgia and medical school in New York. After stints at Oglethorpe University and Franklin College in Georgia, from 1857 he was a professor of chemistry and geography at what is now the University of South Carolina in Columbia.[65]

George Brinton McClellan was making a good living as a railroad executive in Ohio. He still had ties to the beloved army he had joined in 1842 as a cadet at West Point through his father-in-law, also his former commanding officer. Yet the peacetime army was a place of stagnation, of boredom and hard drinking, of frontier isolation far from family, and of few prospects for advancement—all this had already broken an otherwise nondescript Ulysses Simpson Grant—and so McClellan sought better opportunities in civilian life.[66] His father was already a prominent academic physician in Philadelphia, yet McClellan sought opportunities with the burgeoning railroad companies rapidly building new track in the western states. By 1859 he was chief engineer and vice president of the Illinois Central Railroad, only two years after resigning his officer's commission. Presidency of his own railroad loomed ahead, and beyond that perhaps a career in politics, possibly even the presidency of the United States. McClellan duly stepped into the Ohio and Mississippi Railroad's top job in 1860 and married Mary Ellen Marcy on May 22 of that year.[67]

Antebellum American women were deemed to be naturally more religious than men. This stereotype certainly proved true in McClellan's life and the development of his faith. Until he began courting Marcy in the late 1850s, McClellan neither professed nor exhibited adherence to a Protestant denomination. By 1859 he experienced an evangelical rebirth that altered his worldview. "He openly embraced the rigid Calvinistic dogma of mainstream Presbyterianism, particularly the doctrine of predestination," noted Thomas J. Rowland, convictions that McClellan shared with his wife, whom he called his "little Presbyterian."[68]

Sojourner Truth lacked McClellan's economic prospects and Charles Hodge's learning, though born in the same year as Hodge. She was already attempting to raise children as a single mother on the western frontier while speaking out against slavery. Like Tubman, she knew slavery's brutality firsthand, at least as practiced in northern states. Sold away from her family at the age of nine and known as Isabella Baumfree, she spoke only Dutch when she left her upstate New York home to endure a series of masters. One of her sons was sold illegally to Alabama by an abusive master, and she went to court to (successfully) win back her child, who had already been mistreated in the Deep South. Baumfree "walked off" from slavery in 1826 with only one of her boys. New York ended slavery the following year, though her children were still subject to indentured servitude into their twenties under the terms of the state's gradual emancipation policy.[69]

Officially free, Baumfree was still limited in her economic opportunities when she met Robert Matthews in 1832. Matthews was a messianic figure—known as "Prophet Matthias"—and Baumfree agreed to become a housekeeper for his commune. Although she likely never met the founder of another latter-day religious movement, her erstwhile employer ventured west to meet his fellow prophet Joseph Smith in 1835 as Smith built a Mormon community. Baumfree and Matthias were accused of poisoning one of the commune's members in order to steal from him, although they were acquitted at trial.[70]

Others' religious views might have suffered a fatal blow from so many trials in slavery and the hothouse atmosphere of a cult, yet Baumfree—now Von Wagenen to friends—converted to Methodism and on June 1, 1843, was reborn as "Sojourner Truth." She confided in friends: "The Spirit calls me, and I must go," and so she went, speaking against slavery as an itinerant preacher.[71] She dabbled with Millerite Adventists, but when the end of the world failed to arrive in 1843 and again in 1844, she moved on from that, too, though not from her vocation of antislavery public speaking.

RUFFIN PREPARED FOR CIVIL WAR by moving temporarily to Charleston, South Carolina. After all, had he not written in a fictitious book that war between North and South would begin at Fort Sumter in Charleston's harbor? So let it be written, so let it be done. Prominent Virginians took note of his travels and perspective on the developing situation in the Deep South. Evidently on hand as South Carolina's politicians debated secession, Ruffin returned to Virginia to share what he had seen and heard. "Old Mr Ruffin has just arrived here from the south," one Richmonder noted, and "says that on the 18th of next moth So[uth] Carolina will be an independent nation—without a shadow of a doubt."[72] The prophet was merely two days off in his declaration as to the state's departure from the Union.

2

HARRIET TUBMAN'S MILLENNIUM
× × × × × **1861** × × × × ×

GOD WON'T LET MASTER LINCOLN beat the South till he does the right thing," Harriet Tubman commented in relation to the president's rescinding of General David Hunter's abolition decree in South Carolina. The Union could continue to send "the flower of their young men" to die of fever in the summer and ague in the winter for a year or two or three, but all was in vain until the Union fought to free the enslaved. "Master Lincoln, he's a great man, and I am a poor negro; but the negro can tell master Lincoln how to save the money and the young men. He can do it by setting the negro free." Tubman explained the true way to end the war with a parable. "Suppose that was an awful big snake down there, on the floor. He bite you. Folks all scared, because you die. You send for a doctor to cut the bite; but the snake, he rolled up there, and while the doctor doing it, he bite you *again*. The doctor dug out *that* bite; but while the doctor doing it, the snake, he spring up and bite you again; so he *keep* doing it, till you kill *him*. That's what master Lincoln ought to know."[1]

In 1862 Massachusetts senator and abolitionist martyr Charles Sumner echoed Tubman. Ironically, though, he lamented Union battlefield successes in the western theater; the complete defeat of the Confederacy too early would leave slavery intact. "We are too victorious; I fear more from our victories than our defeats," Sumner confessed to his diary. "There must be more delay and more suffering . . . before all will agree to 'let my people go': and the war cannot, must not, end till then."[2] The senator told an aficionado of English Romanticism from Philadelphia that after Fort Sumter fell in 1861, "I went at once to Mr. Lincoln, and told him I was with him now, heart and soul; that under the war power the right had come to him to emancipate the slaves."[3] Yet Lincoln delayed, despite Radicals' constant pressure. By the fall of 1863, the president referred to Sumner and his allies as "utterly lawless—the unhandiest devils in the world to deal with," for "after all their faces are set Zionwards," Zion being a postmillenarian destination of heaven on earth in a slave-free, reborn nation.[4]

A postmillenarian residing in Urbana, Illinois, echoed Tubman and Sumner when he wrote his brother. "For some years, I have thought the signs of the times indicate the approach of the great millennial day. The hand of providence has been overruling and moulding all the affairs of nations to introduce this glorious event, but," he continued, "one obstacle stared me in the face. How the dark lot of human bondage was to be wiped off this christian nation." The mystery "is solved" by the inauguration of civil war, "for tho this dreadful rebellion springs out of the corruption of the human heart, God is directing the storm to wipe out the lot and before 1865 we shall be reinstated as a nation on a firmer basis of christian and republican principles than before."[5] The would-be prophet was only a few months shy of his prediction, though doubtless his sibling dismissed the notion that the war could last four long years.

MOST UNION SOLDIERS DID not view the war in 1861 in Tubman's racial terms. "As he went off to war, the northern farmer-soldier carried with him certain ideas about what a proper farm should look like. These ideas would be just as important as the gun or ammunition he carried," noted historian Lisa Brady, "especially during those campaigns in which destruction of the southern landscape was an integral part of his military duties." The majority of the farms "northern soldiers encountered in the South differed greatly from those they left back home, even though the majority of landholders across the southern United States were yeoman farmers engaged in subsistence production similar to their northern counterparts. Differences in climate" and other factors encouraged southern growers to develop "a unique relationship with the natural environment that did not draw clear distinctions between nature and culture."[6] Another historian argued that the southern farmer developed a laissez-faire attitude toward nature that led him to become "at best an ambiguous friend to the wilderness, and a positive enemy of orderly development."[7]

Although the majority of northern Republicans did not immediately view the escalating sectional conflict as a war that must result in the abolition of slavery or as a religious war, a majority of those who voted for Lincoln were religious. If by no means all evangelical Protestants—even those living north of the Mason-Dixon Line—voted Republican in 1860, they succeeded in "regimenting the moral energies of evangelical churches more effectively than ever before in the cause of political antislavery and civic purification. It was . . . the Republican party which most successfully focused the moral energy of postmillennialist Protestants and exploited the public discourse they had elaborated over three decades," in the words of historian Richard Carwardine. "In part theirs was a negative discourse of anxiety and paranoia, which played on fears of Freemasons and Catholics as conspirators against the Christian republic, and which contributed to Free Soilers' and Republicans' elaboration of a hated 'slave power.' But evangelical perceptions also" contributed to American politics "a more positive stress on conscience, Calvinistic duty and social responsibility," that is, of individual self-control leading to advocacy of industriousness on a national level.[8]

Northern Democrats desired to distance themselves from their antebellum allies, while still maintaining—and defending—their differences from Republicans. A former Democratic mayor from Maine who distinguished himself at First Manassas at the head of his regiment and then won promotion to brigadier and major general in 1862, Hiram Berry proclaimed from Virginia: "I am a Democrat still. I am not, however, a Southern Democrat, for I find Democracy here nothing less than aristocracy, to make the rich richer and the poor poorer."[9] His fellow political general Benjamin F. Butler, when challenged by southerners who remembered him as an antebellum champion of southern rights, declared, "I am a friend of Southern rights . . . but I came here to put down Southern wrongs."[10]

Now that seven southern states were in the process of seceding from the Union and John Brown's body was "a-mouldering" in its grave, Pastor Henry Ward Beecher executed another 180-degree turn regarding slavery, this time in relation to the restriction of the full teachings of the Bible in the southern states. On January 4, 1861, he claimed that "wherever you have had an untrammeled Bible, you have had an untrammeled people," while in most southern states it was now illegal to teach an enslaved person to read the Bible. "Where you have had a Bible that the priests interpreted, you have had a king," and with kings came hierarchy and slavery. Wherever "the Bible has been in the household, and ready without hindrance by parents and children together—there you have had an indomitable yeomanry, a state that would not have a tyrant on the throne, a government that would not have a slave or serf in the field. Wherever the Bible has been allowed to be free," it has been an agent of progress, carrying "light like the morning sun, rising over hill and vale, round and round the world; and it will do it again!"[11]

If most Union soldiers volunteering for military service in 1861 did not have the abolition of slavery in mind, the most vocal prosecessionist voices in the Deep South linked preservation of slavery with preservation of true Christianity, this linked to proper teaching of the Bible. This stood against Beecher's democratic notion that the Bible could be entrusted to the interpretation of any and all readers instead of only properly educated pastors. Foremost among them was a native of secession-pioneer South Carolina, Reverend Benjamin Morgan Palmer, who was now pastor of New Orleans's First Presbyterian Church. Less than a month after Lincoln's election, two thousand Louisianans packed Palmer's church to hear his political Thanksgiving sermon, entitled "Slavery a Divine Trust: Duty of the South to Preserve and Perpetuate It."[12]

Palmer attacked northerners and particularly reformers for their postmillenarian belief that they could perfect the world, for in doing so they would be substituting man's authority for God's. "The Most High, knowing his own power, which is infinite, and his own wisdom, which is unfathomable, can afford to be patient. But these self-constituted reformers must quicken the activity of Jehovah or compel his abdication," Palmer argued. By declaring independence from this heretical Yankee postmillenarian perfectionism, southern Protestants conserved the classical "idea that Providence must govern man, and not that man shall control Providence."[13] The "providential trust" of southern Protestants was *to conserve and to perpetuate the institution of slavery as now existing.*"[14] General Butler, an antebellum Democratic politician, placed a bounty on Palmer's head when his troops occupied New Orleans in 1862, evidently agreeing with a Confederate nationalist who credited the minister with doing more than "any other non-combatant in the South to promote rebellion."[15]

If the majority of Union soldiers did not volunteer to destroy slavery during the war's first year, a majority of Confederate soldiers did not own enslaved people. Yet many of the nonslaveholding yeoman still thought they were fighting to preserve the "peculiar institution." Southern critics of slavery like Hinton Helper thought this was due to the "absolute ignorance among the non-slaveholding whites" perpetuated by the planter "oligarchy."[16] Free public education "for the masses could possibly lead to a large percentage of white Southerners questioning—or even opposing—slavery," wrote a recent historian of poor whites in the antebellum South.[17] The opposition of planter elites to public education certainly worked in the sense that most nonslaveholding volunteers in the Confederate army believed that the enemy aimed to destroy slavery. "Our poor men of the southern army say [Yankees aim] to free the negro and make" them "equal with the poor man of the southern states and have free mixed schools and a negro can marry a white girl and etc.," a member of the Fourth Virginia Cavalry noted. The trooper concluded that "the men are saying they will wade in blood to their chins before such a thing shall happen to our people."[18] These words lend credence to historian George Fredrickson's *Herrenvolk* democracy theory regarding white southern racism, namely that all white southerners were socially equal by virtue of their ownership of white skin even if economically unequal based on whether or not they owned other people.[19] "We trust the time will never come when the children of the poor white man in Georgia shall be . . . humbled or abased" by emancipation, a Whig newspaper noted a month after the Republican triumph in 1860. If the "slaveholding population would . . . lose money" with the freeing of the enslaved, "the poor white man would lose much more, and what is all in all to him and to every man, viz: the consciousness of political and social superiority."[20]

Slaveholders had no doubt that the war was being waged over slavery, and they joined the Confederate armed forces accordingly. Joseph Glatthaar, the chief modern authority on the Army of Northern Virginia, noted that "Southerners who resided in slaveholding households turned out in disproportionate numbers to fight in Virginia, comprising four of every nine men" who volunteered in 1861.[21] If only one in twelve of Confederate enlisted volunteers in 1861 directly owned slaves, more than half of their officers counted fellow human beings among their property.[22]

NOT COUNTING THE ENSLAVED people themselves, there were roughly as many abolitionists as adult male slaveholders in the United States during the secession crisis of 1860–61. 393,975 masters owned 3,950,528 enslaved persons according to the 1860 Census.[23] Roughly 300,000 Americans—black and white, female and male—answered to the publicly disreputable name of "abolitionist" in that same year.[24] Each group—one dedicated to the expan-

MILLENARIAN DREAMS AND RACIAL NIGHTMARES

sion and preservation of the "peculiar institution" and the other devoted to the curtailment and abolition of slavery—represented (slaveholders slightly more and abolitionists slightly less than) 1 percent of the overall population. Yet these diametrically opposed camps were the most vocal parties in the decades-long national debate over slavery leading to secession and civil war.

Planters—masters owning twenty or more enslaved people—dominated the culture and politics of the seven Deep South states that seceded in the immediate wake of the Republican victory of November 1860. William Scarborough wrote a prosopography of 272 major planters—those owning 250 or more people in the 1850 or 1860 Censuses—demonstrating that "elite slaveholders shared certain common social and cultural characteristics." This cohort enjoyed "large families . . . ; an extraordinary degree of intermarriage . . . ; a cosmopolitan life-style and outlook; surprisingly close . . . ties with the Northeast; an emphasis upon quality education . . . [and] intellectual interests; and not least—a confident belief in God as the omnipotent regulator of human affairs."[25] If more of the grand planters were Whigs than Democrats, by 1856 none of them could accept the new Republican Party or its candidate.[26] If by 1862 Confederate yeomen had cause to decry "a rich man's war and a poor man's fight," more than a tenth of the 272 largest slaveholders (and 167 of their close male relatives) served in the Confederate military, with 13 reaching the rank of colonel or above, of whom 7 (Howell Cobb, Philip St. George Cocke, Wade Hampton III, John Doby Kennedy, Gideon J. Pillow, John S. Preston, and Zebulon York) became generals.[27]

Southerners more generally (and slaveholders specifically) dominated the highest echelons of the US government from the first term of George Washington's presidency through the 1850s, constituting the "Slave Power" conspiracy in the minds of northern abolitionists and Republicans. New York Republican William H. Seward and South Carolina Democrat James H. Hammond could agree by 1858 that "the slaveholders of the South" ran the nation.[28] A supermajority of Deep South state legislators were slaveholders, and their human stake hold—and hence state politicians' personal investment in the defense of slavery—increased in the 1840s and 1850s. For instance, the median slaveholding for Alabama legislators was 9 in 1830 and 9.5 in 1840, which rose to 12.5 by 1849 and 17 in 1859.[29] As historian Leonard Richards noted, plenty of evidence existed that, in addition to holding a lock on the state legislatures of fourteen slave states, slaveholders and their planter elite held disproportionate sway in the three branches of the federal government. Prior to 1864, "the only men to be reelected president—Washington, Jefferson, Madison, Monroe, and Jackson—were all slaveholders," as were the three men who served longest as Speaker of the House, not to mention eighteen of thirty-one Supreme Court justices.[30]

Whether planters themselves or not, Protestant ministers in the slave states contributed significantly to the strident defense of slavery in the decade before Lincoln's election. Pastors like Palmer in New Orleans gifted southern politicians with moral and theological justifications for slavery and secession. Episcopalian priest William Prentiss argued that his congregation stood on a precipice as South Carolina debated secession. "We cannot coalesce with men whose society will eventually corrupt our own," he warned his fellow premillenarian southern Protestants, "and bring down upon us the awful doom which awaits them" for their postmillenarian heresy.[31] Charlestonians, in Prentiss's mind, were placed "between the hearse and the cradle, touching as we do the shroud and the swaddling bands of national death and national infancy."[32] In early 1861 the *Southern Literary Messenger* contained similar language about premillenarian nation birthing. The anonymous essayist argued that countries were "not made, but born" by a sacred process. Indeed, "treaties, leagues, [or] constitutions" were of little import in shaping new governments, and the southern Confederacy could therefore be best understood as a creature "of nature and of God."[33]

Presbyterian minister James Henley Thornwell both condemned the Republican victory in 1860 and helped craft a Presbyterian denomination suitable for the Confederacy in 1861. Lincoln's victory was, in Thornwell's words, "nothing more nor less than a proposition to the South to consent to a Government, fundamentally different on the question of slavery, from that which our fathers established."[34] He also cautioned his fellow premillenarians against assuming that the Confederacy could always triumph on the battlefield, lest drawbacks lead to precipitous despair. By the summer of 1862, Thornwell viewed the victories in Virginia mingled with losses in Tennessee as evidence that it was "presumptuous for any one, independently of a special revelation, to venture to decipher" what he designated "the whole end of Providence."[35]

The formation of the southern Confederacy was a consciously premillenarian revolution against politics. In the words of historian George Rable, the Confederate Constitution "embodied the fundamental paradox of the

Confederate experiment—the bold and at the same time circumscribed attempt to make a conservative or even a reactionary revolution, revolution against the old political system."[36] Unlike postmillenarian Republicans, "Confederates did not believe they needed to make new worlds," Emory Thomas wrote, "they were more than content with the world they already had," a worldview they shared with northern Democrats.[37] Yet there was a significant difference between Confederate and northern Democratic premillenarians, as noted by recent historians of the Confederacy, Stephanie McCurry and Anne Rubin. "Confederates' vision of a perfected republic of white men was something new unto this world," McCurry argued, "the only explicitly proslavery nation-state any agrarian elite ever attempted to build in the modern world."[38] Rubin emphasized Confederate ideologues' linking their revolution to that of 1776, in which polemicists like George Fitzhugh argued that not only were southern premillenarians the true heirs to the Founding Fathers' ideology but also were now improving upon the first revolution. Fitzhugh argued that the improvement was by way of "rolling back the excesses" of the American Revolution driven by John Locke's emphasis on liberty, excesses that were now running rampant in the northern "free" states.[39] But the question remained whether Protestant northern Democrats and Republicans were willing to invade the premillenarian Confederacy and shed blood to preserve the Union.

ON JANUARY 29, 1861, Episcopal bishop of Louisiana and prosecessionist Leonidas Polk wrote to the bishop of New York of his confidence that northern Protestants abhorred a war of invasion to "prevent a separation" of the Deep South states "by force of arms." He continued: "I cannot but think and hope that the good sense and Christian feeling of the North will prevail over passion and pride, and that we shall be saved from such a disaster and be permitted to go in peace. It is our very great happiness to know that the [Episcopal] Church has stood firm, throughout all this contest . . . and that she has not contributed in the very least to the causes which have brought these mischiefs upon us." As noted earlier, in contrast to the other national Protestant denominations, the Episcopalians stood strong in permitting slaveholders access to Communion and pulpits.[40]

Yet in the new year, Polk helped preemptively lead his region out of the Episcopal denomination rather than await the outcome of the secular political division.[41] Not only that but he offended northern clergy of all denominations by accepting a commission as a major general of the Confederacy in June 1861. The secular press soon got into the game as well, *Harper's Weekly* printing a caricature of the "Right Reverend Major-General" riding a rearing horse while attired in clerical vestments, crozier, and sword. A southern correspondent for the *Herald* of London noted that Polk's dual office reminded him unfavorably of the Middle Ages, "when the cowl of the priest was combined with the armor of the warrior" during the Crusades.[42] "We fight," the "mitred major general" informed a Richmond newspaper, "for a race that has been by Divine Providence entrusted to our most sacred keeping."[43] Polk earlier told a fellow bishop: "I believe most solemnly that it is for constitutional liberty, which seems to have fled to us for refuge, for our hearth-stones, and our altars that we strike. I hope I shall be supported in the work and have grace to do my duty."[44]

Although unprepared, underresourced, and not intended to hold the command on a permanent basis, Polk gamely took on his new duty until a better man arrived. His Department No. 2 was vast: "an expanse eventually to include portions of West Tennessee and northern Alabama, the Mississippi counties along the Mississippi River, all of Arkansas and Missouri, and the river parishes of northern Louisiana"—a third of the new Confederacy.[45] Polk made his theology crystal clear to his command in his first announcement, composed to be read not only by soldiers but also by the civilians of his department. The "war which has forced us into arms is not of our seeking. We have protested against it in the fair of mankind. We have been the parties assailed . . . for the assertion of our birthright." This war is "of unparalleled atrocity. We have protested, and do protest, that all we desire [is] to be let alone, to repose in quietness under our own vine and fig tree," the desire of God's Old Testament chosen people. Yet on the "shallow pretense of the restoration of the Union," invaders threatened the South with no "motive except lust or hate." This meant the Confederacy faced a "war against heaven, as well as a war against earth." His soldiers defended "nothing less than the security of civil liberty and the preservation of religious truth" and so fought in "the cause of Heaven."[46] The latter-day soldier-bishop sounded like the crusading clergy of yore. Yet Polk's grandiose words and actions also played preemptively into the hands of Union strategy when he ordered the occupation of neutral Kentucky—driving that state into the Union—rather than allow northern forces to get the jump on him.[47]

ALTHOUGH DEMOCRATS AND REPUBLICANS were united in their wish to keep African Americans out of the war in any martial capacity in 1861, Frederick Douglass and others nevertheless offered the services of military-aged men to the country. If Douglass accepted the dismissive words of northern conservatives that it was "a white man's war," Tubman wasted no words and acted instead to join the Union war effort without white permission. She attached herself to one of Butler's Massachusetts regiments in May—likely as a washerwoman—marching around her native Maryland as the general sought to keep order in the divided state. She then moved with Butler's command to Fortress Monroe on the Virginia Peninsula, between the York and James Rivers.[48] While there, dozens and then hundreds of enslaved Virginians sought freedom under the US flag. Ever quick to scent the political winds, Butler the Democratic politician refused to return the self-emancipated people fleeing rebel masters, confiscating them as "contraband of war," and so a nickname was born. Drawing on her antebellum experiencing aiding the self-emancipated in Canada, Tubman helped the fledgling liminal community as a cook, laundress, and nurse.[49]

As elated as many Deep South men of military age were at the news that their states had seceded in the wake of the Republican victory in November 1860, Mary Boykin Chesnut of South Carolina was increasingly agitated during the first half of 1861. "Oh if I could put some of my reckless spirit into these discreet cautious lazy men," she complained of the Confederate leadership in April.[50] Although a native of South Carolina and the daughter of a planter family, Chesnut nevertheless had her doubts about slavery. "I wonder if it be a sin to think slavery a curse to any land—[Charles] Sumner said not one word of this hated institution which is not true—men & women are punished when their masters & mistresses are brutes & not when they do wrong," she reflected in March. "God forgive *us* that ours is a *monstrous* system & wrong & iniquity."[51] Nevertheless, as her biographer notes, Chesnut "wholeheartedly agreed with [her US senator husband's] view that the southern states must not be dictated to."[52]

With Fort Sumter under bombardment, Chesnut's thoughts turned to both her elite white neighbors and the potential enemies at home. Talking to other white Charlestonian women, she found their explanation that "God is on our side" because "of course He hates the Yankees" excessively facile. Perhaps more worrying was the silence of the enslaved people—60 percent of South Carolina's population in 1860—as the Palmetto State loudly declared its independence with deadly intent in the form of cannon fire directed against a federal fort. "Not by one word or look can we detect any change in the demeanor of these negro servants," Chesnut noted on April 13. "They carry it too far," she groused. "You could not tell that they hear even the awful row that is going on in the bay, though it is dinning in their ears night and day. And people talk before them as if they were chairs and tables. And they make no sign. Are they stolidly stupid or wiser than we are, silent and strong, biding their time?"[53] If elite South Carolinians were careful to avoid talk of the politics of slavery and sectional discord in front of their enslaved people after the rise of the immediate-abolition movement in the 1830s, euphoria associated with the declaration of secession and the outbreak of hostilities loosened their tongues. Time would tell as to how the state's black majority responded to civil war.

As the year drew to a close, Chesnut found herself alone in South Carolina as her husband took up duties with the Davis administration in Richmond. If in the spring she had devoted her attention to her black and white neighbors, as winter weather set in Chesnut turned her mind to her fellow southern elites, so vilified by the northern enemy. Yankee intellectuals like Harriet Beecher Stowe, Horace Greeley, Henry David Thoreau, Ralph Waldo Emerson, and Sumner shared many traits with Carolina planters, who "were educated at Northern schools mostly—read the same books as their Northern contemners, the same daily newspapers, the same Bible" as postmillenarian Republicans. Anticipating Lincoln's second inaugural address, Chesnut continued that her peers "have the same ideas of right and wrong—are highbred, lovely, good, pious—during their duty as they conceive it. They live in negro villages. They do not preach and teach hate as a gospel and the sacred duty of murder and insurrection, but they strive to ameliorate the condition of these Africans" in every aspect of life. "They set them the example of a perfect life—life of utter self-abnegation." Yet abolitionists condemned them as unchristian and proclaimed a superior form of self-denial that consisted of "the cheapest philanthropy trade in the world— easy. Easy as setting John Brown to come down here and cut our throats in Christ's name."[54]

Chesnut also received a lesson in how enslaved Protestants perceived southern Christianity as her personal servant combed her hair one evening. Maria compared the theology of two white pastors with respect to their application of the Gospel on racial lines. One, Manning Brown, a relative of

MILLENARIAN DREAMS AND RACIAL NIGHTMARES

Chesnut's husband, was "a gentleman born—and he preaches to black and to white just the same. There ain't but one Gospel for all. He tells us 'bout keeping the Sabbath holy, honoring our fathers and mothers, and loving our neighbors as ourselves." The other, a Pastor Shuford, "he goes fer low-life things—hurting people's feelings. Don't you tell lies—don't you steal—and worse things yet, real indecent. Before God we are white as he is," Maria argued. "And in the pulpit he has no need to make us feel we are servants, repeating poetry about sweeping brooms to the glory of God."[55] Chesnut commented that she "took up the cudgels for Mr. Shuford," noting that he spent many hours attempting to teach a Sunday school full of enslaved children, and from personal experience Chesnut knew how difficult it was to "teach them, for I have tried it, and I soon let my Sunday school all drift into singing hymns." Shuford's patience with "those imps of darkness" was "sublime" in Chesnut's view, despite the fact that "only God saw or heard him" in his efforts, though she gave little thought to the perspective of the little "imps."[56] For all of her perceptiveness, Chesnut failed to note that black Christians like Maria believed that some white Protestants were hypocrites, with the logical next step being for enslaved people to see themselves as the true Christians and at minimum to seek other (white) Christian allies in time of revolution.

Chesnut's husband, James, was the first US senator to resign his seat—even before his state seceded—but he was less ambitious than his wife to take an active role in the new Confederacy. The Princeton graduate passively awaited the South Carolina Secession Convention to select him as one of the two Confederate senators from the first state to secede. He did act as a volunteer aide to Confederate general P. G. T. Beauregard and in this capacity attempted to convince Major Robert Anderson to surrender his garrison at Fort Sumter in April.[57] Chesnut complained that her husband allowed other secessionist leaders to "persuade him that he can be most use to the country in the Senate," but she wished he would "go in the Army."[58] Indeed, by late May she declared, "if I was a *man* I would not doze & drink & drivel here until the fight is over in Virginia."[59] And after the first major battle at Manassas, Chesnut claimed that if she could convince her husband to take "a colonelcy I will go as a *cook*," despite the fact that such a low-status job was reserved for enslaved people and poor yeoman women.[60] Aggravatingly, her husband refused to ask for a generalship or to actively campaign for a Senate seat, failing to win the seat he thought his by right of his (interrupted) US Senate term from 1858. He instead received a colonelcy in December 1861 as President Jefferson Davis's military aide.[61]

The previous December, a senior cadet at VMI wrote his New England–born mother of his pessimism at the possibility "of any pacific settlement of the questions now at issue between the North & the South." Henry King Burgwyn Jr. blamed the "Republican members of Congress" for this situation and their failure "to show the slightest spirit of concession." The North Carolina native rejected a submission "to the domineering rule of those who arrogantly style themselves the interpreters of God's will."[62]

The Pennsylvania native and Presbyterian president of the other institute of higher education in Lexington despaired over the Deep South's secession from the Union in the winter of 1860–61 and then over Virginia's secession in response to Fort Sumter. George Junkin held to the Puritan-inspired tradition that the United States was a "millennial model" for the world, which would be thwarted—and thereby thwart God's mission—by the division of the nation into two states. "If this nation fails in her vast experiments, the world's last best hope expires," Junkin declared, anticipating President Lincoln's views by two years. He wrote Andrew G. Curtin, Republican governor-elect of Pennsylvania, to plead that his home state show grace to the slave states, for if the free states "apply the hellish torch, or fan the flames" of sectional hatred, Junkin feared lest the North "bury beneath the gray ashes of this temple the hopes of freedom for the world."[63] Following the fall of Sumter, Washington College students began raising secession flags and quoting from secessionist politicians' speeches during Friday orations. Junkin invariably ordered the flags lowered and told each orator "to sit down, sir." He characterized Virginia's belated decision to secede rather than contribute soldiers to subjugate the Deep South as "a rebellion without cause."[64] His students' growing resentment of this undiminished Unionism found expression in references to him as "a Pennsylvania abolitionist" and through graffiti on the columns of a college building that could be seen from his classroom: "Lincoln Junkin."[65]

Two of Junkin's sons-in-law, both professors at VMI, literally next door to Washington College, concurred with his condemnation of ultrasecessionists. John T. L. Preston denounced the "hot haste of South Carolina in seceding" at a public meeting, convinced that "Western Virginia sided with Pennsylvania and Ohio!"[66] His colleague Thomas J. Jackson told his staunchly

Unionist sister Laura, "I am strong for the Union at present," agreeing with Preston's view that "the majority in this county are for the Union."[67]

Margaret Preston joined her husband and erstwhile brother-in-law (Jackson) in seceding from the Unionism of her father during the spring following Virginia's withdrawal. Yet while young men throve amid secession and militarization, for Preston the forthcoming war would be "a long, torturous, unrelenting nightmare."[68] Already forty during the secession crisis, she was pregnant for the second time, giving birth to a son on January 24, 1861. Her stepson William Preston helped raise a Confederate flag over the Washington College campus in defiance of her father's orders. Junkin had publicly burned the first such banner, lofted over the statue of George Washington.[69] Unwilling to continue defending her father once Virginia seceded and after her husband and Jackson sided with the Confederacy, Preston stood by as Junkin resigned from the college presidency and hastily left Lexington—leaving behind his papers and books—accompanied by his youngest child. He paused at the Mason-Dixon Line on May 9, wiping the Virginia dust from his wagon's wheels, akin to the biblical injunction of Christ to his disciples to dust their sandals as a sign of judgment upon leaving a faithless community.[70]

The rector of Grace Episcopal Church in Lexington was an 1830 West Point graduate named William Nelson Pendleton. A contemporary of Robert E. Lee's at the military academy, Pendleton accepted a lower salary than he was used to for the opportunity to minister to VMI's cadets. Unlike President Junkin of Washington College, Pendleton found in Virginia's secession an opportunity to temporarily set aside his vestments to don once more a military uniform in defense of the new Confederacy. The pulpit was filled in 1861 by his cousin Robert Nelson, home from missionary work in China for a furlough in 1859 and whose return to Asia was delayed indefinitely by the outbreak of war.[71] Pendleton's son Sandie (Alexander) accompanied his father to the army. A graduate of Washington College, the younger Pendleton left graduate studies at the University of Virginia to join his father's artillery battery, which was attached to a brigade commanded by former VMI professor Jackson. On June 25 Jackson asked the junior Pendleton—whom the general had known in Lexington and whose religious character raised him in the estimation of the pious commander—to join his staff. Pendleton's father approved the appointment, and Sandie accepted the offer.[72]

West Point was another institute of higher education that witnessed sectional turmoil in 1861. Only 64 of 210 cadets supported Lincoln in the 1860 election.[73] Abolitionists were few and far between in the cadet corps and faced regular harassment from southerners. Emory Upton, "the class genius" of the 1861 graduates, spent two years studying at the abolitionist hotbed Oberlin College in Ohio before becoming a cadet.[74] "I had heard but little profanity before I came here," Upton confessed to Lieutenant Oliver O. Howard (whose weekly West Point prayer meetings he attended), "and on my arrival I was shocked." He always felt best "after the performance of any service or duty, which tends to draw off my mind from worldly things," betraying a Weberian sense of the Protestant ethic, a close ally of postmillenarian Republicanism.[75] Upon quizzing from older cadets as he arrived for his plebe year, Upton "openly and frankly declared that he had been at Oberlin and was an Abolitionist," noted a member of the Class of 1862. "Upton's sincere declaration . . . at once made him a marked man."[76]

John Brown's "army" at Harpers Ferry included two black Oberlin alumni, men Upton knew. The duel he fought with Wade Hampton Gibbes over Upton's alleged romantic partners at Oberlin, shortly after Brown was executed, was the talk of barracks.[77] "It was the most thrilling event in my life as a cadet," Morris Schaff wrote of the duel, remembering "that when the fight was over, I saw Upton's resolute face bleeding."[78]

Sharply departing from antebellum practice, West Point graduated two classes in 1861, one in May and the second in June. The second graduating class did not leave after only three years of education, for they were enrolled under the five-year course implemented by Pierce's secretary of war, Jefferson Davis.[79] The goat of the June class was George Armstrong Custer, who wryly noted that "only thirty-four graduated, and of these thirty-three graduated above me."[80]

THE CONFEDERATE EFFORT to convince or coerce the surrender of the garrison of Fort Sumter in Charleston harbor brought several important premillenarian southerners—or their husbands—together. Edmund Ruffin joined Citadel cadets in pulling the first lanyards to send shells arcing toward the fort on April 12. The aforementioned James Chesnut was a volunteer aide on General Beauregard's staff. On April 13, after thirty-six hours of bombardment, Chesnut convinced the garrison commander Major

Anderson—a proslavery and pro-Union Kentuckian—to surrender. He was joined in this mission by Virginia Democrat Roger A. Pryor, another of Beauregard's volunteers. The son of a Presbyterian minister, Pryor was vocally prosecession and assured a supportive Charleston audience that Virginia would join the Confederacy, but as "the Old Mother of Presidents," the "old lady" was "a little rheumatic" and needed time. "Strike a blow!" Pryor exhorted South Carolinians, and "in less than an hour" Virginia must join "this Southern Confederation."[81] Concerned on the visit to Sumter that he did not belong because his home state had not seceded, Pryor accidentally drank iodide of potassium from a bottle he thought contained alcohol. Although other members of the garrison told the fort surgeon Samuel W. Crawford to let the rebel die, the doctor successfully pumped the man's stomach, claiming that he could not permit Pryor to leave the fort with any US government property.[82]

Despite protestations that they did not desire war or any other direct conflict with the United States, the Confederacy surreptitiously sent agents to convince Virginia and other Upper South or Border South states to join it. It also sent commissioned officers to recruit volunteers in states that had not yet seceded. William D. Pender, an 1854 West Point graduate and North Carolina native—having resigned his commission in the US Army and now a captain in the Confederate forces—in late March arrived in Maryland, where he began recruiting volunteers and "sending [them] South to be enlisted in the Southern Army." He assured his wife: "I merely inspect and ship them. I do nothing that the law could take hold of if they wish to trouble me, but Baltimore is strong for secession, and I am backed up by the sympathy of the first men here. The police, Marshall, and nearly all are with us."[83] Pender was a classmate of Howard's.

Although he missed the battle at Manassas, by late August Pender was the colonel of the Sixth North Carolina Infantry. If pleased with his rapid rise in the Confederate military, Pender was troubled by his spiritual state—the lack of peace to be gained by a conversion experience—an anxiety reinforced by his pious wife. "Honey, . . . I am afraid. I know I am unfit," he wrote on September 19. Pender thought "constantly as I have for some weeks . . . of my sinfulness and how much I need the help of my Savior. I want to keep him and his sufferings constantly in mind, but have failed lately. I read and pray but—oh! I fear to no use." He confessed that he had faith, "but not the right kind. . . . I feel that when I reach [a proper relationship to Christ and] understanding I shall have reached a point, from which I may claim to have started a Christian career. May the Lord bring me to that condition. I will read and pray and try to do good works. If I can do more tell me how that I could feel as you do."[84] Pender bowed to Victorian convention by acknowledging that his wife was more naturally religious—women generally were perceived to be—than her husband and also to a premillenarian conviction or resignation that only God could bring him to true faith.[85] "Honey, continue to write me how to do, and all about religious matters," the colonel requested of her two days later. "I do not think that good works are enough, but I think if a man tries to do good he is more likely to try to love his Lord and Savior, for [if] he follows the dictates of his sinful heart he will never give himself to think of anything but what is sinful. . . . I want to be a Christian," he maintained, to appreciate Christ's suffering on his behalf. Yet "it is a hard, I fear an impossible thing for me."[86]

On October 7 Pender was baptized by Reverend Loomes Porter of Charleston, and although he was still "not satisfied with" his spiritual condition, he credited the "pen and Christian life" of his wife to show him "what I ought to be."[87] As winter set in, Pender undertook "a difficult task, that is to Christianize my [enslaved] boy Joe," his army valet. "He seems to be a good boy and desirous of doing right and says he likes for me to read and talk to him, but he is rather unlearned as a darky would say. If I could bring him to a true Christian condition I should feel that I had done some good in this world."[88]

Ten days before the First Battle of Manassas, a Tennessee newspaper argued that civil war "has converted all of the citizens of each of the Confederacies into aliens and enemies. It has disrupted all church connections and all charitable associations, not previously broken up. It puts an end to intermarriages and traveling into the separate nations. It breaks up all private correspondence and friendship." While inspiring "separate systems of municipal laws," war between the sections also "individualizes the blood and race of each branch," sifting the people and driving "Northern men, with Southern ideas and Southern proclivities to the South, where they properly belong," and vice versa. "The war is thus making the whole people in the South homogenous and the people in the North homogenous."[89]

IRONICALLY, FOR THOSE WHO are familiar with the Union and Confederate armies that contested Virginia from 1862 to 1865, the Union army that marched on Manassas in July 1861 was named the Army of Northeastern Virginia, while the Confederate army defending the banks of Bull Run was the Army of the Potomac.[90] Unlike the legions under Lee and McClellan who clashed from mid-1862, the armies that fought at First Manassas were poorly trained, and uniforms were hardly uniform; many Confederate regiments wore blue, while several Union regiments wore gray.

Considering that both belligerent capitals were located in or bordered upon the commonwealth by May 1861, it is no surprise that the American Civil War's first major battle was fought in Virginia. That state's white Protestants were themselves split in the wake of the bombardment of Fort Sumter and President Lincoln's call for 75,000 volunteers (almost 4,000 of whom were to be raised in Virginia) to suppress the Deep South. Presbyterian theologian Robert Lewis Dabney circulated a Unionist petition—signed by Junkin and Jackson in Lexington along with other professors at the University of Virginia, VMI, and Washington College—calling on Protestants to pray and refrain from hasty actions during the secession crisis. Indeed, Dabney held Deep South fire-eaters to be equally culpable as postmillenarian Yankees in stirring up this calamity. "As for South Carolina, the little impudent vixen has gone beyond all patience," Dabney wrote his mother the previous December. "She is as great a pest as the Abolitionists."[91]

Dabney identified "fear" as "the chief element" of the excitement overtaking his fellow Virginians following Lincoln's election and the secession of South Carolina. He opined that "the duty of a minister, and indeed, of a Christian too, in these times, is that he should be the *brake* on the wheels of the machine, to keep it from running too fast."[92] Considering his defense of the Union during the crisis, one might assume that Dabney voted for the Constitutional Unionist platform. Yet he confessed the week before to a fellow Presbyterian pastor that while "we ministers when acting ministerially, publicly, or any way representatively of God's people as such, should seem to have no politics," he had his own personal politics "and at the polls act[ed] on them." He "voted for Breckinridge, fully expecting to be beaten, and therefore preferring to be beaten with the standard bearer most theoretically correct. But if I had seen that Bell, or even Douglas, had a chance to beat Lincoln, I could have voted for either." Yet while wishing for the Republican's defeat, Dabney did not consider "Lincoln's election . . . [a] proper *casus belli*, least of all for immediate separate secession, which could never be the right way, under any circumstances," confident that the president must suffer a "thundering" defeat in 1864.[93]

"All Southern Christians would deplore an unnecessary rupture of the Federal Union bequeathed to us by our heroic sires, as marring their glorious work, and showing ourselves unworthy of their inheritance," read Dabney's "A Pacific Appeal to Christians." Disunion would cover "the claims of American Christianity and republicanism with failure and disgrace before the world," a warning echoed by George Junkin to his college students.[94] But Reverend Dabney also believed that the commonwealth stood undivided in the face of any external threat. "Virginia is united as one man, in the spirit of lofty defiance," he declared to fellow theologian Charles Hodge, "and this includes all classes."[95] Yet Dabney ignored the one-third of the state's 1860 population who were enslaved as well as the more than 300,000 white western Virginians who resented the long-term mastery of Tidewater planters and remained true to the Union despite Fort Sumter.[96]

Dabney was present with the Confederate army in Virginia as a regimental chaplain from its first major battle at Manassas. He wrote his sister on the day of the first skirmish with the Union army at Blackburn's Ford. Responding to her concern about his safety, Dabney admitted: "There is of course some slight risque of wounds or captivity; but I assure you, I am a *non-combatant,* and intend to remain so. I have persisted in refusing to get any uniform or side arms. I shall make it my business to attend upon the wounded, in time of action, if our Regt goes into" battle.[97] Three days later he could write as an eyewitness to the war's first major fight. "The great battle is fought, our Regiment was briefly but splendidly engaged, and I have kept my promise of acting as a non-combatant, and keeping out of harm's way," the minister wrote to assuage the anxiety of his sister and their mother. "We have gained a great victory. Tell Mama not to be uneasy about me," he reiterated, "for I do not intend to expose my life to danger; I do not consider it my duty." To her concern that McClellan, about to win western Virginia for the Union, was going to reverse the verdict of Manassas, Dabney prophesied what most on either side only discovered in 1862: The general "is very much a braggart. If he penetrates the Valley, his army will be destroyed or captured."[98]

Many miles from the site of the battlefield, the residents of Lexington nevertheless heard the sound of artillery fire from Manassas that July day. If her husband was not present, one of Margaret Preston's stepsons was a cannoneer with the Rockbridge Artillery battery while another was a chaplain with an infantry regiment; her brother-in-law Jackson was slightly wounded while winning his immortal nickname "Stonewall."[99] Although a daughter destroyed her wartime letters to her husband years after the war, his responses survived. John Preston's praise of his wife's prose—which transformed his mundane existence into a mystical shelter where "poetry and romance are real"—spoke to the refuge Margaret took in her writing, with so many male relatives away on military service.[100] He wished he "might be able to wield my sword when in battle, as you wield your pen."[101] Reinforced by spousal praise of her "poet nature," Preston composed a poem "All's Well" in response to her husband's account of sentry duty.[102] Her poetic inspiration kindled—or rekindled—by his absence, in 1862 Preston began composing verse for publication and therefore public consumption.[103]

Less than a month after the Confederate victory at Manassas, Unionist pastors in Virginia were seen in a new light by lifelong neighbors. "A Union man is looked upon as the verriest enemy on earth," a Baptist minister in the Piedmont noted. "I have been threatened with the halter, and am now a marked subject for future operations." All he could count on was the "one truth [that] remains—God is judge and He has a purpose to fulfil. Those whom the Gods destroy, they first make mad."[104] Another Unionist from the same county noted after the war that "the few Union men were denounced by the Rebels as being traitors, Abolitionists and black republicans, and every vile epithet that a wicked heart could imagine & a bitter tongue express." Worse, "some of those persons who call themselves Christians indulged freely in the abuse."[105]

If the first battle did not end the war, it hardened the resolve of northern postmillenarians that the conflict would be an extended one that would involve the divine chastening of the people until its true cause was rooted out and the nation transformed. Electa Dawes, wife of a Massachusetts congressman, was confident that if the army "shall fail once, or twice, they only fail, to the more surely in the end accomplish the deliverance of the captive." Defeat at Manassas was punishment for the "national sin" of slavery; the nation must "bleed to atone for its iniquities" until the government adopted emancipationist policies. "God grant that the day may be soon."[106]

x x x

THE FIVE UNION DIVISIONS commanded by 1838 West Point graduate Irvin McDowell at First Manassas contained fifty militia or volunteer infantry regiments and two regular battalions (one each of US Army and Marines) and was heavily northeastern in composition.[107] Fourteen regiments were from the six New England states, and another twenty-eight regiments were raised in the three mid-Atlantic states.[108] Unsurprisingly when one considers the necessity of defending the extensive Ohio River line west of the Appalachians, the midwestern states contributed only eight regiments, while Border South Unionists were unrepresented at this battle.

The Confederate Army of the Potomac under the Louisiana native Beauregard—a West Point classmate of McDowell—was joined on the eve of battle by Virginian Joseph E. Johnston's Army of the Shenandoah. The combined force contained forty-four infantry regiments. The Upper South was overrepresented in units on this battlefield, with exactly half of the Confederate infantry regiments, although not decisively so in demographic terms, as there were 2.9 million free people in those four states compared with 3.4 million free inhabitants in the Deep South in 1860. Twenty-one regiments hailed from the Deep South, and a single regiment (battalion, actually) from the Border South state of Maryland.

If not included among the forty-four infantry regiments that fought at Manassas, Hampton's Legion merits a closer look. Wade Hampton III was the nephew of former South Carolina governor and senator James H. Hammond of "King Cotton" speech infamy. A conditional Unionist and one of historian William Scarborough's elite planters, Hampton undertook to raise and equip an all-arms legion with his own slave-grown wealth. Within weeks of the fall of Fort Sumter at his native Charleston, Hampton began recruiting six companies of infantry, three of cavalry, and one battery of light artillery.[109] Many of the legion's initial officers and men were prominent Carolina planters, several of whom rose to high command in the Confederate armies, including Stephen D. Lee and J. Johnston Pettigrew.[110] If the Confederate government and its constituent states had trouble paying regimental chaplains, Hampton's elite unit faced no such complication in convincing Episcopalian reverend Anthony Toomer Porter of Charleston to minister to its scions of the plantations.[111] Enough men joined the colors for Hampton's Legion to participate in the battle in northern Virginia.

By no means were all available Confederate forces stationed in defense of Manassas Junction or the Shenandoah Valley in July. D. H. Hill—whose

1842 West Point classmates included James Longstreet, John Pope, and the fittingly named Napoleon Jackson Tecumseh Dana—commanded a brigade in defense of Richmond. Hill commented to his wife in regard to Anna Jackson and herself, "If preachers' daughters fancy military men, they must expect all the uneasiness and anxiety incident to a state of war."[112] Less than three weeks later, his brother-in-law and fellow premillenarian Calvinist Jackson won lasting fame and an immortal sobriquet at Manassas, though his wife faced much anxiety over the next two years.

Although he missed the great battle, Hill played a starring role in the first significant skirmish of the war at Big Bethel, Virginia, bringing him within a few miles of Harriet Tubman and her contraband community. Commanding the FirstNorth Carolina, Colonel Hill took up a position within a few miles of General Butler's outposts outside Fortress Monroe on June 6. His goal was to provoke Union forces into attacking him and so draw them into an ambush near Yorktown. Establishing a well-sited defensive position, Hill drove foraging parties away, alerting Butler to his presence and setting the bait. Butler obligingly planned a double envelopment of the Confederates, with the aid of a contraband scout who knew the area. On June 10 Hill's command repulsed several attacks by a force more than twice its size, inflicting almost eighty casualties while losing only eight men, one of the most lopsided engagements in the war and demonstrating the advantages of prepared defensive works. The ten-to-one loss ratio also seemed to bear out the assumption—including in Hill's prewar mathematics textbook—that one southerner was worth any number of Yankees on a battlefield.[113]

GEORGIAN WILLIAM H. T. WALKER also missed Manassas. An 1837 graduate of West Point, Walker gained fame in combat against Mexico with the Sixth US Infantry before serving as commandant of cadets at his alma mater. A slaveholder and lifelong Democrat, Walker resigned his army commission on December 15, 1860, days before South Carolina seceded, the first regular officer to leave the US Army with the intention of defending his home state.[114] "As God is my judge," he wrote to his hometown newspaper in January 1861, "I will raise 'with uplifted arm' against the rule of a renegade southern abolitionist (Lincoln), let Georgia go as she may in her convention." Even before a state of (civil) war existed, he declared, "I war for the South to govern the South."[115] Walker spent the first months of 1861 as colonel of the Second Georgia Regiment (the commander of the first state regiment was his successor as West Point commandant, William J. Hardee). When the state forces were integrated into the Confederate military in March, Walker was insulted that he was only offered a colonelcy, while men who graduated from West Point after him—like Beauregard—were made generals. By June he was commanding a brigade under his West Point classmate Braxton Bragg in the siege of Fort Pickens near Pensacola, Florida, his pride finally (if temporarily) pacified by promotion to brigadier general in late May.[116] The pastor of the Presbyterian church in Walker's hometown of Augusta—the general's wife and mother attended services there—was Joseph R. Wilson. Wilson had a four-year-old son named Thomas Woodrow Wilson.[117]

By early 1862 General Walker sought a draft exemption for his plantation's overseer, fearing that the absence of so many owners and overseers in the Confederate army would lead to "the destruction of the property and the demoralization of the negroes. It does seem to me that as the country will require to be fed and as the agricultural popu[la]tion is the largest and the country actually requires that crops should be made, that overseers should be exempt" in slave-majority counties. "I am willing to make any sacrifice in the cause individually but the country will be ruined if our plantations are deprived of their overseers whilst the owners are off fighting the battles of the country."[118]

Within a week of the debacle along Bull Run, President Lincoln and General Winfield Scott, a loyal Virginian, turned to George McClellan. The Ohioan was authorized to consolidate the Departments of Northeastern Virginia, Washington, Pennsylvania, and the Shenandoah into the Army of the Potomac on July 26. If he was quickly dubbed the "Young Napoleon," the thirty-four-year-old McClellan was actually eight years older than the real Napoleon had been when the Corsican first took command of an army. By November he had engineered the retirement of Scott to become the general in chief of all Union armies. When Lincoln expressed concern that coordinating armies in several states simultaneously would prove too taxing for any one man, McClellan smugly replied, "I can do it all."[119] The president had good cause to fear for McClellan's competency to command so many men in so many armies; by the end of 1861, there were 192,000 men in the Army of the Potomac alone.[120]

As fall turned to winter, premillenarian pastors turned to prophecy in efforts to link the Confederacy to the Old Testament chosen people. A reverend in a Shenandoah Valley county destined to be part of the new state of West Virginia looked at Isaiah 43 as evidence that he belonged to the predicted "People or Witnesses of the Power of the Lord." He trotted out the tried stereotypes of "the northern people and power, raised up with the images of Spiritualism, Mormanism, Socialism, Free-loveism, Abolitionism, Millerism, and every species of Infidelity." He referred to the controversy of the American interception of a British vessel carrying the Confederate emissaries James Mason and John Slidell to Europe and the British demand that the diplomats be freed to carry on their mission as further evidence of prophecy fulfilment. "Thus we are told to press on in the struggle for our rights and independence. If our cause is holy and just to defend our homes, we should carry out the injunction, 'I say to the South, keep not back'; and by the[se] efforts will 'bring my sons from far, and my daughters from the ends of the earth'—meaning England, France and all Europe." Certain European intervention would then break the blockade so that "ships from all parts of the world will come to our ports . . . and [trade] with us. Then, oh! my countrymen, give God the glory, his mighty power is moving in our behalf." Note the premillenarian, though not yet fatalist, bent to this interpretation of prophecy; Confederates need only "stay their murmurs, and [be encouraged] to stand united" as they awaited the advent of God's deliverance.[121] A soldier from the Valley serving with Stonewall Jackson carried a copy of this printed broadside.

WHILE WE ARE NOT LOOKING closely at any of the armies gathering in the western states during 1861, several units and generals bear a second glance. Two days before opposing armies clashed at First Manassas, the Ninth Arkansas Infantry Regiment was formed. It was known as the "regiment of preachers" or "Parson's Regiment" because it initially counted more than forty pastors in the rank and file, including its original colonel and major.[122] Yet the main western Confederate army was less religious than the one in Virginia in 1861 and 1862, according to historian Larry Daniel. A private in the Fifteenth Tennessee attended a July 1861 prayer service at which one hundred of the one thousand men in his regiment were present. "Such is the proportion of God fearing men in the camp," he averred.[123] When President

Davis called a national day of fasting and prayer in November, a lieutenant stationed at Bowling Green, Kentucky, noted: "There was very little of it done in our Reg. as well as others."[124]

Aside from Leonidas Polk, another pious Confederate general in the western army was Alexander P. Stewart. An antisecession Whig and 1842 West Point graduate—his roommate was the now-Republican and Kentucky native John Pope—neither he nor his family owned enslaved people, which made him an oddity among western division and corps commanders in 1863 and 1864.[125] As a West Point plebe Stewart had had doubts about religion, as he confessed to his sister.[126] But while teaching at Cumberland University's School of Engineering in the 1850s, he went through an old-fashioned revival conversion. Stewart was soon well known as a deeply pious man and organized the first college chapter of the Young Men's Christian Association at Cumberland.[127]

FARTHER WEST THAN the Union armies organizing in Ohio under Ulysses S. Grant and other West Point graduates and the rebel forces gathering in Tennessee under Polk and other West Pointers pledged to the Confederate cause, Republican generals tested the boundaries of limited war. John Charles Frémont was the Republican Party's first presidential candidate in 1856. Now he commanded the Union forces in Missouri. In late August 1861—less than three weeks after the disastrous Battle of Wilson's Creek in the southwestern part of the state—Frémont issued a unilateral emancipation proclamation, freeing the enslaved people claimed by Confederate masters in Missouri by military decree.[128] Lincoln attempted to privately convince his fellow Republican to quietly rescind the order in preference to a presidential override and public reprimand of a general in the field. Distance prevented Republican general and Republican president from meeting face to face. "I can but think that if the President had had one interview with Mr. Fremont there never would have grown up this state of injury to the public service," Jessie Benton Frémont later wrote Superintendent of Army Nurses Dorothea L. Dix.[129]

Conservative Republicans, including the Blair family of Maryland, warned Lincoln that Frémont's proclamation could not be allowed to stand, or pro-Union *and* proslavery citizens in Kentucky and Missouri might switch sides.[130] Frémont's wife—the daughter of former senator Thomas H. Benton of Missouri—met Lincoln in the White House, astonishing and offending the president, who argued that the general "should never have dragged the Negro into the war," with her forthright political advice and strongmindedness.[131] Crediting Lincoln with a "good brain and bad heart that made [him] so unjust and deaf to me," Jessie Frémont noted that the "lost time" surrendered by the president could "never be regained for the country." Republican generals like her husband could not "well afford to wait" until the nation recognized that slavery must be destroyed, she believed, referring to scripture in support: "While it is yet day the work should be done."[132] Jessie Frémont interpreted John 9:4 in a postmillenarian, Republican sense that faithful Christians had a duty to live faithfully and not squander the daylight, for night would soon fall, and with it would come judgment.

Next door to Frémont's postmillenarian project in Missouri, abolitionist Augustus Wattles endeavored to bring the Gospel to Native Americans. Fellow abolitionist Sarah M. Grimké wrote to Wattles's daughter Sarah, who had until recently been a pupil at the reformist boarding school run by Grimké's sister, Angelina, and her husband, Theodore Weld, in Eagleswood, New Jersey. Now that war was joined over slavery, Weld's old colleagues begged him to return to lecturing—he had destroyed his oratory voice with a strenuous antislavery speaking campaign in the mid-1830s—but "abolition's golden trumpet" declined to participate.[133] Grimke mentioned two of the sons of the first antislavery presidential candidate, James G. Birney. The youngest Birney son, Fitzhugh, had been a student at the Grimke-Weld progressive school but now was a lieutenant in the Twenty-Third Pennsylvania, commanded by the elder brother, Colonel David Bell Birney.[134]

Well to the south of Virginia, Union forces occupied the Sea Islands of South Carolina, where cotton agriculture had first been introduced in British North America and long-staple cotton, which could be processed without the use of a cotton (en)gin(e), thrived.[135] In early November 1861, Union naval and ground forces, most importantly three brigades of more than ten thousand infantry under General Thomas W. Sherman of Rhode Island, occupied Port Royal and surrounding islands. Left behind by Confederate forces in their hasty evacuation were thousands of enslaved people and thousands of acres of cotton ripe for picking and processing.[136]

If General Sherman was keen to avoid a radical transformation of Sea Island society—planters could return unmolested so long as they pledged allegiance to the Constitution—black islanders wasted little time before beginning their own revolution in Union-occupied territory. Many gins on white-abandoned plantations were broken in a postmillenarian initiative to prevent the cotton that lay ready to pick from being processed, and some enslaved residents no doubt dared hope that freedom followed the US flag.[137]

A volunteer officer in Sherman's force—another Rhode Islander—contacted the former governor of Ohio and present Treasury secretary Salmon P. Chase, whose department was responsible for the abandoned property. Chase had hoped to be the 1860 Republican presidential candidate, but his reputation as the legal advocate of the self-emancipated in Ohio (in direct combat against the 1850 Fugitive Slave Law) preceded him, and a more moderate candidate was deemed necessary to be nationally viable.[138] William H. Reynolds of the First Rhode Island Artillery, the "religiously principled" antebellum leader of his state's cotton trade, used Governor William Sprague—who would marry Chase's daughter Kate in 1863—to convince the secretary that the US government should intervene; contraband cotton should be picked by contraband labor. Lieutenant Colonel Reynolds was duly appointed the US agent to collect the Sea Island cotton by December 20.[139] Invited by Massachusetts governor John Andrew, Harriet Tubman joined this postmillenarian experiment the following April, along with dozens of postmillenarian volunteers from the state sent to teach or otherwise aid the islands' black population.[140]

Secretary Chase's presidential ambitions might never be fulfilled, but, in the meantime, he could transform Washington, the loyal states, and the occupied portions of the south in postmillenarian ways. A devout man, he worked to undermine enforcement of the Fugitive Slave Law in the capital and appointed antislavery clerks to his department. "All I can do to advance the cause of *God* & Humanity shall be done free of charge as I have an appointment in the Treasury Department under Sec. Chase," one clerk reported to an abolitionist running the American Missionary Association.[141] Anticipating the changes that Chase and other antislavery Republicans in Lincoln's administration later enacted, Washington abolitionist Gulielma Breed expected a "moral revolution" to follow.[142]

Chase also actively promoted the career prospects of soldiers from (or otherwise employed in) Ohio, including McDowell, McClellan, William S. Rosecrans, and William Tecumseh Sherman. "It was in my power to secure your original appointment as Brigadier [General]; and thus give you some opportunity of proving your capacity and courage," Chase reminded Rosecrans shortly before he took command of the Army of the Ohio in 1862. "You are my debtor for little more than friendship," he modestly demurred, as Rosecrans's subsequent performance in the field in western Virginia and Tennessee—and Secretary of War Edwin Stanton's assessment of the same—were responsible for his current prominence.[143]

Thomas Sherman was transferred to the western theater in early 1862, and his replacement—transferred *from* the west—was David Hunter. The 1822 West Point graduate followed in Frémont's emancipatory footsteps in that spring, garnering a similar response from Lincoln as the Pathfinder received. His brother-in-law was Princeton theologian Charles Hodge.

Wounded at First Manassas while commanding one of McDowell's divisions, Hunter was transferred to Missouri in August 1861, and when Frémont was relieved from command after his abortive emancipation project, he took over the Western Department in November. Hunter was transferred again to Kansas that winter but in March 1862 took over the Department of the South on South Carolina's seacoast.[144] By May he was also recruiting a black regiment from the Sea Islands contraband community, a postmillenarian project uniting the desires of white Republicans for black freedom and African Americans' desire for liberty through service with the (mostly) white Republican cause. The First Contraband Regiment—soon to be the First South Carolina Volunteer Infantry (African Descent)—was initially commanded by the general's nephew, Arthur M. Kinzie, who was replaced in June by James D. Fessenden, son of the US senator from Maine.[145]

SYMBOLS MATTER, PARTICULARLY in revolutions against or within existing nation-states. Southerners who supported the Confederacy had to craft a new flag or flags distinct enough from the Stars and Stripes while claiming some of the democratic symbolism that the US national flag once held for them. Aside from stars and stripes, secessionists considered crosses crucial in proposing a Confederate national flag. South Carolinian Christopher Memminger invoked the Roman emperor Constantine, who established Christianity as his empire's new religion in the 300s CE. Explicitly adopting a cross into their new flag, Memminger argued, "in this [Christian] sign we will conquer." This was linked to the Confederacy's declaration of Christianity (without denominational specification) as the recognized national religion, for it was "by the aid of revealed religion" that the South defeated radicalism to achieve "over fanaticism the victory which we this day witness."[146]

Memminger's rhetoric was reinforced by St. George Tucker's poem "Southern Cross"— also invoking Constantine—in the unsuccessful (in 1861) effort to design an explicitly Christian Confederate flag.[147] They had to wait two years before great suffering and sacrifice and a major shift in Union policy inspired a Georgia newspaper editor to design a new flag linking premillenarian belief with white-supremacist nationalism. In the meantime, premillenarians theologians pointed to northern ministers' alleged "worship [of] the [American] flag" as evidence of postmillenarian idolatry: "How many have perished in sustaining that flag, even as the symbol of oppression and fratricidal war!"[148]

Nationalism and religion marched hand in hand in the warring sections. "Confederates considered themselves to be God's chosen people in much the same way as the majority of antebellum Americans" considered the United States, noted Paul Quigley.[149] Premillenarian Methodist W. H. Seat attempted to reconcile biblical prophecy with Confederate reality. Writing in late 1861, Seat linked the division of the Old Testament Israelites into northern and southern kingdoms to the current conflict in North America. Just as the northern Israelites forsook God, "substituting opinion and sentiment for Divine authority," so present-day northerners cut themselves off "from the heritage of God." The Almighty permitted them to "go into captivity to the old monarchical principle" and foreign invasion, while the faithful "remnant" of the south enjoyed God's blessing. The "new nationality" of the Confederacy, "the highest ideal of human government and . . . under the control of the Saviour of the world, will stand central and preeminent among the nations," inaugurating a "thousand years of the peaceful millennial reign."[150] Jesus must assume his Confederate throne *before* the millennium commenced, the crux of premillenarian conviction. Yet southerners' "continued status as God's chosen people was not necessarily guaranteed. With tremendous advantage came tremendous responsibility. Confederates reminded each other that in order to be good citizens, they must be good Christians."[151]

3

ROBERT L. DABNEY'S APOCALYPSE
××××× **1862** ×××××

DURING THE WINTER AND EARLY spring of 1862, Robert Dabney's fellow Richmond premillenarians were more concerned with warfare out west than with enemy forces in Virginia. J. Lansing Burrows rewrote the Confederate defeat at Shiloh in Tennessee into a spiritual victory for his Baptist congregation. He noted that the first major victory on Virginian soil the previous July (First Manassas) had "cause[d] us to forget, too guiltily, that our strength and dependence were in God" and to assume that "we might forget the toils and struggles that led to it, and anticipate henceforward rest and peace."[1] Burrows noted the recent defeats in North Carolina and at Forts Henry and Donelson in Tennessee, asking: "Why . . . have [we] been humbled before our enemies? Perhaps in His sovereignty God sees that unmixed prosperity will not be best for our future good."[2] The pastor summed up the two-day battle thus: "An army comparatively poorly clad and poorly armed, has met and mastered an army of at least equal numbers, said to have been one of the best equipped and prepared for battle that the world has ever seen."[3] Burrows was certainly correct that the western Confederate army was inferior in numbers, arms, and equipment than the host defending Richmond but woefully inaccurate in terms of the outcome of Shiloh. His congregation soon had more pressing and geographically closer concerns than military accuracy, however, in the form of Union forward movements in the Shenandoah Valley and the Virginia Peninsula. In the meantime, enslaved postmillenarians in coastal North Carolina rejoiced over the arrival of Union soldiers.

× × ×

THE SLAVES ALONE SEEMED rejoiced at our coming, and looked upon our victorious banners as signs of their approaching millennium," a colonel from New Jersey wrote his governor in March 1862 while on occupation duty in coastal North Carolina.[4] He was part of a 10,000-man force under Ambrose Burnside recruited to land on the barrier islands and eastern mainland of the state. It was in that same month that Mary Chesnut noted that the Republican-majority Congress "is down on us. The talk largely of hanging slave-owners. They say that they hold Port Royal" and the Sea Islands of South Carolina along with about 10,000 enslaved persons "as we did when we took it originally from the aborigines, who fled before us. So we are to be exterminated and improved à l'Indienne—from the face of the earth."[5] Chesnut betrayed a premillenarian fear of the intentions of postmillenarian northerners as Congress debated a confiscation act permitting Union forces to take rebel property—including enslaved persons—as somehow linked to a Republican ideology to "improve" southern society by destroying it.

CAPTAIN WILLIAM DUNHAM, on occupation duty in Virginia with the Thirty-Sixth Ohio Infantry, wrote his wife to complain that "our army is doing nothing and the Spring Campaign is destined to pass away without any decisive results—I am satisfied of one thing and that is that this war has thus far *developed no great military character* [like] Napoleon," a figure much invoked by Protestants on both sides. Yet this officer—as did so many others—referred to the French military genius without noting the problematic civil policies of the dictator. Regardless, Captain Dunham claimed that Napoleon "would have done more in one month than we have done in one year, but the finger of Providence is in all this, and never until every *shackle* is knocked off the slave will this country be redeemed"—never mind that the historical emperor sought to restore slavery in Haiti from its self-emancipated Caribbean revolutionaries. "Mark that Congress may fight off the day—and Presidents may set their feet upon it but it *will come*. The North is alike guilty with the South, she is 'particeps cominis' as lawyers say, and must suffer alike with her." He continued: "You may think me extreme but such are my honest convictions and I am not singular in them, as these are the views of sensible and reflecting men that I have talked with lately—and they seem rather to desire a consummation of these views men who were conservative heretofore." The captain presented as evidence "Judge Alderson a prominent and intelligent man of Lewisburg, [who] told me in conversation a few days ago that all well informed men he had talked with regarded Slavery as gone up. He said they thought Providence was overruling this war for the destruction of slavery." Dunham continued, "It is a matter of great concern to many what disposition will be made with the Colored race when freed, but 'sufficient' unto the day is the evil thereof I shall not be troubled much about that question."[6] The premillenarian general in chief of Dunham's and all other Union armies was not keen to fulfil the captain's postmillenarian vision of the destruction of slavery, nor was he living up to his nickname Young Napoleon.

The grand army that George McClellan trained in the fall and winter of 1861–62 was a far cry from the rabble that McDowell led to Manassas, both in the precision of its regimental drills and the professionalism of its officers. The 50 regiments of ninety-day volunteers had ballooned to 140 infantry regiments of mostly three-year volunteers by June 25, 1862.[7] Only 26 of McClellan's regiments hailed from the Republican stronghold of New England, compared with 101 mid-Atlantic, 10 midwestern, and 1 Border South regiment. In other words, the bulk of the army originated in the mid-Atlantic states, more specifically in the urban centers of those states that tended to vote Democratic and to hold premillenarian mindsets.[8]

Joseph E. Johnston and then Robert E. Lee—West Point classmates and scions of Virginia—commanded a similarly enlarged Confederate army in Virginia in 1862, which by June 25 numbered 170 infantry regiments defending Richmond.[9] Eighty-five regiments hailed from the Deep South, 84 originated in the Upper South, and 1 regiment came from the Border South. Of that total, 92 regiments saw combat between early April and early July. Exactly half of these blooded units were raised in North Carolina. Tar Heel regiments suffered a higher casualty rate—nearly a quarter of total reported losses—than Virginia units during the Peninsula Campaign. Casualties aside, North Carolina had been virtually denuded of regiments in order to defend the Confederate capital, while a Union force of nearly 10,000 men roamed at will through the state's coastal region.[10] North Carolinian William D. Pender wrote his wife in March of the melancholy case of an Alamance County woman who "spent her last cent" to travel to the army's camp in Virginia to visit her husband, whom she assumed to be in hospital, only to find that "he had been buried four or five days." Pender gave five dollars for her return trip. "Wasn't her case a hard one. Many is the poor heart that will be broken by this war. May God spare yours is my daily prayer."[11] His daily prayer was denied on July 1, 1863, north of Gettysburg, Pennsylvania.

BY 1860 THE SHENANDOAH Valley was Virginia's most diverse region in terms of religious belief. From the earliest years of white settlement, it was characterized by the lack of the Anglican and later Episcopalian dominance of the early coastal colony and state. Composed of eight counties—two now in West Virginia—the Valley by the Civil War years was mostly Presbyterian and Lutheran, reflecting the westward movement of Ulster Scots and the southwestern movement of "Pennsylvania Dutch" settlers in the late eighteenth century. Historian James Leyburn claimed that two Valley counties, Augusta and Rockbridge, were the most "Scotch-Irish counties" in the United States, based on the overwhelmingly Presbyterian membership of their churchgoing inhabitants.[12] Stephen Longenecker provided a strong sense of the "salad bowl" of Protestant belief here. This Protestant bowl, by 1861, comprised a mixture of Anabaptists and Anglicans, Friends and Mennonites, and (English) Baptists and Methodists, all in addition to the aforementioned Scotch-Irish and disciples of Martin Luther.[13] By the 1850s, Valley Protestants joined with the rest of the commonwealth's evangelicals in defending slavery from northern abolitionists so that "evangelicalism . . . became the chief cornerstone of Virginia's slave society," as historian Charles Irons observed.[14]

If George Junkin was the most prominent Unionist in the Valley, there were plenty of other less prominent and less vocal loyalists, many of them women. Julia Chase of Winchester, daughter of the town's postmaster, was born in Maine and attended the local Presbyterian church. Even before the war's first major battle, Chase anticipated that her town, and by extension the Shenandoah Valley, "will now be the battle ground" of Virginia.[15] Winchester's Methodist pastor was a conditional Unionist. "The reason I am for the Union grows out of the influence of America on the ultimate civilization of the world," Benjamin Brooke preached in 1861, echoing Junkin in Lexington.[16]

Another Unionist was David Hunter Strother, a Martinsburg native and, by the outbreak of the Civil War, a well-known author and illustrator for *Harper's Monthly* under the penname Porte Crayon.[17] Strother's Unionism led him to join the military, in which his Valley expertise elevated him to advise generals on how best to invade and occupy his native land. "Let him go down to infamy doubly damned!" cursed a Confederate captain.[18] Burning with righteous anger for the mistreatment of his Unionist father, Strother returned to the Valley in 1864 with his cousin, an abolitionist Union general whose brother-in-law was the theologian Charles Hodge.

Alexandria aside, Winchester was the first significant Virginia town to fall under long-term Union occupation. Several thousand northern soldiers arrived in early March under the command of Nathaniel Banks, formerly the Republican Speaker of the House of Representatives. Principal John Peyton Clark of Winchester Academy was particularly incensed by the abolitionist rhetoric and advocacy of racial mixing by New England regimental chaplains. Less than a week after the Yankees' arrival, Winchester's black Methodists were sufficiently emboldened to declare at a prayer meeting that "no white man should preach to them who did not go it for President Lincoln and the war for the liberty of the slaves!"[19] Laura Lee noted of Winchester's enslaved population, "The sauciness of the servants is very hard to bear." The "premil" Protestant continued, "The streets are filled with runaways who have flocked to the town from all around the country and who lounge about in everybody's way" without regard to their erstwhile masters. This situation must have seemed like the manifestation of a "postmil" paradise to black Protestants. "The Yankees walking and talking with [runaways and Winchester's enslaved people alike] in the most familiar way" was anathema to Lee.[20] Worse than black-white social familiarity was the sight of black women walking arm in arm with Union officers, who seemed unconscious to the "depth of their degradation" thorough interracial romance, with its implications of sexual miscegenation.[21]

Abolitionist chaplains accompanying Banks's regiments held interracial gatherings in the town's churches, where they mixed postmillenarian politics with prayer. Four New England chaplains visited Reverend Brooke on March 15. With them was "a minister who used to travel a circuit in this county—and was reared within 7 miles of Winchester."[22] Chaplain Charles Denison declared in a local church that "every black and white before him, negroes and soldiers, would be presented by the Government with at least ten acres of the fine land of this Valley," a most "postmil" reconstruction of the region via wealth redistribution if carried out. Worse still from the perspective of shocked Winchester premillenarians was the chaplain's suggestion that the New England soldiers "could marry some of these pretty girls about here." He did not clarify whether he meant by "these . . . girls" the rebellious "premil" Protestant women or the enslaved women in the audience, thereby sanctifying miscegenation.[23] Denison, a Baptist minister from upstate New York, had been a vocal abolitionist since the 1830s.[24] A May prayer meeting in the Methodist church involved appeals to divine intervention for President Lincoln and his administration to introduce African Americans "into the rights and privileges which properly belong to [them]." The explicitly "postmil" position was voiced, too, that "the time had come when the perfect equality of the white and black race was to be established." The meeting concluded with black women throwing "their arms around [soldiers'] necks and . . . other acts equally disgusting and revolting," as one disapproving resident put it.[25]

Winchester's women were the most vociferous—if unarmed—enemies Banks's men faced while occupying the town. An officer in the Tenth Maine noted that he "had already seen rebel women [elsewhere], but in all our travels we never saw any so *bitter* as those of Winchester. They were untiring in their efforts to show how they hated us." Shared Protestant religion in the form of respect for the Bible could not bridge the divide between premillenarian Virginians and postmillenarian New Englanders. "A lady of one of the very 'First Families' [of Winchester] dropped her bible or prayer book on going to church," noted the same Maine lieutenant, but "it was instantly picked up by one of our boys who stood near and handed [it] to the lady, who scowled at him and refused to take it."[26]

The postmillenarian occupation of Winchester came to an abrupt end in late May thanks to Stonewall Jackson. When General McClellan acted on his plan to avoid the direct overland route to Richmond by setting in motion an amphibious assault via the Peninsula involving over 100,000 Union soldiers, the Lincoln administration was justifiably concerned. Although he claimed to be leaving roughly 75,000 troops to defend the Union capital as well as the approaches to the Shenandoah Valley, in reality McClellan spared forces only about a third that size, far too few to prevent the Confederate army under Johnston from waltzing into Washington (had most of it not rushed south to defend Richmond).

The Confederate military took advantage of the situation by dispatching Jackson into and down the Valley with a small force—never more than 17,000 strong—to attack Union forces there to worry authorities in Washington and further disrupt McClellan's offensive. After each battle except for the first at Kernstown, Jackson's army held the field and so could claim victory. At Winchester, however, the Union army was not merely defeated but driven through the streets. The women there not only appeared on their porches to jeer the Union forces fleeing their town but also, as northern soldiers testified, several picked up firearms and shot at their erstwhile occupiers.[27]

Jackson's campaign gave the best example of a forerunner of the blitz-krieg warfare of the Second World War, though done at the pace of hard-marching infantry who earned the nickname "foot cavalry." Inflicting 4,000 casualties on three separate Union forces (for two-thirds their loss), these Confederates marched over 600 miles in forty-eight days. Yet the casualty figures pale in comparison to the over 50,000 Union soldiers the Lincoln administration ordered to chase Jackson, half of whom were meant to rein-force McClellan outside Richmond.[28] General Banks was convinced that his force was outmatched by "an enemy five times our number," thus his army's escape from the Valley was nothing short of "miraculous."[29]

Nathaniel Banks—his fleeing soldiers were those reportedly fired upon by Winchester's female furies—reflected in July 1862 on what he sup-posed were the religious origins of the difference between men and women. "Women—we owe them much but we ought not to forget that they cost us the 'original garden,'" he confided to his diary, referencing the fall of Adam and Eve in the book of Genesis. "A commentary about man, 'The woman gave me and I did eat.'" Banks then added a non sequitur comment, "A French-man s[ai]d he admired women but had the greatest respect for horses," be-fore returning to ruminations over transportation and rations.[30] Later that month the general wrote his wife to confess that—his prominent antebel-lum political career notwithstanding—"I do not think of public affairs and so feel quite easy" in light of the frustrations of the campaigns in the Valley and against Richmond. "God is very great and will bring about just results. If our People are so much surrendered to lying and fraud as to forget their country, they won't have one. If it is otherwise nothing can defeat us."[31] He here testified to the antebellum gender convention that properly educated Protestant men could exhibit superior self-control over non-Protestants, let alone women. Already convinced that he was the only general to forbear from complaining to the president and secretary of war about the disas-trous campaign, Banks stoically credited himself with resisting the advice of regular army officers to resign or otherwise "make a row."[32] Whether or not he realized it, the advice may have originated in West Point graduates' ulterior motive to replace him with a professional soldier.

Banks's private thoughts about gender and self-control were in line with premillenarians and most postmillenarians of the nineteenth century. American Protestants accepted that women were more emotional than men, who tended in their turn toward reason (when properly educated) over emotion. Perhaps these notes helped convince him that women should remain at home or in church, not as combatants on the battlefield, for as he believed that the first woman helped the first man rebel against God's laws, so rebellious southern women were throwing society into chaos by taking up arms like men.

EVEN AS UNION SOLDIERS loped into the Valley, Richmonders lamented the loss of western territory, culminating in the fall of Nashville and the slaughter at Shiloh (that Reverend Burrows attempted to gloss over). Some of them were disposed to blame Jefferson Davis, particularly those who had voted Whig in antebellum elections. The Whigs, after all, stood for progress, while Democrats like Davis emphasized the preservation of old ways and the expansion of slavery into new territories. With the capture of Fort Donelson in February, the *Daily Whig* asked whether "more energetic men" than Davis "might not have effected far more important results."[33] In mid-May one war clerk journaled: "Our army has fallen back to within four miles of Richmond. Much anxiety is felt for the fate of the city."[34]

If President Davis was criticized for a lack of manliness in defense of Richmond, including for his baptism that February, the women of Richmond and Petersburg fulfilled their gendered calling by encouraging their fathers and husbands, their brothers and beaux, to fight on. Frances Brockenbrough used religious language to emphasize that even as Confederate women engaged in soul-searching as to how shortcomings in their faith displeased God and therefore the war effort, Confederate men should do the same, even writing a tract to that effect. In *A Mother's Parting Words to Her Soldier Boy*, the titular woman reminded her figurative sons that, "of all men," soldiers had "the greatest need for piety" and argued against the male criticism of their president for his adult conversion as unmanly: "Piety will not make you effeminate or cowardly."[35] By the end of the year, over 150,000 copies of Brockenbrough's tract were in soldiers' hands.[36] Some of its readers were encouraged to see faith and masculinity as intertwined—the evidence: reduced profanity, increased bible reading, and nightly prayer meetings. Although there was "no great public demonstration in the way of revival meetings," Melvin Dwinell admitted that August, "a quiet but deep work has evidently been going [on] in the hearts of large numbers" of men in the army in Virginia over the past half year. Part of the revival was likely due to God's "gracious mercy shown in preserving their lives from the ravages of disease, and the awful conflicts of the bloody field," noted this member of the Eighth Georgia. "May the good work go on, until not only profanity, but all other immoralities shall cease in the Confederate army, and . . . every man feel a calm and holy reliance in the protection of Providence, and be willing to live or die as an all wise and just God shall determine."[37] If this was moral progress in an army fighting for its very survival, it was also manly progress.

Oliver O. Howard arrived on the Peninsula a brigadier general in command of four regiments. As slow as McClellan was to advance on Richmond, his opponent was similarly reluctant to counterattack. Finally, with the Yankee host "within four miles of Richmond," as the *Daily Whig* noted, Johnston was compelled to fight. The result was a poorly executed slugfest at Seven Pines at the end of May. Among the casualties were Howard and, as the battle sputtered out on the first of June, Johnston.

Akin to his brother-in-law Thomas J. Jackson, by the 1860s Daniel Harvey Hill was a dour Calvinist. Having joined the Confederate army and now commanding a brigade, in late April 1862 Hill wrote his wife that if he fell in battle, she was to keep their children free from "high, fastidious and aristocratic notions," teaching their offspring that "the salt of the earth is in the lower ranks of life." He noted tenderly, "May God bless you my darling, ever, ever more," then bluntly admitted that she had "been virtually a widow for a year and you may be so very soon in fact."[38] During the Seven Days Battles, Hill sought to live out this faith that God would take his life when it suited the divine will. Colonel John B. Gordon at one point found the general using a tree for a backrest, facing the fire of Union artillery. When Gordon urged him to get on the "safe" side of the tree, Hill replied: "Don't worry about me; look after my men. I am not going to get killed until my time comes." A shell then exploded next to the officers, knocking them down but not seriously wounding either man. Hill brushed the dirt from his uniform and, on second thought, sat down on the other side of the tree.[39]

Hill and his brother-in-law competed for the services of a Presbyterian theologian in April. If the prominent Presbyterian theologian Robert Dabney canvassed Virginia's religious and educational leadership to unite the Old Dominion against a rash act of secession in 1861, in the new year he threw himself wholeheartedly into the Confederate war effort. Dabney did so at the behest of the most prominently pious Confederate general in Virginia, Stonewall Jackson, or rather Jackson's wife, the daughter of a Presbyterian-college president. If initially envisioning a role as Jackson's chaplain, he accepted the position of major and chief of staff when Stonewall's adjutant general resigned. While the minister was still pondering active service compared to a simple chaplaincy, Hill offered him the chaplaincy of his division. But in the end, Jackson's wife prevailed upon the professor to accept her husband's offer. If Dabney worried about "how unfit" he was to become a serving officer and preferred "to get a chaplaincy again," Mrs. Jackson persuaded him otherwise.[40] "Our parson is not afraid of Yankee bullets," the hard-bitten Colonel Andrew Jackson Grigsby of the Stonewall Brigade noted of the new staff officer, "and I tell you he preaches like hell," whatever limitations Dabney possessed as a military administrator.[41] Acting as Jackson's secretary during the week and preaching to the soldiers on Sundays, Dabney accompanied Stonewall through his now immortalized Valley Campaign and east to Richmond to reinforce Lee, though he noted a worrying flaw in Jackson's aggressiveness. "Jackson's *great* fault is that he marches and works his men with such disregard of their physical endurance. His victories are as fatal to his own armies as to his enemies." The "rigidity of his character," Dabney groused, rendered him "in too much of a hurry to attend to the physical needs of his soldiers."[42] Jackson's strenuous campaign style nearly proved fatal to Dabney, who left the army in late August after weeks of severe illness despite the general's reluctance to approve his resignation.[43]

The chaplain of a regiment in John B. Hood's Texas Brigade compared the postbattle announcements of the opposing armies. Lee's words contrasted "well with that of the infidel Yankee leader of Northern fanatics," McClellan, "whose crusade upon the South is as unholy and unjust as that of Northern Europe, which sacked the cities and deluged the Southern States in blood. They claimed that their cause was holy, and upon their banners was emblazoned the cross—which is the star of hope to a sin cursed earth." In asserting that these "enemies boast a superior religious morality, and demand a holier Bible and purer religion than was taught by Prophets and Apostles," the chaplain accused all northerners of postmillenarian heresy, though Mc-Clellan could protest that he was a premillenarian conservative, just like Confederate Protestants. In contrast to the "bombastic . . . self-conceit . . . [that betrays] the large pretensions, high profession and extravagant pomposity" of McClellan—words that the general's Democratic allies used against their Republican opponent John Pope—Lee acknowledged "the supremacy of his God" in humble piety.[44]

While the opposing generals with a shared premillenarian mindset waged their respective campaigns to capture or defend Richmond, thousands of enslaved people—particularly those not evacuated from the path of McClellan's host—watched the Union army in expectation of deliverance. As the Army of the Potomac marched through Williamsburg in May, Seventh Maine officer Thomas Hyde noticed "crowds of contrabands [who] passed to our rear, looking like so many old clothes-bags, but in great joy, as they believed the millennium had come."[45] Yet McClellan did not wage war on Richmond to bring about the sort of millennium the enslaved sought, but rather to save the Union with slavery intact, to preserve the status quo antebellum.

McClellan's grand campaign against Richmond failed. He never grasped what increasing numbers of Republican generals in the West understood: Confederate cities fell once Confederate armies were destroyed, but the capture of rebel cities did not necessarily result in the destruction of rebel armies. At least in private—in letters to his wife—McClellan could confess that pride might have led him to this fall. "I hope and trust that God will watch over, guide & protect me—I accept most resignedly all the adversity he has brought upon me—perhaps I have really brought it upon myself," he wrote Ellen, "for while striving conscientiously to do my best, it may well be that I have made great mistakes." Such errors could be due to blindness caused by "my vanity."[46] These were the words of a premillenarian Calvinist who saw in the surprising Confederate offensive and the Lincoln administration's failure to properly reinforce him a double portion of judgment rather than opportunities to do better. But in public McClellan seemed resolute in prosecuting a Democratic limited-war strategy, particularly when faced with the threat of a Republican, postmillenarian way of war. After all, in the same letter to his wife, the general perceived that a "crisis will soon be upon us" if the administration "adopts those radical & inhuman views to which it seems inclined" instead of the "Christian" war he advocated.[47]

UNION ARMIES IN THE West were everywhere on the attack in the spring of 1862. Having captured Nashville in early April, later that same month the Confederacy's largest city—its one true metropolis—fell to the combined assault of Union naval and land forces. Erstwhile Democratic politician Benjamin Butler took charge of the 160,000 people of New Orleans. Aside from earning the nickname "Beast" for his policies toward disrespectful "she rebels," Butler cracked down on pro-Confederate clergy who failed to pray for President Lincoln or appealed to the Almighty on behalf of the rebellion. Three of the greatest offenders credited (or shifted the blame to) their bishop, Confederate general Leonidas Polk, for their anti-Union actions. W. T. Leacock, one of the Episcopal priests hauled before Butler, accused the Massachusetts general of "eating up God's people, as it were bread. You have possessed them with such fear, that they are rushing, innocent and weak women . . . guiltless and timid men, most ingloriously . . . to their destruction, through fear of being deprived of their substance or of their personal liberty." Leacock also protested at requiring citizens to swear an oath of loyalty to the Constitution before receiving desperately needed food rations, proclaiming that Butler thus placed his "will above the law for people to bow down and obey; and in their obedience they deny God and rush into the arms of Satan—and whose is the sin?" The general thought that "nine years of [Leacock's] preaching" brought his congregation to rebellion and now dependence on the Union army of occupation. When Leacock asked if the general was going to shut down the churches, Butler replied, "I am more likely to shut up the ministers." Leacock and the others were soon enough sent to a prison in New York.[48]

The capture of Nashville in the spring of 1862 was a welcome liberation for Unionist Tennesseans like William G. Brownlow. An erstwhile Methodist itinerant preacher turned Whig newspaper editor, Brownlow had damned abolitionists and fire-eaters alike before the war and—like most voters from his home state—supported the Unionist Whig John Bell in the 1860 presidential election. Continuing to preach Unionism in Knoxville after Tennessee seceded, he was imprisoned and threatened with execution. Brownlow beseeched God in January 1861 to defend the nation from "men of corrupt minds, evil designs, and damnable purposes, such as are seeking to upturn the best form of government on earth." He prayed for God to protect the Union men of Tennessee, granting them "the spirit of true patriotism, enlightened wisdom, and [the power] of persevering hostility toward those traitors, political gamblers, and selfish demagogues who are seeking to build up a miserable Southern Confederacy, and under it to inaugurate a new reading of the Ten Commandments, so as to teach that the *chief end of man is Nigger!*"[49]

Finally released to go to Union lines in 1862, Brownlow went straight to the state capital. Inundated with lucrative invitations to speak to appreciative audiences, "Parson" Brownlow toured northern cities in 1862. Still critical of abolitionists, the Tennessean claimed in Cincinnati, Philadelphia, and New York that he was always "quite a politician," although he never sought public office.[50] His wartime fame as a suffering southern Unionist awakened in him an aspiration for a career in state politics. Although he had to await the liberation of his home state and the elevation of its first occupation governor—Andrew Johnson—to the presidency, Brownlow longed for a political position empowering him to "point out to the triumphant Federal army such men as deserve to hang." Indeed, he was tempted "to tie the rope around some of their infernal necks" himself.[51] Revolutions, such as the "most fearful one" the nation was now embarked upon, could transform old foes into new friends. "I have fought that man for twenty-five long and terrible years," Brownlow said of "Andy Johnson," and was proud to have "fought him systematically, perseveringly and untiringly; but it was upon the old issues of whiggery and democracy; and now we will fight for one another."[52]

BEFORE RETURNING TO VIRGINIA and the first large-scale political showdown pitting postmillenarian Republicans against premillenarian Confederates *and* northern Democrats, we must turn to the major western armies campaigning in Tennessee in the spring of 1862. On April 6 the Confederate Army of the Mississippi under Albert Sidney Johnston caught Ulysses S. Grant's Union Army of the Tennessee in camp on the west bank of the Tennessee River by Pittsburg Landing. Grant was waiting for reinforcement by Don Carlos Buell's Army of the Ohio after its easy capture of Nashville before the combined armies marched against Johnston; Grant was certainly not expecting to be attacked at Pittsburg Landing. Near the landing was Shiloh Church, a Methodist meetinghouse bearing a Hebrew name meaning "place of peace." Ironically it would witness the bloodiest battle of the war to date, which also happened to begin on a Sunday. The 3,500 Confederate and

Union soldiers killed in combat during the two-day battle nearly equaled the battlefield fatalities of the War of 1812 and the Mexican-American War combined. Among the casualties was General Johnston, who had bled to death for lack of a tourniquet on the first day of fighting, replaced by First Manassas victor Beauregard. Another 20,000 combatants were wounded or captured before the battle ended.

"At Shiloh," wrote historian David Goldfield, "soldiers witnessed the destructive potential of modern weaponry,, and "every moment threw someone into a profound moral dilemma that neither the Bible nor conventional ethics addressed back home."[53] The unprecedented thousands left lifeless or writhing in their blood on the battlefield seemed not to herald the dawn of a new Christian era purchased by young American lives, but rather it presaged a long and remorseless war. "The real battle was often not against the enemy but against oneself," against fear, and the facile assumptions of country and Christ that motivated soldiers to march into battle might not sustain them through the second or third bloody campaign. These conflicts led to existential questions. "Could such misery produce a greater end? Are we doing the work of God or the devil?"[54]

The unprecedented 13,000 casualties that Grant and Buell's armies suffered in defeating Johnston raised cries of "butcher" against Grant, and their superior Henry W. Halleck took charge of the combined armies, further reinforced by John Pope's Army of the Mississippi before Halleck advanced on Corinth, Mississippi, to which Beauregard's army retreated after the battle. To simultaneously sidestep continued outcries against Grant and prevent his subordinate from gaining credit for any success in the upcoming campaign, Halleck kicked Grant upstairs to be his second in command, relieving him of direct command of troops in the field. If Grant commanded 73 infantry regiments at Shiloh—reinforced by 35 volunteer regiments and three regular battalions from Buell's army for the second day of the battle—the three armies Halleck led in a glacial advance on Corinth comprised more than 150 infantry regiments.[55] Eventually, the 160 volunteer infantry regiments and four regular battalions under Halleck's command added up to an effective force of about 120,000 men (including artillery and cavalry units) deployed against Corinth by mid-May.[56]

Johnston had taken seventy volunteer infantry regiments, two regular regiments, and nine battalions into battle at Shiloh on April 6.[57] Beauregard now led eighty-nine volunteer regiments, one regular regiment, and eight infantry battalions after the arrival of Braxton Bragg's Army of Tennessee and Earl Van Dorn's Army of the West as he endeavored to defend Corinth in May.[58] Johnston had roughly 45,000 effectives on April 6, Beauregard 65,000 in May. Unlike the bloodbath of Shiloh, each side lost only about 1,000 men in skirmishes before Beauregard abandoned Corinth on May 29 in preference to losing his army along with the town.

General Polk had led one of the three full-sized Confederate corps at Shiloh, where he lost his friend, army commander, and West Point contemporary Sidney Johnston. What enraged him even more than the loss in Tennessee was the fall of New Orleans. He was absolutely livid when he heard that the Union military governor of the seat of his ecclesiastical diocese had declared war on the city's women. Presbyterian minister Benjamin Palmer of New Orleans alerted Polk when he arrived at the army to read General Butler's "Woman Order" to a brigade of Louisianans. One of Palmer's audience recorded, "the resolute look, the compressed lip, the flashing eye of every soldier, said plainer than words could say that the insolent invaders of our sacred soil should never cross our entrenchments without walking over the dead bodies of sixty thousand determined and indignant men."[59] For his part, Polk promised the men that the army "would go into battle with this motto: 'Our mothers, our sisters, our daughters, our wives, our country and our God.'"[60]

Polk neglected to include "our slaves" in his motivational litany. Yet enslaved people in the western Confederacy sought Union defenders. Colonel James Garfield of Ohio noted that when his regiment passed "fine plantations" in northern Alabama where African Americans were "toiling for masters and masters sons who are in the rebel army fighting us," his men were compelled to "let [the enslaved people] stay at their toil." Yet the enslaved viewed the arrival of Union regiments as the arrival of freedom, begging, "Take us with you, we will work, we will do anything for you," only to be rebuffed by officers, compelled to respect rebel property. "I could chill your blood with the recital of horrors that have resulted to slaves from their expectation of deliverance and their being abandoned to death at the hands of their overseers," the Republican Garfield wrote his wife.[61] Other western officers later overturned this injustice.

If Shiloh is considered in conjunction with the siege of Corinth, the Grant-Halleck campaign of April and May was a significant (if costly) Union victory. Yet in its aftermath Halleck threw away the advantages of concentrating a grand western army, dispersing its component parts to defend railroad lines along the Mississippi-Tennessee border or to operate against the Confederate railroad junction of Chattanooga in southeastern Tennessee.[62] Pope's flawless capture of 7,000 Confederates on the Mississippi River at Island No. 10 and his aggressive actions during the Corinth operation, despite Halleck's efforts to rein him in, made him an attractive candidate for army command in Virginia, where the premillenarian Democrat McClellan's eastern grand army was floundering.

VIRGINIA IN THE SUMMER of 1862 witnessed a struggle within the Union high command over the meaning of the war. There was a struggle between the premillenarian Democratic ideology of McClellan and the postmillenarian Republican ideology of Pope (supported by Radical Republicans).[63] The Army of Virginia, the second major Union army in the Virginia theater during the summer of 1862, provides a focal point for an analysis of political millenarianism. The internal affairs of the Army of Virginia consisted of the command relationship between the citizen-soldiers and elected volunteer officers of the roughly 50,000-man force and its generals, a mixture of West Pointers and political generals. As to external affairs, the army's commanders and its common soldiers communicated with Republican politicians in the nation's capital as well as with disgruntled civilians in the region that they occupied. Officers and soldiers influenced the hardening of Union policy toward southern civilians via military decrees and petty theft or confiscation of rebel property (such as chickens) alike.

The Army of Virginia—a remarkably understudied unit from a remarkably overstudied war—presents a useful contrast to the more durable and scrutinized Army of the Potomac as it contained a significant number of general officers appointed for political reasons, and generally Republican appointees at that. The Army of the Potomac by contrast was an organization dominated by military professionals who leaned conservative (read Democratic) and intentionally shaped to be such a partisan military institution by McClellan from its 1861 formation. The Army of Virginia was led by Republicans who saw in the restoration of the Union an opportunity to reconstruct the southern states. The alliance between Republican generals and citizen-soldiers of the Army of Virginia with their likeminded representatives in the District of Columbia clashed with conservative professional generals in the Army of the Potomac in the summer of 1862. By then it was evident that more severe military and political policies seemed necessary to restore the Union in the face of Confederate intransigence. This conflict took on apocalyptic proportions in Congress and in the field as political postmillenarians and premillenarians clashed over the future of the nation.

PROMOTED TO COMMAND the newly designated Army of Virginia at the end of June, John Pope took over the three corps-sized units that unsuccessfully chased—and in turn were chased by—Stonewall Jackson up and down the Shenandoah Valley that spring. Numbering 50,000 men on paper, this force possessed low morale from its uncoordinated campaign against Jackson and a disproportionate number of partisan Republicans among its generals. By contrast the dominant ideology of amateur generals in McClellan's Army of the Potomac by this juncture was Democratic, not to mention the political views of its West Point–educated commanders, from McClellan on down. Pope devoted the month of July to meetings with Radical Republican politicians in the capital while sending decrees to his army, which boasted of western armies' aggressiveness and promised that the kid gloves were coming off.

In order to clearly differentiate between the Republican Army of Virginia and the Democratic Army of the Potomac, our snapshot is taken on August 9. On that date the Second Corps of Pope's army attacked Stonewall Jackson's wing of the Army of Northern Virginia at Cedar Mountain, despite being outnumbered more than two to one. However tactically unsound—indeed Jackson's forces recovered from their initial surprise to drive Banks's forces back on the rest of Union army—the battle represented Pope's more aggressive form of warfare in Virginia in contrast to McClellan's caution. Pope counted seventy-three volunteer infantry regiments, one sharpshooter regiment, one regular battalion, and two volunteer battalions in his three corps on August 9, of which seventeen regiments and the regular battalion were engaged at Cedar Mountain.[64] Those regiments under Banks included three from New England, six from the mid-Atlantic region, six from the Midwest, and two from the Border South, making it a fair microcosm of the Union states by mid-1862 in a demographic sense. Pope's overall army contained forty mid-Atlantic, eighteen midwestern, five New England, and seven Border South regiments. (The division comprising thirteen volunteer Pennsylvania Reserve regiments in McDowell's corps is not included as they were still attached to McClellan's Fifth Corps on the Peninsula at this date.)[65] Jackson's wing of three divisions counted sixty-three infantry regiments and three battalions at Cedar Mountain and was evenly split between Deep and Upper South states.[66]

A few months before his regiment—particularly his fellow Harvard alumni among the officers—was eviscerated at Cedar Mountain on August 9, Robert Gould Shaw exulted in the adventure that the war provided. "What a blessing that we happened to be born in this century and country!"[67] John Brown and his fellow Calvinists did not perceive any accident in the timing of their birth or country of origin; God determined that their generation should stand up and fight in this war, yet such could still be seen as a blessing.

Pope's new policies of warfighting reflected what he had learned in Missouri the previous year while fighting a frustrating counterinsurgency campaign against the arson of federal property and murder of Union personnel perpetrated by guerrillas. Worked out with Radical politicians in July, Army of Virginia soldiers could now confiscate civilian property (payable after the war upon demonstration of loyalty to the government) and impose loyalty oaths upon men of military age on pain of expulsion from their homes. Many of the common soldiers welcomed the aggressive rhetoric in comparison to the conservative, limited-war policies established by McClellan. Volunteers in Pope's army—particularly those who voted Republican—increasingly saw what generals like McClellan did not, that Virginia's white citizens materially and morally aided the Confederate war effort. By targeting them the war might be brought to a speedier close, thus extra-battlefield policies like Pope's might be necessary to damage the Confederacy's ability to continue to fight. Some of these soldiers bordered on the vindictive; ordered to protect the property of rebel families for the past year, now they were unleashed to wreck it. One lieutenant wrote a Radical politician how "dreadful" it was "to behold the state of prostration" his army now visited upon Virginia, the "Eden of America," through the "hard hand of war." He noted with relish the "abundant harvest for the support of treason" in "her fertile valleys" was now "trampled under foot by those whose lives are pledged to support our free & glorious Constitution."[68]

Professional generals and genteel officers were taken aback, seeing in these new policies a declaration of war against Virginia's civilian population.

McClellan also saw this as a declaration of war against him and his policies. Less than a week before the winnowing of the Second Massachusetts's ranks at Cedar Mountain, Shaw credited his new army commander with being "bold and rapid, but likely to lay himself open" to surprise by the enemy and liable to lose his current fame with northern civilians as McClellan had after the recent defeat before Richmond. "The American public are following their usual course of praising and expecting wonders of a man, before he has shown himself worthy of it, and if he fails in anything he undertakes, they will come down on him like an avalanche. That has been McClellan's fate, you know." Shaw found in Pope's criticism of McClellan evidence that he was a man of poor taste, "a great *blow-hard.*"[69]

The slaughter of Banks's corps at Cedar Mountain (2,300 casualties from less than 8,000 men engaged to 1,300 Confederate losses) gave the lie to the utter uselessness of West Point professionals in the assessment of Radical postmillenarians. Although "Grecian heroes never stood by their guns better" and pushed Jackson's first line rearward, Banks's aggressive advance fell afoul of Stonewall's second line.[70] If Banks at times outnumbered Jackson's force in the Valley, here it was the Confederate who enjoyed the two-to-one numerical advantage. One of Banks's soldiers wrote of his near escape from typhoid fever, which had carried away sixty of the three hundred comrades in his regiment who contracted it. He exhibited a premillenarian faith. "It is but according to the pleasure and will of the Great Ruler of all worldly events that these things," such as the typhoid epidemic, "are so, and we can do nought but murmur 'thy will be done' and submit to such chastenings as he may inflict."[71] If his bout with typhoid spared him from the debacle at Cedar Mountain, this man may well have attributed that escape to Providence as well.

Pope's order for his army to subsist itself on the countryside was interpreted by many volunteer soldiers as a license to plunder. Even when he and other West Point generals revised their instructions in order to condemn plundering as beyond the intended interpretation of confiscating civilian property only of use to the Union war effort, officers struggled to rein in their men, some exerting little effort to do so. "The ord[er]s seem to have done no good," the colonel of the Ninth Pennsylvania Reserves noted. "Little pigs, chickens and corn come in as fast as ever. The men seem to think they have a right to assume the responsibility of destroying every thing in Virginia."[72]

Stonewall Jackson perceived in Pope's hard-war policies an existential threat to the Confederacy. In a meeting with his brother-in-law, the general recalled a chat they had in Lexington during the 1860 election campaign, which included discussion of the possibility of civil war should Lincoln triumph. Jackson claimed no "special concern for slavery, but . . . agreed that if the sword was once drawn, the South would have no alternative but to defend her homes and firesides, slavery and all," a northern triumph forcing the "dissolution of the bonds of all society." He wanted "the black flag" of total war raised against invaders, but "the people of the South were not prepared for such a policy" in 1861. Now "the cruel and utterly barbarous orders of Pope" changed everything.[73] Lee forwarded Jackson's plans "to check Pope's dastardly system of warfare and plunder" to President Davis.[74] Jackson wanted to use Pope's policies against northern cities and civilians but more realistically suggested that "noted leaders [in Pope's army be held] as hostages for ransom or for retaliation."[75] He credited the decrees with "fast opening [the] eyes" of southerners to "the scope and design of the Abolition element" of postmillenarians "Ben Butler, Fremont, and Pope."[76]

Jackson convinced Lee and Davis that Pope represented a new kind of threat to the Confederacy. The general and his army were to be destroyed before their ideology spread throughout the Union war effort. Pope and his officers were declared outlaws to be held separately from other Union prisoners of war for potential execution in reprisal for depredations inflicted by their men on Confederate civilians. This separate and unequal treatment of Army of Virginia officers was an unintended rehearsal for the differential handling of the officers and men in black Union regiments due to the revolutionary threat they posed to the Confederacy from 1863 onward.

A staff officer in Pope's army, William Wilkins, catalogued the different treatment that these officers received in captivity from that given to McClellan's officers held in Richmond. Captured at Cedar Mountain in early August, Captain Wilkins was a member of the Fifteenth US Infantry Regiment. Initially he was treated well and held with his fellow captive West Point regulars General John F. Reynolds and Colonels Robert Stockton and Jacob Sweitzer. Yet his prisoner-of-war experience changed dramatically when he was separated from the officers captured during the Peninsula Campaign. He objected to being kept in a "room 70 by 30 filled with deserters, captured teamsters, idiots, lunatics, thieves, [and] counterfeiters." The arrival of Wilkins and the other initial captives from Pope's army "swelled the numbers in the room to about 200: giving us barely space to lie down." But this was only the beginning of the ordeal.[77] On August 23 another 160 prisoners arrived from Staunton, Virginia. A captain of the Twenty-Eighth New York informed Wilkins that even the wounded men in this coffle were "handcuffed! not for any resistance or attempt to escape but because they were of Pope's Army."[78] Although Wilkins did not draw the comparison, these new arrivals were treated like common criminals or enslaved people, not white soldiers.

A Lieutenant Fisher, an ailing officer from the Army of Virginia, was clapped in irons for daring to write home to complain that Pope's officers were not allowed entry into the hospital and for wishing "he could exterminate the rebel Confederacy." A sharp-eyed censor in the prison's office of the commandant caught this passage. "I pity the fate of any Southern prisoners who may ever fall into the hands of the officers confined here, when released," Wilkins continued. "But Gen. [Henry] Prince thinks we will be held as prisoners during the war, as a standing menace to our Gov't: and that the rebels are anxious to make the war, a contest of bloody retaliation, in order that the shocked moral sense of the European communities may compel them to interfere."[79] On the last day of August—the day after Pope's army faced decisive defeat at Second Manassas—Wilkins noted the sentries' desire "to kill us and [they] fired at us repeatedly for standing near the windows, fortunately without effect." He was convinced of their "wish to reduce us to rags, wretchedness and disease as rapidly as possible; and this they are fast effecting. . . . And this; I believe, the fiends desire, in order that we may be disabled from rendering further service to our Gov't." If no theologian, Wilkins nevertheless pondered the racial and religious nature of the war that such inhumane treatment brought to mind even before the Lincoln administration officially rendered the abolition of slavery a Union war aim. "And yet these [fiends] are white-men like ourselves, and pretend to be civilized and *call themselves* christians."[80] If left out of Wilkins's account, the comparison between the shackling of slave coffles and the treatment of prisoners of war from Pope's army as a hidden link between the war to preserve the Union that Wilkins set out to fight in 1861 and the war of emancipation that emerged from 1863 is striking to the modern reader.

Not all members of the Army of Virginia were so fortunate as Captain Wilkins to survive Pope's attempt to impose a Republican way of warfare in Virginia. On Sunday, August 17, 1862, another captain celebrated his twenty-second birthday. "Another of the years of my life have begun & am parting with my youthful days," noted George Hyer Brayton of the Seventh Wisconsin in his diary. "Thank God the past year of my life has all been spent in my countries service. I ought indeed to be thankful that I have been saved while so many thousands of my brethren in arms have fallen. My fervent prayer shall be that he who presides over the destinies of nations will ere another year free ours from this unholy rebellion & restore our union as it was."[81] This was Brayton's final diary entry, for eleven days later the captain was killed during his regiment's baptism of fire at Groveton, the combat that kicked off the Second Battle of Manassas. Although he did not live to see it, the war continued for well more than another year, not least because the Union could not be restored "as it was."

Richard S. Ewell was one of the most prominent casualties in the final showdown at Second Manassas between Pope's Republican ideology and the premillenarian Democratic faith shared by Stonewall Jackson and George McClellan. Ewell, one of Jackson's three division commanders, was less than ten miles from his family's Belleville, or Stony Lonesome, farm in Prince William County when he was wounded in the leg on August 28; upon medical examination the leg was amputated. If godly wives impelled generals like McClellan and Hardee to find faith in adulthood, pious fellow soldiers could also play a significant role. The conspicuous piety of Jackson certainly exerted some influence on his subordinate generals. While Ewell recuperated in Richmond from the loss of his leg, a family friend frequently visited the general with the purpose of accomplishing his conversion, with the blessing of Lizinka, Ewell's wife, who lived with the Hoge family in Richmond.[82]

Reverend Moses Drury Hoge convinced the general to stop swearing, a habit that came second nature to officers on long garrison tours in the peacetime army; a man who met Ewell in the 1850s claimed that he "could swear the scalp off an Apache."[83] Indeed, when his brother told the religious skeptic of his intention to become a missionary in the 1840s, then-Lieutenant Ewell disapprovingly commented on the wife beating, adultery, and theft practiced by the missionaries to Native Americans he had met while on frontier duty.[84] "I was quite shocked at the thought of William's turning Missionary," the recent West Point graduate wrote. "I have seen so much injury done the Indians here by them that I am rather skepti[c]al as to their utility. Some of the greatest scamps we have are Missionaries."[85] But in the summer of 1863, following his Richmond convalescence, Ewell returned to the Army of Northern Virginia a changed man. The Sunday after his arrival, the new corps commander attended, along with Lee, A. P. Hill, William Pendleton, and other generals, a worship service conducted by Reverend Beverly Tucker Lacy. A few days later he met with General Pendleton and Episcopalian bishop of Virginia John Johns to discuss the evangelization of the soldiery.[86] Bishop Johns reported that the interview "assured me . . . the good providence and grace of God had prepared the way . . . for the extension of the Gospel in the army."[87]

Before his life-threatening wound at Second Manassas, Ewell joined with prosecession Virginians (and not a few premillenarian Unionists) in his prejudices against German American soldiers in the Union army. Whether such men were Catholics, Lutherans, or atheists, premillenarian Americans saw invading German soldiers through the lens of past behavior. This prejudice stemmed from the depredations of "Hessian" soldiers—mercenaries hired by the British to help suppress the American Revolution—in the eighteenth century. "The Hessians destroy all the fruits of the Earth without regard to Loyalists or Rebels," one British officer noted in 1776. He observed that their pillaging was conducted "unmercifully," so it was "no wonder . . . the Country People [of New Jersey] refuse to join us."[88] Of course, many of these mercenaries sought freedom from draconian military discipline and even citizenship in the new United States. Yet Ewell and other Virginians brought this past characterization forward and saw the German Americans, who made up perhaps a quarter of the Army of Virginia, as disproportionately representative of Union pillagers.

Aggressive action by Lee and Jackson enabled the Army of Northern Virginia to defeat Pope at Second Manassas before the Potomac army could fully reinforce him. "All this has been brought about by *West Pointers,*" concluded one of Pope's abolitionist generals. "Soulless, brainless, Selfish Villains who having made their *Profession*—Care nothing for the country, so they can be hoisted into high places."[89] Yet Pope's brand of ideological, postmillenarian warfare was only temporarily defeated in Virginia. Confederate politician Charles Russell noted as Second Manassas raged that "the Federal government had repudiated all restraints upon violence, and waged upon the South a war of extermination, to which history presents no parallel."[90] That parallel was reached—and exceeded—in two summers.

x x x

IF HE DID NOT join the Baptist Church until 1868, artillery battalion commander Stephen D. Lee of South Carolina—present with James Chesnut and Roger Pryor for the negotiations with Major Anderson at Fort Sumter in 1861—traced the first significant religious thought in his life to Second Manassas. Watching Pope's army charge across the open fields on August 29 and 30, Lee thought, "well there is hell to play here, for sure, and . . . nothing but some unseen and superintending power, can tell where this thing is going to end."[91]

A lieutenant in the Pennsylvania Reserves who had already survived McClellan's abortive campaign against Richmond was saved from a musketball wound in the shoulder at Second Manassas by a gum coat he had rolled over his shoulder.[92] "We suffered more in the 14 days that we was under Pope than we did all the time on the Peninsula," Benjamin Ashenfelter wrote home. Although he rejoiced at the return of McClellan to army command on the eve of the deadliest day of the war, the evidently Catholic lieutenant unconsciously gave evidence in favor of the idea that Pope's Republican way of war was more aggressive than McClellan's Democratic style. He was confident that McClellan would lead the army to victory. "I Do feel thankful to Almighty God that I have been spared and not been wounded as many are that I have seen."[93]

The Army of Virginia was the military arm of Radical Republicans' quest to transform the war into a postmillenarian crusade regardless of Lincoln's efforts to slow the engine of millennial progress. Its defeat only energized their political wing. Radical voices trumpeted forth from the pages of Horace Greeley's *New York Tribune*. Even as Pope wrestled with Lee and McClellan in August, Greeley grabbed Lincoln's equivocation over slavery by the horns. In "The Prayer of Twenty Millions," Greeley declared that Lincoln could answer the prayers of loyal Americans and African Americans yearning for freedom by ending slavery via executive order. Such an act would also declare to the world—most importantly the antislavery, if procotton, British Empire—that the Union was fighting for principle and moral progress, not just territorial integrity. Yet Greeley's public letter backfired when the president answered with his declaration that he fought to preserve the Union, promising to do so by freeing all, none, or some of the enslaved as best sustained that primary goal.

Privately, Lincoln had already informed his cabinet that he intended to free the enslaved, although he accepted their advice that he wait to make this public until a Union victory, lest his declaration sound like a last *"shriek, on the retreat."*[94] Lincoln's evasiveness over emancipation as a military measure during the first year and a half of the war provided plenty of fodder for generations of historians since. Various scholars have speculated that he was a moderate constantly weighing public opinion, a radical waiting for events to provide public cover for personal intent, or a conservative forced by events out of his control to bow to emancipation. A division between Lincoln's political philosophy and his personality may hold the answer to this debate. "Certainly," argued Richard Carwardine, "his values and ideals placed him much closer to the radical-progressive side of his party than to the conservatives, while his temperament, his aversion to self-righteousness, and his gritty political realism kept the distance between them."[95]

MCCLELLAN'S HOPES FOR a war conducted on "limited, Christian principles" were resurrected by Pope's defeat and Lee's invasion of Maryland. Yet he took over the combined forces of the Potomac and Virginia armies with the knowledge that influential members of Lincoln's cabinet thought he should be shot for failing to intervene at Second Manassas with his full command instead of passively watching Pope get out of his scrape. With two Confederate armies now marching northward (Lee's into Maryland and Bragg's into Kentucky) and midterm elections nigh, Republican representative Thaddeus Stevens lamented the situation. No traditional Protestant he—Wheaton College founder Jonathan Blanchard tried unsuccessfully to convert him—Stevens nevertheless had been converted to the antislavery crusade by the white evangelical.[96] "The symptoms give no promise of good," the Pennsylvanian observed on September 5. "The removal of Hunter and Butler," and he might have added the replacement of Pope with McClellan, as well as "the continued refusal to receive negro soldiers convince me that the Administration are preparing the people to receive an ignominious surrender to the South. It is plain that nothing approaching the present policy will subdue the rebels." The social revolution that McClellan feared was required. Stevens doubted whether someone could be found "with a sufficient grasp of mind, and sufficient moral courage, to treat this as a radical revolution, and remodel our institutions," for it must "involve the desolation of the South as well as emancipation; and a repeopling of half the Continent."[97]

What counted at that moment of crisis for Lincoln was that the common soldiers of the army still believed in McClellan, even if the chief executive increasingly doubted the general's competence. "The army is now better contented than it was," a staff officer wrote from Maryland during the pursuit of Lee. "Gen. McClellan their idol is restored to command. He is, in the opinion of all the soldiers, the only honest and skillful leader we have had. None other can replace him in the affection of the men."[98] Left unsaid was the proper place of idols and idolatry in an ostensibly Christian land.

A Connecticut sergeant in Ambrose Burnside's Ninth Corps noted the difficulty of reconciling faith and nation.

> My Family is as dear to me as any mans family can be to him, but I have left them at the call of my country and God only knows whether I will ever see them on earth again. If I do not I know that He will take care of them and I trust I shall meet them in a better world. Jimmy wrote me something in one of his letters that I think will please Mother and you as much as it did me. He said he had learned to trust in God for all good things and he found more pleasure in so doing than he had ever known before. I often wish I could feel more implicit confidence in God such as would lead me to leave all the events of my life for his direction. Tis a hard place for a Christian in the army.[99]

The next month many of this New Englander's fellow soldiers—devout Christians or otherwise—discarded their playing cards as they marched into a cornfield, advanced on a wagon-wheel-rutted sunken road, or charged across a bridge spanning Antietam Creek. A sergeant of the Seventh (West) Virginia found a corpse still clutching a deck of cards over his face, the man evidently dying while in the act of tossing them away so that his family might never learn of his gambling. James Murdock found the dead "fallen on the field in every conceivable shape, grasping ramrods, photographs of loved ones, and Bibles."[100]

JAMES S. WADSWORTH, AN ARISTOCRATIC landowner and abolitionist from upstate New York turned general, ran for governor of the state in 1862 as a Republican. Commandant of Washington's defenses that summer while McClellan and Pope battled with Lee and each other, the gubernatorial candidate reveled in the Preliminary Emancipation Proclamation even as his Democratic opponent used Wadsworth's antislavery credentials against him. "Gentlemen, I stand by Abraham Lincoln," the general told an audience at the Cooper Union in his one campaign speech in New York, for, referring to the president's response to Greeley, "he has never said to you that if he could not save slavery he would let the country go." Therefore, it is "just, it is holy" to defend Lincoln's policy.[101] "How long are we to ear the insolence of this Southern aristocracy?" Wadsworth asked in a speech given in Washington, still faithfully at his military post. "Have we not borne it long enough?" This minority of landed bullies has too long "paralyzed the energies of the country" and, "in the eyes of the other civilized nations of the world, covered us with infamy." The general turned to the language of spiritual warfare to discuss how the planter class's armed rebellion and slavery were to be defeated. "We are in the pangs of dissolution, or we are in the pangs of exorcism. If we would save ourselves, we must cast out the devil which has tormented and disgraced us from the hour of our national birth."[102] With thousands of postmillenarian citizens serving in the ranks and moderate Republican leaders loathe to support a Radical, Wadsworth lost the election by over ten thousand votes and thus remained in the army.

Major factors in Wadsworth's gubernatorial defeat were the influential Tammany Hall political machine and the Irish American populace of New York City. While thousands of brave Irish New Yorkers served in the ranks—many fell at Antietam and later that winter at Fredericksburg following Lincoln's proclamation—they and their families did not welcome emancipation or the prospect of thousands of self-emancipated African Americans arriving to compete with them for jobs. The Irish-born editor of the most widely read American Catholic newspaper attacked the proclamation. Patrick Donahoe ("Apostle of the Irish"), editor of the *Boston Pilot* (the "Irishman's Bible"), ridiculed an act of political tyranny that could only redouble Confederate resistance.[103] He claimed that no more than one in twenty of the enslaved would seek freedom under the new executive order, for they "love their masters, as dogs do."[104]

"Do you know for what I enlisted?" a Connecticut man who dropped out of Yale College to join the Sixth New York Cavalry asked his mother. "*It was to free the slave. And though neither the army nor the government were ever particularly imbued with the spirit of Liberty yet I trusted that they would be. I thought that the process of events must surely bring about universal*

Emancipation," either as an incidental result of "our subduing the rebels, or a direct result of the light which would dawn on men's minds. It has not resulted *indirectly* because of traitors at home[,] the imbecility of the government, and blundering generals," while "those sentiments of duty and high honor and love of Liberty and regard to God's law which would make a strike at Slavery *directly* because it is wrong and every way abominable, seem to be waning more and more."[105]

The young soldier went on to warn his mother: "You cannot expect me, then, much longer to remain with this army as it is. If it does not change *soon* either in its principles or its actions, I trust in God that I shall have the moral courage to desert it. I did not join it to get a living or to escape the penalties of the civil law at home. I trust I shall not remain with it against every impulse of conscience to be beaten and disgraced with those who desire to enslave the bodies and souls of men."[106] Fortunately for the Union cause and Uriah Parmelee, less than ten days after he penned this letter, the Battle of Antietam gave President Lincoln the victory he needed to issue the Preliminary Emancipation Proclamation and start the Union down the road to fighting a war to destroy slavery as well as to preserve the Union.

A number of political generals and volunteer soldiers converted from the Democratic Party to the postmillenarian vision of Radical Republicans during the war. Among the most prominent in their ranks were Generals Butler and John Geary. The six-foot-six Geary was from Pennsylvania, fought in the Mexican-American War, moved to California as a postmaster appointed by President James Polk, served as the final alcalde and first American mayor of San Francisco, and fought for order in Kansas as territorial governor in 1856–57. He did all of these things as a partisan Democrat. Geary recruited and led a regiment of Pennsylvanians into the Shenandoah Valley. The frustrations of occupation duty—generally due to obstreperous secessionist women—helped set him on the path to Republican postmillenarianism in the face of the depth of southern disunionism. Promoted to general in 1862, by September Geary was reluctantly reconciled to the Radical view that emancipation must accompany the restoration of the Union. "The President's proclamation is the most important public document ever issued by an officer of our Government," he wrote his wife, though "I tremble for the consequences." While he anticipated "the opposition of the *delectable*," fearing "our country is on the verge of anarchy and despotism,"

Geary looked to God to "save us individually and, our country from the treason which surrounds us on every hand."[107]

In the wake of Antietam and Lincoln's proclamation, a sergeant from Indiana thought that "the rebellion will be put down this winter" but nevertheless hoped

> the war will last untill the last slave shall be free. I am in for the war till liberty be established in every part of our country: till every man shall be free. We will never have peace till this be accomplished. We had had war on the subject of slavery ever since our existence as a nation and now we are having bloodshed by the ocean on its account and no other. Now let us make away with the barbarous corrupt and wicked institution and we shall be free indeed. Our people are getting their eyes opened and are working in the right direction now, but it has cost a great deal to accomplish just the beginning. O that the end may be as sweet as the beginning has been bitter.[108]

Not all northern Protestant soldiers in Virginia shared the optimism of the Yale dropout and the sergeant from Indiana. Robert Gould Shaw, a fortunate survivor of the slaughter at Cedar Mountain, Second Bull Run, and now Antietam, did not share his parents' excitement at Lincoln's proclamation, "or rather, its forerunner." He failed to see the "*practical* good it can do now. Wherever our army has been, there remain no slaves, and the Proclamation will not free them where they don't go." Shaw feared that "Jeff Davis will soon issue" a retaliatory "proclamation threatening to hang every prisoner they take, and will make this a war of extermination." If emancipation was the right policy as a matter of morality, the young officer anticipated that "the evil will overbalance the good for the *present*."[109] Ten days later, after receiving his mother's objections to his dim view of the immediate prospects of the proclamation, Shaw emphasized that "as an act of justice, and to have real effect," emancipation "ought to have been done long ago. I believe, with you, that the closer we adhere to Right and Justice, the better it will be in the end, and that, if we want God on our side, we must be on His side." He was convinced that "the slaves are sure of being free at any rate, with or without an Emancipation Act" but that "much of the moral force of the act has been lost by our long delay in coming to it."[110] A Calvinist might retort that God's timing and the bloodbath at Antietam determined emancipation's dawn, not Lincoln's vacillation.

Confederate forces hoped their counteroffensives into Maryland and Kentucky would spur the British and French into recognition of their nationhood as well as encourage twenty thousand recruits from the two "Union-occupied" states to join their ranks. They were looking for a Saratoga moment, akin to the Patriot victory in upstate New York in 1777 that not only compelled the surrender of a British army but also convinced France that the American Revolution was viable and worthy of open support. "If Antietam was the Civil War's Saratoga moment," however, "it was so in reverse: a critical battle [that] thwarted, rather than hastened, the internationalization of a North American civil war."[111] If Prime Minister Viscount Palmerston was ready to strike "while [the iron] is hot" and intervene should "the Federals sustain a great defeat," now he shelved his plans to recognize Confederate independence.[112]

Methodist William Taylor, an American missionary residing temporarily in London, published a brief essay to explain the causes and likely results of the present war for his hosts in the fall of 1862. Although born in Virginia's Rockbridge County, both of Taylor's grandfathers had freed their enslaved people after participating in the American Revolution. He traveled to California as the gold rush boomed, founding the first Methodist church in San Francisco. "If 'not a sparrow falleth to the ground without our heavenly, Father,' it is not at all likely that such a war as is now raging in the United States could occur without Him," Taylor began. He held that the war constituted a "severe chastisement of the American nation for national sins" and did not mince words as to the chief of those sins. "We have sinned grievously against God and humanity, not only by our complicity with slavery, but in numerous ways besides."[113] The "providential end" he anticipated emerging from the war was no less than "the final overthrow of the 'institution of slavery.'"[114] He heard "many on this side of the Atlantic who claim for the South the right of revolution under the precedent of the revolution of the American colonies in 1776," responding that the situation was in no way analogous. "The colonies stated their grievances, and prayed long and loud for legal redress. The seceding states did neither." While the colonies were three thousand miles "across the sea, [and] had no voice in her halls of legislation, the kingdom of Great Britain" neither needed the colonies to maintain constitutional integrity nor was it jeopardized by their independence. The seceding states, in contrast, were "integral parts of the government, helped to create it, and by the most solemn compact were sworn to maintain it."[115] Taylor speculated that if Britain's abolitionist hero William Wilberforce attempted to speak against slavery in the antebellum South, he would "have been hung most likely."[116] Then he came to the solution: "The cheapest and shortest way out of the difficulty is the most direct way through it—the overthrow of its cause, slavery. Let honest Abraham untie the knot if he can, cut it if he must. As the light of Christianity and civilization have gradually increased their" influence, "have not the developments of Providence all been in favor of human freedom. Look at the glorious emancipation policy of England; see the abolition of serfdom in Russia."[117]

To the query of well-meaning Englishmen that many slaveholders must be "good men," Taylor related a story from his native Rockbridge County. There a neighbor suspended one of his slave women from a pole in the barnyard, "whipped till she was unable to moan aloud, and had an ear of Indian corn stuck in her mouth as a gag." Her master also allowed his three children—aged five to ten—to whip her at will to teach them the absolute "authority" of white over black.[118] Taylor emphasized the undemocratic nature of the planter oligarchy's domination of society until the present war. "The churches should pray, not that three hundred thousand persons should rule or ruin thirty millions . . . but that God would be gracious to the oppressed millions of the South, both white and black . . . and extend to them and their posterity, free schools, [and] . . . freedom of speech." A Union victory would guarantee the freedom to enjoy the golden rule, that "whatsoever ye would that men should do to you, do ye even so to them."[119] From 1863, Taylor's missionary journeys took him through the British Empire and around the globe, starting with Australia and South Africa.

RIDING UP TO an Indiana regiment by mistake at the Battle of Perryville, Leonidas Polk ordered the Union colonel commanding the unit to stop firing on his men, realized his mistake, and then followed through with the charade. Surviving this close call with death or imprisonment and making it safely back to his own lines, the bishop-general then ordered his own forces to fire on the unsuspecting Indianans, for "every mother's son of them is a Yankee," he told a dubious subordinate. The Twenty-Second Indiana suffered over 50-percent casualties. Polk was criticized for allegedly ordering "give them Hell, General!"[120] He was roundly condemned too at the northern Episcopal convention held in New York. Charles McIlvaine, who led Cadet Polk to saving faith at West Point years ago and was now bishop of Ohio, gave the most damning comment on his spiritual protégé. "When the ordained ministers of the Gospel of Christ . . . do so depart from their sacred calling as to take the sword and engage in the fierce and bloody conflicts of war," then the church had arrived at a dangerous place. McIlvaine continued, "when especially one comes out from the exalted spiritual duties of an Overseer of the flock of Christ, to exercise high command in such awful work—we cannot, as ourselves Overseers of the same flock, . . . refrain from placing on such examples our strong condemnation." The northern bishop repeated the words of Christ: "They that take the sword shall perish with the sword."[121]

Two Presbyterian ministers met with Lincoln late in the year. J. R. W. Sloane and A. M. Milligan presented two petitions for constitutional amendments, "one to end slavery forever, the other to submit the nation to God."[122] An hour-long conversation ensued, during which these two abolitionists "of the most radical school" pleaded with the president to grant "immediate, unconditional and universal emancipation" instead of the limited liberation of enslaved people held by Confederate masters. While shelving their petitions, Lincoln discussed at length the philosophical conundrum of differing sectional convictions regarding slavery and Christianity. If personally antislavery, Lincoln confessed that he recognized "that men were preaching and praying on both sides of the controversy."[123] In his view—publicly stated in his second inaugural address—providence punished both sides with this war.

A lieutenant from upstate New York added a religious dimension to the Union war's new purpose post-Antietam, echoing George Junkin's 1861 concern about the divine purpose of the United States. "I have always felt that the American people had a greater mission among the nations of the earth than to show the old crumbling despotisms of the old world how to depopulate whole communities and to shed seas of blood," William Walling wrote his sisters in October. "We have held up our institutions, and extended a call to the oppressed and downtrodden of all nations to take refuge under them." Though lakes of American blood had been shed, at least "the real mission of our government," namely "to be instrumental in the spread of the Gospel, in the publication of salvation to a world lying in sin and wickedness and in gathering in the heathen whom God has declared he would have for an inheritance," could now advance. "I believe we have too much at stake in crushing out this rebellion to become disheartened though every household in the land is thrown into mourning for the slain in battle," the lieutenant confessed. "And in this if it be necessary I would not make an exception even of the representative you have in this war."[124] Although his life was not required of him, Walling's conviction was sorely tested when, in mid-December, over ten thousand Union soldiers were killed or wounded in a seemingly needless bloodbath at Fredericksburg.

THE SAME DIVISIONS OVER occupation policy between McClellan's and Pope's armies in Virginia could be seen too in the western armies. The Army of the Ohio was divided into "hard war" and "soft war" factions by the fall of 1862.[125] "Hard war" postmillenarians like Mead Holmes Jr. perceived the link between slavery and southern rebellion. "But for slavery, Middle Tennessee would be densely populated. This 'peculiar institution' curses whatever it touches. It is truly wonderful, to see the difference between free and slave territory." Holmes was sure that now that the Union cause was synonymous with the antislavery cause, "the God of battles is on our side."[126] Commanded by the former slaveowner Don Carlos Buell—"a McClellan without charm or glamor"—army policy under his leadership followed McClellan's example of returning self-emancipated African Americans seeking safety with the army to their rebel masters.[127] Buell "desired to have as little to do with the slaves as might be" and "that loyal men should have their negroes." On June 21 he ordered one of his division commanders to prevent any fugitive African Americans from crossing the Tennessee River with his command while advancing on Chattanooga, leaving them to the tender mercies of rebel forces or local authorities.[128] Unlike the widespread lamentations in the Army of the Potomac when Lincoln removed McClellan following the fall elections, celebrations broke out when soldiers in the Army of the Ohio heard that General William S. Rosecrans was replacing Buell. "The whole army was electrified by the news that 'Don Carlos' was relieved, [and] the change raised the spirits of the troops."[129] Yet Colonel John Beatty darkly noted that within a year Rosecrans stood "as unpopular as Buell."[130]

The western hard-war policies of confiscating civilian property that Pope applied to Virginia in July and August were also liberally practiced in the western theater by the fall of 1862—with dire consequences for southern farmers. "We are obeying your christian exhortation 'to kill them' but prefer to let them die by inches to shooting them down," a Union officer wrote his wife after returning from a harsh foraging expedition in Middle Tennessee.[131] Civilians in that region of the state—occupied by Union forces since February—looked to the Bible and apocalyptic language to explain their severe treatment by northern troops. "I think it is a fulfilment of the bible, as the learned of all denominations admit that their [sic] is some important event to take place between this and 1866 the melanial year," a woman from Rutherford wrote Military Governor Andrew Johnson. "And if that be a correct opinion we all should be ready to appear before the juge to receive our final doom," although she thought it proper to warn that governor that he too faced an impartial judge. "Mr. Johnson you have power now but recollect the bible says whatsoever measure we meete out it will be measured back again."[132]

Two days before the Union debacle at Fredericksburg, a sergeant in the 20th Massachusetts watched the bombardment of the city by massed Union artillery. "Our batteries on the banks opened fire throwing into the devoted city perfect showers of shell and solid shot, and the din of the exploding shell, and the reports of one hundred and thirty pieces of artillery," John Summerhayes noted, "together with the crashing of the shot through the empty houses, and the falling of the walls of houses partially burnt, caused one to imagine the millennium had come."[133] Summerhayes found only apocalyptic language appropriate to describe such hitherto unprecedented destruction of civilian property.

On the last day of the year, Rosecrans's newly named Army of the Cumberland approached the Confederate Army of Tennessee in its winter quarters on the banks of Stones River in Middle Tennessee. Although the Union army was on the offensive, Bragg's forces counterattacked viciously, almost cutting off Rosecrans from his line of supply (and retreat) to Nashville. "Never mind me," the Catholic convert Rosecrans replied to a staff officer's concerns about the general's safety, "make the sign of the cross and go in." He repeatedly muttered, "This battle must be won." Soon afterward, the same friend and aide was decapitated by Rosecrans's side, spattering the general with gore, yet the army commander persisted in closely coordinating the fight.[134]

x x x

WHILE ROSECRANS'S ARMY FOUGHT to wrest Murfreesboro and Middle Tennessee from Bragg's tenacious force, Virginian Robert Scott desired the Almighty's swift judgment upon the invaders who murdered his father and despoiled his home state. "No set of miscreants, barbarians, thieves and scoundrels, disgraces of humanity, as the *Yankees,* can ever succeed," the 1854 University of Virginia graduate wrote. "I some times think the avenging angel of a righteous and just God will ultimately bolt them out of existence."[135] Along with his father, a Unionist Whig, gone was Scott's hope of the war's first year that northerners "would have a sudden epiphany in which they would see their evil ways" and cease fighting.[136]

Only a few miles away from Scott on that same New Year's Eve, an officer's servant from Philadelphia wrote the *Weekly Anglo-African* newspaper. George Stephens noted that the start of a new year "has always seemed like a period for moral and religious reckonings, when the errors and misdeeds of the past year are tearfully and prayerfully remembered, and a new leaf is turned over and we resolve to live better in the future." For religiously observant Protestants like Stephens, the last day of the year was a time for watch-night church services, when Christians prayed for a blessed new year. But this was a crucial watch night for African Americans like Stephens, who prayed for an end to slavery. "This December 31st, the watch-night of 1862, may be the watch night which shall usher in the new era of freedom," he penned.[137] Church bells and cannon blasts touched off by Unionist hands a few hours later indicated to millions of Protestant Americans that a postmillenarian new year was dawning. Yet Lincoln's fulfillment of his preliminary proclamation freed no enslaved people by itself; postmillenarian Protestants like Harriet Tubman and Oliver Howard would have to do that by force of arms.

4

SOJOURNER TRUTH'S MILLENNIUM
××××× 1863 ×××××

THE YEAR OF UNION EMANCIPATION dawned along with a new periodical devoted to the kind of millennial expectation that swirled around the young Sojourner Truth. "A New Serial devoted to the exposition and inculcation of the doctrine of the speedy coming and the reign of the Lord Jesus Christ, and related subjects," proclaimed the first issue of the *Prophetic Times*.[1] Published in Philadelphia and boasting an editorial board of evangelical pastors from five denominations concentrated in New York, New Jersey, and Pennsylvania, *Prophetic Times* joined the *Quarterly Journal of Prophecy*, printed in Scotland since 1849.[2] Charles Hodge warned his fellow Presbyterians of this kind of speculation in 1861.[3] Yet unlike Truth, who with other black postmillenarians observed in national events the initial fulfilment of their efforts, this periodical was premillennial and dispensationalist. The editors condemned the postmillenarian "expectation of a Millennium of universal righteousness and peace before the return of the Saviour" as an "unchristian delusion."[4]

The inaugural publication of the *Prophetic Times* followed by a few months the arrival in North America of the founding father of modern dispensational premillennialism, John Nelson Darby. Born in London, Darby studied classics at Trinity College, Dublin; embraced evangelicalism; and dropped his legal career when convinced of its inconsistency with his faith. As with Methodist founder John Wesley, Darby possessed "magnetic, electric personal qualities" and spent much of his ministry as an itinerant preacher.[5] He arrived in Canada in the fall of 1862. Spending almost half of the next sixteen years in North America, Darby was unimpressed by Protestantism in the United States. "The church is more worldly in America than anywhere you would find it, that is, the professing bodies, the world—professedly such—

inordinately wicked," he wrote following his first four-week tour of the northern states.[6] In 1863 Darby criticized American Protestants for living up to the "nation of joiners," or the voluntarist observation of Alexis de Tocqueville in the 1830s. "People join churches for respectability, but christian life is feebleness itself."[7]

From its first issue the *Prophetic Times* exhibited the pessimism of many northern premillenarians as to the reunion of the warring sections. "What is going to become of us as a nation?" the editors queried. "We have been long expecting and predicting that the rotten and tottering dynasties of the Old World would fall" without anticipating the sundering of "our government, so free, so just, so liberal, so enlightened, so Christian." Permanent separation loomed in light of the continued military stalemate in Virginia, and anarchy or military rule of the northern states seemed plausible in 1863. Should either catastrophic declension occur to northern democracy, what could "reconcile us so well to such calamities, as the belief that Christ is coming to set up his long-prayed-for kingdom upon earth."[8] Whatever northern premillennial theologians theorized, Union soldiers continued their advances into Confederate territory, operating in a truly postmillenarian, abolitionist, and armed institution.

SOLDIERS AND GENERALS in all armies began the 1863 campaigning season very aware that the war was now being waged over the future of slavery as much as the future of the Union. Postmillenarian civilians—particularly pastors—saw God's almost-chosen (northern) people entering a new covenant with the advent of emancipation. The son of missionaries who grew up in India and now resided in Iowa wished "that this dreadful [war] was near its end. But we are marching along," like John Brown's truth and Julia Ward Howe's lyrics, "God and truth are gaining ground, and will assuredly come off triumphant at last. Uncle Abe aides by his Proclamation tens of thousands of shackels have fallen . . . every yoke must soon be broken. All this chastisement was needed . . . for us as families, churches, and as a country."[9] Fifteen years previously his missionary father had written from a far "distant heathen land" that he labored for "the fruit of Gospel seed" that that "distant land might yield" as it threw off the shackles of idolatry in favor of freedom in Christ.[10] Furloughing in Iowa to recover his health, he saw no inconsistency in joining the efforts of the Underground

Railroad to help spirit African Americans to freedom with his foreign-missionary work.[11]

Even premillenarian Confederates could sympathize with the plight of enslaved persons known to be well behaved and merely endeavored to keep their families together. General Pender wrote his wife that his brother had tried to purchase a neighbor's slave but learned that he had been sold in Richmond for running away from his master. The general was actively seeking to purchase the man from his new owner, not because he wanted to "own him, but Beck [a female slave of Pender's brother] is dear to me, and I hate to see her husband whom she seems to love, torn from her in that way. This separating man and wife is a most cruel thing and almost enough to make one an abolitionist. I know you will approve my trying to buy him."[12]

The new year was less than three weeks old before three enslaved people held by Alabama Baptist minister Basil Manly, chaplain of the Confederate Congress during its initial residency in Montgomery, sought freedom. They "evidently started with the idea of getting to the Yankees, in North Ala[bama], or Miss[issippi]." One of the three young men, having accompanied Manly on his prewar missionary tour, "had been all through the valley of the Tennessee in North Ala[bama] where the enemy were some months ago; and he supposed he should find them there still." They were quickly apprehended. Ten days after they absconded, Pastor Manly "took them out of prison . . . on their promise to be good boys; and sent them down to the plantation."[13]

Charlestonian Emma Holmes spent the first month of the new year reading Virginia secessionist Beverly Tucker's *The Partisan Leader*. She was impressed by how his "prophecies" were remarkably close to the reality of "Secession, Virginia's course, & many other minor points . . . , and how well he understood the baleful influence of the Federal government as well as its despotism." The "unholy war" pursued by their former brethren, "such reiterated acts, of *Re-construction*," led her to pray that "every man, woman and child [would] perish in one universal self-immolation and our blessed country become a wide-spread desert than become the slaves of such demons as they have shown themselves." Holmes resorted to the English Civil War analogy to identify Confederates as "the free-born descendants of the Cavaliers," who must "'Never!'" submit "to the descendants of the witch-burning Puritans, whose God is the Almighty Dollar."[14]

Some Border South Unionists proudly recorded their conversion to the emancipationist cause. A soldier in the First West Virginia wrote home in January 1863 to declare, "I am in for the proclamation 'heart and soul,' and you know what my sentiments were at home."[15] Indeed, the previous year he had recorded his disgust that one of his fellow diners at the National Hotel in Washington was "that infernal abolitionist from Illinois, Owen Lovejoy," and had he been aware of the fact at the time, "I do not believe I would have eaten with him."[16] This soldier was reasonably devout, claiming: "We spend [Sundays] as best we can. When there is preaching," every other Sunday, "I attend, in 'God's first temples, the groves.'"[17] Emancipation arrived with economic benefits for the soldier's family; a contraband slave now worked at his home.[18]

Yet plenty of other Union soldiers—particularly those who voted Democratic in 1860—were displeased by the new war aim. Two members of the Fourteenth Indiana, a regiment that campaigned in Virginia, illustrate this perspective. "I think the Union is about played out," one Hoosier wrote home after Christmas. "I used to think we were fighting for the Union and Constitution but we are not. We are fighting to free those colored gentlemen," he jibed. Just how sarcastic his reference to "gentlemen" was emerged in his next sentence. "If I had my way about things I would shoot all the niggars I come across." One of his comrades wrote his hometown newspaper to complain about "Old Abe's 'free papers' to all including Africans and the rest of mankind, also the apes, orangutangs and monkies in South America caused me an hour's hearty laugh two hours tender cry, [and] four hours big with mad," he recorded in a style more florid than most common soldiers achieved. "I am swearing in all the languages known to Americans and Europeans," he concluded.[19] These views were in line—if more colorfully expressed— with the findings of historian Gary W. Gallagher that Union soldiers referenced a desire to preserve the Union far more often than they did any ambition of ending slavery.[20]

"Will it have much effect I wonder?" a northern premillenarian in the Army of the Potomac pondered of Lincoln's proclamation. "I fancy not," the cosmopolitan officer—educated in Berlin and London—decided, for he did "not believe the people of the North susceptible to unity to a degree which will be required to put down the Rebellion. Could we have unity of purpose as the South has, we could easily accomplish all we desire. Now you see by the Proclamation that we are fighting, not for the Union but for the *nigger*," anticipating Gallagher's claim regarding Union and emancipation relatively as motivating factors. "I however am *not* fighting for the nigger," but "having once gone into it, I will not back out."[21] This officer's grasp of military realities was somewhat tenuous; the day before recording the above reaction to presidential emancipation, he expressed widespread desire for replacing Ambrose Burnside with the exiled founder of the Army of the Potomac. "*Everyone is longing for McClellan*" was an understandable sentiment following the disaster at Fredericksburg. Yet to claim that McClellan "could lead us up & take those Fredericksburg batteries, considered now impregnable," strains credulity, even if the army might be willing to try with their idol.[22]

IF THEIR PREMILLENARIAN FOES claimed that Republicans made an idol out of the Union and emancipation, antislavery postmillenarians like John Hight, chaplain of the Fifty-Eighth Indiana, fired back with the argument that premillenarians made an idol out of slavery. Even in Unionist Kentucky the people "love slavery better than the National Government," Hight alleged. "Slavery is a sin against man—against God," he declared, and one of the "most vile of all crimes," hindering "all virtue" while breeding "all vice." As "the great crime of America," the Methodist pastor was convinced that the Union "can not be successful until [slavery] is utterly overthrown. Many wrongs have been, and still are, heaped upon the negro race. We must change our course and repent before God, and make restitution, before we can hope for complete success. We must conquer ourselves before we can conquer others." If it took Lincoln two years before he shared most of the above sentiments in his second inaugural address, he could agree with Hight that his native state "seems the slowest to learn" that slavery must die if the Union was to live.[23]

Not only did Union forces officially fight to end Confederate slavery in 1863, but now their ranks also included African American soldiers in segregated regiments, however much white generals sought to keep them out of the front lines. Colonel Nathan W. Daniels, commander of a regiment of free blacks from New Orleans, waxed eloquent that not only the men but also the company-grade officers of his unit were black. "I have yet to learn that a noble heart may not beat beneath a sable covering as of one of [another] tint. That a manly soul may not exist within the being of its darkest of Ethiop race as of those of snowy skin and Caucasian extraction." He turned to the postmillenarian mission of which his regiment was an integral part. "Thank God it hath been my fortune to be a participator in the grand idea of proclaiming freedom to this much abused and tortured race. Thank God my Regiment an African one, that I have been permitted to assemble them under the banner of freedom to do and die for their country and liberty."[24]

Yet postmillenarian advances for black Americans in 1863 nevertheless met with reverses, sometimes caused by Republican allies. "I have no confidence in General Banks," Colonel Daniels confessed in September in the wake of the Republican political general's efforts to purge black regiments of black officers. "I believe him to be a thorough Demagogue and only intent upon reaching the Presidential chair and little does he care by what means." Banks's predecessor, fellow Massachusetts politician Benjamin Butler, was little better in Daniels's mind, but he had at least acquiesced in the commissioning of African American officers. "The opposition accuse Butler of all manner of wrong deeds—but let him be ever so guilty (and I do not believe him as he is anything else but an honest one)—still has he the consciousness of doing his duty towards the poor enslaved race." This Daniels placed in contrast to Banks's good words but lack of comparable deeds.[25]

White abolitionist officers and civilians advocated the recruitment and use of black soldiers, sometimes expressing a willingness to "sacrifice" their command of veteran white troops to take on this postmillenarian project. David and William Birney, the elder sons of former slaveholder turned Liberty Party presidential candidate James Birney, were at the forefront of this effort. David Birney rose to the rank of major general and the command of a Union army corps at the Battle of Gettysburg.[26] William Birney gained the colonelcy of a "colored" regiment. While his elder brother achieved prominence and high command at the head of white troops, William focused on the "good work" of aiding the "contrabands" who sought protection in Union army lines as he recruited his black regiment. "The slaves have been coming in daily. . . . Several Hundred have come in altogether. I think I have enlisted in this state not less than five hundred, besides what I got in Washington." He echoed the impatience of his father's generation of abolitionists at the president's ambivalence toward African Americans. "Now is the time to strike slavery in Maryland. The slaveholders are panic-stricken, humbled and fearful. My officers go in among them and recruit their slave boldly and without guards. If Lincoln had the nerve, the blessings of the poor would be upon him," the younger Birney declared to J. Miller McKim.[27]

Colonel Birney appealed to the older abolitionist generation's evangelical sensibilities and commitment to biracial reform efforts in asking McKim to find "a colored chaplain" for his black regiment, "the best one you can possibly get. I want a man of education and eloquence, and a good man." His superiors were inclined "toward refusing the colored [regiment] the office of chaplain," probably on the grounds that a black chaplain had to be commissioned as an officer like his white counterparts. "This seems to me useless and cruel rapacity of the white man. Why should the colored soldiers be deprived of spiritual guides and literary teachers who sympathise with them?" Birney sought "a colored man eminently qualified" to present to the secretary of war—Elizabeth Cady Stanton's cousin—as "a test case." He found the black ministers in Baltimore to be too "timid" to pass the rigorous test of prejudice on the part of white officials and generals. The colonel hoped that if abolitionists could recommend an excellent black candidate, that preacher could "carry this point" and open the door to the commissioning of black chaplains for all "colored" regiments. "The great difficulty now is the supposition that the better class of colored preachers will not go," Birney noted, although hoping that assumption would be "promptly" disproved.[28]

Secretary of the Treasury Salmon Chase—who once stood up to a Cincinnati mob in defense of the right of William's father to print an antislavery newspaper—visited a dress parade of Birney's black recruits in late September 1863. Chase "expressed himself delighted with all he saw," though he did not register an opinion as to the colonel's efforts to appoint an African American regimental chaplain. Birney followed his appeal for a qualified black chaplain with a request for "a good teacher," noting that "these ex-slaves are deplorably illiterate: in my three companies, there are only four who can read and write, and these do it poorly." McKim's ongoing recruitment efforts for the American Missionary Association (AMA) to send white abolitionist teachers to the Deep South to educate contrabands in regions occupied by Union forces qualified him to find one more teacher for black soldiers. The colonel also asked for aid from McKim's Philadelphia associates to provide (or "appeal to the public" through the newspapers for) high-quality India rubber blankets and knapsacks to his regiment, supplies that Birney evidently could not persuade state or federal authorities to provide.[29] David and William's younger brother Fitzhugh—a graduate of the New Jersey school run by the Grimké sisters and Theodore Weld—left Harvard College to serve with his eldest brother, making a war fought by and for freed enslaved people a truly Birney family affair.[30] "I must go to the war," Fitz wrote a friend. "My father sacrificed all for freedom. My brothers are already in the field. Am I not dishonoring my name and the cause with which it is identified?" While on a visit with his uncle Gerrit Smith in upstate New York, he received an officer's commission in the Twenty-Third Pennsylvania from David, the commander of that unit.[31]

If he later commanded an entire corps of black troops only briefly—at the end of his life before felled by illness—David Bell Birney confessed that from time to time it had "occurred to me that I should offer to the Government to lead and organize the 'blacks.' As I have gained the highest Military rank, and enjoy a splendid command of whites, the '3d Corps' my motives would not be misconstrued into dubious ones," the general wrote to one of John Brown's Harpers Ferry financiers. "It has occurred to me, that the deep sacrifices made by my father for their race has gained their confidence, which they might the more readily transfer to the son. And their confidence would induce the Northern and Western free blacks to enlist the more readily, than under Generals unknown to them."[32]

A white staff officer's reflections of General Birney as a "Puritanical" figure remind one of Emory Upton or Francis Barlow. If he had "many enemies, . . . few officers could command 10,000 men as well as he. He was a pale, Puritanical figure, with demeanor of unmovable coldness; only he would smile politely when you spoke to him." While he looked after his staff officers, Birney also "looked out for his own interests sharply and knew the mainsprings of military advancement. His unpopularity among some persons arose partly from his promotion" above West Point graduates as well as his "cold covert manner."[33] If Stonewall Jackson could be descried in similar terms as to personality, Birney fit well with other postmillenarian political generals whose ideology and self-worth rubbed premillenarian professional soldiers the wrong way. Premillenarian Union generals thought promotion should go only to gentlemen who earned their rank by bravery in action and quiet patience.

IF DAVID BIRNEY ENVISIONED himself a George Washington of sorts to black soldiers, the original Washington inspired devotion on both sides during the 1860s. "Secession is nothing but revolution," Robert E. Lee wrote to his son in 1861, while mulling over the "calamity" of the current crisis. "The framers of our Constitution [would] never [have] exhausted so much labor, wisdom and forebearance in its formation . . . if it was to be broken by every member of the Confederacy at will. It was intended for 'perpetual union' so expressed in the preamble." Rather than the permanent government intended by "Washington . . . and the other patriots of the Revolution," anarchy would reign. Yet a "Union that can only be maintained by swords and bayonets . . . has no charm for me," leaving him to "mourn for my country and for the welfare and progress of mankind."[34] What might Washington do in this situation? As the first president warned of in his 1797 farewell address, sectional divisions had now flown home to roost. Celebrations of Washington's Birthday occasioned the first public singing of Julia Ward Howe's "Battle Hymn of the Republic" on February 22, 1862. In New York the following year, Reverend William Adams urged his congregants to "measure our nationality as related to that kingdom of Christ, which is paramount, permanent, and universal." That nation represented a "new order of men: of a church ransomed and free from all political alliance—a church reformed and untrammeled in soul and limb, of liberty regulated by law, of institutions established by the people for self-government, self-protection, and self-improvement."[35] Yet it was a nation founded upon Washington's antipartisan (his opposition to "factions") principles.

THE CAMPAIGN AND BATTLE of Chancellorsville in May 1863 was apocalyptic for both armies in Virginia. "I have the finest army the sun ever shone on. I can march this army to New Orleans. My plans are perfect," declared Union army commander Joseph Hooker, "and when I start to carry them out, may God have mercy on General Lee, for I will have none."[36] General Hooker sounded every bit the postmillenarian in his go-ahead rhetoric, except for his distinct lack of piety or humility, not to mention his questionable lifestyle. "Fighting Joe" had quite the task in transforming an army demoralized by the pointless slaughter at Fredericksburg in December 1862, a project that he tackled with zest and plenty of luster. Part of the task was psychological; Hooker had to convince his oft-beaten army that they were just as good as Lee's.[37] "I know the South, and I know the North. In point of skill, of intelligence, and of pluck, the rebels will not compare with our men, if they are equally well led. Our soldiers are a better quality of men,"

Hooker wrote one of his cavalry officers. "They are better fed, better clothed, better armed, and infinitely better mounted," not least due to the general's reforms. "Now, with such soldiers, and such a cause as we have behind them—the best cause since the world began—we *ought* to be invincible, and by God, sir, we *shall* be!"[38] Hooker seemed to take everything into account as he prepared for his offensive except God and General Lee. The 135,000 highly motivated and well-drilled men that Hooker marched from the vicinity of Fredericksburg in May were a far cry from the 100,000 dispirited survivors of the assaults on the heights west of Fredericksburg that shivered through the winter of 1863–64 and cursed Burnside. McClellan never concentrated so many men.

Enjoying his first corps command during this campaign was O. O. Howard, although "enjoy" was probably not the word he would have used. Recovering from his wounding and the loss of an arm on the Peninsula, Howard returned to the army in time to lead a Second Corps division at the Fredericksburg bloodbath. He did not approve of his bachelor army commander's proclivity for keeping young women of questionable repute around his headquarters, which allegedly led to their nickname of "Hooker's division" and more tenuously still to the use of the term "hooker" (or "Hooker's") for a prostitute. Neither did Howard enjoy his new command—or frankly, they him—the preponderantly German American Eleventh Corps. For all the later criticism of their battlefield performance at Chancellorsville and Gettysburg—both under Howard's command—these men had fought through the Shenandoah and Second Bull Run Campaigns with no less courage than their Anglo-American comrades.[39] They were accustomed to the leadership of Radical Republicans like John Frémont or the German revolutionary veterans Franz Sigel and Carl Schurz. The resignation of Sigel when he failed to receive a command commensurate with his seniority in rank left Hooker with the unpalatable choice of Schurz, however postmillenarian his politics and however popular with his men. The army commander "would consider the services of an entire corps as entirely lost to this army were it to fall into the hands of Maj. Gen. Schurz," however, and handed the corps to Howard instead.[40]

If Howard was antislavery like Sigel and Schurz, he was a dour teetotaler sent to the corps along with some fellow New England division and brigade commanders (West Point alumnus Adelbert Ames and Harvard graduates Francis Barlow and Charles Devens). All were deemed aliens brought by Howard to teach the Eleventh Corps proper soldiering, and they were resented accordingly. The "most earnest and devoted Christian I ever saw," according to one of his former colonels, "Old Prayer Book" Howard's piety struck a poor chord with the free-thinkers among the German-speaking generals.[41] "I was not at first getting the earnest and loyal support of the entire command," Howard commented understatedly.[42]

Francis Channing Barlow—who tutored the scion of Boston abolitionists Francis Gould Shaw in preparation for Harvard—enlisted as a private in 1861, leaving his wife of one day. He rose meteorically through the ranks and by May 1863 commanded one of Howard's brigades.[43] Recuperating from a wound suffered at Antietam, he still, in his wife's view, "loves fighting for the sake of fighting, and is really bloodthirsty," returning to duty though not yet fit and appearing "very frail."[44] His erstwhile pupil now commanded the first all-black Massachusetts regiment (the Fifty-Fourth). Barlow was impressed with the soldiers' deportment, expressing interest in commanding a brigade of black troops, including Robert Gould Shaw's Fifty-Fourth Massachusetts. "I hope Frank Barlow can get the command," Shaw wrote home. "He is just the man for it, and I should like to be under him."[45] Yet Barlow had to help recruit the brigade, taking him north and removing him from combat.

While in Boston, Barlow met the Howe family, describing Julia Ward Howe as "not only very bright & clever but most amiable & kindhearted & an earnest and good woman."[46] Howe's husband offered Barlow another opportunity to work with African Americans as the superintendent of the Freedmen's Bureau to help educate former enslaved people. Although it was a civilian instead of a military role, Barlow requested more information. "Politically it would be a great advantage to me," he wrote his mother around this time, "but I doubt my ability to fill the place and I dislike the idea of leaving the active service for which I am well fitted."[47] Yet if he seriously weighed the opportunities of commanding or otherwise leading African Americans, Barlow still used the terms "darkey" and "nigger" when discussing them with relatives.[48]

CHANCELLORSVILLE'S LONG CASUALTY LIST severely affected Lexington, Virginia. "Of the mothers in this town," Margaret Preston wrote on May 5, "almost all of them have sons in this battle; not one lays her head on her pillow this night, sure that her sons are not slain . . . oh! The sickness of soul with which almost every household in this town awaits the tidings to-morrow may bring."[49] The wives (and mothers) of Lexington were very well represented in Lee's high command at Chancellorsville—Stonewall Jackson's Second Corps, particularly—and suffered accordingly from Lee's costly triumph. Including Jackson, the town was represented by Generals Raleigh E. Colston (a colleague of Jackson's on the VMI faculty), Elisha F. Paxton, and William N. Pendleton. Paxton, commanding the famed Stonewall Brigade, was a Rockbridge County native who attended Washington College and Yale.

"We neither sought, nor provoked" the present war, John Tucker claimed to an audience of Richmond's Young Men's Christian Association members two weeks after Jackson's death.[50] The attorney general of Virginia emphasized that the commonwealth was fighting a defensive war, placing it firmly in the Christian just-war tradition.[51] Richmond's Protestants cherished such a reminder less than two weeks after their "idol" Stonewall succumbed to illness and wounds inflicted by his own men at Chancellorsville. Ironically, two weeks after Tucker's speech about defensive war, the Army of Northern Virginia embarked on its second invasion of the Union states.

The fall of the pious Jackson to friendly fire ignited more than a little soul-searching among premillenarian Virginians. Richmond resident Sarah Brock's admission that the general had been Confederate Virginians' "hero-idol" as well as "the terror of the enemy" highlighted a danger for premillenarians who placed their faith in fallible men, mortals who could be snatched away by fatal accident.[52] Three days after Attorney General Tucker's Richmond address, James Ramsey of Lynchburg compared the death of his fellow Presbyterian to the "mighty fallen" Jonathan, companion of ancient Israel's King David. Jackson succumbed "at the very zenith of his fame and usefulness."[53] Pastor Ramsey claimed that Jackson, as a true man of God, was immune to the "worldly honors" that surrounded him as he achieved fame, for he knew such honors were empty and mere "baubles."[54] Premillenarians must avoid the temptation to turn Stonewall into the idol that Brock mourned. God gifted Jackson to the Confederacy but now took him away. "He finished his work just when we thought he was about to enter upon a still more glorious set of triumphs. We are all bereaved," Ramsey noted.[55] The pastor then fell prey to the idolatry he had warned against. In setting Jackson up as an eminent and holy leader, he emphasized that faith and action in the name of "Jackson's God" must lead to "victory over our country's foes, over all of the foes of the Church of Christ, over sin and hell and death."[56]

The commanders of the Army of the Potomac engaged in plenty of self-recrimination and finger-pointing after the disaster at Chancellorsville, Hooker and Howard more than most. His corps positioned on the far Union right flank, Howard was assured—and failed to question—that there was no threat to the Eleventh Corps in its reserve position. Yet Jackson marched half of Lee's army past Hooker's supine host and rolled over and through Howard's panicked command. Hooker knew, thanks to his Bureau of Military Intelligence, that he had over 130,000 men in his army; he also knew that Lee had less than half that number with him.[57]

At one point during the rout, grabbing a regimental flag and conspicuously attempting to rally his men on horseback, Howard "felt . . . that I wanted to die. It was the only time I ever weakened that way in my life, before or since, but that night I did all in my power to remedy the mistake, and I sought death everywhere I could find an excuse to go on the field."[58] He reflected on the demise of his fellow "Christian general" and foe, praying God to grant the postmillenarian cause "more men and more leaders than we now have, who possess the virtues of that man."[59] Decades later he embellished Jackson's legacy: "even his enemies praise him; but, providentially for us, it was the last battle that he waged against the American Union."[60]

Seeking a scapegoat for his unanticipated debacle, Hooker attacked Howard's sense of honor and manliness after the war. Questioned about Howard's courage by a Californian journalist, Hooker in 1872 called his former subordinate "a very *queer* man. . . . He was always a woman among troops. If he was not born in petticoats, he ought to have been, and ought to wear them. He was always taken up with Sunday schools and the temperance cause. Those things are all very good, you know, but have nothing to do" with military command.[61]

HOOKER'S ARMY MARCHED into the Wilderness with a new code for conduct. A week before the Chancellorsville Campaign kicked off, Lincoln signed General Order No. 100, implementing a set of military ethics developed over the previous nine months by Francis Lieber. A veteran of the Prussian army wounded in battle against Napoleon near Waterloo, Lieber moved to South Carolina to become a professor of politics. He moved to New York's Columbia University to help establish a new law school in the 1850s. His family was divided like the nation; his eldest son fought and died for the Confederacy, while two others served in Union armies. "God has given us this great country for great purposes," Lieber wrote the attorney general in 1861—sounding like George Junkin and anticipating Lincoln—thus the Union "must be maintained at any price under any circumstances."[62] The code that Lincoln authorized was founded upon the master principle of "military necessity," which could justify the execution of prisoners in extraordinary circumstances as well as the confiscation of private property (including enslaved people) and even the endangerment of hospitals.[63] "The more vigorously wars are pursued, the better it is for humanity. Sharp wars are brief"—this was the crux of Lieber's moral vision for a justly and morally prosecuted war.[64] He anticipated Sherman's stated policy views as he besieged Atlanta and then marched on Savannah in 1864. Yet there must be limits to the sharpness of military policy. "Men who take up arms against one another in public war do not cease on this account to be moral beings, responsible to one another and to God."[65]

LEE'S ARMED PREMILLENARIANS LEFT Virginia behind again in June 1863, invading Maryland first and then southern Pennsylvania. They returned south in July, with twenty-five thousand fewer men in the ranks. The Baptist chaplain of an Alabama regiment viewed the invasion's defeat as the result of hubris born out of the long list of victories and providential survivals since the previous spring. "We have failed to confide in the God of our mercies, we have trusted in our own strength" and in the piety of the lamented Jackson.[66] The solution was clear: "We need to be deeply convinced that the battle is not ours, but God's."[67] Their path to Gettysburg and the misnamed "high water mark of the Confederacy" again took them through the Shenandoah Valley.

Despite Stonewall Jackson's lightning campaign the previous spring, Union forces had reoccupied the lower Shenandoah Valley and were enforcing the Emancipation Proclamation upon rebellious slaveowners. The new Union general who took up his post in Winchester on New Year's Day, 1863, promised the full execution of the Lincoln administration's new antislavery policies. During the march to Winchester on the first day of 1863, General

Robert Huston Milroy made a short speech to his men: "This day President Lincoln will proclaim the freedom of four millions of human slaves, the most important event in the history of the world since Christ was born. Our boast that this is a land of liberty has been a flaunting lie. Henceforth it will be a veritable reality." He explained that the Union had yet to win the war because until now "we waged a war to protect and perpetuate and to rivet firmer the chains of slavery." If his men enforced presidential emancipation, "the Lord God Almighty will fight on our side . . . and the Union armies will triumph."[68] Milroy spoke pugnaciously enough and backed up words with action in his personal religious life; he was expelled from the Presbyterian denomination in 1861 for brawling and questioning church doctrine, yet he "firmly believed in God."[69]

Milroy's military superiors and civilian victims concurred that the abolitionist general was "restless excitable and impulsive."[70] A graduate of Norwich Academy rather than West Point, Milroy had fought in the Mexican-American War and was a lawyer in Indiana when the Civil War broke out.[71] As with Radical politicians, he deemed West Point–trained generals the reason why the Union was failing to win in Virginia. "Scientific West Point Generals and their Science is proving as detrimental to the Nation as Treason," the general wrote his wife in 1862.[72] Milroy's contempt of West Point boiled over during Pope's summer campaign: "if the Devil had swallowed that institution 40 years ago, this rebellion would have been crushed Months ago—Our Genls. would now have been governed by common sense instead of West Point Slavery."[73]

Milroy used Old Testament analogies freely when he confronted the citizens of Winchester. "It does me good to [proclaim] Heavens anathemas upon them especially the preachers, Methodist and Presbyterian, who call upon me for passes and other favors and I have had several bouts with them," the general confessed to his wife. He particularly relished calling southern pastors' attention to the fact "that in ancient times the cry of a nation of slaves went up to God out of Egypt and He heard them and sent Moses and Aaron to reason with the slave holders . . . , but all arguments . . . were received by the slave holders with scorn and ridicule." Now Milroy, the latter-day Moses, was only too happy to confiscate Winchester's enslaved people from rebel masters. He was offended that southerners "even insulted God by trying to prove that slavery was His institution" and predicted that, like pharaoh, southern slaveholders would persist in their "Hell[-]deserving iniquity until . . . overwhelm[ed] in total destruction."[74] Milroy would be only too happy to serve as the instrument of that divine devastation, complaining particularly about the frustrating behavior of the women of Winchester. "H[ell] is not full enough, there must be more of Secession women of Winchester to fill it up."[75]

During this occupation of Winchester, African Americans were the only civilians "who have any rights or liberty, and of the latter they have an undue share," complained a premillenarian Presbyterian woman. "Negroes can assemble in any numbers, and if they choose can jostle and crowd ladies off the pavement into the gutter as may suit their convenience," Cornelia McDonald further groused. She comforted herself with the notion that most of the black population were "loyal and faithful to the white people if they do love freedom, and who can blame them if they do" appreciate this shift that temporarily expanded their civil liberties.[76] General Milroy practiced in private what he preached to soldiers and civilians, a consistency upheld by the prophet John Brown if flaunted by many genteel abolitionists' private segregation from their public allies. General Schurz, the radical German revolutionary, noted a "touching scene" at Milroy's tent when the commander entertained self-emancipated African Americans recently fled from Culpeper.[77] "The colored people of America should erect a monument to his memory," wrote one of Milroy's officers. "He was their friend when to be so drew upon him much adverse criticism."[78] Yet if Joseph Keifer respected the general's racial iconoclasm, he also frankly assessed him as "a rashly brave and patriotic man" who "risked his own person unnecessarily and without exercising a proper supervision over his entire command" in battle.[79] The Valley's white Protestants could certainly agree with Colonel Keifer's assessment of Milroy's aggressiveness, although not with the merit of setting up a monument to him.

Winchester witnessed a second battle and second rout of Union occupation forces in the late spring of 1863. The victim this time was a Republican general even more fiercely detested than Banks or Frémont by Valley Protestants. If the victor was not Stonewall Jackson, who now permanently occupied a plot in a Lexington cemetery, among those who defeated and then captured most of Milroy's force were the remnants of Jackson's old Stonewall Brigade.

Milroy remained in town too long as the Confederates approached, disregarding the instructions of superiors to avoid superior enemy forces. A woman in Staunton noted on June 26 that Winchester had been retaken by Lee's army as it moved northward. "The old brute [Milroy] narrowly escaped," while several thousand of his men were taken prisoner "and stores without number" captured.[80] Other pro-Confederate Virginians regretted that the abolitionist general had not been captured and hanged as a barbarian vandal.

THE UNION AND CONFEDERATE armies that fought the Battle of Gettysburg on July 1–3 are the obvious candidates for close organizational study in 1863. George Gordon Meade was in command of the Army of the Potomac for less than a week before battle was joined at the southern Pennsylvania crossroads town. Marching to intercept the invading rebels were 226 volunteer infantry regiments, two sharpshooter regiments, eleven regular battalions, and two volunteer battalions, with the sixty-six Pennsylvania regiments probably the most determined of the lot.[81]

Harvard graduates and 20th Massachusetts officers Henry Ropes and Henry Livermore Abbott found the replacement of Hooker by Meade a welcome improvement in the moral tone of the army high command. "We were all delighted yesterday afternoon to hear of Hooker's removal and hope well for Meade," Ropes noted on the last day of June.[82] "Every thing one hears of Meade is so honest, so well-conducted, there is such an absence of drunkenness, *whores,* etc which marked Hooker's head-quarters," Abbott wrote to Ropes's brother, "there is so much of the old McClellan style and feeling that men think they are in the hands of an honest and God-fearing gentleman."[83] Abbott and Ropes's regiment was commanded during this campaign by the grandson of Boston revolutionary Paul Revere and largely officered by Harvard alumni.

The highest command echelons of Lee's Army of Northern Virginia in July not only included a disproportionate number of Upper South generals but also a significant overrepresentation of Virginians. Apart from Lee himself, two of three corps commanders, the cavalry chief, and five of nine division commanders were natives of the Old Dominion.[84] In contrast, the 162 infantry regiments and seven battalions of his army were mostly from the Deep South. The previous June the Deep and Upper South contingents had been on a virtual parity in the army, but now North Carolina, Tennessee, and Virginia units were outnumbered by their western comrades. This increasing share of Deep South regiments seems counterintuitive when one considers that the states of Alabama, Louisiana, Mississippi, and Texas were significantly closer to the western Confederate army's theater of operations in Tennessee and Georgia than to Virginia.[85]

The meeting engagement on the morning of July 1 spiraled out of the control of Lee and his corps commanders. The youthful commander of the Twenty-Sixth North Carolina—at nearly 850 officers and the men, the largest regiment in either army—was shot through the lungs during the hottest fighting of the day. Twenty-one-year-old Colonel Henry King Burgwyn Jr., an 1861 VMI graduate, was carried to the rear, where he mixed religious and nationalistic language as he prepared for death. "The Lord's will be done," were among his last words. "We have gained the greatest victory in the war."[86] The colonel did not live long enough to realize that the second and third days of the battle turned out rather worse for his command, which suffered the highest number of casualties for a regiment during the battle, and his cause.

Meade was new to army command but not to the army. If he commanded the only (and all-Pennsylvanian) division to pierce Lee's defenses at Fredericksburg, he "almost always erred on the side of caution in military operations," according to his most recent biographer; this tendency shone through in his defense of Pennsylvania.[87] In his initial announcement to the army as its commander, Meade emphasized the duty of the men to defend their homes and drive the enemy out of the northern states. William Kepler of the Fourth Ohio and other veterans "seemed to think the order too tame, that we ought to destroy our invader instead of driving him back. There was an apparent distrust on the part of the men, who had always seemed more anxious for 'real business' than their general officers."[88] Kepler's sentiment was echoed by President Lincoln, who became frustrated with Meade's premillenarian satisfaction that the Army of the Potomac had driven Lee's army from "our soil." Lincoln, in an unsent postbattle letter written upon learning of Lee's escape back into Virginia, reminded the victorious general that the entire country—North and South—was "our soil," and driving precluded the real goal of destroying the rebel army.[89] The president also wrote General Howard, the one postmillenarian Republican among Meade's seven corps commanders after the new army commander purged his top lieutenants of Radicals *during* the battle (replacing the antislavery Abner Doubleday and David Bell Birney with conservative West Pointers).[90] Although he expressed gratitude for Meade as a "brave and skillful officer, and a true man," Lincoln confessed he was "deeply mortified" that Lee was allowed to escape, "for the substantial destruction of his army would have ended the war, and . . . such destruction was perfectly easy."[91]

"THE FUTURE IS UNCERTAIN," LaSalle Corbell Pickett remembered George Pickett saying after the disastrous repulse of his division at Gettysburg. "With all the graves I have left behind me, and with all the wretchedness and misery this fated campaign has made, we would not wish anything but a very silent, very quiet wedding . . . and after that, back to my division and to the blessing of those few of them, who by God's miracle, were left."[92] Historian Lesley J. Gordon noted, "Marriage to the vivacious, outgoing Sallie Corbell was perhaps his only salvation."[93] General Pickett was lost in premillenarian despair after July 3, 1863, with the vibrant love of his adoring young fiancée his only hope left in a life surrounded by death.

Pickett's army commander turned to God's sovereignty over the Confederacy's future and its present sorrows. "Let us confess our many sins," Lee urged his men a month after the battle in Pennsylvania—the costliest single battle for the Army of Northern Virginia—"and beseech Him to give us a higher courage, a purer patriotism, and more determined will," the general instructed on August 13. Lee included the foe in his address, encouraging his men to pray that God "will convert the hearts of our enemies; that He will hasten the time when war, with its sorrows and sufferings, shall cease, and that He will give us a name and a place among the nations of the earth." President Davis seconded Lee, declaring August 21 a day of fasting and prayer.[94]

One of Pickett's regimental commanders, wounded at the onset of the famous charge on July 3, was troubled by the losses suffered by his unit and the devastation of his Virginia plantation while he was campaigning in Pennsylvania. Inspired by the postmillenarian destruction inflicted on Virginia by Pope's army the previous summer, William Aylett was initially disposed to ignore Lee's orders to respect private property at the outset of the June campaign. "I don't mean to obey & the Army will not." Yet he could not "help feeling sorry for the people, bad as they have done us," he confessed to his wife after seeing a Pennsylvania wheat field trampled by another regiment.[95] Aside from his unit's losses on July 3, Aylett noted, "we hear of nothing but trouble & distress on every side, truly God [has] afflicted us as a people, but he has some good & wise purpose for so doing. Our recent disasters have made us sad, together . . . [with] the loss of so many of our noble soldiers."[96] The colonel's attempt to preserve his premillenarian sense of God's discipline as a step to future blessing was brought to breaking point when he heard that Yankee raiders had visited his plantation and threatened his wife. Never in his life had he been "more moved," and upon finishing his wife's letter, "by way of retaliation he selected twelve of the eighty Union prisoners under his care to be "shot on the spot."[97] Only the intervention of a staff officer who was thinking of national rather than personal concerns convinced the colonel that such executions constituted murder. "For myself," Aylett vowed, "I'll fight them as long as I have a leg to stand on or an arm to strike. Conquer them we must and will, for God cannot intend that such wickedness should succeed."[98]

Confederate defeats at Antietam and now Gettysburg inspired not only much soul-searching in the Army of Northern Virginia but also seeded the spiritual soil for revival. One clergyman motivated to win over the troops to right religion told his colleagues that once Lee's army was evangelized, "the foundation of a wide religious power over the country is now lain," for this army was increasingly the great hope of Confederate independence. "We, then, here and now, stand at the fountain head of the nation's destiny. We lay our hands upon its throbbing heart. Never again shall we come so near having the destiny of a great nation in our own hands."[99]

The suffering and dying at Gettysburg continued well after the two armies marched southward again. Rev. Israel Silvers joined the US Christian Commission in late July specifically to relieve the wounded left behind in the town as the war shifted back to Virginia. Arriving a full three weeks after the battle had scarred the community, Silvers spent part of his first day in Gettysburg sending supplies to the thrice-wounded septuagenarian John Burns, a veteran of the War of 1812 who helped fight the invaders on July 1 and was lucky to avoid execution if caught under arms but without a uniform. Burns's defiance of the Confederacy was undiminished by wounds or age; Silvers noted, he "hopes to recover to fight them again if they come here."[100] The minister observed the zeal—and "peculiar dress"—of the Catholic Sisters of Charity who "are the best of nurses at the hospital the [surgeons] say. They are however converting our men to Romanism, proselyting all they can, they are authorized to administer the sacrament, and the ord[inance] of baptism."[101]

Silvers noted the arrival of the exile from Virginia (and Pennsylvania native) George Junkin in August. Junkin preached at the hospital, and "many Rebel Off[icer]s came up to speak with him after service."[102] The former college president traveled to the battlefield from Philadelphia—the city of brotherly love, ironically for him a refuge from fratricidal strife—and walked with the aid of a gold-headed cane given him by his now-deceased son-in-law Stonewall Jackson. The cane not only aided his mobility but also was wielded as evidence to Confederate prisoners and enemy wounded of his relationship to their premillenarian hero. Encountering several of his own former students, Junkin surprised them by reading their academic records from an old class roll.[103]

The twin victories of Gettysburg and Vicksburg in the first week of July did not convince Union veterans that the rebellion was on its last legs, however welcome the news. The "fall of the Confederacy" was a long way off, a lieutenant in the Fifth Iowa wrote on the day Vicksburg's garrison surrendered. "Many hard battles are yet to be fought, and months, perhaps years, of fighting stand between us and peace." This he believed because "the chastisements of the Almighty are not yet ended" upon Christians of both sections for the sin of slavery. "The nation has not yet been brought down into the dust of humility and will not *let the oppressors* go free. . . . [T]he Almighty has taken up the cause of the oppressed and . . . he will deny us peace until we 'break every yoke' and sweep every vestige of the cursed institution from our land."[104]

TWO WEEKS AFTER the Fourth of July and less than a month after his friend General Barlow was wounded and captured at Gettysburg, Colonel Shaw and the Fifty-Fourth Massachusetts stormed Battery Wagner near Charleston. Harriet Tubman witnessed the failed attack, claiming later to have served young Shaw his last meal.[105] Among the regiment's missing—and presumed dead—soldiers from this campaign was James Leggett, Sojourner Truth's grandson.[106] Tubman was in South Carolina because Union generals occupying the coastal islands actively recruited black soldiers, an action that preempted Lincolnian or congressional policies. As noted earlier, David Hunter not only attempted to free the enslaved population of South Carolina but also ordered the arming and training of black men. Although Hunter was eventually replaced by Rufus Saxton, the Department of the South was now authorized to raise five regiments of self-emancipated African Americans by the secretary of war. After a few command changes and a temporary disbanding, the First South Carolina Volunteers now was led by Tubman's ally Thomas Wentworth Higginson, who arrived at Beaufort in November 1862. The colonel found Tubman already in Beaufort, serving "as a sort of nurse & general caretaker."[107]

WITH VICTORIES AT GETTYSBURG and Vicksburg, Rosecrans's nearly bloodless Tullahoma Campaign, and black soldiers proving themselves in combat in the successful siege of Port Hudson, President Lincoln had much cause to proclaim a day of thanksgiving in August. Short weeks before Davis called for fasting and prayer in light of Confederate reverses, Union clergymen like N. G. Collins, the chaplain of the Fifty-Seventh Illinois, reviewed "the history of the past two years" and found "we have abundant cause to exclaim, 'Behold, what hath God wrought!' We have conquered more than half the rebel territory, which we still hold, have been successful on almost every battle-field." Blaming the Confederacy for instigating the war, the chaplain congratulated the assembled soldiers for "the pleasing fact to us that the North are fighting for the right, the perpetuation of intelligence and human freedom, while the South are fighting for human bondage as the chief corner-stone of their government," which Confederate vice president Alexander Stephens himself had declared in April 1861. As of the third summer of the war, "the Southern Confederacy has been weighed in the balance and found wanting." As Union forces were now fighting to free African Americans too, God must be on their side; "when the cause (slavery) which has produced this war shall have been removed and not till then, shall we have a permanent peace." Collins thanked God, "that he has caused light to shine out of darkness, and brought order out of confusion, upon the subject of American slavery which has hitherto darkened almost every ray of light in our political heavens."[108]

Whether in response to victories or defeats, Union and Confederate days of fasting and thanksgiving acknowledged the ever-mounting numbers of war dead that affected ever more northern and southern families with each passing month. As historian Drew Gilpin Faust noted, the unprecedented death and destruction led to new mass acts of commemoration of the dead and the spread of a market of mourning.[109] A "new religion of sacrifice emerged from the prayers, fasts, and funerals that were celebrated in town after town across the North and the South," noted historian Jon Pahl.[110]

THE ARMY OF TENNESSEE lagged behind the Army of Northern Virginia in everything: modern firearms, reinforcements, brilliant generals, morale, and last but by no means least, battlefield victories. It also trailed Lee's army by several months in its religious revival. The western army's first wave of evangelical enthusiasm began in the spring of 1863, following its unceremonious turfing out of winter camp by the Union army at Murfreesboro.[111] As many regimental chaplains went home the previous year due to the Confederacy's inability to pay them as well as the frustration at the lack of progress among their charges, visiting "missionaries" (civilian ministers) helped fan the flames of repentance. "There has been a general revival going on in this army for the past month and there have been a great many professions of faith," noted the assistant surgeon of the Forty-Seventh Tennessee. "I think some 30 or 40 in this regiment and a great deal more in others."[112] "It seems quite strange to see so many men who were a few weeks ago swearing, gambling, cockfighting and now praying and reading their bibles," wrote a surgeon, impressed by the transformation of the army into "one perpetual camp meeting."[113] A convert during this revival wrote home, expressing the hope its influence might spread well beyond the Army of Tennessee, casting "a great blessing nationally as well as Spiritually."[114]

One of General Polk's fellow Episcopal bishops was a key player in this movement. Steven Elliott told his listeners that the war was "as much a moral as a political necessity" while defending the Confederacy's peculiar institution. Southerners should be lauded for their treatment of the enslaved: "we are elevating them in every generation." Yet he did not hint as to what the logical endpoint of that progress might be.[115] On June 1 the bishop of Georgia addressed an assembled brigade on the "religious aspects of the war." He attacked the enemy as "lovers of pleasure rather than lovers of God." Loyal southerners were "warring with hordes of unprincipled, ignorant and brutal men, who, having cast off at home all the restraints of order and of belief, have signalized their march over our . . . country by burning the churches of Christ . . . and by fanning into fury the demoniac passions of the ignorant and vile."[116]

Polk put a brave face on his army's prospects despite the loss of Vicksburg and Lee's retreat from Gettysburg, yet he blamed the Confederate president for failing to provide the main western army with the materials it needed to win. "It is the law of God's providence to aid those who aid themselves," he wrote to a fellow bishop. "This is as true in efforts to succeed in things temporal as things spiritual."[117] Polk's problematic theology could be just as easily embraced by northern abolitionists frustrated with their own president's tardiness in the freeing and arming of black postmillenarians.

Southern losses aside, the seasons continued to progress, and Episcopal chaplain Charles Todd Quintard looked forward to the Christmas holiday following yet another military disappointment at Chattanooga. As historian Benjamin Miller has noted, Episcopal chaplains paid more attention to martial hierarchy than their more egalitarian Baptist and Methodist counterparts.[118] Quintard was no exception, recording his frequent preaching "before distinguished congregations . . . when Generals Johnston, Polk, Cheatham and nearly all the general officers . . . were present." During advent, Quintard presided over services held at army headquarters and in Polk's parlor, where he did not neglect two other high-ranking officers awaiting communion.[119]

Two days before Christmas of this year, Polk again invoked the virtues of God helping those who helped themselves. Echoing his sentiments of 1861, when he temporarily commanded the western army while awaiting the arrival of A. S. Johnston, Polk assailed the two sources of Union fanaticism he most abhorred: New England abolitionists and midwestern "infidels of German descent." In case they needed reminding, his soldiers were told that these barbarians sought to rob them of their political and property rights as well as their wives—particularly their wives—"who everywhere regard our invaders with loathing and abhorrence." The men did not need a priest to tell them what God thought of this. "It was a maxim of the religion [even] of the heathen that the gods helped those that helped themselves. The teachings of purer and truer faith have served to confirm and establish" the truth of this idea.[120]

If the war east of the Appalachians was anticlimactic after Gettysburg, the second half of 1863 was the more dramatic season for the western armies. The Roman Catholic General Rosecrans, who spent the winter months debating the finer points of theology with his Methodist Chief of Staff James A. Garfield, was prosecuting the war against the Army of Tennessee in the southeastern part of the Volunteer State.[121] His Army of the Cumberland advanced on the key rebel railroad link between the eastern and western theaters at Chattanooga, a goal of western Union forces since the capture of Corinth the previous May. Rosecrans commanded 140 regiments of volunteer infantry, five regular battalions, and two volunteer battalions in September.[122]

Bragg's Army of Tennessee received crucial reinforcements on the eve of battle at Chickamauga. Adroitly maneuvered out of defensive positions in June and July by Rosecrans until compelled to abandon Chattanooga, Bragg took two newly arrived divisions from Lee's Army of Northern Virginia into combat on September 19 and 20. With the addition of two more divisions under James Longstreet and an additional division sent from Mississippi under Bushrod Johnson, Bragg finally achieved numerical superiority over Rosecrans. The western Confederate army had not enjoyed such an advantage over its foe since April 1862 at Shiloh, taking 115 volunteer regiments, one regular regiment, and twenty-two battalions into battle on the nineteenth.[123] The following day Bragg's force had grown to 127 volunteer regiments with the arrival of Lafayette McLaws' division of Longstreet's corps.

If the Roman Catholic commander of the Army of the Cumberland spent the previous winter debating the finer points of theology with his Protestant chief of staff, the gruff commander of the Army of Tennessee discouraged conversation on any nonmilitary matter. In early June 1863, the Tennessee Episcopalian Quintard, chaplain of his home state's First Infantry Regiment, found the courage to approach Bragg about the general's faith. Persuading a headquarters sentry that he had urgent business with the army's commander, Quintard "was very much frightened [when Bragg appeared], but I asked the General to be seated, and then, fixing my eyes upon a knot-hole in the pine-board floor of the tent, talked about our Blessed Lord and about the responsibilities of a man in" Bragg's position. "When I looked up after a while I saw tears in the General's eyes and took courage to ask him to be confirmed. At last he came to me, took both my hands in his and said: 'I have been waiting for twenty years to have some one say this to me, and I thank you from my heart. Certainly, I shall be confirmed if you will give me the necessary instruction.'"[124]

Victory on the battlefield—and Chickamauga was the first and last time that the Army of Tennessee succeeded in driving (most of) the enemy's army from the field—did not end Bragg's problems with his senior lieutenants or the enlisted men. "Several of us were drilled today for swearing. I was one of their number," Lieutenant Robert Watson noted in October. "I told [my captain] that when I joined the Confederate Army that I did not intend to become a Methodist preacher and if he thought he could make me a preacher or hypocrite of me by punishment that he was mistaken."[125]

The hero of Chickamauga was not a Confederate general, but rather the loyal Virginian, George H. Thomas, a man "never . . . tempted to question what came to [him] so sweetly," his Christian faith. "I cannot see how a man can be an infidel and remain a brave man," Thomas commented, anticipating the twentieth-century claim that there are no atheists in foxholes. "Belief in God is like confidence in one's general, it holds us to the front. We feel that the power above has a wise design in making us face the deadly peril. I doubt whether any sane mind ever does positively disbelieve. One may have painful doubts," the general admitted, "for we are brought continually face to face with mysterious and apparent contradictions, but back and above all these, we feel that there is an overruling power ever wise and just."[126]

Farther west than the furious campaigns of Chickamauga and Chattanooga, and even beyond the Mississippi where Grant lay siege to Vicksburg, guerrilla violence dominated the war experience. A guerrilla band led by William Quantrill rode into the antislavery stronghold of Lawrence, Kansas, at dawn on August 21, 1863. When proslavery ruffians sacked the town in 1856, the only fatality was one of the raiders, killed when his comrades pulled down upon him the building he was looting. This time all resident males of military age were marked out for death. At least 150 teenagers and men were gunned down in front of their distraught families on the streets of Lawrence. James Henry Lane, now one of Kansas's US senators, escaped the carnage and used his rhetoric to stir up a spirit of vengeance.[127]

The previous summer Lane declared: "If to oppose the using of American volunteers for the protection of rebel property; if to favor the confiscation of rebel property constitutes radicalism, then . . . I am a radical. If opposing the use of American soldiers for the return of fugitive slaves to rebel masters" makes one a radical, then Lane was one; "if opposition to the policy of driving from our lines the loyal men of the rebellious States because of their color renders me an abolitionist, then . . . I am one. Radical and abolitionist, . . . I say crush out this rebellion, even if human slavery should perish in the land."[128] The senator's rhetoric and sentiments echoed among eastern postmillenarians. A marksman from rural Pennsylvania captured when his division—commanded by General Meade—temporarily broke through Lee's lines at Fredericksburg, suggested that a younger friend take Lane for the subject of a school project and oral presentation. "Would it not be [a good] policy to abolish slavery before peace shall be made with the South? It has been so called a sacred institution but the time has come when it is no more a divine institution." As Lane called for emancipation now, peace later, "I think it is time for that curse to be removed from the nation."[129]

LIKE D. H. HILL, General Howard served both in Virginia and the western theater. Howard went west in 1863 after the debacle at Chickamauga, joined by other Union generals who failed in Virginia, including Burnside and Hooker. Although many eastern generals used profanity, his new army commander, William T. Sherman, encouraged the especially profane General Jefferson C. Davis—who murdered his commanding officer in cold blood at Louisville in 1862 yet escaped a court-martial—to let loose in front of Howard. Eventually Howard, with "distress all over his face, left, whereupon Sherman and Davis made the house ring with laughter." When another officer protested at this display, held expressly to discomfort Howard, Sherman replied, "that Christian-soldier business is all right in its place, but he needn't put on airs when we are among ourselves."[130] The famously secular Ohioan failed to notice that Howard's piety was not for public consumption only, but for the benefit of impressionable citizen-soldiers as well.

On at least two occasions Howard all but ordered his subordinates to hold their tongues than to give vent to profanity. With the two major Confederate armies on the ropes, he still lectured his command in March 1865 that "every insult to Him is a scourge to ourselves and invites disaster to our noble cause."[131] God might see (and hear) the blue cloud of profanity ascending from Union army camps and withhold his favor from the postmillenarian cause. Howard took seriously the legislation of morality in the Army of the Tennessee after becoming its commander.

ANNA DICKINSON COMMANDED WARTIME public influence belied by her second-class civilian status. More than one hundred Republican senators and congressmen gave evidence of this when they signed a letter to thank her for her speeches on behalf of their candidates in New Hampshire, Connecticut, Pennsylvania, and New York. Most importantly, they invited her "to deliver one or more addresses this winter at the Capitol."[132] The new year was less than a month old when she mounted a temporary platform in the House of Representatives next to the Speaker of the House's desk as Abraham and Mary Todd Lincoln took their seats in the chamber.[133]

Dickinson devoted much of the summer and fall of 1863 to the twin causes of recruiting black soldiers and getting out the Republican vote. She shared a stage with Frederick Douglass in Philadelphia to encourage black men to join an army that now wanted their services yet only paid them two-thirds of the monthly salary white soldiers received.[134] Two days after the Fourth of July, Dickinson admitted the awkwardness of a white woman saying "Anglo-Africans, we need you," despite the unequal treatment they faced after enlisting. "My cheeks would crimson with shame" if her recruiting efforts were for whites alone, yet she asked her audience to seize a better future with their war service. "You hold the hammer which, upheld or falling, decides your destiny," for if they did not have homes, "gain them. You have not liberty!—gain it. You have not a flag!—gain it. You have not a country!—be written down in history as the race who made one for themselves, and saved one for another."[135] If not allowed herself to enlist in the Union army, Dickinson nevertheless nearly lost her life speaking on behalf of her postmillenarian cause. The Republican leadership of Pennsylvania thought she might fare better than a man in the Democratic stronghold of the state's coal-mining region, promising her a thousand dollars a day for her efforts to persuade voters to switch parties for the looming election. On October 5 one of those miners allegedly fired a pistol, missing her face but clipping off a lock of her hair. The state party also failed to pay her the promised twelve thousand dollars for her perilous efforts.[136]

FREDERICK DOUGLASS DECLARED in December that the northern premillenarian goal of fighting for the status quo antebellum—the Union as it was—was dead. "What business, then, do we have to fight for the old Union? We are not fighting for it. We are fighting for something incomparably better than the old Union." The new Union would be a postmillenarian one beyond even Lincoln's progress-oriented dreams, but one that would require over a century to truly arrive, when Democratic presidents grasped Cold War realities to embrace Douglass's postmillenarian dreams. "We are fighting for unity: unity of object, unity of institutions, in which there shall be no North, no South, no East, no West, no black, no white, but a solidarity of the nation, making every slave free, and every free man a voter."[137] Nevertheless, in the new year of 1864, George McClellan would fight one last time for the old Union.

5

GEORGE B. McCLELLAN'S APOCALYPSE
× × × × × **1864** × × × × ×

THE REALITY THAT TENS of thousands of formerly enslaved men served as fully armed—if unfairly paid—soldiers in the Union war effort was a recurring nightmare for northern and southern premillenarians in 1864. George McClellan sought election as president of the United States to roll back the revolutionary initiatives of the Republican Congress, while D. H. Hill and Leonidas Polk sought to crush any prospect that black soldiers would make salient achievements in the field, so vindicating wider use of this apocalyptic force. A nonslaveholding Confederate general even forced a debate over the selective emancipation and arming of slaves still in southern control; if Confederates did not utilize military-age black men in this fashion, then they would continue to join the Union war effort.

In late 1863 Army of Tennessee division commander Patrick Cleburne met with his brigade commanders and a few other generals. In light of the Lincoln administration's active recruitment of enslaved southerners for labor and to swell Union military ranks, Cleburne thought it only logical that the Confederacy offer freedom to enslaved men of military age in return for Confederate service rather than see them run to Union lines. "The idea of abolishing the institution at first startles everyone, but every person with whom I have conversed readily concurs that liberty and peace are paramount questions and is willing to sacrifice everything to obtain them," noted Captain Thomas Key, to whom Cleburne had personally confided his plan. "All, however, believe the institution [of slavery] a wise one and sanctioned by God."[1]

Yet most of Cleburne's colleagues reacted vehemently to his proposal. "I am satisfied that the North is in earnest and that the whole energies of her people will be brought to bear to destroy us as a people, to enslave us, to desolate our fields, and [to] put a yoke on our necks that will crush the proud spirit of the South. That is their object," General William H. T. Walker wrote his wife on New Year's Day, 1864. "Heaven and earth are raised to accomplish this object. Let us then buckle on our armor. Let us prove [to] them and the world that we are not the degenerate sons of a noble race but that we will dare everything, suffer everything but a loss of our honor and liberty," he closed on a premillenarian note.[2] The very next day Walker joined seven division or corps commanders of the Army of Tennessee at army headquarters by invitation of General William Hardee. With the army's new commander, Joseph E. Johnston, present, Hardee introduced General Cleburne, who then read a paper—already circulated among his brigade commanders—arguing that slaves who were willing to fight for the Confederacy should be immediately freed and armed.[3]

Walker vocally opposed the plan in the ensuing debate. Afterward all present (except Walker) agreed to keep silent on the subject of their meeting with their subordinates. Walker approached Cleburne to ask for a copy of the plan, with the clear object of forwarding it to Richmond, to which Cleburne acquiesced.[4] Within a week of this extraordinary meeting, Walker first approached Hardee as to his views on the plan. When the corps commander dodged his questions, he then addressed a circular to the other generals present at the meeting. Three of Walker's peers expressed their opposition to the idea of enlisting black soldiers to fight a white man's war. Presbyterian General Alexander P. Stewart of Tennessee found Cleburne's proposal "at war with my social, moral and political principles."[5] Others supported Cleburne or refused to discuss the subject further, citing the agreement to table the matter at the end of the meeting.

Walker then defied his army commander's wish to end the debate there, sending the proposal to the civil authorities in Richmond. Confederate secretary of war John Seddon and President Davis thanked Walker for forwarding the document but emphasized to he and General Johnston that they wanted the matter to remain a private one, that it should not appear in the press for public consumption and debate.[6] "No power except the Power above could keep [me] from marching to fight an enemy who has come to . . . make free men of our blacks and blacks of our free men," Walker wrote his wife, feeling fully vindicated by the Confederate leadership in Richmond in his condemnation of Cleburne's revolutionary plan.[7]

Robert Dabney's denomination formally resolved in 1864, "we hesitate

not to affirm that it is the peculiar mission of the Southern Church to conserve the institution of slavery, and to make it a blessing both to master and
slave."[8] Their pastoral letter the next year returned to the "question of social
morality" to declare "that the dogma which asserts the inherent sinfulness
of [the enslavement of African Americans] is unscriptural and fanatical." Indeed, they deemed the postmillenarian view of the equality of races "one of
the most pernicious heresies of modern times," warranting perpetual separation from northern Calvinists.[9]

West of Virginia the Unionist Presbyterians of Kentucky affirmed the
link between the divisions within the Protestant denominations and secession as well as the Confederacy's continued resistance to federal authority.
Robert L. Stanton of the seminary at Danville argued in an 1864 book that
the South's defiance of lawful authority was rooted in "the Church of God."[10]
The Protestant churches, as "its greatest social institution . . . , constituted
the major resource of the Confederacy in the building and maintenance of
civilian morale. As no other group, Southern clergymen were responsible for
a state of mind which made secession possible, and as no other group they
sustained the people in their long, costly and futile War for Southern Independence."[11] Stanton singled out D. H. Hill as an exemplar of "the schemes
for 'peculiar education' at the South to foster the 'peculiar institution.'" A
lay leader of the Presbyterian Church, an educator, and now a Confederate
major general, Hill was described as "a South Carolinian in all his feelings,
principles, and prejudices. . . . He has nursed his hatred to the North to
such a degree, that it has become as near to a passion as his cold nature
permits."[12]

REVIVALS SWEPT THE ARMY of Northern Virginia's winter camp, continuing the work of the previous year. Lee's chaplains transcended denominational lines to reap the spiritual harvest. The two young chaplains in one
North Carolina brigade—Presbyterian William S. Lacy of the Forty-Seventh
Regiment and Methodist Richard S. Webb of the Forty-Fourth Regiment—
both "excellent young men" in the assessment of one pious soldier, held regular meetings in the brigade's chapel. If few attended at first, soon services
were held daily at noon as well as in the evenings.[13]

x x x

REVIVAL STRUCK THE ARMY of the Potomac during the winter of 1863–64, months after religious passions overflowed in its rival. "I have never witnessed anything like it," a colonel from New Jersey observed. "When our regiment is not on picket, our church is crowded for preaching and prayer every night. After the regular meeting is over, a large number" stays for prayer and conversation on spiritual matters.[14] A soldier from Vermont made a connection between the foreign-missions field and the heathen army, claiming that no missionary "can receive a heartier welcome than the soldier is willing to accord the delegates of the [US] Christian commission." Nothing "more can be accomplished" for Christianity in India or China than in the army, Wilbur Fisk continued, recording his gratitude for the material and spiritual aid offered by the volunteers of the Christian Commission.[15] Accompanying the revival was a new acceptance of the role of slavery in the rebellion that kept them from home. "There is a great change in the army . . . on the subject of slavery," a Maine chaplain wrote. "Its overthrow was a military necessity. We destroy tanneries, flour-mills, and other fixtures," so why "not then weaken and destroy the strong arm of slavery, which has been used to raise food for the army of the Confederates, to dig rifle pits, and throw up earthworks?"[16]

"The Fates seem against this Army of the Potomac," a disgusted Michigander wrote days after the 1862 disaster at Fredericksburg. "We have tried strategy under McClellan, dash under Pope, bulldog fighting under Burnside & failed with all. Who shall we find combining all?"[17] Lee, by contrast, commented humbly enough in late 1862 that he worried the Lincoln administration might someday find a general whom "I don't understand" and cannot therefore confound.[18] The fall of Vicksburg and the relief of Chattanooga gave country and Congress a man to promote to the highest rank, who hopefully combined the necessary qualities of generalship to win the war.

Congress revived the rank of lieutenant general—bestowed since George Washington's day only in brevet form to the general of three wars, Winfield Scott—to confer it upon "Unconditional Surrender" Grant. Now the commander of all Union armies, Grant intended to unleash five of them in a coordinated offensive, three in Virginia and two in the West. Yet three of them were led by postmillenarian political generals with checkered records—Nathaniel Banks, Benjamin Butler, and Franz Sigel—leaving only the two largest under veteran West Pointers. "For coping with" this all-out offensive, "Lee had no elaborate plans even though he saw 1864 as the critical year for the Confederacy because of the northern presidential election. He had as his objective to 'resist manfully' until the South had sapped the North's will-to-win."[19] Read in an eschatological light, the words "resist manfully" could only be seen as premillenarian fatalism. Lee's Army of Northern Virginia must bleed the three Union armies in Virginia long and hard enough to keep Grant away from Richmond. Failing a reverse like those of Second Manassas or Fredericksburg, attrition at unprecedented levels could energize Democratic voters to knock Lincoln, running on a fusion Union ticket, out of the White House in November. Then President George McClellan as a political neophyte could be maneuvered by savvier Peace Democrats to accept a peace with separation, whatever the general promised on an ostensible platform of peace with reunion and slavery (the premillenarian status quo antebellum).

Mere days before Grant brought the western Republican way of war home to Virginians via his Overland Campaign, North Carolina Presbyterian and Confederate brigade commander Stephen Dodson Ramseur still hoped that one major victory could secure southern independence. The 1860 West Point graduate was influenced during his academy days by the efforts of Oliver O. Howard—then a lieutenant and, from autumn 1857, an academy instructor—to encourage religious revival via twice-weekly prayer meetings for cadets after supper; Cadet Ramseur joined Howard's movement as a prayer leader.[20] Knowingly or otherwise, in April 1864 General Ramseur echoed the New England Puritan leader John Winthrop in his desire that the Confederacy might be viewed as a new chosen people. "I do pray that we may be established as an independent people, a people known and recognized as God's Peculiar People!"[21]

Rather than look at the Armies of Northern Virginia and of the Potomac at the inception of the spring Overland Campaign, we will take a snapshot of them in mid-May 1864, when both sides had taken heavy casualties and received reinforcements. Major General Meade was still technically in command of the Army of the Potomac, but Lieutenant General Grant chose to follow his army's progress personally rather than remain in the western theater, where he entrusted Major General Sherman with an ambitious campaign from Chattanooga to Atlanta, yet another key western railroad junction. By mid-May Meade led 184 volunteer infantry regiments, two sharpshooter regiments, five regular regiments (or parts thereof), one heavy artillery regiment from Vermont, and three infantry battalions.[22]

Another thirty-seven volunteer, three regular, and two heavy artillery regiments served in Major General Burnside's Ninth Corps, which was technically independent of Meade's command as Burnside was senior to him by commission date but was still under Grant's overall command.[23] Whatever their individual religious beliefs, the presence and participation of six black regiments (and by the time of the tragic Battle of the Crater on July 30, there were eight such units in Burnside's command) was a sign of the postmillenarian character of the Army of the Potomac after mid-1864. Thousands of former enslaved men were now armed, paid, and free, and their job was not only to kill their former masters but also to liberate Virginia's enslaved population.

Lee's army endeavored to oppose the latest Union offensive against Richmond from the latest Union general that Lincoln had found to send against him with largely the same army (at least in an organizational sense) that had marched to Gettysburg, including all three of the corps commanders of the previous July. By mid-May Lee's "Old War Horse," James Longstreet, had been wounded—by friendly fire, ominously like Stonewall Jackson at Chancellorsville the previous May—and on May 11 the flamboyant if erratic cavalry chief J. E. B. Stuart was mortally wounded. Nevertheless, Lee's 172 infantry regiments and ten battalions that fought Grant to a standstill at Spotsylvania Court House were at least half full of veterans.[24]

The Army of the Potomac—a mixture of seasoned veterans (some of whose three-year terms of enlistment expired that summer) and dubiously reliable draftees—experienced an unprecedented crucible as it advanced on Richmond. The army sustained more than 50,000 casualties in barely a month of fighting at the Wilderness, Spotsylvania Court House, and crossing the North Anna River, culminating in a senseless assault at Cold Harbor in which several thousand were killed or wounded in less than an hour. Aside from the loss of half its original strength since launching the campaign, the army had lost hope. "Hope is a vital element to morale, or the will to fight," observed historian Steven Sodergren, "for without hope why would a soldier continue risking his life on the field of battle? There are different kinds of hope on the battlefield, such as the hope in the survival of oneself or one's immediate comrades, the hope for the triumph of one's cause, and the hope" that generals' leadership will lead to the victory of their cause.[25] Hope, as applied in this book, also relates to the postmillenarian optimism or premillenarian fatalism of northern soldiers fighting to end the war on their ideological terms. As of June 1864, the Army of the Potomac, despite 30,000 reinforcements, temporarily despaired of all of these kinds of hope until the mobile warfare of the Overland Campaign ceased and the men could regain some sense of control within the environment of the siege of a static city.[26]

Grant never despaired of this campaign, however, grimly preparing to fight it out all summer or for the next year, if necessary. He was nevertheless disgusted by the premillenarian pessimism that was McClellan's lasting legacy to the Army of Potomac's general and staff officers. When a staff officer prophesied in the face of a Confederate counterattack that Lee was about to cut the army off from the Rapidan in May, Grant exploded. "Oh, I am heartily tired of hearing about what *Lee* is going to do. Some of you always seem to think that he is suddenly going to turn a double somersault and land in our rear and on both flanks at the same time," the general exclaimed. "Go back to your command and try to think what we are going to do ourselves, instead of what *Lee* is going to do."[27] John Pope noted a similar syndrome in the army's high command in 1862; Grant in 1864 was gifted with more time and authority to try to stamp it out and replace pessimism with postmillenarian optimism and aggressiveness.

Having bypassed the Richmond defenses, the Army of the Potomac now besieged the city of Petersburg, south of the Confederate capital. Grant was keen to break through the rebel defenses, split Lee's army in two, and end the war. Northern morale could hardly accept another 60,000 casualties, so a new tactic was needed.

The colonel of a regiment from Pennsylvania's anthracite-coal-mining region went to General Burnside with the proposal that a mine could be excavated and a breach blown in the rebel line. A successful exploitation of the breach could capture Petersburg. Richmond must then fall, and with the destruction of Lee's army, the war was won. For a month the men of the Forty-Eighth Pennsylvania dug their tunnel.[28] By the end of July, the mine was ready.

But there remained the selection of the assault's vanguard. As Burnside's corps was tasked with the assault, he picked an all-black division for special training, which included diverting on either side of the crater to widen the breach instead of running into the depression. Yet Burnside's superiors worried that if the green US Colored Troops (USCT) failed in the attack, the northern press might claim that the black soldiers were expendable, that "we were shoving those people ahead to get killed because we did not care about them." The troops were also largely untested in battle, further worrying General Meade.[29] A white division was substituted at the last minute.[30]

When the mine exploded and the division went forward, its commander was nowhere to be found. Leaderless and untrained, the troops poured into the crater rather than widening the breach. The eight USCT regiments of Edward Ferrero's division followed them, and in the face of growing rebel resistance, also poured into the crater. This first major collision between black and white soldiers in Virginia was more charged than ever due to the massacre of over one hundred African American soldiers by Nathan Bedford Forrest's troopers a few months before in Tennessee. Over a month before the attack on the Crater, white soldiers of the Seventh West Virginia found Confederate soldiers fearful of murder if overcome by USCT forces following word of Fort Pillow. Lieutenant James Murdock discovered a dozen rebel soldiers lying face down, hiding from vengeful USCT bayonets, as his unit stormed the defenses outside Petersburg on June 16.[31]

The USCT attackers allegedly yelled, "*No quarter for the d—d rebels. Remember Fort Pillow,*" as they reached the Confederate works. Rebels from Virginia determined the black soldiers "would give no quarter to us and rest assured received none."[32] Neighboring South Carolinians bellowed, "Kill 'em! Shoot 'em! Kill the damned niggers!"[33]

Two brigades of William Mahone's Confederate division—including several units from Petersburg—rushed to seal the breach. The commander of the Sixty-First Virginia "never felt more like fighting in my life" after he saw the race of his foe.[34] "Our men were maddened and wild with rage," the colonel remembered, "deep and loud curses were hissed between clinched teeth as bayonets were thrust into men and drawn from the bleeding bodies of the dying or as the butt thud brought strong men to their knees."[35] The fighting was certainly face to face and hand to hand. "Our men would drive the bayonet into one man, pull it out, turn the butt and knock the brains out of another, and so on until the ditch ran with [the] blood of the dead and dying," another officer recalled.[36] William Stewart of the Sixty-First Virginia noted that the bloody mud was "shoe-sole deep" in places.[37] A veteran of the Twelfth Virginia recalled after the war that "Gen'l Mahone had remarked very emphatically that he wanted all the [enemy regiments' flags, and "sixteen stands," or eight regiments' worth, were visible of] colors and no prisoners."[38] A captain in one of Burnside's white brigades heard the rebels yell, "Save the white men but kill the damn niggers."[39] Race mattered as to which Yankees were allowed to surrender.

Artillery officer and Petersburg resident William Pegram noted the "ever ready Mahone" endeavored "to retake the line with his fine troops, which he did, with . . . great loss to the enemy. I never saw such a sight. . . . For a good distance in the trenches the Yankees, white and black, principally the latter, were killed two or three or four deep." He claimed that the black soldiers "threw down their arms to surrender, but were not allowed to do so." Pegram deemed this massacre "was perfectly right, as a matter of policy." While it "seems cruel to murder them in cold blood," he thought it justified, having long "wished the enemy would bring some negroes against this army. I am convinced, since Saturday's fight, that it has a splendid effect" on morale.[40] Pegram believed that the slaughter of trapped soldiers could result in the Union's abandonment of its postmillenarian experiment in employing black soldiers.

IF GENERALS GRANT AND Philip H. Sheridan generally avoided using black regiments as frontline troops, armed black postmillenarians nevertheless affected the Shenandoah Valley in 1864. In early April elements of the Nineteenth USCT Regiment marched into Winchester on a recruiting mission. The premillenarian residents of the town were less pleased at the arrival of armed African Americans than they were with Banks's and Milroy's white soldiers each of the past two years. "It's horrible to think of" black men ordering white people off their own streets, Kate Sperry noted.[41] "We have witnessed a sight today that I never expected to see. A Negro regiment came into town," causing "great excitement among" black and white residents, Julia Chase recorded, conceding that such apocalyptic scenes were now commonplace. "We shall expect to see almost anything after this."[42] If few recruits resulted from this mission, the regiment and others posted on occupation duty elsewhere in Virginia served notice to premillenarian Confederates that postmillenarian ideology was in the ascendant. The men of the Nineteenth USCT were tragically numbered among the eight regiments eviscerated at the Crater in July.

Three separate Union offensives pushed into the Shenandoah Valley in 1864, successively led by Sigel, Hunter, and Sheridan. If Valley denizens breathed a sigh of relief after the German radical Sigel's army fled the battlefield at New Market in May, his successor posed a greater threat. David Hunter, a West Point graduate *and* an abolitionist, sought to restore his military reputation after mediocre performances in Missouri and South Carolina. "Should I ever have another command," the general wrote in 1863, "I shall be as absolute as a Turk, and consult nobody on the face of the earth."[43]

Rockbridge County was spared the direct attention of Banks and other Union generals in 1862, but postmillenarian Hunter—having sought to free South Carolina's enslaved population in 1861 without Lincoln's permission—dramatically altered Lexington's war experience in 1864.[44] The lackluster attempt by two thousand Confederate soldiers to defend Lexington against Hunter's host gave the avenging general all the excuse he needed to burn VMI and Governor John Letcher's house. Colonel David Strother—Hunter's cousin and staff officer—encouraged the general to destroy the institute, a school fostering treasonous instruction which over the past three years had produced a long "list of capable military officers . . . raised up against the government" to destroy the Union. Strother charged that VMI was "fostered by the state authorities" to spread disunionist sentiments and other poisonous ideas among elite southerners.[45]

Hunter's soldiers, in contrast, turned their attention to Lexington's farms and houses. Margaret Preston told the men who entered her home that she was a northern woman "but confessed that I was ashamed of my northern lineage when I saw them come on such an errand." Some of the intruders started to carry away the china in the dining room until a soldier from Philadelphia intervened. The family's breakfast was appropriated, so when Preston's children cried for something to eat, she "had nothing to give them but crackers."[46] The pastor of Lexington's Presbyterian church—Preston's minister—lost "36 bushels of corn—a ton of hay and my favorite riding horse" to his "Yankee Brethren," who also damaged his carriage. Reverend William White noted that Hunter's officers justified the "cruel treatment" of Lexington's citizens for their persecution of the antebellum president of Washington College, Margaret's father George Junkin, a Unionist from Pennsylvania.[47]

The Lexington residence of the town's antebellum Episcopal clergyman received even more hostile attention from the occupiers. Reverend William Pendleton had become commander of the artillery in Lee's army as a general officer in 1862, while his son Alexander then served as a staff officer to Stonewall Jackson. Only the elder Pendleton's wife and daughters remained in Lexington in the summer of 1864. Items hidden away in their residence by VMI cadets—three rifles among them—were quickly discovered by the occupying troops. The Pendleton women should not have been puzzled at the rapid exposure of the contraband, they needed only to look to their enslaved people for the source of the intelligence. But only after one of the Union soldiers detailed to protect the house from looting admitted that "a Negro" had told him where the rifles were hidden did Rose Pendleton begin to "suspect one of our own servants." Yet the family remained oblivious to the observational powers of people they assumed were happy with their lot, as Mrs. Pendleton told a guard who lectured her on treating her servants well, for "they is as free as you." Her hand still shaking with anger, she lambasted Hunter's men as "brutes" and "wretches" in a journal of the occupation she penned less than a week after the "vile Yankees" departed. Pendleton particularly noted that when her mother—a clergyman's wife—attempted to talk "about the Saviour" with one Union soldier, he damned her for a secessionist and refused to discuss the "Saviour" with her, presumably because Virginians were beyond the pale of Christianity to him. Yet the man's response reinforced Rose Pendleton's view that it was the Yankees who were beyond salvation.[48]

Reverend White noted that Union soldiers looted Washington College—if sparing it the fiery fate of VMI—and what they did not destroy or take was offered to local African Americans.[49] General Hunter's brother-in-law Charles Hodge was the foremost Presbyterian theologian at Princeton Seminary, well known to Reverend White and Robert Dabney. Hodge won the latter's respect for his antebellum refusal to claim that the Bible and Christian tradition militated in favor of the abolition of slavery, yet he now supported military efforts to crush the rebellion as well as Lincoln's Emancipation Proclamation.[50] In other words, the war had converted Hodge from amillennial neutrality on American slavery to postmillenarian radicalism, at least from the perspective of southern Presbyterians.

As Hunter's men unleashed their wrath on Lexington, Margaret Preston worried that the mostly bloodless occupation was a precursor to a deadlier, total war to be waged primarily on civilians. She attempted to intimidate one soldier, warning him of the "deadly earnestness among our men which would make the last remnant of them fly to our mountain fastnesses and fight like tigers till the last inch of ground was taken from them," that "there could be no yielding." The soldier retorted that no such spirit existed in the

Confederate army. This two-hour conversation "with an intelligent and seemingly Christian man" filled Preston "with entire despair for the Confederacy."[51] And even if Lee's army fought on as guerrillas, how long could it persist if Union armies turned fire against and plundered their way through all the cities and towns of Virginia to destroy civilians' will to resist? This principle of fiery retribution was carried out elsewhere in the Valley before the year was out.

Lexington escaped the worst damage inflicted by Union forces in the Shenandoah that year, namely Sheridan's scorched-earth campaign in the fall. If Grant warned Sigel in the spring to avoid "indiscriminate marauding," the Union general in chief in the fall instructed Sheridan to "eat Virginia clear and clean as far as [the Confederate army there retreats], so that crows flying over it for the balance of the season will have to carry their provender with them."[52]

Sheridan and his army did their best to carry out these instructions. "We have done a business for the confederacy during this campaign th[r]ough the Valley of Va that 'I Rec[k]on' wont be forgotten very soon," a soldier from Vermont wrote home.[53] George Howard noted the destruction "by fire from Staunton to Strasburg, of the principal property of those persons who are engaged in this rebellion." Expecting the rebels to "call us very bad names," he argued that such arson was justified "in view of the atrocities committed by these infernal traitors." The destruction of barns and bridges, haystacks and mills, all commingled "in one grand, vast and gigantic conflagration" over seventy-five miles. Howard read of the fiery destruction of Jerusalem by the Romans in school but thought it "pale[d] into insignificance and littleness before the burning of" hundreds of farms in Virginia. This was just recompense for "those three hundred thousand fresh soldiers' graves in these slave states [that] call for redress at our hands."[54]

Already engaged in burning barns, Sheridan's men were unleashed for widespread property damage following what their general termed the murder of Lieutenant John Meigs. Sheridan—if no Calvinist—considered Meigs's death in an alleged ambush by John Mosby's guerrillas nothing short of murder. All the people of the Valley were culpable, so all now suffered. "This, every living soldier who was in this campaign knows to be true," the chaplain of the Tenth Vermont wrote in concurrence with Sheridan's view. "The people were meek-faced citizens by day, and in the presence of any considerable body of Union troops; but as soon as the troops were out of sight . . . they became desperate and bloodthirsty guerrillas." In this guise "they stole upon our men like savages, and shot them down or dragged them away to the woods." If ostensibly good Protestants, Valley residents were bad Samaritans. "Could anything justify their course? Could any punishment be too severe?"[55] His colleague in the Fifth New York Cavalry noted that George A. Custer's cavalry division was tasked with burning "every building within a circle of three miles from the scene of the murder" of Meigs.[56] Yet one of Sheridan's infantry brigade commanders managed to talk the general down from destroying the whole town of Dayton; nevertheless, some outlying houses were put to the torch.

David Silkenat raised an interesting point regarding Sheridan's all-out reaction to an alleged murder of one of his protégés by guerrilla action. Grant already instructed the general that August to hang any member of Mosby's band he caught—without a trial. Given this decree of extermination or total war against them, rebel guerrillas "had little incentive to surrender and increasingly fought to the death"; with little incentive also to abide by any laws of war, the resorted to "torture, arson, and pillage with abandon."[57]

"Sheridan is making thorough work here in the Valley, destroying every thing that would help feed the rebel army. The town of Dayton . . . was burned yesterday afternoon in retaliation for the Murder of a Union officer there," wrote a soldier of the Tenth Vermont, erroneously believing that the army had carried out his commander's threat to destroy Dayton. "I believe Gen. Sheridan to be the man for this place after all. It will not do to trifle with him. Though it may seem brutal to burn the homes of women and children, justice to our own brave men sometimes demands it."[58] The Harvard-educated commander of a Massachusetts cavalry regiment wrote his wife in a similar vein. He noted the new moon looked "almost reproachful in the west last night . . . lighted up by burning barns and houses." While his unit had not yet taken part in the arson, "if it would help end bushwhacking . . . I would cheerfully assist in making the whole Valley a desert from Staunton northward."[59]

A trooper of the Second Virginia Cavalry witnessed the vengeance of Sheridan's men as he rode in pursuit of the Union army. "All along our route were burning barns houses etc. The beautiful and fertile Valley of Virginia is in one vast cloud of smoke, and the very air is impregnated with the smell of burning property." He found a plank left by the Union troopers, which read simply "Remember Chambersburg."[60] The biblical principle of an eye for an eye was being applied not only to murdered officers but also to burned towns. As Valley resident Joseph Waddell noted with foreboding when he heard of the burning of that Pennsylvania town by General John McCausland—the cavalry commander who failed to defend Lexington in June—the "Yankees will come back and burn a hundred for one."[61]

General Jubal Early, commander of the Army of Northern Virginia's Second Corps and sent by Lee with his troops from Petersburg to defend the Valley and threaten Washington, DC, tried once more to turn Confederate fortunes around in the Shenandoah and influence the northern elections, striking Sheridan's unsuspecting army at Cedar Creek in October. Yet if half of the Union force fell back before the onslaught, the rebels' hunger and the stalwart veterans of the Sixth Corps halted and then shoved Early's army back. Two years of "retreats and defeats in the Shenandoah valley . . . have at last been redeemed by a decisive victory," the newspaper of the African Methodist Episcopal Church noted, trusting Sheridan's success must "aid materially Grant's operations against Petersburg and Richmond."[62]

Four Union battlefield victories in the Valley and the ongoing siege of Petersburg only reinforced a feeling of helplessness among Virginia's white premillennial population in the face of the triumphant ideology of northern postmillennials and their black allies. "This is the darkest and most trying time we have ever seen," Laura Lee noted after news arrived of more disasters in the West to add to those in the East. "Everything seems depressing and almost hopeless."[63] Northern Democratic newspapers condemned Sheridan's tactics, for all the good that did anyone. "Sheridan intends to continue the destruction all the way north to Martinsburg," the *Philadelphia Age* noted. "The people, deprived of food and homes, will have to wander off" to uncertain fates thanks to Grant's strategy as carried out by Sheridan.[64] The *Valley Spirit* of Chambersburg, Pennsylvania, summed up Sheridan's actions in one word: "Vandalism."[65] A motley army of mercenaries—"German, Irish, negro, and Yankee wretches"—so inferior to Virginia's knightly defenders, had lain waste to Virginia, the gloomy assessment of Lexington clergyman and Confederate general Pendleton.[66]

WHILE TENS OF THOUSANDS of soldiers fell in combat between the Battle of Fredericksburg and the Siege of Petersburg, thousands of formerly enslaved Virginians (mostly women and children) were held in contraband camps like Craney Island near Norfolk. Freedom aside, these unarmed post-millenarians sought work and a reunion with families torn asunder by slavery and the disrespect of southern premillenarians for the institution of marriage when applied to the enslaved. Union army chaplains and AMA missionaries at these camps spent a significant amount of time and energy officiating weddings—an institution they believed served to "civilize" their charges—as well as catechizing the self-emancipated.[67]

Although slaveowners often encouraged their human property to marry, sometimes officiating over ceremonies that could be as simple as jumping over a broom, such unions were broken up the moment that one spouse was sold away, with masters expecting the forcibly separated couple to take up new partners. Lucy Chase, an abolitionist from New England now serving as a missionary teacher at Craney Island, recorded the reunion of one such couple. Both had remarried, yet they embraced and cried, with the second wife looking on jealously. "My [second] husband is so kind, I shouldn't leave him if he hadn't had another wife, and of course I shouldn't now. Yes, my husband's very kind, but I ain't happy," this woman, "wise and faithful in her home relations" and trusted by Union authorities, remarked afterward. "White folk's got a heap to answer for the way they've done to colored folks!" she told Chase regarding the involuntary separation from her first, still-beloved husband. "So much they won't never *pray* it away!"[68]

ASIDE FROM CONVERSION and marriage, white postmillenarians emphasized the importance of education for the improvement of the freedpeople. General Banks created a system of Sunday schools in the Department of the Gulf "for the purpose of giving greater care, industry, and intelligence to the laboring classes of freedmen, and inspiring them with a higher sense of their obligations to society, to their race, and to all rightful authority."[69] An AMA leader in the Department of the Gulf concurred with the general's view of the civilizing purpose of education. E. M. Wheelock wrote that missionaries followed the military's "pioneering work of blasting the rock and felling the forest . . . to sow the grain and raise the golden harvest." The AMA's "small pacific army of teachers and civilizers" were the vanguard of postmillenarian progress, for the "schoolhouse takes the place of the whipping post and scourge" wherever these missionaries went in the footsteps of the wilderness-cleansing army.[70]

An army captain serving as superintendent of contrabands in Virginia testified to African Americans' desire for self-determination as well as their eagerness to work for that independence. C. B. Wilder wrote of their disposition to work "if they could be reasonably paid" and noted that their efforts exceeded his antebellum prejudice. "I did not think that they had so much brain. They have got as much brains as you or I have, though they have an odd way of showing it." He now accepted that "the [premillenarian] dogma that negroes are very valuable as slaves, but when free, worthless, and unable to take care of themselves, is now exploded." What made "all the difference" was whether "they are forced, or encouraged to work."[71]

A southern premillenarian and loyal Unionist expelled from North Carolina argued against emancipation unless it followed significant improvement to African Americans' education and morals. If authorities were to "turn them out in their present ignorant condition," Bryan Tyson "feared disastrous consequences would follow."[72] Anticipating Lincoln's speculation over slavery in his second inaugural address, Tyson argued from his exile in the District of Columbia that "God is on [one] side or the other of the question." That debate was whether slavery "is just and lawful, having been instituted under a Theocracy," or "that it is unjust, inhumane, and ought to be abolished."[73] Tyson ostensibly echoed postmillenarian support for education and religious proselytization. "I wish to do these people justice throughout, and I, therefore, desire that they should be sent to school, and at least taught to read, so as to be able to read the Scriptures. It has been thought by some emancipationists that such a course would lead to enfranchisement. If it would, I am for it."[74] He extolled the virtue of marriage, believing that slave marriages were honored by their masters, however extralegal, and claimed that very few cohabiting slave couples were forcibly parted, though he favored a law that forbade such separation.[75] "The negro is as yet but a child in intellect. I therefore think it should be our duty as a Christian people to treat them kindly, and place them in whatever position they thrive best. I think the white race at least owes that much. . . . Therefore, as we have plenty of room for them," and they had the potential to "occupy a useful position in society, why exterminate the poor creatures?"[76] Why commit genocide, indeed?

Tyson's "only plea . . . for retaining these people a day longer in servitude, is that, under existing circumstances, I don't think their condition would be bettered by changing their social position." He favored "first applying to them the anointing oil of learning and Christianity; and, whenever it shall have been clearly demonstrated that they are in a fit condition to take care of themselves, I am then for their going out free. But"—of course there was a but—if "after exhausting these means, it should be discovered that they had not made proper advances in the sciences and civilization, we might then fairly infer that God never intended that they should be placed on a level with the Caucasian or white race." In line with the Confederate vice president Stephens, Tyson objected to Thomas Jefferson's assertion that "all men are created equal" in the Declaration of Independence. Yet his objection was laid on the basis of a postmillenarian interpretation to "date back and apply as an interpretation of the Scriptures written by inspiration thousands and thousands of years before. No such doctrine is inculcated in the Scriptures, and it cannot be found within the lids of the Bible that all men were created equal, such an idea being wholly of human origin."[77]

Two postmillenarian pastors provided a counternarrative to Tyson's story of complacent slaves. The classically educated chaplain of the Sixth Massachusetts wrote from near Suffolk, Virginia, of "the long files of dusky pilgrims" arriving in his army's camp, "dragging the household penates" like Aeneas fleeing Troy en route to founding Rome. However poor their appearance, he "found them intelligent as, and every way the equals of, the white people left in our neighborhood."[78] He was touched by their prayers for his soldiers and, on at least one occasion, preached alongside a black Methodist minister. Standing before "an audience of white and black, of ministers and laity, and of many denominations, we, a Universalist and Methodist preacher, administered the communion," the chaplain—ironically named for the founder of Methodism—enthused. "It seemed a foregleam of the millennium, as we all worshipped together; for, though speaking many sectarian dialects, we were united in one spirit."[79]

Farther south, another clergyman sympathetic to the formerly enslaved wrote of his fellow Protestants' hopes for the future. "There is no part of the Bible with which they are so familiar as the story of the deliverance of Israel," Chaplain William Kephart wrote of the freedpeople near Decatur. "Moses is their ideal of all that is high and noble, and perfect, in man. I think they have been accustomed to regard Christ not so much in the light of a *spiritual* Deliverer, as that of a second Moses who would eventually lead them out of their prison-house of bondage."[80] If Kephart and other white Protestants envisioned Lincoln as the most evident exemplar of a latter-day

Moses, by 1864 enslaved people could look to the already self-emancipated Harriet Tubman—and to themselves.

Tubman began 1864 in Florida, where Union forces were attempting to reclaim the sparsely settled state. If she was not present at the disastrous February battle at Olustee, where wounded black soldiers were massacred following the Union army's retreat, she likely tended to the survivors who made it to Jacksonville.[81] Paid very little over two years' employment with the Department of the South even as she paid scouts and spies for intelligence, Tubman sought and received a furlough to return northward in June.[82] White abolitionists noted that while "the country owes her much," she was not receiving just compensation.[83] Allies in the New England Freedmen's Aid Society arranged for Tubman to be hired as a "practical teacher" in the Hilton Head area of South Carolina.[84]

OUR APOSTLE SERVING IN Sherman's western army was visiting Philadelphia on a religious mission at the beginning of the year. He gave a speech at the US Christian Commission's rally held at the Academy of Music in January 1864. General Howard represented the men serving at the front. The mother of one of his fallen friends wrote Elizabeth Howard that when her husband "came forward . . . with his empty sleeve . . . the whole people rose and echoed their welcome."[85] The general compared the tenuous progress of the war to the troubled state of the national soul. The defeats suffered so far were the product of a "fearful power of evil," which carried in its train "demoralizing tendencies [that] crushed out the principles of good in the soldier's heart."[86] The secular—or premillenarian—goal of preservation of the Union was insufficient to overcome Confederate determination. Only the work of the Christian Commission and other devout postmillenarians to convert Union soldiers and grant them a moral purpose and crusade could equip them to win the final victory.[87] Julia Ward Howe's literary contribution to the postmillenarian war effort featured in the Christian Commission's next annual meeting.

We will take a snapshot view of the major western armies in mid-July, as John Bell Hood took command of the Army of Tennessee on July 18. Hood replaced Joseph E. Johnston, who for the past two and a half months had failed to halt Sherman's advance on Atlanta or force the Union army into a decisive battle. Hood replaced Johnston's defensive tactics along rivers and ridgelines with frontal offensives against the invader, throwing 154 volunteer infantry regiments, three regular regiments, and eleven battalions against Sherman's forces.[88] As a result, Hood's army declined from almost 60,000 effectives in mid-July to less than 52,000 by the end of the month.

The 301 volunteer infantry regiments, six regular battalions, and three volunteer battalions in Sherman's three armies from the Military Division of the Mississippi weathered Hood's assaults.[89] His army group counted roughly 106,000 effectives in mid-July prior to the beginning of Hood's attacks outside Atlanta.

Bishop Polk's ministrations to his fellow generals in the Army of Tennessee bore fruit this year. As Sherman began his campaign through northern Georgia toward Atlanta, Polk baptized Hood at Dalton on May 12 and army commander Johnston six days later.[90] The bishop's influence, combined with that of Mrs. Hardee, convinced Polk's fellow corps commander William Hardee to be confirmed in the Episcopal denomination. Hardee's first wife and all of their children were Episcopalians, so the Episcopal bishop did not have to work hard to convince the general which denomination to join. "I am trying hard to lead a godly life," the new convert wrote his wife. "In time I hope to conquer the old Adam."[91]

As June 13 turned into June 14, Polk conversed with his friend Randall Lee Gibson, a Louisiana sugar planter turned general. The bishop was by turns postmillennial and premillennial in his view of the state of the war. Despite the advance of Sherman's army, Polk averred that the Confederate states "would surely achieve our independence, and what a day it would be when we could all return to the dear city of New Orleans, bringing peace and liberty to our people." Then he seemed to abruptly realize the postmillenarian fantasy of his words. "Rising up in bed," the bishop-general backtracked: "No, my dear boy, even this may never be. For experience in life and true philosophy have taught me to set my heart upon nothing, nothing in this world. Our triumphs, our joys can be celebrated only in the world and life to come."[92]

Polk's death—assassination by rifled artillery shell by order of General Sherman—later on the fourteenth shook Hardee. He and Johnston too were almost killed by the same Union battery that hit Polk with its third shot. William Harrison Polk, a distant kinsman of the general serving in the Twenty-First Illinois, witnessed a Confederate deserter identify Generals Johnston, Hardee, and Polk standing at a cleared rebel artillery position atop Pine Mountain via field glass for General Sherman. The latter ordered a nearby battery to "give the bishop a morning salute!"[93] Sherman matter-of-factly noted "That will do" as the third shot stuck. Later he just as perfunctorily wired his superiors: "We killed Bishop Polk yesterday, and made good progress today."[94] The latter-day Leonidas died like his namesake, defending a noted rocky prominence, while his secular enemy focused on forward progress.

The next night General Hardee received a religious pamphlet that Polk had intended to give him, now soaked in the blood of his friend and spiritual mentor.[95] The pamphlet—a just-published tract by the Episcopalian missionary to the Army of Tennessee Charles T. Quintard entitled *Balm for the Weary and Wounded*—was written for common soldiers, and Polk had copies for each of his fellow corps commanders and General Johnston. Fittingly, Reverend Quintard delivered the bishop's funeral address.[96] "I thought the death of our dear old friend Genl. Polk would cause you to feel uneasy about my safety," Hardee attempted to reassure his other spiritual mentor a few days later. "According to the doctrine of chances, I am in less danger now than before, there being but three Lieut. Genl's & one being killed the chances for the safety of the other[s] are greatly increased."[97] Polk's men left a more prosaic memorial of their commander for the Yankees to find at the fatal site, a sign that read, "You damn Yankee sons of bitches has killed our old Gen. Polk."[98] A *New York Herald* correspondent picked up fragments of Polk's ribs and arm bones, while Union soldiers dipped handkerchiefs in the blood-matted grass where Polk fell, as if he was a martyred saint of old whose relics merited preserving.[99]

Bishop Stephen Elliott used the occasion of the fighting bishop's funeral to condemn the "Christians of the North," particularly the northern Episcopalian clergy "who have lent yourselves to the fanning of the fury of this unjust and cruel war," in "the presence of the body of my murdered brother." The presiding Episcopal bishop of the Confederacy challenged his fellow Protestants "to meet us at the judgment seat of Christ . . . , that awful bar where the multitudes whom you have followed to do evil shall not shield you from an angry God." In the name of "sacred Liberty which you have trampled underfoot" and the "glorious Constitution which you have destroyed," Elliott summoned them to see "the temples of God which you have desecrated" and the "Christian virgins whom you have violated . . . [and] our slaves whom you have seduced and then consigned to misery."

Yet he left "justice and vengeance to God." Invoking the memory of God's judgment of Cain for murdering his brother, Abel, the "blood of your brethren" such as General Polk "crieth unto God from the earth, and it will not cry in vain. It has entered into the ears of the Lord God of Sabaoth, and will return upon you in that day of solemn justice and fearful retribution."[100] In the meantime, bloody retribution continued to pour out upon the rebel Protestants of Georgia and Virginia.

Other clergymen fell in battle after Polk's death as Sherman's host advanced inexorably on Atlanta. At Resaca the chaplains of two regiments facing each other perished. Rev. John M. Springer of the Third Wisconsin joined the regimental battle line, asking for use of a musket, although told to act as a lieutenant initially, for "there would soon be plenty of muskets, if there was much of a battle. He did so; and was the first man hit."[101] After the fighting ended for the day, soldiers of the Third Wisconsin found the body of the elderly chaplain of the Georgia regiment that fought them. Wounded members of that regiment claimed "that this chaplain's son was a captain and had been killed; and the father was shot while on the field to recover the body of his son." Father and son lay only "a few rods from the place where Chaplain Springer fell."[102]

While campaigning in the western states, Corporal Frederick Pettit of Pennsylvania condemned the "poison of slavery," which "kills energy, enterprise, sociability, and all that makes a people enlightened and happy."[103] Noting that white southerners failed to respect the sabbath—possibly because pastors were ordered to include a prayer for Lincoln during their services or see their churches shuttered—Pettit believed "there are people here who do not know what the Sabbath is. The whole south is in this ignorant, heathenish condition." Again, slavery was to blame. "It appears to me there is no other means of reaching the root of all this but through war and bloodshed." With the peculiar institution destroyed, "a wide field will soon be opened for Christian labor." Yet Pettit envisioned a white nation after the war. "The masses of poor whites will need to be educated and christianized. The negroes must be colonized sooner or later."[104]

The butt of Sherman's antipious humor, O. O. Howard, was also the beneficiary of his prejudice against political generals. When Sherman decided to replace his fallen protégé James B. McPherson with a professional instead of the temporary stand-in John Logan, who had acquitted himself well in close combat before Atlanta, Howard was the choice to command the Army of the

Tennessee. Another West Point graduate, former Army of the Potomac commander Joseph Hooker, left the army in a huff after he was passed over.[105] Howard realized how fortunate he was to gain this elevation, knowing "after the reverse at Chancellorsville," a specter that also haunted Hooker, "it was hard for me to cherish a feeling of confidence in the whole of the old corps" of West Point graduates.[106]

One of the division commanders who traveled west with Howard from Virginia the previous year was John Geary. Having "trembled" while contemplating the ramifications of the emancipation proclamation, Geary now observed the doleful consequences of the siege of Atlanta upon its civilian population. A young mother "with a starving child so poor as scarcely to live" sought bread at his headquarters. "Her husband was a conscript in the rebel ranks, and this is but a specimen of Davis' work. If there is one spot in hell hotter than another, why should it not be reserved for him who has brought such evils on his fellow man."[107] The general's transition to Republicanism was now far advanced, and he was proud to proclaim, "'Old Geary' is [now] as much of a terror to the Georgians as he used to be [to] the Virginians."[108] Confident that "nine-tenths of the soldiers in this Army will vote for Lincoln," Geary anxiously awaited the election results from Pennsylvania and the rest of the loyal states in November.[109]

IF NORTHERN PREMILLENARIANS HAD decisively lost control of the Union armies by 1864, they earnestly contended with postmillenarian Republicans to wrest away control of the White House, for 1864 was an election year. Yet the Democratic Party was deeply riven between one faction that wanted victory and the status quo antebellum and another that demanded peace at any price. Finding a candidate acceptable to both sides was critical. The Republican incumbent summed up their dilemma perfectly: "They must nominate a Peace Democrat on a war platform, or a War Democrat on a peace platform."[110] Yet if this divide worked to Lincoln's benefit, the president still needed to convince radical postmillenarians that he deserved four more years.

In the summer of 1864, Sojourner Truth and Harriet Tubman met for the first time in Boston during the latter's visit north from Florida. Both born to enslaved families and very religious, Truth and Tubman nevertheless differed "in their assessment of Lincoln. Truth had campaigned for Lincoln and believed he had done much for the betterment of African Americans. But Tubman still did not care for Lincoln."[111] Unlike Frederick Douglass, Martin Delany, and other black middle-class (or upwardly mobile) reformers, Truth and Tubman remained working women. "Truth's membership in unorthodox religious sects, disinterest in politics," illiteracy, and "most important, her failure to conform to respectability's tenets likely alienated her from" the male-dominated black-reform community.[112]

The months Tubman spent in Boston were a welcome relief from her irregular military career. Not only did she receive material aid from sympathetic abolitionists, but she also was able to receive critical medical treatment. Although only thirty-nine, she looked visibly older due to a deteriorating physical condition. The fracture of her skull at the hands of an overseer during her Maryland youth now evidently affected her in the form of narcolepsy, causing her to suddenly fall asleep during the day, at times midsentence. Although there was no formal medical diagnosis for her condition at the time, Tubman sought medical treatment at Massachusetts General Hospital, where surgery reduced her discomfort, although the sleeping spells continued at a reduced rate.[113] She also remained north long enough to hear of the passage of the Thirteenth Amendment, which meant that she, her relatives, and all those black postmillenarians she had sought to aid over the past years were now forever free.

Truth and Douglass again shared the speaker's stage—twenty years after their first meeting in Northampton, Massachusetts—during this election year. Douglass had met the president the previous year and now agreed with Truth that Lincoln was fulfilling prophecy. They each quoted from Isaiah as "a howling jeremiad—a bloodletting fulfillment of divine justice because the nation would not let the oppressed go free," in the words of historian Margaret Washington. Peace could not prevail until all enslaved people were free. Truth castigated northern premillenarians who kept communion with slaveholding southerners; she would rather eat out of a trough with hogs than take "the sacrament with . . . devils" who burned, hunted, and mauled with bloodhounds her brothers and sisters "for a century." Yet she also emphasized postmillenarian hope. "After the blood and smoke and storm of battle are gone, this country will be beautiful [with] justice and freedom." Douglass acknowledged their 1852 confrontation over whether white Americans could be convinced by God and moral suasion to end slavery or if they must be forced into it by the armed rebellion of the enslaved ("Frederick, is God dead?"). In a way, they were now both right.[114]

As summer turned to fall, Truth traveled from upstate New York to Manhattan and then to "Copperhead New Jersey," where she played her part to win votes for Lincoln in a state expected to favor the Democratic candidate. She gave speeches in Trenton, Newark, and Orange, where General McClellan now lived. Continuing on to Washington, Truth enjoyed an audience with the president thanks in part to Elizabeth Keckley—Mary Todd Lincoln's black seamstress—and to her own Radical Republican contacts George W. Julian and Charles Sumner.[115]

One of the Republicans' most important orators struggled with her conscience about deploying her voice on behalf of a compromising incumbent. Anna Dickinson considered sitting out this campaign, for Lincoln was "the wisest scoundrel in the country, & I would rather lose all the reputation I possess & sell apples & peanuts on the street than say aught—that would gain a vote for him." Yet neither could she support the ostensibly more radical John Frémont.[116]

Anticipating McClellan's Democratic nomination and viewing the growing public frustration with the bloody stalemate at Petersburg following the high casualties of the Overland Campaign and the ongoing siege of Atlanta, Lincoln worried about his prospects for reelection. "This morning, as for some days past, it seems exceedingly probable that this Administration will not be re-elected," he wrote in a memo to his cabinet on August 23. "Then it will be my duty to so co-operate with the President elect, as to save the Union between the election and the inauguration; as he will have secured his election on such ground that he can not possibly save it afterwards."[117] He did not allow his administration's officers to see the memo but had them sign the outside of the sealed document. He later divulged that if McClellan had won, he would have been compelled approach the general and say "let us together . . . try to save the country" in the next four months. "You raise as many troops as you possibly can for this final trial, and I will devote all my energies to assisting and finishing the war."[118] Lincoln intended to order his armies to occupy as much Confederate territory as possible while encouraging enslaved southerners to flee to Union lines; President McClellan could not be expected to help African Americans not already in Union custody.[119]

Crucial to Lincoln's reelection were the tens of thousands of otherwise eligible adult men serving in the Union armies, a predominance of whom (if of age) voted for Republicans in 1860. Governors of key swing states like Indiana encouraged generals to furlough men home so they might add the weight of their ballots to the election.[120] McClellan enjoyed little exposure among the western armies, so it was no surprise that two-thirds of those veterans supported their laconic commander in chief. A Wisconsinite in Sherman's command thought that if the North compromised with the Confederacy "by letting them have their slaves" and electing McClellan, they must "fight them again in ten years. But let Old Abe settle it, and it is always settled."[121]

McClellan was more responsible for the tone and personality of the Army of the Potomac than any other man, molding it over the first year of its existence. He might have at least expected to split the soldier vote of that army. But *three-quarters* of the army commanded by Meade and accompanied by Grant voted the postmillenarian ticket of Union and emancipation. Veterans of a Vermont regiment agreed with one of their number who said he "was a McClellan man clear to the bone, but he couldn't vote for him on the Chicago platform. Rather than have peace by surrendering to the rebels, he would let his bones manure the soil of Virginia."[122] The survivors of the Second Wisconsin, the lynchpin of the Iron Brigade of Antietam fame, voted seventy to one for Lincoln, the one ballot for their old general cast so that "he would know that we have not entirely forgotten him."[123] Historian Jonathan White has determined that while there was significant intimidation of McClellanites in the armies, it was not enough to challenge the overall support for Lincoln's reelection.[124]

An enemy of McClellan's premillenarian, proslavery way of warfare slaughtered hundreds of Native Americans in Colorado Territory weeks after the election in the name of postmillenarian progress. An abolitionist and a Methodist minister, Colonel John Chivington allegedly faced down a proslavery mob in Kansas who opposed his giving an antislavery sermon in the 1850s. Placing two revolvers on the pulpit next to his text, Chivington delivered his sermon. He accepted a commission as major of the First Colorado in preference to a another unit's chaplaincy in 1861. Now in late 1864 he ordered an attack on Cheyennes and Arapahos, seeking the protection of the Union military, on the pretext of avenging the murder and scalping of a family of white settlers. The leader of the Cheyennes, Black Kettle, even flew an American flag over his lodge as a testament to his community's peaceful intentions. Historian Ari Kelman theorized that Chivington ordered the attack—"one of the most bloody battles ever fought on these plains," according to the colonel, as opposed to the massacre it was in fact—in order to win promotion or grease the wheels for postwar political election.[125]

ATLANTA FELL TO UNION forces in early September, winning for Lincoln a major military victory two months before the election. Eastern Georgia and the Carolinas now beckoned to Sherman, though he waited nearly two months before setting off on his March to the Sea. The president was concerned by the plan when presented to him, leaving Hood's still-dangerous Army of Tennessee threatening northern Alabama and Tennessee, but Grant convinced him that Sherman was equal to the campaign and that George Thomas had sufficient troops to defend Tennessee. "Don't even know whether we are starting a campaign or not," mused an Illinoisan in Georgia. "Hood is reported across the Tennessee [River]. We understand that Thomas has men enough to attend to him, and that Sherman intends us to Christianize this country."[126] The proselytization the general and this soldier had in mind left Atlanta a fire-purged, uninhabited shell. With the smoking ruins of the city behind them, the Union host marched on Savannah, "relying on our strength and the Providence of God," in the words of the Thirty-First Missouri's major.[127]

Discipline was an issue from the beginning of this march, for Sherman wanted to "make Georgia howl." But so long as his forces were prepared to face whatever paltry rebel forces opposed them, he did not worry much about the troops' behavior. "The army will forage liberally on the country during the march," read Sherman's orders, yet not enter private residences. He levied a class basis on loyalty, with accompanying policies to leave sufficient food for civilians to survive, discriminating "between the rich, who are usually hostile, and the poor and industrious, usually neutral or friendly."[128] Indeed, each of his brigades had an assigned officer-led foraging detail of twenty-five to fifty men who ranged ahead or on the flanks of their unit, taking gathered supplies to a collection point on their parent unit's path. Yet legitimate requisition of food to feed the army easily bled over into looting of jewelry, watches, and other valuables.[129] Howard, as commander of the Army of the Tennessee, issued strict orders that any man found stealing was to be tried by a drumhead court-martial and executed if convicted.[130]

Volunteer officers were not willing to enforce such draconian discipline, docking pay instead. Confederate soldiers who caught such looters enforced their own form of justice, hanging or shooting the "bummers."

As Sherman's army neared Savannah in mid-December, General Geary wrote of the impending doom not just of that city but also what was left of the Confederacy. After a month "cut off from the world and 'the rest of mankind,'" the army learned, "through rebel sources, of Mr. Lincoln's [re]election. I hope the friends of 'little Mac' are satisfied now."[131] Two years and two months earlier, when Geary was still counted among "the friends of 'little Mac,'" the general wrote his wife about "this horrible unnatural war [that] has been forced upon our beloved country and the little of happiness that Satan saw looming in the world must be by him . . . destroyed." The war was tearing apart not only the Union but loving spouses as well. With elections looming in 1862, the "intriguer, the liar, and slanderer, all join to produce hell upon earth generally, and fair finds they are of his Satanic majesty to produce his desires."[132]

Now Satan's plots were upturned, with disastrous results for premillenarians in both sections. The aged "dogmas" of northern and southern Democrats "are not in keeping with the progress of the age, in which our lots have been cast, away up in the noon of the nineteenth century. They seem [to] be antiquated fossils, and like the Jews in the Christian era, cannot discern the signs of the times." For it is "now certain that the United States must be all *free* or all *slave,* and the momentous question has been decided in favor of freedom by the edict of the people in November." Geary anticipated Lincoln's forbearance with the nearly crushed Confederacy in his second inaugural address, writing that the president could now "afford to make *peace* by the offer of most generous terms." Yet peace only arrived after more destruction of biblical proportions at the hands of Sherman's command. "This last campaign of Sherman's has almost disembowelled the rebellion. . . . Georgia is about as badly damaged as some of the tribes of the land of Canaan were by the Israelitish army," Geary noted, and South Carolina was next in the line of march.[133] South Carolina's chief city, Charleston, was considered "the citadel and capital of American slavery," while the state as a whole could expect less mercy than Georgia for its having pioneered secession.[134]

Sherman's marches—from Atlanta to Savannah and from Savannah through the Carolinas—bring us to our twelfth, and youngest, apostle. Emma Florence LeConte was a teenager by 1864. As historian Victoria Ott noted, the lives of LeConte and other premillenarian white adolescents in the Deep South were severely disrupted by the war generally and by Sherman's destructive offensive particularly.[135]

LeConte's first diary entry was composed at the close of 1864. Noting that the last day of the year was "always a gloomy day," it was "doubly so today." Not only were the skies dark and rain pouring down, but the war also was going poorly. "A fit conclusion for such a year—'tis meet, old year, that thou should'st weep for the misfortunes thou has brought our country! And what hope is there to brighten the new year that is coming up?" Nothing. "Georgia has been desolated. The resistless flood" of Sherman's host swept through that state, with only a desolate waste to mark its path.[136] LeConte queried without irony whether 1865 would see South Carolina "enslaved and subjugated by those Yankees" when "Lee's noble army alone stands firm." The Army of Northern Virginia, not the capital or the government, was now the embodiment of the Confederacy. Her fellow teenagers, "boys of sixteen[,] are conscripted" to replace their dead elders. She could not accept any discussion of surrender to the Yankees. "How we hate them with the whole strength and depth of our souls!" If a new year usually inspired thoughts of bright prospects, she found no comfort in such musings for 1865. "Hope has fled, and in its place remains only a spirit of dogged, sullen resistance."[137]

THE TWIN DEFEATS at Franklin and Nashville in late November and mid-December (respectively) broke Hood's confidence, and the general confessed his sinful pride to the Episcopalian chaplain who was now his denomination's official missionary to the Army of Tennessee. Hood, reported Reverend Quintard, "says he is afraid he has been more wicked since he began this retreat than for a long time past—that he had so set his heart upon success—had prayed so earnestly for it—had such a firm trust that he should succeed—that his heart has been very rebellious—but said he, 'let us go out of Tennessee singing hymns of praise.'"[138] Yet Emma LeConte and the other women of Columbia, South Carolina—along with their sisters in Savannah—had even less cause to sing hymns of praise thanks to Hood's quixotic, premillenarian march on Nashville while Sherman marched his postmillenarian host to the sea.

6

OLIVER O. HOWARD'S MILLENNIUM
xxxxx **1865** xxxxx

EVEN AFTER THE ELECTION granted Lincoln four more years with which to wage postmillenarian war against the Confederacy, plenty of northerners questioned the war's winnability. When White House visitors raised their concerns with Lincoln in January 1865, the president took them to a map to show the ongoing siege of Petersburg and—more importantly—the destructive progress of Sherman through the Carolinas, with Virginia his ultimate destination. Lincoln viewed his current situation—with two presidential victories in the bag—as reminiscent of "an old fellow in the early days of Indiana who had been a wicked and lascivious sinner but he had joined a church and was getting baptized." When the pastor baptized him, he demanded to be immersed again, despite the minister's assurance that "once was enough. The old fellow insisted. So the preacher dunked him again. As he came up and rubbed the water out of his eyes and mouth and got his breath," the man exclaimed, "Now I've been baptized twice and the Devil can kiss my ass." The president pointed to a spot on the map and said that once Sherman's army arrived at the place where Grant besieged Lee, the war was won. "And then," Lincoln said, "the Southern Confederacy can kiss my ass."[1]

Premillenarian Virginians sensed that the war was beyond human agency to redeem. "God save us! we seem incapable of saving ourselves," a Richmond clerk moaned.[2] "It is time for thee, Lord, to work," a Virginia newspaper beseeched the Confederacy's premillenarian deity in February.[3] It was almost past time, given "the fall of Atlanta and the reelection of Lincoln, and certainly after Sherman's march to the sea." These disasters motivated most Confederates "to face the inevitable" in 1865. With Bishop Polk dead and buried, few of his confederates still held to the principle of "God helps those who help themselves" and reluctantly prepared for defeat. "Their religious views made this process easier. Their brand of Christianity and the religious fatalism they espoused allowed them to overcome more easily than otherwise the dissonance created by the knowledge of the attractive features of rejected alternatives," such as the dissolution of the field armies into roving guerrilla bands. "God's will became a psychological bridge to the acceptance of defeat."[4]

THE NEW YEAR BEGAN with sunshine in Columbia, South Carolina. Emma LeConte struggled with the pessimism she had expressed in her diary the day before, trying "to throw off the sad memories I was brooding over and hope for better things."[5] She was relieved to receive word from her father, who was somewhere near Savannah looking for his widowed sister's family (as well as his fourteen-year-old daughter) due to the threat of Sherman's advancing army.[6] If for three years sheltered from the Union forces that had constantly threatened Virginians in the Shenandoah Valley and the northern counties (not to mention Carolinians along the coast), impelling many to seek refuge with family in Richmond or farther south, now (inland) South Carolinians faced exile or abuse. And Sherman's veterans intended to target them as the true fomenters of the rebellion and the reason for *their* own three years of exile from home (in the ranks).

LeConte's father was more concerned about the mental—expressing he "greatly feared the effects on her mind"—than the material or sexual threats to his sister of the arrival of "the plundering Yankee soldiery" in Savannah.[7] Yet by setting out on what wound up being a prolonged odyssey to deliver his sister's family and his daughter to safety, Joseph LeConte exposed his family in Columbia—putatively safe when he departed in late 1864—to the dangers of Yankee occupation without his protection. While still twelve or thirteen miles from the state capital, LeConte heard from refugees that the city had fallen on February 17. He fell asleep after "an ejaculated prayer for the loved ones at home," yet "while we thus slept in peace Columbia was wrapped in flames! If we had even looked at the sky in that direction before going to bed and seen its ruddy glare, we would have slept none that night."[8] All he could do was continue home and continue praying that his wife and daughters left at home were safe. In noting this LeConte tacitly admitted that he had failed to deliver on the male end of the social contract that Confederate women accepted in 1861; as historian Drew Faust argued, women stayed at home while men marched off to war to defend the new nation. Men were active agents in politics and warfare, women the prayerful supporters. Yet in Columbia in February 1865 as in Savannah the previous December, Confederate women were at the mercy of Sherman's troops, while Confederate men were powerless to save them, breaking the bonds of the social contract.

While the LeConte family worried about the impending arrival of Sherman's avenging host, Lincoln agreed to attend the anniversary meeting of the US Christian Commission held in the House chamber of the Capitol. The president joined in the singing of Julia Ward Howe's "Battle Hymn of the Republic" during the ceremony. Attendees noted tears in Lincoln's eyes, and toward the end of the event, he scribbled a note on his program for the chairman to request the reading of one of his favorite poems, "Your Mission," which included an injunction to those who "cannot in the conflict Prove a soldier true, . . . [they should] bear away the wounded . . . [or] cover up the dead."[9]

Margaret Preston contributed a rather different kind of verse to the Confederate cause that January than the lines that drew tears from Lincoln's eyes. She celebrated a flag that incorporated the St. Andrew's cross of the Confederate battle flag into a "pure" field of white. Regardless of its similarity to a flag of truce or surrender when flapping in a heavy wind or in poor light, Preston composed an ode to William Tappan Thompson's "Stainless Banner," the new Confederate national flag. "Shelter Freedom's holy cause, Liberty and sacred laws, Guard the youngest of the Nations—Keep her virgin honor bright," read her "Hymn to the National Flag."[10] It is worth noting that when Thompson designed the Stainless Banner in 1863, he explicitly intended the "White Man's Flag" to proclaim to the world that "as a people, we are fighting to maintain the heaven ordained supremacy of the white man over the inferior or colored race."[11]

Preston began her postwar career of writing the "Lost Cause" into being during the same dark winter of 1864–65 that Emma LeConte experienced and recorded farther south. During these months, Preston composed the epic poem *Beechenbrook: A Rhyme of the War,* the protagonist of which loses her "gallantly brave" husband in the Confederate service. Yet "his death on the battle-field" gifted her with a renewed faith both in God and the conviction "that her glorious South MUST BE FREE!"[12] Although she did not lose her husband, the deaths of her beloved "idol" and brother-in-law Stonewall

Jackson and a stepson were perhaps inspiration enough for this paean to the passing of the premillenarian torch from male to female hands in 1865. She eventually sent a copy to Jackson's widow—like her the daughter of a Presbyterian college president and sister-in-law to D. H. Hill—who thanked Preston for "the beautiful copy of Beechenbrook."[13] As historian Alice Fahs noted, the wide dissemination of this inaugural wartime Lost Cause publication was thwarted by postmillenarian military action. The initial run of two thousand copies was printed in Richmond (despite paper shortages, though the quality of copy suffered), yet only fifty copies made it out of the capital before fires destroyed the bulk of this sole Confederate edition.[14]

GENERAL PATRICK CLEBURNE DIED along with five other generals while attempting to storm the Union defenses at Franklin, Tennessee, in November 1864, proving once more the folly of frontal assault on defenders in prepared positions, some of them now armed with repeating rifles. Yet his controversial idea submitted before Atlanta bore fruit in 1865, with Robert E. Lee throwing his weight in favor of recruiting enslaved men into the Confederate army. There was still plenty of resistance to training black soldiers, an action that flew in the face of the Confederate national experiment to demonstrate that (as Vice President Stephens had said in 1861) the black man was not equal to the white. Now, however, many Virginians wanted to replace President Davis with General Lee as a dictator—Lee rejected such a notion—and Lee's change of mind dictated that some black men were offered freedom for fighting for the Confederacy.[15] Acceptance of necessity did not mean enthusiasm, however. A colonel invalided to Richmond from active duty observed black recruits "walking on the streets with their uniforms. Quite military, I say, but ah! how funny." How "I hate the idea of having to buy Cuffee and Sambo into the ring very much."[16]

Meanwhile, the siege of Petersburg—and by proxy, Richmond to its north—ground on. If Emma LeConte envisioned the Army of Northern Virginia as the embodiment of resistance to Yankee rule in 1864, in the new year that symbol of Confederate defiance shrank to Lee alone. Former governor of Virginia Harry Wise—serving as a general since 1862—told Lee in early April 1865: "There is no country. There has been no country, General, for a year or more. You are the country to these men."[17]

The anaconda-like vise broke in the Union's final favor when five brigades holding Lee's right flank were crushed on April 1 at Five Forks, leading to successful assaults at other points of Petersburg's defenses. The Confederate leadership was at Sunday services when news of the disaster arrived. Reverend Charles Minnigerode was preaching at St Paul's Episcopal Church when Davis received word that Richmond must be evacuated. As he left, other leaders received similar notification. Minnigerode attempted to stem the flood of departing notables, but to no avail. A few returned for communion, but the priest "could no more stop his congregation from leaving St. Paul's than Lee could stop the Union forces from pushing through his lines."[18]

GEORGE McCLELLAN ADDED EXILE from national politics and the nation itself to his separation from the Army of the Potomac. "I can imagine no combination of circumstances that will draw me into public life again," he wrote his mother after his election defeat in November 1864.[19] A month later he turned thirty-nine, no longer qualifying—if he ever did—as the "Young Napoleon."[20] Struggling to attain an executive rank in a civilian firm similar to the one he had enjoyed with western railroads in the final antebellum years, McClellan looked abroad for renewed military opportunities. "I suppose I must make up my mind now to shake the dust off my shoes"—as George Junkin did when leaving rebellious Virginia in 1861— "and go elsewhere—so be it." He considered, among other things, offering his services to the tsar of Russia or the French puppet-emperor in Mexico.[21] Instead of these, he settled for a comfortable self-exile in Europe for the better part of four years, sailing on January 25, 1865.[22] McClellan's wife wrote her father that the English "look upon [George] as *the* American General."[23] Not the humblest of men, McClellan admitted that Italians "seem disposed to exaggerate very much the importance of my part in the war," at least to his face. This was a situation far preferable to the "exile in Nevada or Utah for some years" he could expect should he remain home while "Uncle Abraham" was in office.[24]

ABRAHAM LINCOLN HAD SPENT four years frustrating and in turn frustrated by the most radical postmillenarians. A wartime convert to faith— never a church member, however—the president delivered his last major speech in a more postmillenarian vein than he previously allowed. It was particularly postmillennial because it admitted a third party to the sectional struggle: the formerly enslaved. Even free African Americans in many northern states had been disenfranchised, so the president's reference to millions as yet unable to vote—and to whom he owed no formal obligation for his reelection—was the rhetorical move of a statesman. For if they could not vote in a traditional fashion, the enslaved postmillenarians in the Confederacy forced the Democrats and Republicans of the Union armies to take them into consideration by voting with their feet and seeking refuge with blue-clad forces. Those who fled plantations denied their labor to erstwhile masters and contributed materially to the Union war effort, however reluctant northern premillenarians were to accept it. Now almost 200,000 of them served in the army and navy. Not only did Lincoln bring up the enslaved millions, but he also referred to them in the context of the Protestant deity that millions of Americans—black and white—prayed to. The majority of both sides worshiped the same God, read the same Bible, and invoked the same deity's blessing to empower their side to victory. And yet the war continued. Did the Almighty allow the death and suffering until the generations of torture and unrequited labor were repaid upon the present generation of Americans so that the enslaved could go free? Ever the Whig, Lincoln constantly thought about the future, about the progress of the United States, and now that future required the nation as a whole to take responsibility for slavery rather than relegate it to a guilty (now-treasonous) southern section.[25] The "Uncle Abraham" scorned by his 1864 rival was transformed into a latter-day Moses, alongside Harriet Tubman.

A MONTH AFTER CONGRESS passed the Thirteenth Amendment—starting the process of the rehabilitation of the president in her mind—Tubman traveled to Washington, where she received permission to board a military transport to South Carolina. Yet Sanitary Commission representatives in Philadelphia convinced her that the freedpeople living near Fortress Monroe in Virginia were in desperate need of medical aid.[26] She was in Virginia when Richmond fell, Lee surrendered, and Lincoln was assassinated. Although the war was over, the suffering of the state's freedpeople at Fortress Monroe continued in May and June. With supplies low and sickness mounting, Tubman traveled to Washington in July to win the aid of prominent Republicans. When the promised supplies failed to materialize, she decided that her parents—"entirely dependent on her"—needed her more than the country, and she returned to upstate New York.[27] Yet the postmillenarian paradise of the northern states was not without its warts; plenty of premillenarians remained. While taking a train through New Jersey en route to her parents, a conductor disbelieved the authenticity of Tubman's soldier's pass. When she declined to leave her seat, he enlisted three other men to force her into the baggage car for the rest of the trip.[28]

IN SPITE OF JOSEPH LECONTE'S prayers, Union soldiers entered Columbia shortly after noon on February 17. Emma's father failed to return to his anxious family until a week after Sherman arrived, two days before his own birthday.[29] In microcosm LeConte's involuntary absence from his wife and daughters represented the helplessness of military-aged premillenarian men to protect female relatives in Atlanta, Savannah, and now Columbia from postmillenarian invaders. Were he home, the middle-aged professor could have done nothing to avert the avenging postmillenarians from rampaging through the capital of the first state to secede.

The black postmillenarians of Columbia did not even wait for Sherman's army to fall into criminality, as Emma LeConte snidely recorded. The sound of explosions—presumably Confederate authorities destroying government property—and the approaching sound of cannon fire were sufficient for "the negroes all [to proceed] uptown to see what they could get in the general pillage" of the Confederate withdrawal.[30] Yet unexpectedly, when they returned with their plunder, the LeConte's enslaved people were "very kind and faithful," sharing meat, rice, and crushed sugar with her family. "How times change! Those whom we have so long fed and cared for now help us."[31] For at least the liminal moment before the arrival of armed postmillenarians, the postmillenarians who lived as LeConte's property demonstrated a pacific and generous new order of life.

In the vanguard of the army of postmillenarian liberation and judgment was Howard's Army of the Tennessee. "Two corps entered town—Howard's and Logan's—one, the diabolical 15th [Corps commanded by John Logan] which Sherman has hitherto never permitted to enter a city on account of their vile and desperate character," LeConte recorded.[32] She prayed that "retributive justice will find" Sherman, "the lying fiend," for failing to protect the city's private property as he promised.[33] She referred frequently to the occupiers as "fiends" and was grateful that on only one occasion was she compelled to speak to one of the "blue-coated" invaders.[34]

Although guards were posted around the city to prevent looting or arson of private homes, they "were rarely of any assistance—most generally they assisted in the pillaging and firing" of Columbia's dwellings. If in the early evening LeConte discerned "the burning of Gen. Hampton's residence a few miles off in the country," soon fires blazed in the city itself.[35] "A quivering molten ocean seemed to fill the air and sky," with the college buildings—workplace of LeConte's father—catching fire but saved to prevent the fiery death befalling the wounded Confederate inmates. Watching "the drunken, fiendish soldiery in their dark uniforms, infuriated, cursing, screaming, exulting in their work, came nearer realizing the material ideal of hell than anything I expect to see again." In LeConte's mind they thoroughly earned the nickname of "Sherman's Hellhounds."[36] Her own home was in danger of catching fire on multiple occasions, but each time it was saved by vigilant African Americans.

LeConte's 1864 conviction that "Sherman the brute" promised to level all houses and allow "his licentious troops—white and negroes . . . —[license] to ravage and violate" was hardly borne out.[37] Nevertheless, they brought war home to LeConte and the premillenarian women of Columbia, a war of words and arson. "From what I can hear, their chief aim, while taunting helpless women, has been to 'humble their pride'—'Southern pride,'" LeConte recorded, plausibly enough. "'Where now,' they would say, 'is all your pride—see what we have brought you to! This is what you get for setting yourselves up as better than other folks."[38] The premillenarian women of Winchester in the Shenandoah Valley gloried in their resistance to postmillenarian occupation, yet LeConte noted with pride that "Yankee officers while here paid the tribute to the women of this State" as the worst secessionists. Her sisters "were the most firm, obstinate, and ultra-rebel set of women they had encountered." If only "the men . . . prove equally so!"[39] Although many private dwellings were destroyed along with Columbia's public buildings, few of the city's premillenarian women suffered more than verbal abuse and property loss. Postmillenarian women—ostensibly now freed by Howard's army—faced greater dangers from their liberators.

Although at least one of the LeConte family's enslaved persons, Mary Ann, expressed her wish to remain with the family, most seemed determined to accept the freedom offered by Sherman's postmillenarian army.

"They have been dressed in their Sunday best all day," LeConte journaled, a premillenarian interpretation that some African Americans saw entering freedom as akin to attending church, setting out with one's best foot forward.[40] When a soldier entered the LeConte yard, looking for one of the enslaved men, the sought-for Henry locked himself in his room rather than leave. When Emma's mother asked "the mean filthy devil if he wished to make Henry go against his will," the soldier denied this, yet still asked to talk to Henry, to which Mrs. LeConte replied she would only accept an officer's order to free Henry, and the soldier left.[41]

THE SIEGE OF PETERSBURG ground on while the LeConte family tried to rebuild, although April Fool's Day proved a fitting occasion to mark the breaking of the siege and the doom of the proslavery, premillenarian cause in Virginia. On that day the cavalry and infantry of the Army of the Potomac crushed the right flank of Petersburg's defenses.[42] Realizing that with the collapse of the line at Petersburg Richmond was also lost, Lee sent word to Davis that the Confederate government must abandon the capital and join the Army of Northern Virginia in flight toward North Carolina.[43]

Lee's army struck westward, seeking supplies at Amelia Court House and Danville prior to joining forces with the remnants of the Army of Tennessee, again under Joseph Johnston, in North Carolina. Grant's cavalry and infantry followed quickly, the cavalry managing to cut ahead of Lee's army and corral it at Appomattox Court House. Although some of the younger officers such as E. P. Alexander argued in favor of dispersing the remaining troops into guerrilla bands to continue the war as an insurgency, Lee decided to surrender his entire army on April 9.[44] Older generals such as Lexington's William Pendleton sided with Lee; guerrilla warfare was a young man's game, and the families of any who decided to fight on would face vengeful Union armies imprisoning and possibly executing civilians as reprisals against guerrilla violence.[45]

Bad news travels quickly, and Lexington heard of Lee's surrender the very next day. "We are struck dumb with astonishment!" Margaret Preston journaled. To her, the loss of Lee's army signaled the end of the Confederacy. "Why then all these four years of suffering—of separations—of horror—of blood—of havoc—of awful bereavement! Why these ruined homes—these broken family circles—these scenes of terror that must scathe the brain of those who witnessed them till their dying day! Why" was her stepson Willy "in his uncoffined grave? Why poor Frank to go through life with one arm? Is it wholly and forever in vain? God only knows!"[46] There was no room in Preston's mind for the possibility that God sided at last with the postmillenarians and—as Lincoln had said recently—had repaid the blood drawn by premillenarian lashes with blood drawn by postmillenarian swords.

GENERAL HOWARD NOW WENT to war with a female academy whose recent alumnae included Mildred Lee and Lucia Polk. Lee's father had already surrendered to Grant at Appomattox, but the other students of St. Mary's School in Raleigh objected to the Union soldiers encamped in the grove next to the school as well as the flag they hoisted every morning. General Lee had sent his daughter from a school in Winchester to North Carolina in 1862 to keep her safe from Union incursions into the Valley. The first lady of the Confederacy, Varina Davis, herself moved into the school in the summer of 1862.[47] St. Mary's was therefore a refuge for the daughters and spouses of prominent rebel generals and politicians, but now their fathers and husbands could not protect them. Noticing that the students drew the curtains of their classrooms to avoid looking upon the Stars and Stripes, "Howard gladdened their hearts by making them martyrs to their" now lost "cause. He sent in word to the principal that unless all such expressions of dislike to the United States flag were stopped he would close the school."[48] When General Sherman, his superior, arrived at the school in April, the students treated their visitor respectfully. Yet when leaving he turned once more to look at the school, Sherman saw the girls "all making such mouths as only angry school girls can make, while some more daring ones were absolutely shaking their pretty little fists at him."[49]

If they resented the premillenarian students of St. Mary's School, Howard and Sherman acted to prevent arson and murder in Raleigh following the shocking news that Lincoln had been assassinated, confining their troops to camp. "The men are fearfully angry, and I don't know what they may do," a veteran sergeant observed.[50] But a brigade's worth of men knew exactly what to do. A mob of 2,000 soldiers set out for Raleigh with fiery devastation as their object. General Logan rode up, placed himself in their path, and ordered them back to camp. The men ignored him until he deployed a battery of artillery and warned that he would disperse them with canister, which convinced them to desist.[51] Raleigh owed Logan "a debt it never can pay."[52]

Aware that his fellow (former) Democrat Andrew Johnson was born near Raleigh, John Geary wrote of the reaction of North Carolinians to the death of Lincoln. "The murder of the President creates a most profound sensation among the better class of people of this state, and the act is most bitterly denounced," Geary wrote home. Defeated rebels knew the new president to be "a more determined and implacable man than Mr. Lincoln, they also feel that they have now a *Rowland for an Oliver*, and that they are not now so safe and so perfectly secure," which could lead to more violence rather than a quick peace.[53] As keen as he was to return home, Geary declared darkly, "if we have to fight anymore, woe be to Rebeldom! The cowardly assassins are only exhibiting the same" behavior that "so greatly embittered me towards them" in Kansas. He would not treat the new insurgents with the patience he had displayed in 1856.[54]

EMMA LECONTE FRETTED at the news of an armistice between Johnston and Sherman around April 20, following swiftly in the wake of the notice that Lee's army had surrendered. The "Grand Army of Virginia which has heretofore never known defeat, but has stood like some great rock against which the huge waves of our enemies have dashed themselves in vain, is now melted away. All that is left is Johnston's small army, cooped up between Grant's hordes" in Virginia and Sherman's in North Carolina. Yet if armed premillenarian men manifestly failed to defend Virginia and the Carolinas from the postmillenarian "hordes," LeConte wanted total mobilization of the southern white population, meaning a chance for her sex to take up arms. "Why does not the President call out the women?" She was convinced that "we would go and *fight* too—we would better all die together" than submit to humiliation and worse by "such horrible and contemptible creatures."[55] LeConte could not yet grasp the revelation rudely forced upon Margaret Preston's mind the previous June in conversation with a Union soldier who doubted the "deadly earnestness" of Confederate men to "fight like tigers [for] the last inch of ground" in their "mountain fastnesses."[56] If premillenarian men lost the will to fight, their wives and daughters must accept surrender, though their pens and diaries, nightmares and dreams, remained to them.

"Hurrah! Old Abe Lincoln has been assassinated! It may be abstractly wrong to be so jubilant," LeConte admitted, "but I just can't help it."[57] Many of her premillenarian elders disagreed—as General Geary noted—for they knew the war was lost and the assassination as hostilities wound down could only inflame postmillenarian desire for vengeance and a harsh peace. Yet LeConte at least understood that Lincoln's successor boded ill for the planter class. "Andy Johnson will succeed him—the rail-splitter will be succeeded by the drunken ass. Such are the successors of Washington and Jefferson, such are to rule the South."[58]

Anna Dickinson mulled over how best to memorialize a president whose policies she often attacked. "Of course I cannot feel that sorrow which his admirers do, but I have little trust in [Andrew] Johnson," one of her fellow Radicals wrote presciently of the administration's policy once the anti-Confederate *and* anti-black Tennessean took over.[59] Dickinson visited Cooper Institute in New York—Lincoln had given a speech there in 1860 that gave him eastern visibility—to deliver "Our Martyred President" in May.[60] Three thousand attended, hearing Dickinson's admission of her criticism of Lincoln in life. She also called for the prosecution of Confederate leaders, including "the leading spirit of the rebellion," Robert E. Lee. As her biographer noted, Dickinson's rhetoric differed to the last from Lincoln's call to "bind up the nation's wounds" in his second inaugural address.[61]

Julia Ward Howe was plunged into a double grief with the assassination. John Wilkes Booth's elder brother, Edwin, was a friend and neighbor of Howe's. She had attended the funeral of the Shakespearean actor's young wife.[62] The "Battle Hymn of the Republic" gained new resonance in the wake of Lincoln's violent death—a seeming martyrdom symbolically executed on Good Friday—for mourning postmillenarians could now equate the president with Christ. If Jesus died to make men holy, Lincoln died to make men free. Paid five dollars by the *Atlantic Monthly*—roughly half the monthly pay of the lowliest soldier—which published the hymn anonymously on its cover in February 1862, Howe's singular literary contribution at last outweighed her husband's public work.[63]

EMMA LECONTE TURNED to the church for solace. Her pastor was Benjamin M. Palmer, an antebellum secessionist and clerical Confederate exiled from his pulpit in New Orleans by Union occupation forces. On April 23

Palmer preached against despair, for "even if we should be overthrown—not conquered—the next generation," LeConte's generation, "would see the South *free* and independent."[64] Yet despair was hard to stave off. The more LeConte thought of Lee's surrender, "the harder it is to bear. That army—that General—we idolized Stonewall Jackson, worshipped Lee." Despite the passage of two years, how fresh was "the death of Stonewall Jackson! I can never forget my feelings when I heard of it." She had heard that the general was unwell yet had no conception that he was a mere mortal, that "*he* could *die*."[65]

If LeConte felt unmoored by the surrenders of Lee and Johnston, with weeks now passing between diary entries, she was hardly the only Confederate woman who scrambled for purpose. Georgia plantation mistress Gertrude Thomas wrote a letter to General Sherman's wife as Union soldiers despoiled her plantations. Unable to deploy the male weapons of war, Thomas lashed out in the time-tested war of words and rumor that was the preserve of elite women. She claimed that the general had had an affair with a "Mulatto girl" and threatened to publish the story and ruin the Shermans' marriage. Now that "*your* husbands are amongst a colored race whose reputation for morality has never been of the highest order," northern women could drink from the same "bitter cup of humiliation" as generations of southern planters' wives.[66] In the assessment of historian Stephanie McCurry, for Thomas and many other premillenarian women, "emancipation (like slavery itself) was always about sex, adultery, and inevitably, sex between white men and black women."[67]

SHORTLY AFTER JOHNSTON'S ARMY surrendered to Sherman, now-former lieutenant general William J. Hardee, previously a West Point commandant, discussed what the end of the war meant for the former slave states with *New York Herald* correspondent Theodore C. Wilson. "I accept this war as the providence of God. He intended that the slave should be free, and now he is free," Hardee affirmed, concurring with President Lincoln's speculative remarks in his second inaugural address. But the general claimed that "slavery was never a paying institution." His wife had owned a hundred African Americans, but "forty of the hundred were useless for work, yet she had to feed these forty, in order to get the work of the other sixty. The negro will be worse off for this war." Hardee doubted northern abolitionists' willingness to "feed and clothe half-a-dozen little children, in order to get the work of a man and woman," a scenario that must be multiplied thousands of times to get four million freedpeople to continue to cultivate cotton.[68] It was up to General Howard and the agents of his newly established Freedmen's Bureau to prove Hardee wrong. Howard had already learned from white teenagers in Raleigh the opposition he would face from unreconstructed rebels.

The unreconstructed rebel LeConte wrote disparagingly of the Fourth of July, the first holiday observed by the black postmillenarians of Columbia as free people. "The white people shut themselves within doors and the darkies had the day to themselves—they and the Yankees," their northern postmillenarian allies. "It was a fearfully warm day and some four or five thousand negroes assembled," while two Union regiments were stationed nearby to prevent any unrest. "Most of the gentlemen of the town were invited," including her father, "but of course not one *real* gentleman was present." When her parents showed her the invitation, LeConte "was highly indignant and regarded it as a piece of insolent impudence, but Father said he thought it was meant kindly." She judged the festivities unworthy of a true Fourth of July celebration. Fireworks were set off, and a brass band played, yet once "the pyrotechnics were exhausted, the band ceased and the negroes were left to make their own music. Hundreds of voices singing strange negro songs and hundreds of feet dancing weird negro dances made a terrible noise." This "strange" holiday was "too humiliating and made [her] realize our condition too keenly" to watch. Premillenarian "order" had been replaced by postmillenarian "anarchy." Only when the white colonel commanding the occupation forces ordered an end to the frolic at midnight was she able to sleep. Colonel Haughton "has been all kindness and consideration to the [white] citizens," LeConte admitted. "The negroes dislike him, and say he is no Yankee but half a rebel," or at least a premillenarian and thus sympathetic to white southerners in the manner of George McClellan.[69]

The moderate rule of Colonel Haughton in Columbia—keeping the peace between former masters and former enslaved people—highlighted the second and only slightly simpler issue than how to incorporate freedpeople into society Howard faced in the postwar months: military occupation. In 1847 Lieutenant D. H. Hill thought that reconstruction under Protestant American guidance would benefit Roman Catholic Mexico. "I look upon the present movement as full of promise for Mexico," hoping it could be "the precursor of the down-fall of the present corrupt hierarchy and the [onset of] universal freedom of conscience" through annexation and assimilation via benevolent Protestants to Mexico's north.[70] In 1865 Major General D. H. Hill rejected any insinuation that his section's "corrupt hierarchy" needed any education in or forced implementation of "universal freedom of conscience" by northern postmillenarians on behalf of black postmillenarians. Fittingly, just as he had served as the tactical commander of the war's first significant combat at Big Bethel in Virginia in 1861, Hill had a major role in the final major engagement at Bentonville in North Carolina in 1865. He had no intention of giving up the war, although he was forced to change tactics.

GENERAL HOWARD BECAME SUPERINTENDENT Howard in the summer of 1865. On March 3 Congress approved an initiative of Lincoln's to address the immediate needs of the freedpeople and refugees, namely the creation of the Bureau of Refugees, Freedmen, and Abandoned Lands as part of the War Department. On May 8 General Grant asked Howard to join him in Washington to discuss plans for the federal reconstruction of the South. Arriving in the capital the following evening, Howard met with Secretary of War Stanton, who offered him leadership of the new agency.[71]

Postmillenarian evangelicals such as Henry Ward Beecher desired that the bureau's responsibility for uplift—"Christianization and civilization"— be entrusted to their benevolent empire (including the AMA and the US Christian Commission), not a secular government agency. As historian William McFeely delineated more than five decades ago, Stanton (rightfully) distrusted the new president's devotion to this mission as opposed to revenge against the planter class, which he (Johnson) considered the oppressors of white yeomen. As such, Stanton hoped that a sufficiently devout general known to be sympathetic to the freedpeople could convince the "Christian public" to provide active aid to the bureau. Such voluntary support from postmillenarian missionaries, teachers, and donors could minimize the costs of the agency, winning Johnson's support in the face of other budgetary demands. Stanton also preferred a general previously considered by Lincoln—rejected then since his military expertise was needed by Sherman to close out the war—suitable for the post.[72] Howard fit that bill to a "T."

Although he fully endorsed Howard for the post just as he picked him to take over the Army of the Tennessee, General Sherman warned his former lieutenant not to allow the bureau to become part of a "New Revolution" driven by Radical Republicans, which could only result in yet another war. "I am tired of fighting," Sherman confessed, and the "North West may take a different side" next time. Sherman sounded ominously like McClellan two years before when the Napoleon-who-was-not lectured Lincoln about avoiding a remorseless revolution via emancipation and draconian occupation policies. Peace could only be preserved if "the theorists of New England" were prohibited from forcing "the Negro on the South" beyond being a second-class citizen allowed to "have his own labor."[73] A postmillenarian project of full citizenship and political equality—with the threats of economic and sexual equality in the wings (and minds of premillenarians around the country)—guaranteed more violence.

Howard rode beside Sherman at the head of the triumphal procession of the western armies through Washington on May 24. The audience knew that he was the chosen leader for the bureau tasked with raising four million formerly enslaved people to some aspect of American citizenship. When a little girl stepped from the crowd with a wreath of flowers for Howard's horse, the general politely declined, for he could not handle both horse and wreath.[74] This moment reminded the victorious nation of the sacrifices Howard had made in its service.

THE NEW LEADER of the Freedmen's Bureau received support and offers of aid from the postmillenarians among his former officers and men. Francis Channing Barlow, his subordinate at Chancellorsville and Gettysburg, wrote of his interest in combining military occupation duty with the uplift of African Americans. "You know the interest I have always taken in these Freedmen affairs & I have just written to the Secretary of War to ask him to assign me a command in the Southern States & suggesting that at the same time I might be made Superintendent of Freedmen in my District."[75]

If never explicit in his criteria for bureau-agent selection, it was clear that Howard considered sympathy with the freedpeople a prerequisite for service. He did not succeed in placing—or maintaining—sympathetic former Union officers in all of his districts, nor was he expected to do so. Howard confessed to a Congregationalist minister working with the AMA that he proposed to "give the freedmen *protection, land & schools,* as far and as fast as he can."[76]

ROBERT DABNEY SECEDED from his antebellum and wartime paternalism for the African "race," doing so in a public letter to General Howard, whom he addressed as the "Chief of the Freedmen's Bureau." God had taken from premillenarian southerners the responsibility of civilizing and Christianizing the "heathen" in their midst, Dabney wrote, symbolically washing his hands of the matter. Now let the postmillenarians of the North—more successful in the past four years at destroying the premillenarian South than raising up the enslaved—try their hand at what the reverend deemed a thankless task.[77]

Edmund Ruffin's Apocalypse, June 1865

EDMUND RUFFIN WAS DONE. He was done with the war, done with Yankees, and done with life. And his family knew it. Despite their vigilance, on June 17, 1865, Ruffin took advantage of his daughter and son-in-law's distraction with departing houseguests to climb up to their study with a forked stick and a rifle. A literary man—Protestant in practice if not in creed—to the end, Ruffin set pen to paper one last time to record in his diary: "And now with my latest writing and utterance, and with what will near to my latest breath, I here repeat, and would willingly proclaim, my unmitigated hatred to Yankee rule—to all political, social and business connections with Yankees, and to the perfidious, malignant, and vile Yankee race."[1] With the business end of the rifle in his mouth, Ruffin used the stick to pull the trigger. As happened all too often on the battlefield, the percussion cap cracked yet failed to ignite the powder. Hearing the ominous sound, Ruffin's hosts raced to the room. But by the time they arrived, he had successfully reloaded, and this time the rifle barked, sending Virginia's prophet of secession into eternity. His children found the body seated upright in a chair, "defiant and unyielding even in death."[2]

ALTHOUGH HE DID NOT pull the trigger on his life, D. H. Hill nourished Ruffin's ire. Accepting the fall of the Confederacy as a fact and therefore part of God's will, he never rejected the cause he fought for nor accepted the draconian domination of the southern states as implemented during Reconstruction. Hill's self-admitted "great sin" was "hatred of the Yankees."[3]

Margaret Preston and Hill, linked by antebellum ties to Lexington, Washington College, and Thomas Jonathan Jackson, collaborated in a literary effort to defend the Confederacy's legacy. Starting in 1866, Hill edited the magazine *Land We Love*. Over the next three years, Preston contributed seventeen poems to the purportedly nonregional periodical and its 12,000 subscribers.[4] Preston's early pieces for the magazine—in its first volume—belied Hill's claims of neutrality. "Hero's Daughter" was written about one of Robert E. Lee's daughters, while "Regulus" expressed anger at the alleged mistreatment of Jefferson Davis in federal custody.[5]

In Lexington former Confederate general William Pendleton, now returned to his antebellum calling of Episcopal rector, was placed under house arrest in July 1865 for omitting the prayer for the president of the United States from Grace Episcopal Church services. Federal officials closed the church, but Pendleton defiantly held services and administered Communion in his rectory. The church was allowed to reopen in January 1866 after Pendleton took the oath of allegiance and agreed to pray for the southern-born Democratic president. Yet federal troops remained in town for a few more months.[6]

GILES BUCKNER COOKE, 1859 VMI graduate and wartime convert to Christianity, felt called to minister to African Americans while serving as one of General Lee's staff officers.[7] Settling in Petersburg after the war, Cooke established a private school for freedmen under the auspices of the Episcopal Church, emphasizing the importance of religious instruction for children. His open advancement of freedpeople's interests during the 1870s did not sit well with his white neighbors. He responded that Lee and Jackson were his inspiration: "Lee had provided religious instruction to his slaves and Jackson had taught a Sunday school class for slaves before the war."[8] Ignoring the work of the freedpeople themselves and of the northern black and white abolitionists' initiatives via the Freedmen's Bureau, Cooke believed that if he did not get involved, "no one else would." Indeed, Lee, president of Washington College in Lexington during his last five years, wrote Cooke to commend him for his labors with African Americans.[9]

While a few former Confederates such as Cooke joined postmillenarian Republicans (as well as the AMA and the Freemen's Bureau) in evangelizing the freedpeople, many African American postmillenarians took this moment to secede from white churches. As historian William Montgomery noted, "thousands of blacks began organizing their own autonomous congregations. The months that followed emancipation marked the beginning of an exciting new era for the black church, a time during which it began to mature and to take on new forms and functions."[10]

PROTESTANT SOUTHERNERS SOON CONSTRUCTED a Lost Cause ideology to explain and justify the premillenarian act of secession and the Civil War that they began to preserve a white man's Christian. Temporarily sidelined by their failure to defend the Confederacy and attempting to rebuild their shattered lives and economy, veterans ceded the field of Confederate memory to clergy and women in the immediate postwar years. Both groups, deemed suspect or at least weak by the more secular advocates of wartime southern nationalism, now held the initiative to defend the Confederate endeavor, minimize the role of slavery, and combat Republican slander and occupation. Among the front ranks of these literary defenders of the Confederacy stood Preston and Dabney, with D. H. Hill playing a supporting role.

Not all former Confederates clung to the raft (or ark) of the Confederacy as New Israel. Elite male Virginians who came of age in the decade before the Civil War—they led many of the Old Dominion's regiments to initial victory and ultimate defeat—could no longer subscribe to "the idea that Southerners were God's chosen people." Historian Peter Carmichael made this argument on the basis that this premillenarian faith was "conspicuously absent in their post-1865 writings," which paradoxically "gave them more freedom to critique their own society during Reconstruction" and seek some accommodation with their postmillenarian conquerors to remake the commonwealth.[11]

Yet the majority of white southerners who supported the Confederacy did not want to accommodate their conquerors more than absolutely necessary, particularly the women. Unarmed premillenarian women confronted armed postmillenarians in occupied territories beyond formal battlefields. Confederate women bought into the social contract that their men left home to defend their way of life, a contract that was broken in 1865 (or well before, in places like New Orleans and the Shenandoah Valley).[12] If generally unarmed, these women resisted Union occupation by word and deed, constantly frustrating federal soldiers and generals. Their wartime resistance and the failure of husbands, brothers, and fathers to defend them gave premillenarian women the license to lead the effort to construct the Lost Cause narrative.

Gender conflict raises the issue of sexual assault, particularly in light of the "black beast rapist" stereotype of African American men of the later nineteenth century and the accompanying epidemic of lynching. In plantation counties premillenarian women and children were exposed to any potential physical and sexual violence as never before since black men faced less supervision from the departed military-age white men. Despite the lynching culture that spread through the southern states during Reconstruction, "Confederates were not convulsed with fears of slave rape," at least not in Virginia. Historian Diane Sommerville found fewer than ten wartime cases of enslaved persons convicted of rape or attempted rape, and the "leniency accorded to accused black rapists . . . indicates that white southerners felt little compulsion to make examples of convicted slave rapists." Wartime pressures did not compel Virginians "to forgo the custom of giving accused slaves at least the appearance of a fair public hearing."[13]

SOUTHERN DEMOCRATS GAMBLED BADLY and paid the price. By wagering the future of a white man's republic on a cast of the dice that involved secession and civil war, premillenarian southerners gave up their antebellum dominance of US politics and the profitable institution of slavery. Their white northern allies also lost, not only the chance to preserve the status quo antebellum but also any hope of restoring Democratic power at the national level for a decade. Postmillenarian Republicans and enslaved African Americans—now freedpeople—won a war started by their pessimistic foes. "In a way, the Civil War was post-millenarianism's greatest triumph," historian Eugen Weber wrote at the end of the twentieth century. "Like many triumphs, however, it marked the beginnings of its own decline and the return in force of rivals indifferent to social reforms that did not address the vital problem of original sin."[14]

Robert Lewis Dabney adhered to the hardline positions of Edmund Ruffin and D. H. Hill on the prospects of Reconstruction. He could not forgive northern postmillenarians—particularly fellow Presbyterians—for waging a war "precipitated by treachery, aggravated by every measure of barbarity condemned by the laws of nations, by the agency of multitudinous hordes of foreign mercenaries, and [by] semi-civilized slaves seduced from their owners."[15] Yet he did not "dream of affecting the perverse judgments of the great anti-slavery party which now rules the hour" of the waking nightmare he now inhabited. "Nothing but the hand of a retributive Providence can avail to reach them."[16]

Those southern premillenarians either too young or excluded by gender conventions from fighting in the war found it difficult to accept an outcome they had no role in resisting. Professor Joseph LeConte wrote his daughter while on a trip to see his dying sister in Georgia, concerned both about Emma's mental and spiritual health. He was convinced "it would do you much good if you could be here and could witness the death bed of your Aunt. Your life darling has been one of almost unalloyed happiness," a claim that Emma's diary entry on the last day of 1864 refuted. "You know nothing of either pain or suffering. Do not forget . . . to be sincerely grateful for these blessings. I have no wish, wantonly to interfere with the happiness . . . but I am sure the contemplation of suffering and approaching death borne with resignation and cheerfulness" shall "give you insight into the real significance of human life and the reality of the life to come." His sister's "triumphant faith" dispelled "human doubts . . . , and human speculations sink into insignificance." Sister Ann "talked cheerfully and almost joyfully of going home, of meeting friends long dead. Our father and mother. Our brothers . . . and many others." Sure of his sister's saving faith, he was less so about his daughter's. He beseeched, "while your life is still in its prime do not forget to be grateful to the giver of all blessings—do not fail to love and reverence the Foundation of all goodness and nobleness and purity and to dedicate your young heart to the service of our spiritual Father," closing with the desire that God will "make you his own child."[17]

LeConte's tender love for his daughter and admiration of his dying sister did not extend to Reconstruction. He objected to South Carolina's "carpet-bag governor, scalawag officials, and a negro legislature controlled by rascals," a premillenarian assessment of the ascendancy of postmillenarian politics. He ignored the fact that three-fifths of the state's population were recently emancipated, and so most (male) voters were only now exercising their rights, claiming that the "sudden enfranchisement of the negro without qualification was the greatest political crime ever perpetrated by any people."[18] The LeContes left the conquered South for the boundless western frontier in 1869, when Professor LeConte was hired by the University of California.

x x x

WHAT ABOUT THE VICTORS? The dentist Thomas Bayne, a self-emancipated native of Norfolk, Virginia, returned to his home state from Massachusetts at the end of the war. In 1865 he led a gathering of Norfolk freedpeople to discuss and publish *An Address . . . to the People of the United States*. Reminding white Americans of the labor of Africans alongside white British colonists on tobacco plantations on the James River and of Crispus Attucks's sacrifice in opposing English tyranny, Bayne and his neighbors argued that African Americans deserved the vote and first-class citizenship. National honor was at stake in the postwar debate over the status of freedpeople, "but is that honor advanced, in the eyes of the Christian world, when America alone, of all Christian nations, sustains an unjust distinction . . . on the senseless ground of a difference in color?"[19] An itinerant preacher as well as a dentist, Bayne, along with his community, argued in language that most white American Protestants accepted, that the United States was a Christian nation and as such must act accordingly or be judged wanting by the rest of the "Christian world."

Carl Schurz toured the newly defeated southern states during the summer of 1865. What the general saw and heard of erstwhile Confederates warned all northerners who blissfully assumed that the defeated meekly accepted their fate and the progress offered by the victors. Schurz remained a Republican during Reconstruction, although his devotion to liberal principles in the face of partisan corruption led him to extend the olive branch to seek compromise with southern voters in 1872 along with Horace Greeley.

Although John Geary considered a gubernatorial run in Pennsylvania with the Democrats in 1866, Simon Cameron recruited him for the Republican ticket.[20] His Democratic challenger resorted to the worst antebellum or wartime premillenarian propaganda, using racist posters to claim that a vote for Geary was a vote for the "negro," while a vote for Hiester Clymer— who failed to serve in the war—was a vote for the "white man." One poster highlighted Geary's speech of August 11, 1866, in which the candidate stated, "there can be no possible objection to negro suffrage," to tar him with the "black Republican" and promiscegenation brush.[21]

OLIVER HOWARD FACED an impossible task. Although considered the best possible man to lead the Freedmen's Bureau by both sympathetic and skeptical observers, Howard was leading a postmillenarian mission in the guise of a secular government agency. Despite much support from northern missionary-teachers and the hopes of millions of freedpeople, the bureau was doomed by persistent opposition from southern premillenarians and their northern counterparts—Unionist Democrats like President Johnson—who opposed societal change. Emancipate the enslaved? Fine. Make them the political equals of white people? No, never. Johnson could agree on this score, nor could Generals McClellan and Sherman as well as former Confederates Dabney, Hill, and Nathan Bedford Forrest. In 1903 historian W. E. B. DuBois judged that Howard's agency failed to make African Americans truly free due to outside forces. It "did not do because it could not."[22] In William McFeely's analysis, DuBois made "prophecy of history," wanting "the beginnings he thought had been made by the Bureau to predict the great changes necessary if the Negroes were to gain their freedom," a postmillenarian perspective, if true, that accorded with much of Howard's own worldview.[23]

As McFeely noted, Howard made a good general to a great army commander, however he lacked the initiative to make his own policy of lasting reforms in the form of land redistribution, which was so crucial to the freedpeople's future. This was particularly the case when the commander in chief was Andrew Johnson, who pardoned most Confederate leaders, allowing the planter class to reclaim the land that African Americans deemed rightfully theirs. Radical Republicans in Congress were still a year away from decreeing Military Reconstruction, and conservative occupation generals such as Howard's former commander George Meade, who sided with former Confederates in land disputes, doomed Howard and the bureau.[24]

Howard's legacy as an advocate of educational reform stands on firmer ground than his social-reform efforts. He was one of thirty-odd members of the First Congregational Society who met at a rented facility in Washington in mid-November 1866. Dr. Charles Boynton, presiding, exhorted his congregation on the nation's responsibilities to the freedpeople. They discussed the potential benefits of founding a theological seminary for black men. On November 20 ten Congregationalists convened at the residence of a deacon to follow up on this proposal. Howard, recently returned from a trip to visit freedpeople in the southern states, was convinced that advanced-education institutions should be founded for the elevation of African Americans; one of the men present thereafter won approval for the formation of Howard Theological Seminary.[25] The general closed the meeting in prayer. Two months later the proposed seminary had been twice reenvisioned, first as a seminary and teachers college, then as an institute for the training of teachers, which stood to gain more congressional support than a strictly religious one. The third iteration of the proposal was for a full-fledged university that "a hundred years later [stood as] the foremost institution in the world for the higher education of a predominantly colored student body."[26] Unable to escape the farming communities of rural Maine herself, Howard's mother "chose a superior education" as the path for her sons to "advance in the world."[27] Oliver Otis graduated from two colleges and bequeathed to generations of African Americans a university that embodied the goal of improvement and progress that black and white postmillenarian allies had fought for during the Civil War.

TWO YEARS AFTER HER husband's assassination, Mary Todd Lincoln moved to New York and into a hotel room with her former seamstress, Elizabeth Keckley. Pensionless—despite her arguable status as the war's last widow—Lincoln attempted to auction off various possessions to support herself. She failed to gain sufficient funds from these sales, so Keckley wrote to black leaders to see if they might help organize a lecture tour, with proceeds to go to the widow. Frederick Douglass and Henry H. Garnet agreed to this venture in October 1867. "If the thing is done," Douglass advised Keckley, "it should be done on a grand scale. The best speakers in the country should be secured for the purpose. You should not place me at the head or foot of the list, but sandwich me between, for thus out of the way, it would not give *color* to the idea." Yet Lincoln's premillenarian prejudice torpedoed Keckley's project, despite her desire that Douglass remember "how deeply my feelings were enlisted in the cause of freedom" during the war. "I want neither Mr. Douglass nor Garnet to lecture in my behalf," she told Keckley.[28]

If neither resided in the former Confederate states, the postwar lives of Sojourner Truth and Harriet Tubman testify to the challenges aging formerly enslaved persons encountered despite and due to Reconstruction. Suffering from the new injuries inflicted in New Jersey while defending her right to her seat on a train, Tubman struggled to make a living and to persuade federal authorities that her variegated wartime service warranted a pension. As early as July 1865 she sought the assistance of Secretary of State William Seward—through whom she purchased her home in Auburn,

New York—for aid in receiving compensation for her espionage and medical services. Seward was favorably disposed and asked General David Hunter to forward the matter; still, no pay was authorized.[29] When asked if she thought women deserved the vote, Tubman replied: "I suffered enough to believe it."[30] For her part, by 1870, after decades of public speaking on behalf of emancipation and racial integration, Truth embraced separatism—still decrying expatriation to Africa or the Caribbean—"as the most viable means of black progress in the wake of virulent racism." Like Tubman, she favored women's suffrage. At an 1870 American Woman's Suffrage Association meeting held in Boston, Truth held that women needed equal rights not just for themselves but also for the benefit of the entire world. When younger (and whiter) feminists attempted to limit her speech, she held to her prophetic character, reminding her audience that she "spoke when the spirit moved her—not when the people moved her."[31]

OLD SOLDIERS ALWAYS REFIGHT wars. Plenty of generals on both sides were left with bitter legacies and shared them with trusted allies or waged a war in which ink rather than blood was spilt in the pages of the *Century Magazine* during the mid-1880s, eventually filling four thick volumes with their articles and accounts. Although he did not live to contribute to this paper contest, Joseph Hooker stayed true to his wartime bluster, criticizing Sherman as "crazy," claiming Grant "had no more moral sense than a dog," and charging that Howard could "command a prayer meeting with a good deal more ability than he did an army."[32] Howard's elevation to command of the Army of the Tennessee during the Atlanta Campaign occasioned Hooker's huffy resignation—much to Sherman's relief—from his western chance at military relevance. Howard, of course, led the unbeaten army forged by Grant and Sherman through the March to the Sea and the Carolinas rather better than the corps he commanded under Hooker at Chancellorsville.

Margaret Preston was one of the few women asked to contribute publicly to the outpouring of Civil War accounts in the 1880s. *Century* published her "Personal Reminiscences of Stonewall Jackson" in 1886. As historian Sarah E. Gardner noted, Preston emphasized the general's faith, compassion, and devotion to Virginia in preference to cataloguing his martial achievements. Jackson's widow later plagiarized much of this article in her biography of the general.[33] Following acclaim for Preston's piece about a man she deemed "the popular idol of the South," the magazine's editors asked her to compose a similar biographical sketch of Lee.[34]

Let us leave the "Poet of the Confederacy" with her observations of the postmillenarian raid on Lexington. She noted that several Union soldiers related to her through her relationship to Stonewall Jackson. One asked her to relinquish some possession of the general's, while another showed her leaves taken from his gravesite.[35] She saw some of Hunter's officers and enlisted men pay respect at Jackson's tomb, moving her to write "Stonewall Jackson's Grave." Although she labeled the invaders "Pagans," Preston acknowledged that Union and Confederate soldiers were linked in respect— "the love of friend or foe"—for the fallen general, who inspired fighting men of both sides to make pilgrimages to his apparently "holy sepulchre."[36] In other words, this poem—published in England—gave Preston some hope that American "Christians and Pagans" could find reconciliation via appreciation of their mutual wartime loss, albeit at the grave of a Confederate hero and on southern (premillenarian) terms. The Lost Cause was born from the tomb via Preston's pen.

Julia Ward Howe continued her progressive literary crusade into the twentieth century. After the Mexican-American War she wrote Francis Lieber that when he visited her, she strictly prohibited discussion of "insane hospitals, idiots, educated or otherwise, and madness of every description . . . Philanthropy—philanthropic enterprizes—workhouses—relief and vigilance committees—interests of the African race—disgusts of the Mexican War—every kind of philanthropy" and "every description of philanthropist," how different was the second half of her life.[37]

Manuscripts held at the Library of Congress include the texts of postwar speeches and sermons. Months after the United States joined the western European powers in the quest for overseas empire around the turn of the twentieth century, Howe addressed in secular terms the postmillenarian-premillenarian dichotomy at the core of this book. "Optimism and Pessimism as Efficient Social Forces" occasioned for Howe—long past youthful evangelicalism—an engagement with the antagonism of good versus evil, even as she reflected that she knew "very good and intelligent people" on either side of the pessimist-optimist divide. She was puzzled to observe "people more comfortable under the hypothesis that all things tend to evil than under the opposite supposition," though perhaps less so when she commented that this was a "class" primarily composed of men. Regardless, these people "seem to hug the conviction of the general folly and meanness of mankind as a comfort that cannot be dispensed with," betraying the fact that many of them "do not take the trouble to think." Yet rejecting overly simple dichotomies, she admitted that "the same individual [may] sometimes [be] an optimist, sometimes a pessimist."[38]

Howe betrayed the fact that, four decades following emancipation, she had cooled on the progress of the freedpeople, although her analogy was also applied to the peasants who had supported the French Revolution. "Extravagant hopes had been entertained of the height to which the oppressed classes would rise when once liberated from the yoke of despotic sway. It was forgotten that the slave in revolt has still the habits and passions of the slave." Tutored by "wild nature" on how to "overthrow, rend and trample," yet "the heavenly art of reconstruction is unknown to him, and must be supplied by another agency than his." Who was to provide that agency? In the era of Max Weber's *The Protestant Ethic and the Spirit of Capitalism* and the perceived need of "backward" Filipino, Cuban, and Puerto Rican Catholics for Protestant uplift, it was the white man who must act to develop in passive pupils "the heavenly art of reconstruction."[39] The active opposition of white southern premillenarians had doomed this postmillenarian Reconstruction in the former Confederacy.

Yet Howe did not provide a facile view that Protestantism was the answer to pessimism, for although "eminently a religion founded upon faith in the inherent power and spiritual tendency of man, much of its administration has told of reasoning in the opposite direction." The "forceful and despotic" tendencies of many Christian churches started "from the assumption that man is a superstitious, selfish and ignoble being, incapable of the disinterested pursuit of good," from which "early Protestant and Puritan beliefs show little or no improvement." Looking back on more than eight decades of life, Howe concluded that "a long experience of life reveals to us many reasons for painful anxiety, and many for uplifting hope. I think that we may well be pessimistically anxious on the one hand," yet "also . . . optimistically hopeful," for hope was not only "one of the Christian trio of graces, but the very condition of all availing effort, of all true progress." Even "when tossed on the troubled seas of doubt and difficulty," she advised holding on "by that anchor of the soul, both sure and steadfast. Its hold is beyond the stars, but that way, too, lies our destiny."[40]

If Howe temporarily disdained to discuss the "interests of the African race" as late as the last year of her life, former enslaved persons—and their children—commemorated her contributions to their emancipation.[41] On the occasion of her ninety-first (and final) birthday, the Westside Literary Sunday Club of Chicago—"composed entirely of descendants of some of the ex-slaves of the U.S.A."—congratulated her "for a life spent in behalf of a despised and maltreated race." They perceived "a DIVINE influence in the circumstances" that motivated Howe "to assist in the emancipation of our parents from the shackles of human slavery," resolving to follow her example "in edifying those that sit in darkness of ignorance and superstition."[42]

"We live in a world of many glories," Howe wrote in an undated sermon on the persistence of divine providence. Here she gave some credit to the patriarchs of the Old Testament. "Abraham had a glimpse of it. Moses had the moral law by its light on Mt Sinai," which appeared "from time to time to [later] prophet-priest[s]." She continued, "At last in the fulness of time it came in a form which could never pass from the mind and memory of man," that is, Jesus Christ. Despite living "a life of poverty and privation" and dying "a death of bitter . . . humiliation," his legacy was "a new . . . divine revelation, the glory of God in the face of Jesus Christ."[43]

In Howe's telling, Christ's glory was that "God is love, the source of unwearied, unbounded beneficence. God is love, and man is his child, dear to his heart, and heir to the true glory of his kingdom." Although sounding a unitarian note at the close of the sermon—Jesus was lumped in with "the saints and heroes who have lit up the whole history of human action, the steadfast martyr, the visionary prophet, the fervent apostle"—Christ was still central. If "human they are and were," their word, "written or spoken, does not pass away. It remains to give as much assurance as we need of the eternity and omnipotence of goodness."[44] Howe's sense of the symbiotic nature of pessimism and optimism here was tempered with a conviction of the progressive arc of God's providence.

Emma LeConte and Anna Dickinson—teenagers when the war began—survived the rest of our apostles by more than two decades. Neither surpassed their wartime careers as diarist or lecturer. LeConte followed planter-class convention, marrying Confederate veteran Farish Carter Furman—Citadel alumnus, Georgia planter, judge, and great-grandson of the Baptist minister for whom Furman University was named—yet outliving him by nearly a half century.[45] When her prospects as a lecturer declined, Dickinson began writing novels and plays, climbed several Rocky Mountain peaks, allegedly took up romantic relations with other women, and struggled with mental-health issues and alcoholism.[46] Both women died in 1932, several years into the Great Depression and just before the election of Franklin Delano Roosevelt and the launching of the New Deal.

AMERICAN NATIONALISM WAS BIFURCATED during the 1860s into post-millenarian and premillenarian branches. "All self-conscious nations develop a sense of their peculiar self-worth," wrote Charles Reagan Wilson, "but a few have gone beyond that to develop true messianic zeal."[47] Wilbur Zelinsky found "a symbiotic embrace between state and orthodox church" in monarchical nations such as Spain, "Japan (especially before 1945), Czarist Russia, and the United Kingdom in which a single dynasty reigns over, or controls, both entities, but where the state assumes the task of propagating and executing the civil religion."[48] Nations founded in revolutionary violence such as France, Nazi Germany, Maoist China, the Soviet Union, and North Korea often established their government's secular faith around a cult of the founder (Hitler, Mao, Lenin). "What may be distinctive about the United States," Wilson concluded, "is that throughout the nation's history a folk civil religion that saw transcendent meaning in the national experience has existed apart from both church and state."[49] The victorious postmillenarian optimists evolved into liberal Protestants in the northern states, whose "confidence in the progressive nature of history and revelation" paved the path to their "acceptance of the evolutionary and experiential nature of truth."[50]

The fractured American civil religion was imperfectly reunited as the United States joined Europe in the scramble for overseas empire in 1898 at the behest of postmillenarian industrialists and media moguls and premillenarian southern agrarians. Charging at their head was the scion of Union professionals and Confederate planters, Theodore Roosevelt, a Manhattan cowboy who championed the construction of a modern navy.[51] Decidedly a Progressive—note the twentieth-century translation of the Whiggish nineteenth-century "progress"—Roosevelt's main rival for the rightful legacy of progress-oriented presidential reformer was Woodrow Wilson, the southern-born son of a northern pastor. Wilson's ascendancy to the White House fifty years after the Emancipation Proclamation also represented the South's rising again to national prominence after decades in the political wilderness following the war.[52] This pair—two men born just before the Civil War and whose earliest memories were shaped by that conflict—were the star-crossed rivals and dynamic duo aptly dubbed the warrior and the priest (interchangeably in my mind) by historian John M. Cooper.[53]

By 1900, as "American imperialism and militarism crested, the contributions of black women to the Civil War, such as those made by Harriet Tubman, Susie King Taylor, and the dozens of black women who fought in disguise as men, seemingly merited no mention in the celebrations of black wartime valor."[54] As historian W. Fitzhugh Brundage noted, turn-of-the-century black-male commemorators emphasized the courageous manliness of soldiers in the 54th Massachusetts and the USCT regiments. This was partly understandable as a reaction to the crisis in black masculinity posed by the lynching epidemic throughout the former Confederacy, explained and justified by white premillenarians as a response to uncontrollable black sexual predators.

WITH HINDSIGHT, THE CIVIL WAR was only the most deadly part of white southern Protestants' premillenarian revolt. Two years after Lee's surrender, Republican general John Pope wrote future Republican president Ulysses S. Grant to express his concern that future generations of white southerners might learn that the Confederacy fought to defend individual (or states') rights, not the truth. "The rebellion was the result of a tremendous conspiracy," Republicans like Pope knew, "to destroy the nation's life. It sought to obliterate civil liberty through[out] the South—to reduce the Southern white laborer to the condition of the free negro, and the free negro to slavery; to re-open the African slave trade, and to establish over the South the despotism of an oligarchy" grounded in slavery as well as "the interests and ambition of those interested in slave property. How cruel and remorseless its career was—how little it respected individual rights and the common laws of humanity when they stood in the way of its remorseless schemes."[55] Pope was right to fear the losers might rewrite the history of the war, portraying themselves as victims rather than perpetrators. "If the North won the military battles of the Civil War, the South won the culture war," argued historian Jon Pahl.[56] Or, as I prefer to word the situation, the postmillenarians won the war, but the premillenarians won the peace.

Notes

Abbreviations

AMA   American Missionary Association Archives, Amistad Research Center, Tulane University, New Orleans

BC   George J. Mitchell Department of Special Collections and Archives, Hawthorne-Longfellow Library, Bowdoin College, Brunswick, ME

BRPR   *Biblical Repertory and Princeton Review*

CU   Kroch Library, Cornell University, Ithaca, NY

DU   David M. Rubinstein Library, Duke University, Durham, NC

HL   Huntington Library, San Marino, CA

HRL   Stewart Bell Jr. Archives, Handley Regional Library, Winchester, VA

LC   Library of Congress, Washington, DC

NA   National Archives, Washington, DC

OR   US War Department, *The War of the Rebellion: A Compilation of the Official Records of the Union and Confederate Armies*, 129 vols. (Washington, DC: Government Printing Office, 1880–1901). All citations are to series 1 unless otherwise stated.

RU   Alexander Library, Rutgers University, New Brunswick, NJ

UM   William L. Clements Library, University of Michigan, Ann Arbor

UNC   Southern Historical Collection, Wilson Library, University of North Carolina, Chapel Hill

USAHEC   US Army Heritage and Education Center, Carlisle, PA

UVA   Albert and Shirley Small Special Collections Library, University of Virginia, Charlottesville

VMHC   Virginia Museum of History and Culture, Richmond

WLU   Special Collections, James G. Leyburn Library, Washington and Lee University, Lexington, VA

Prologue: The Civil War as an Eschatological Crisis

1. See Alan D. Gaff and Donald H. Gaff, eds., *A Corporal's Story: Civil War Recollections of the Twelfth Massachusetts* (Norman: University of Oklahoma Press, 2014), 29, 33; Christian

McWhirter, *Battle Hymns: The Power and Popularity of Music in the Civil War* (Chapel Hill: University of North Carolina Press, 2012), chap. 2; and John Stauffer and Benjamin Soskis, *The Battle Hymn of the Republic: A Biography of the Song That Marches On* (New York: Oxford University Press, 2013), chap. 2.

2. Rufus R. Dawes, *Service with the Sixth Wisconsin Volunteers* (Marietta, OH: E. R. Alderman & Sons, 1890), 28–29.

3. Julia Ward Howe, *Reminiscences, 1819–1899* (Boston: Houghton, Mifflin, 1900), 274–75; Jonathan W. White, *Midnight in America: Darkness, Sleep, and Dreams during the Civil War* (Chapel Hill: University of North Carolina Press, 2017), xi–xii; and Richard M. Gamble, *A Fiery Gospel: The Battle Hymn of the Republic and the Road to Righteous War* (Ithaca, NY: Cornell University Press, 2019), 44–45.

4. Julia Ward Howe, "The Battle Hymn of the Republic," *Atlantic Monthly* 9:52 (Feb. 1862): 10, https://www.theatlantic.com/magazine/archive/1862/02/the-battle-hymn-of-the-republic/308052/.

5. Elaine Pagels, *Revelations: Visions, Prophecy, and Politics in the Book of Revelation* (New York: Viking, 2012), 1–6.

6. Drew Gilpin Faust, *This Republic of Suffering: Death and the America Civil War* (New York: Alfred A. Knopf, 2008), 6–10.

7. Kathryn Gin Lum, *Damned Nation: Hell in America from the Revolution to Reconstruction* (New York: Oxford University Press, 2014), 202.

8. Harry S. Stout, *Upon the Altar of the Nation: A Moral History of the Civil War* (New York: Viking, 2006), xvi.

9. Mark A. Noll, *The Civil War as a Theological Crisis* (Chapel Hill: University of North Carolina Press, 2006), 13.

10. Richard Landes, *Heaven on Earth: The Varieties of the Millennial Experience* (New York: Oxford University Press, 2011), 27–28; William G. McLoughlin, *Revivals, Awakenings, and Reform: An Essay on Religion and Social Change in America, 1607–1977* (Chicago: University of Chicago Press, 1978), chap. 2. Benjamin Lynerd briefly referred to millenarian influences on evangelical political theory without disaggregating. See *Republican Theology: The Civil Religion of American Evangelicals* (New York: Oxford University Press, 2014), 50, 88.

11. See Landes, *Heaven on Earth,* chap. 12.

12. Randall Balmer and Lauren F. Winner, *Protestantism in America* (New York: Columbia University Press, 2002), 57–58.

13. Jack P. Maddex Jr., "Proslavery Millennialism: Social Eschatology in Antebellum Southern Calvinism," *American Quarterly* 31:1 (Spring 1979): 52.

14. Paul E. Johnson, *A Shopkeeper's Millennium: Society and Revivals in Rochester, New York, 1815–1837* (New York: Hill and Wang, 1978), 8.

15. Stephanie McCurry, *Masters of Small Worlds: Yeoman Households, Gender Relations, and the Political Culture of the Antebellum South Carolina Low Country* (New York: Oxford University Press, 1995), 147.

16. Drew Gilpin Faust, "Christian Soldiers: The Meaning of Revivalism in the Confederate Army," *Journal of Southern History* 53:1 (Feb. 1987): 63–90.

17. David Goldfield, *America Aflame: How the Civil War Created a Nation* (New York: Bloomsbury, 2011), 8.

18. Robert M. Calhoon, *Evangelicals and Conservatives in the Early South, 1740–1861* (Columbia: University of South Carolina Press, 1988), 188.

19. Calhoon, *Evangelicals and Conservatives*, 190.

20. Robert L. Dabney, *A Defence of Virginia, in Recent and Pending Contests Against the Sectional Party* (New York: E. J. Hale & Son, 1867), 303–4.

21. James O. Farmer Jr., *The Metaphysical Confederacy: James Henley Thornwell and the Synthesis of Southern Values* (Macon, GA: Mercer University Press, 1986), 201.

22. Kenneth Moore Startup, *The Root of All Evil: The Protestant Clergy and the Economic Mind of the Old South* (Athens: University of Georgia Press, 1997), 34.

23. *Semi-Weekly Richmond Enquirer*, July 14, 1863, 1.

24. See Kellie Carter Jackson, *Force and Freedom: Black Abolitionists and the Politics of Violence* (Philadelphia: University of Pennsylvania Press, 2019), 20.

25. Keri Leigh Merritt, *Masterless Men: Poor Whites and Slavery in the Antebellum South* (New York: Cambridge University Press, 2017), 152–53.

26. For Douglass's appreciation of education, see David Blight, *Frederick Douglass: Prophet of Freedom* (New York: Simon & Schuster, 2018), 40. For the importance of education in Howard's family, see William S. McFeely, *Yankee Stepfather: General O. O. Howard and the Freedmen* (New Haven, CT: Yale University Press, 1968), 28.

27. Kenneth G. C. Newport, *Apocalypse and Millennium: Studies in Biblical Eisegesis* (New York: Cambridge University Press, 2000), chap. 4; William M. Shea, *The Lion and the Lamb: Evangelicals and Catholics in America* (New York: Oxford University Press, 2004), 37.

28. Elizabeth Fenton, *Religious Liberties: Anti-Catholicism and Liberal Democracy in Nineteenth-Century U.S. Literature and Culture* (New York: Oxford University Press, 2011), chap. 2; Katie Oxx, *The Nativism Movement in America: Religious Conflict in the Nineteenth Century* (New York: Routledge, 2013), 32–35. For Beecher's own anti-Catholic rhetoric, see Lyman Beecher, *A Plea for the West*, 2nd ed. (Cincinnati: Truman & Smith, 1835).

29. Tyler G. Anbinder, *Nativism and Slavery: The Northern Know Nothings and the Politics of the 1850s* (New York: Oxford University Press, 1992), chap. 5.

30. Anne M. Boylan, *Sunday School: The Formation of an American Institution, 1790–1880* (New Haven, CT: Yale University Press, 1988), chaps. 4 and 5; Richard Carwardine, *Evangelicals and Politics in Antebellum America* (New Haven, CT: Yale University Press, 1993), chaps. 7 and 8.

31. For American Catholics' ambivalent views on slavery, see Paula Kane, "The Supernatural and Slavery: Catholics, Power, and Oppression," in *The Problem of Evil: Slavery, Freedom, and the Ambiguities of American Reform*, ed. Steven Mintz and John Stauffer (Amherst: University of Massachusetts Press, 2007), 199–209; and John T. McGreevy, *Catholicism and American Freedom: A History* (New York: W. W. Norton, 2003), chap. 2.

32. See James H. Moorhead, *American Apocalypse: Yankee Protestants and the Civil War, 1860–1869* (New Haven, CT: Yale University Press, 1978).

33. See Moorhead, "The Erosion of Postmillennialism in American Religious Thought, 1865–1925," *Church History* 53:1 (Mar. 1984): 61–77.

34. Richard L. Bushman, *From Puritan to Yankee: Character and the Social Order in Connecticut, 1690–1765* (Cambridge, MA: Harvard University Press, 1967), chap. 10; Mark A. Noll, *America's God: From Jonathan Edwards to Abraham Lincoln* (New York: Oxford University Press, 2002), chap. 3.

35. William B. Skelton, *An American Profession of Arms: The Army Officer Corps, 1784–1861* (Lawrence: University Press of Kansas, 1993), 160–63.

36. Lafayette College, Miami University, and Washington College in Lexington were helmed—in that order –by Presbyterian reverend George Junkin, father of Margaret Preston. Mary Price Coulling, *Margaret Junkin Preston: A Biography* (Winston-Salem, NC: John F. Blair, 1993), 24–55.

37. Ryan B. Jordan, *Slavery and the Meetinghouse: The Quakers and the Abolitionist Dilemma, 1820–1865* (Bloomington: Indiana University Press, 2007), 3.

38. Joseph C. G. Kennedy, *Population of the United States in 1860; Compiled from the Original Returns of the Eighth Census, Under the Direction of the Secretary of the Interior* (Washington, DC: Government Printing Office, 1864), vii.

39. David S. Reynolds, *John Brown, Abolitionist: The Man Who Killed Slavery, Sparked the Civil War, and Seeded Civil Rights* (New York: Alfred A. Knopf, 2005), 56–57, 61; John Stauffer, *The Black Hearts of Men: Radical Abolitionists and the Transformation of Race* (Cambridge, MA: Harvard University Press, 2002), chap. 5.

40. David F. Allmendinger Jr., *Ruffin: Family and Reform in the Old South* (New York: Oxford University Press, 1990), 48, 57, 77–79.

41. See Luke E. Harlow, *Religion, Race, and the Making of Confederate Kentucky, 1830–1880* (New York: Cambridge University Press, 2014), 145–48; and April E. Holm, *A Kingdom Divided: Evangelicals, Loyalty, and Sectionalism in the Civil War Era* (Baton Rouge: Louisiana State University Press, 2017), 91–92.

42. Lloyd A. Hunter, "The Immortal Confederacy: Another Look at Lost Cause Religion," in *The Myth of the Lost Cause and Civil War History,* ed. Gary W. Gallagher and Alan T. Nolan (Bloomington: Indiana University Press, 2000), 185–218.

43. Hal Bridges, *Lee's Maverick General: Daniel Harvey Hill* (New York: McGraw-Hill, 1961), 23–27; Alfred L. Brophy, *University, Court, and Slave: Pro-Slavery Thought in Southern Colleges and Courts and the Coming of Civil War* (New York: Oxford University Press, 2016), 57.

44. See Bridges, *Lee's Maverick General,* chap. 10.

45. Michael Todd Landis, *Northern Men with Southern Loyalties: The Democratic Party and the Sectional Crisis* (Ithaca, NY: Cornell University Press, 2014), 249. For a similar argument, see Joshua A. Lynn, "Preserving the White Man's Republic: The Democratic Party and the Transformation of American Conservatism, 1847–1860" (Ph.D. diss., University of North Carolina at Chapel Hill, 2015), 47–51.

46. Ethan S. Rafuse, *McClellan's War: The Failure of Moderation in the Struggle for the Union* (Bloomington: Indiana University Press, 2005), chap. 11.

47. Milton C. Sernett, *Harriet Tubman: Myth, Memory, and History* (Durham, NC: Duke University Press, 2007), chaps. 2 and 3.

48. Nell Irvin Painter, *Sojourner Truth: A Life, a Symbol* (New York: W. W. Norton, 1996), 160. For a more recent claim that Douglass became more secular as he aged. see Christopher Cameron, *Black Freethinkers: A History of African American Secularism* (Evanston, IL: Northwestern University Press, 2019), 30–34.

49. Margaret Washington, *Sojourner Truth's America* (Urbana: University of Illinois Press, 2009), 285–86.

50. Margaret Washington, ed., *Narrative of Sojourner Truth* (New York: Vintage, 1994), xvi.

51. J. Matthew Gallman, *America's Joan of Arc: The Life of Anna Elizabeth Dickinson* (New York: Oxford University Press, 2006), 1.

52. Earl Schenck Miers, ed., *When the World Ended: The Diary of Emma LeConte* (New York: Oxford University Press, 1957), xxiv–xxx.

53. John A. Carpenter, *Sword and Olive Branch: Oliver Otis Howard* (Pittsburgh: University of Pittsburgh Press, 1964), 13.

54. Rowland Howard to Oliver Otis Howard, Sept. 8, 1853, Oliver Otis Howard Papers, BC.

55. Huston Horn, *Leonidas Polk: Warrior Bishop of the Confederacy* (Lawrence: University Press of Kansas, 2019), 20–21.

56. Glenn Robins, *The Bishop of the Old South: The Ministry and Civil War Legacy of Leonidas Polk* (Macon, GA: Mercer University Press, 2006), 112.

57. Stacey Jean Klein, *Margaret Junkin Preston, Poet of the Confederacy: A Literary Life* (Columbia: University of South Carolina Press, 2007), chaps. 1 and 3.

58. Elaine Showalter, *The Civil Wars of Julia Ward Howe: A Biography* (New York: Simon & Schuster, 2016), 5–18.

59. Walt Whitman, *Specimen Days in America* (London: Walter Scott, 1887), 125.

Introduction: Harriet Tubman's (Pre)Millennium, 1850–1859, and the Fugitive Slave Act

1. Julia Rush Junkin to Jane Dickey, Oct. 3, 1831, quoted in Coulling, *Preston,* 23.

2. Coulling, *Preston,* 23.

3. Stephen E. Maizlish, *A Strife of Tongues: The Compromise of 1850 and the Ideological Foundations of the American Civil War* (Charlottesville: University of Virginia Press, 2018), 21–25; Andrew Delbanco, *The War before the War: Fugitive Slaves and the Struggle for America's Soul from the Revolution to the Civil War* (New York: Penguin, 2018), 248–61, 346–47.

4. R. J. M. Blackett, *The Captive's Quest for Freedom: Fugitive Slaves, the 1850 Fugitive Slave Law, and the Politics of Slavery* (New York: Cambridge University Press, 2018), xi.

5. Barry Joyce, *The First U.S. History Textbooks: Constructing and Disseminating the American Tale in the Nineteenth Century* (Lanham, MD: Lexington Books, 2015), 81–82; Nina Baym, "The Ann Sisters: Elizabeth Peabody's Millennial Historicism," *American Literary History* 3:1 (Spring 1991): 29–30.

6. Bruce Ronda, *Elizabeth Palmer Peabody: A Reformer on Her Own Terms* (Cambridge, MA: Harvard University Press, 1999), 237.

7. Elizabeth Peabody, *Chronological History of the United States, Arranged with Plates on Bem's Principle* (New York: Sheldon, Blakeman, 1856), 7.

8. Holt Merchant, *South Carolina Fire-Eater: The Life of Laurence Massillon Keitt, 1824–1864* (Columbia: University of South Carolina Press, 2014), 53.

9. Laurence M. Keitt, *Address Delivered before the Two Literary Societies of the Virginia Military Institute, July 4, 1856* (Richmond, VA: MacFarlane and Ferguson, 1856).

10. Merchant, *South Carolina Fire-Eater,* 45–46.

11. Jennifer R. Green, *Military Education and the Emerging Middle Class in the Old South* (New York: Cambridge University Press, 2008), 106.

12. Cecil D. Eby Jr., ed. *A Virginia Yankee in the Civil War: The Diaries of David Hunter Strother* (Chapel Hill: University of North Carolina Press, 1961), 255 (June 12, 1864).

13. Wayne Wei-siang Hsieh, *West Pointers and the Civil War: The Old Army in War and Peace* (Chapel Hill: University of North Carolina Press, 2009), 91–92.

14. George B. McClellan to John H. B. McClellan, Jan. 21, 1843, George B. McClellan Papers, LC.

15. Oliver Otis Howard, *Autobiography of Oliver Otis Howard: Major General, United States Army,* 2 vols. (New York: Baker & Taylor, 1907), 1:81.

16. Stephen E. Ambrose, *Upton and the Army* (Baton Rouge: Louisiana State University Press, 1964), 7.

17. Thomas Rowland, "Letters of a Virginia Cadet at West Point," *South Atlantic Quarterly* 15 (Jan. 1916): 3.

18. Morris Schaff, *The Spirit of Old West Point, 1858–1862* (Boston: Houghton Mifflin, 1907), 143–47.

19. Charles Russell Lowell Jr., "Oration at Commencement 1854," Records of the Harvard College Class of 1854, Harvard University Archives, Pusey Library, Harvard University, Cambridge, MA.

20. Robert Gould Shaw to Sarah Blake Sturgis Shaw, Mar. 19, 1858, Robert Gould Shaw Collection, Houghton Library, Harvard University, Cambridge, MA.

21. Edmund Ruffin Diary, Jan. 10, 1859, Edmund Ruffin Papers, LC.

22. Blight, *Douglass,* 299–301.

23. Mark Peterson, *The City-State of Boston: The Rise and Fall of an Atlantic Power, 1630–1865* (Princeton, NJ: Princeton University Press, 2019), 511.

24. Peterson, *City-State of Boston,* 515.

25. Louis A. DeCaro Jr., *"Fire from the Midst of You": A Religious Life of John Brown* (New York: New York University Press, 2002), 264.

26. Reynolds, *Brown,* 349–59.

27. John Brown, note, Charlestown, Dec. 2, 1859, quoted in Reynolds, *Brown,* 395.

28. Peterson, *City-State of Boston,* 620.

29. Edmund Ruffin, *Anticipations of the Future, to Serve as Lessons for the Present Time* (Richmond, VA: J. W. Randolph, 1860), 85, 89.

30. Ruffin, *Anticipations of the Future,* 2–3.

31. For English and North American Puritans as "the hotter sort of Protestants," see Michael P. Winship, *Hot Protestants: A History of Puritanism in England and America* (New Haven, CT: Yale University Press, 2018), 1.

32. Goldfield, *America Aflame,* 1–3.

33. Thomas B. Buell, *The Warrior Generals: Combat Leadership in the Civil War* (New York: Crown, 1997), xxxiii.

34. Beth Crabtree and James Patton, eds., *Journal of a Secesh Lady: The Diary of Catherine Ann Devereux Edmondston, 1860–1866* (Raleigh: North Carolina Department of Archives and History, 1979), 733.

35. Horn, *Polk,* 60–61.

36. Benjamin Franklin Cooling, *Forts Henry and Donelson: Key to the Confederate Heartland* (Knoxville: University of Tennessee Press, 1987), 41.

37. Albert Sidney Johnston to William P. Johnston, Jan. 19, 1851, Albert Sidney Johnston and William Preston Johnston Papers, Mrs. Mason Barret Collection, Howard-Tilton Memorial Library, Tulane University, New Orleans.

38. Charles P. Roland, *Albert Sidney Johnston: Soldier of Three Republics*, 2nd ed. (Lexington: University Press of Kentucky, 2001), 9.

39. Eby, *Virginia Yankee*, 22.

40. Peter S. Carmichael, *The Last Generation: Young Virginians in Peace, War, and Reunion* (Chapel Hill: University of North Carolina Press, 2005), 19.

41. William R. Aylett, "Temperance Speech," Aylett Family Papers, VMHC.

42. Carmichael, *Last Generation*, 105.

43. David Watson, "Notebook," Lecture Notebooks, 1827–1882, Student and Alumni Papers, UVA.

44. Watson, "Notebook," 105.

45. Watson, "Notebook," 25.

46. Robert Rives, "Crusades—Some of Their Causes and Effects" (master's thesis, University of Virginia, 1859), University of Virginia Master's Theses, Student and Alumni Papers, UVA.

47. The following is a state-by-state breakdown of the four Union regions. New England: Connecticut, Maine, Massachusetts, New Hampshire, Rhode Island, and Vermont; mid-Atlantic: New Jersey, Pennsylvania, and New York; Midwest: Illinois, Indiana, Iowa, Kansas, Ohio, Michigan, Minnesota, Nebraska, and Wisconsin; and Border South: Delaware, District of Columbia, Kentucky, Maryland, Missouri, and (West) Virginia.

48. William Gillette, *Jersey Blue: Civil War Politics in New Jersey, 1854–1865* (New Brunswick, NJ: Rutgers University Press, 1995), chaps. 4 and 9; William J. Jackson, *New Jerseyans in the Civil War: For Union and Liberty* (New Brunswick, NJ: Rutgers University Press, 2000), 29–30, 40, 82, 107–24.

49. Michael Barkun, *Crucible of the Millennium: The Burned-Over District of New York in the 1840s* (Syracuse, NY: Syracuse University Press, 1986); Whitney R. Cross, *The Burned-Over District: The Social and Intellectual History of Enthusiastic Religion in Western New York, 1800–1850* (Ithaca, NY: Cornell University Press, 1950); Milton C. Sernett, *North Star Country: Upstate New York and the Crusade for African American Freedom* (Syracuse, NY: Syracuse University Press, 2002).

50. The Deep South states seceded after the election of 1860 and prior to the bombardment of Fort Sumter, while the Upper South states seceded after President Lincoln called for volunteer soldiers to suppress the rebellion in the wake of Sumter's surrender. The Border South states never seceded but provided regiments to both Confederate and Union armies. Deep South: Alabama, Florida, Georgia, Louisiana, Mississippi, South Carolina, and Texas; Upper South: Arkansas, North Carolina, Tennessee, and Virginia; Border South: Kentucky, Maryland, and Missouri.

1. John Brown's Apocalypse, 1859–1860

1. James M. W. Yerrington, "The Fourth at Framingham," *Liberator*, July 8, 1859.

2. Albert J. Von Frank, *The Trials of Anthony Burns: Freedom and Slavery in Emerson's Boston* (Cambridge, MA: Harvard University Press, 1998), 68.

3. Ednah Dow Littlehale Cheney, "Moses," *Freedmen's Record*, Mar. 1865.

4. See DeCaro, *"Fire from the Midst of You,"* 261.

5. Debby Applegate, *The Most Famous Man in America: The Biography of Henry Ward Beecher* (New York: Doubleday, 2006), 281–82.

6. Ian Michael Spurgeon, *Man of Douglas, Man of Lincoln: The Political Odyssey of James Henry Lane* (Columbia: University Press of Missouri, 2008), 92.

7. Henry Ward Beecher, *Patriotic Addresses in America and England, 1855–1886,* ed. John R. Howard (Boston: Pilgrim, 1887), 214.

8. Richard J. Hinton, *John Brown and His Men* (New York: Arno, 1968), 433.

9. John Thompson Brown to Henry and John Brown, Petersburg, 1833, J. Thompson Brown Papers, VMHC.

10. Brown to Mary Brown, Harpers Ferry, Nov. 27, 1859, Brown Papers, VMHC. I am indebted to Jason Phillips for bringing my attention to this collection in his *Looming Civil War: How Nineteenth-Century Americans Imagined the Future* (New York: Oxford University Press, 2018), 1.

11. On Nat Turner's prophetic proclivities, see Patrick H. Breen, *The Land Shall Be Deluged in Blood: A New History of the Nat Turner Revolt* (New York: Oxford University Press, 2015), chap. 1.

12. Jackson, *Force and Freedom,* 25–26.

13. Michael F. Holt, *The Election of 1860: A Campaign Fraught with Consequences* (Lawrence: University Press of Kansas, 2017), chap. 3.

14. Walter Stahr, *Seward: Lincoln's Indispensable Man* (New York: Simon and Schuster, 2012), 124.

15. John Niven, *Salmon P. Chase: A Biography* (New York: Oxford University Press, 1995), chap. 5.

16. William E. Gienapp, *The Origins of the Republican Party, 1852–1856* (New York: Oxford University Press, 1987), 445.

17. David Herbert Donald, *Lincoln* (New York: Simon and Schuster, 1995), 33.

18. Donald, *Lincoln,* 152.

19. Donald, *Lincoln,* 81.

20. Jean H. Baker, *Mary Todd Lincoln: A Biography* (New York: W. W. Norton, 1987), 62–63, 131–32.

21. Holt, *Election of 1860,* chap. 5.

22. Donald, *Lincoln,* 255.

23. Holt, *Election of 1860,* chap. 7.

24. Wilson Jeremiah Moses, *Alexander Crummell: A Study of Civilization and Discontent* (New York: Oxford University Press, 1989), 92, 145.

25. Alexander Crummell, "Examination, Etc.," in *The Future of Africa: Being Addressses, Sermons, Etc., Etc., Delivered in the Republic of Liberia* (New York: Charles Scribner, 1862), 328.

26. Edward Jones to Henry Venn, Fourah Bay, Dec. 19, 1857, Edward Jones Papers, Original Papers–Missionaries, Reel 85, Church Missionary Society Archive, Cadbury Library, University of Birmingham.

27. Jones to Venn, Sierra Leone, Oct. 21, 1859, Edward Jones Papers, Reel 85.

28. James T. Campbell, *Middle Passages: African American Journeys to Africa, 1787–2005* (New York: Penguin, 2006), 58.

29. Mia Bay, *The White Image in the Black Mind: African-American Ideas about White People, 1830–1925* (New York: Oxford University Press, 2000), 65.

30. Campbell, *Middle Passages,* 74.

31. Campbell, *Middle Passages,* 91.

32. Campbell, *Middle Passages,* 92.

33. Campbell, *Middle Passages,* 92–94.

34. *Weekly Anglo-African,* Oct. 5, 1861.

35. Ernest R. Sandeen, *The Roots of Fundamentalism: British and America Millenarianism, 1800–1930* (Chicago: University of Chicago Press, 1970), 115.

36. Paul C. Gutjahr, *Charles Hodge: Guardian of American Orthodoxy* (New York: Oxford University Press, 2011), 205.

37. Charles Hodge, "Slavery," *BRPR* 8 (Apr. 1836): 292; Hodge, "Abolitionism," *BRPR* 17 (Oct. 1844): 580–81.

38. Hodge, "Emancipation: Art. VI.—*The Question of Negro Slavery and the New Constitution of Kentucky.* By Robert J. Breckenridge, D.D.," *BRPR* 21 (Oct. 1849): 581–66.

39. A Presbyterian in the Far South, *A System of Prospective Emancipation, Advocated in Kentucky, By Robert J. Breckenridge, D.D., and Urged and Supported in the Princeton Review, in Article VI.—October, 1849* (Charleston: Walker & James, 1850), 16, 22.

40. Ira Berlin, *Many Thousands Gone: The First Two Centuries of Slavery in North America* (Cambridge, MA: Belknap Press of Harvard University Press, 1998), 8.

41. Balmer and Winner, *Protestantism in America,* 56.

42. James Henley Thornwell quoted in *God's Almost Chosen Peoples: A Religious History of the American Civil War,* by George C. Rable (Chapel Hill: University of North Carolina Press, 2010), 13.

43. Robert Lewis Dabney to Israel P. Warren, Union Theological Seminary, Pr[ince]. Edward County, Va., Dec. 13, 1859, Dabney Family Papers, UVA.

44. Israel P. Warren to Dabney, American Tract Society, Boston, Dec. 26, 1859, Dabney Family Papers, UVA.

45. Rable, *God's Almost Chosen Peoples,* 14.

46. George Junkin to Francis McFarland, Lexington, Jan. 19, 1861, Francis McFarland Papers, WLU.

47. Robert Patterson to McFarland, Philadelphia, Jan. 30, 1861, McFarland Papers, WLU.

48. Thomas J. Jackson to Margaret Junkin, Lexington, Feb. 14, 1855, Margaret Junkin Preston Papers, UNC.

49. Margaret Junkin to Elinor Junkin, ca. 1853, Preston Papers, UNC.

50. Margaret Junkin, *Silverwood: A Book of Memories* (New York: Derby & Jackson, 1856).

51. *Knoxville Whig,* Oct. 13, 1860.

52. Robins, *Bishop of the Old South,* 117.

53. Robins, *Bishop of the Old South,* 122–24.

54. Horn, *Polk,* 144.

55. Horn, *Polk,* 149–50.

56. Horn, *Polk,* 151.

57. Leonidas Polk to James Buchanan, Dec. 26, 1860, Leonidas Polk Papers, UNC.

58. Horn, *Polk,* 107.

59. Samuel Wilberforce, *A History of the Protestant Episcopal Church in America* (London: James Burns, 1844), 422–25.

60. Robins, *Bishop of the Old South,* 125.

61. Bridges, *Lee's Maverick General,* 27; Daniel Harvey Hill, *A Consideration of the Sermon on the Mount* (Philadelphia: William S. and Alfred Martien, 1858), 152–53.

62. R. L. Stanton, *The Church and the Rebellion: A Consideration of the Rebellion against the Government of the United States; and the Agency of the Church, North and South, in Relation Thereto* (New York: Derby and Miller, 1864), 194.

63. See *Liberator,* Feb. 22, 1856.

64. *New York Herald,* June 19, 1892. See also Elizabeth Cady Stanton, "Anna Elizabeth Dickinson," in *Eminent Women of the Age; Being Narratives of the Lives and Deeds of the Most Prominent Women of the Present Generation,* by James Parton et al. (Hartford: S. M. Betts, 1869), 485–86.

65. Thomas Walter Reed, "History of the University of Georgia" (n.p., 1949), 404, Hargrett Rare Book and Manuscript Library, University of Georgia, Athens.

66. Stephen W. Sears, *George B. McClellan: The Young Napoleon* (New York: Ticknor and Fields, 1988), 49.

67. Sears, *McClellan,* 56, 63.

68. Thomas J. Rowland, *George B. McClellan and Civil War History: In the Shadow of Grant and Sherman* (Kent, OH: Kent State University Press, 1998), 27.

69. Washington, *Sojourner Truth's America,* 60.

70. Paul E. Johnson and Sean Wilentz, *The Kingdom of Matthias: A Story of Sex and Salvation in 19th-Century America* (New York: Oxford University Press, 1994), 3–5, 149.

71. Painter, *Truth,* 73.

72. Robert Williams to Richard H. Meade, Richmond, Nov. 26, 1860, Section 6, Meade Family Papers, VMHC.

2. Harriet Tubman's Millennium, 1861

1. Lydia Maria Child to John G. Whittier, Jan. 21, 1862, Lydia Maria Child Papers, LC.

2. Edward L. Pierce, ed., *Memoir and Letters of Charles Sumner,* 4 vols. (Boston: Roberts Brothers, 1877–93), 4:142–43.

3. Ellis Yarnall, *Wordsworth and the Coleridges: With Other Memories Literary and Political* (New York: Macmillan, 1899), 8.

4. John Hay Diary, Oct. 28, 1863, in *Letters of John Hay and Extracts from Diary,* comp. Clara S. Hay, 3 vols. (Washington, DC, 1908), 1:112. See also David Herbert Donald, "Devils Facing Zionwards," in *Grant, Lee, Lincoln, and the Radicals: Essays on Civil War Leadership,* ed. Grady McWhiney (Evanston, IL: Northwestern University Press, 1964), 72–91.

5. "Dear Brother," Aug. 10, 1861, Edward and Mary Ann Craig Papers, Illinois State Historical Library, Springfield, quoted in *While God Is Marching On: The Religious World of Civil War Soldiers,* by Steven E. Woodworth (Lawrence: University Press of Kansas, 2001), 97.

6. Lisa M. Brady, *War upon the Land: Military Strategy and the Transformation of Southern Landscapes during the American Civil War* (Athens: University of Georgia Press, 2012), 18.

7. Albert E. Cowdrey, *This Land, This South: An Environmental History,* rev. ed. (Lexington: University Press of Kentucky, 1996), 83. I am indebted to Lisa Brady for this reference.

8. Richard J. Carwardine, *Lincoln* (Harlow, UK: Pearson Longman, 2003), 129–30.

9. Hiram Berry to unknown, Mar. 23, 1862, in *Major-General Hiram G. Berry: His Career as a Contractor, Bank President, Politician, and Major-General of Volunteers in the Civil War, Together with His War Correspondence, Embracing the Period from Bull Run to Chancellorsville,* ed. Edward Kalloch Gould (Rockland, ME: Press of the Courier-Gazette, 1899), 104.

10. Benjamin F. Butler, *Autobiography and Personal Reminiscences of Major-General Benjamin F. Butler* (Boston: A. M. Thayer, 1892), 378.

11. Henry Ward Beecher, "Peace, Be Still," in *Fast Day Sermons; or, The Pulpit on the State of the Country* (New York: Rudd & Carleton, 1861), 289.

12. Wayne C. Eubank, "Benjamin Morgan Palmer's Thanksgiving Sermon, 1860," in *Antislavery and Disunion, 1858–1861: Studies in the Rhetoric of Compromise and Conflict,* ed. J. Jeffrey Auer (New York: Harper & Row, 1963), 291–95; Richard T. Hughes, "A Civic Theology for the South: The Case of Benjamin M. Palmer," *Journal of Church and State* 25:3 (1983): 447–67; Goldfield, *America Aflame,* 192; Mitchell Snay, *Gospel of Disunion: Religion and Separatism in the Antebellum South* (New York: Cambridge University Press, 1993), 177–79. For the full text of Palmer's sermon, see *Fast Day Sermons,* 57–80; or "Benjamin Morgan Palmer's 'Thanksgiving Sermon,'" Sermons and Other Religious Tracts, Causes of the Civil War, http://www.civilwarcauses.org/palmer.htm (accessed Nov. 11, 2015).

13. Goldfield, *America Aflame,* 192–93.

14. Palmer, "Slavery a Divine Trust," in *Fast Day Sermons,* 62 (emphasis in original).

15. Snay, *Gospel of Disunion,* 179.

16. Hinton Rowan Helper, *The Impending Crisis of the South: How to Meet It* (New York: Burdick Brothers, 1857), 373.

17. Merritt, *Masterless Men,* 158.

18. John E. Armstrong Reminiscence, n.d., *Civil War Times Illustrated* Collection, USAHEC.

19. George M. Fredrickson, *The Black Image in the White Mind: The Debate on Afro-American Character and Destiny, 1817–1914* (New York: Harper & Row, 1971), 61–64, 94.

20. "The Practical Workings of Abolition," *Southern Banner,* Dec. 13, 1860, 2.

21. Joseph T. Glatthaar, *General Lee's Army: From Victory to Collapse* (New York: Free Press, 2008), 30.

22. Glatthaar, *General Lee's Army,* 20.

23. Online 1860 U.S. Census table, http://www.civil-war.net/pages/1860_census.html (accessed Nov. 14, 2015; page discontinued).

24. Ronald G. Walters noted that by 1838 the American Anti-Slavery Society claimed a quarter of a million members. See *American Reformers, 1815–1860,* rev. ed. (New York: Hill and Wang, 1997), 81.

25. William Kauffman Scarborough, *Masters of the Big House: Elite Slaveholders of the Mid-Nineteenth-Century South* (Baton Rouge: Louisiana State University Press, 2003), 19.

26. Scarborough, *Masters of the Big House,* 251, 280.

27. Scarborough, *Masters of the Big House,* 317–18.

28. *Congressional Globe,* 35th Cong., 1st sess., 1857–58, 962.

29. J. Mills Thornton III, *Politics and Power in a Slave Society: Alabama, 1800–1860* (Baton Rouge: Louisiana State University Press, 1978), 296–97.

30. Leonard L. Richards, *The Slave Power: The Free North and Southern Domination, 1780–1860* (Baton Rouge: Louisiana State University Press, 2000), 9.

31. Goldfield, *America Aflame,* 191.

32. William Prentiss, *A Sermon Preached at St. Peter's Church, Charleston and Repeated on Sunday, and at Meeting of Legislature* (Charleston, SC: Evans and Cogswell, 1860), 3.

33. "Disfederation of the States," *Southern Literary Messenger* 32 (Feb. 1861): 119.

34. James Henley Thornwell, *The State of the Country: An Article Republished from the Southern Presbyterian Review* (Jackson, MS: E. Barksdale, 1861), 55.

35. Thornwell, "Our Danger and Our Duty," *De Bow's Review* 33 (May–Aug. 1862): 50–51.

36. George C. Rable, *The Confederate Republic: A Revolution against Politics* (Chapel Hill: University of North Carolina Press, 1994), 4.

37. Emory M. Thomas, *The Confederate Nation, 1861–1865* (New York: Harper & Row, 1979), 65.

38. Stephanie McCurry, *Confederate Reckoning: Power and Politics in the Civil War South* (Cambridge, MA: Harvard University Press, 2010), 82.

39. Anne Sarah Rubin, *A Shattered Nation: The Rise and Fall of the Confederacy, 1861–1868* (Chapel Hill: University of North Carolina Press, 2005), 17–18.

40. Leonidas Polk to Horatio Potter, Jan. 29, 1861, quoted in *General Leonidas Polk, C.S.A.: The Fighting Bishop,* by Joseph H. Parks (Baton Rouge: Louisiana State University Press, 1962), 158–59.

41. Sydney E. Ahlstrom, *A Religious History of the American People,* 2nd ed. (New Haven, CT: Yale University Press, 2004), 670.

42. *Harper's Weekly,* July 27, 1861; *London Herald,* Aug. [?], 1861.

43. *Southern Illustrated News,* Nov. 15, 1862.

44. Polk to Stephen Elliott, June 22, 1861, quoted in *Leonidas Polk: Bishop and General,* by William M. Polk, 2 vols. (New York: Longmans, Green, 1893), 1:325.

45. Horn, *Polk,* 163.

46. General Orders No. 1, Headquarters, Headquarters Dept. No. 2, Memphis, July 13, 1861, *OR,* 4:368–69.

47. Larry J. Daniel, *Conquered: Why the Army of Tennessee Failed* (Chapel Hill: University of North Carolina Press, 2019), 11.

48. Catherine Clinton, *Harriet Tubman: The Road to Freedom* (New York: Little, Brown, 2004), 148.

49. Clinton, *Tubman,* 148–49.

50. Mary Boykin Chesnut Journal, Apr. 27, 1861, South Caroliniana Library, University of South Carolina, Columbia (hereafter referred to as USC).

51. Chesnut Journal, Mar. 18, 1861, USC.

52. Elizabeth Muhlenfeld, *Mary Boykin Chesnut: A Biography* (Baton Rouge: Louisiana State University Press, 1981), 67.

53. C. Vann Woodward, ed., *Mary Chesnut's Civil War* (New Haven, CT: Yale University Press, 1981), 48 (Apr. 13, 1861).

54. Woodward, *Mary Chesnut's Civil War,* 245 (Nov. 27, 1861).

55. Woodward, *Mary Chesnut's Civil War*, 260 (Dec. 8, 1861).

56. Woodward, *Mary Chesnut's Civil War*, 260 (Dec. 8, 1861).

57. Muhlenfeld, *Chesnut*, 106.

58. Chesnut Journal, Aug. 19, 1861, USC.

59. Chesnut Journal, May 30, 1861, USC.

60. Chesnut Journal, Aug. 26, 1861, USC.

61. Muhlenfeld, *Chesnut*, 113, 115, 117.

62. Henry King Burgwyn Jr. to mother, Dec. 9, 1860, Burgwyn Family Papers, UNC.

63. "A Voice of a Pennsylvanian in the Heart of Virginia" to Andrew G. Curtin, Dec. 1860, quoted in Coulling, *Preston*, 109.

64. "Exodus of Dr. Junkin," *Presbyterian Standard*, May 17, 1861, quoted in *The Reverend George Junkin, D.D., L.L.D., A Historical Biography*, by D. X. Junkin (Philadelphia: J. B. Lippincott, 1871), 518–26; A. T. Barclay, "The Liberty Hall Volunteers from Lexington to Manassas," in Washington and Lee University, *Historical Papers, No. 6—1904* (Lynchburg, VA, 1904), 124.

65. John Newton Lyle, "Stonewall Jackson's Guard, the Washington College Company," Special Collections, WLU, 27; W. G. Bean, *The Liberty Hall Volunteers: Stonewall's College Boys* (Charlottesville: University Press of Virginia, 1964), 6.

66. William Couper, *One Hundred Years at V.M.I.*, 4 vols. (Richmond, VA: Garrett and Massie, 1939), 2:62–63.

67. Thomas J. Jackson to Laura Arnold, Dec. 29, 1860, Thomas J. Jackson Collection, Preston Library, Virginia Military Institute, Lexington.

68. Coulling, *Preston*, 112.

69. Coulling, *Preston*, 114.

70. Coulling, *Preston*, 116.

71. W. G. Bean, *Stonewall's Man: Sandie Pendleton* (Chapel Hill: University of North Carolina Press, 1959), 59n17.

72. Bean, *Stonewall's Man*, 43; William Nelson Pendleton to Anzolette E. Pendleton, Harpers Ferry, June 25, 1861, William Nelson Pendleton Papers, UNC.

73. William Woods Hassler, *Colonel John Pelham: Lee's Boy Artillerist* (Chapel Hill: University of North Carolina Press, 1960), 7.

74. J. Brent Morris, *Oberlin, Hotbed of Abolitionism: College, Community, and the Fight for Freedom and Equality in Antebellum America* (Chapel Hill: University of North Carolina Press, 2014), chap. 9.

75. Emory Upton to Howard, Oct. 1860, Oliver Otis Howard Papers, BC. On the Protestant ethic in the eighteenth and nineteenth centuries, see Max Weber, *The Protestant Ethic and the Spirit of Capitalism*, rev. ed., trans. and ed. Stephen Kalberg (New York: Routledge, 2012), chap. 5.

76. Schaff, *Spirit of Old West Point*, 145.

77. Ralph Kirshner, *The Class of 1861: Custer, Ames, and Their Classmates after West Point* (Carbondale: Southern Illinois University Press, 1999), 7.

78. Schaff, *Spirit of Old West Point*, 147.

79. Kirshner, *Class of 1861*, 3.

80. George A. Custer, "War Memoirs: From West Point to the Battlefield," *Galaxy*, Apr. 1876, 454.

81. *Charleston Mercury*, Apr. 11, 1861; *Charleston Daily Courier*, Apr. 11, 1861.

82. Samuel Wylie Crawford, *The Genesis of the Civil War: The Story of Sumter, 1860–1861* (New York: Charles L. Webster, 1887), 442; Abner Doubleday, *Reminiscences of Forts Sumter and Moultrie in 1860–'61* (New York: Harper & Brothers, 1876), 169–70.

83. William D. Pender to Fanny Pender, Mar. 26, 1861, in *One of Lee's Best Men: The Civil War Letters of General William Dorsey Pender,* ed. William W. Hassler (Chapel Hill: University of North Carolina Press, 1999), 12.

84. Pender to Pender, Sept. 19, 1861, in Hassler, *One of Lee's Best Men,* 64.

85. Karin E. Gedge, *Without Benefit of Clergy: Women and the Pastoral Relationship in Nineteenth-Century American Culture* (New York: Oxford University Press, 2003), 103–5, 175; Lori D. Ginzberg, *Women and the Work of Benevolence: Morality, Politics, and Class in the Nineteenth-Century United States* (New Haven, CT: Yale University Press, 1990), 11–13; Daniel S. Wright, *"The First of Causes to Our Sex": The Female Moral Reform Movement in the Antebellum Northeast, 1834–1848* (New York: Routledge, 2006), 30–32.

86. Pender to Pender, Sept. 22, 1861, in Hassler, *One of Lee's Best Men,* 66.

87. Pender to Pender, Oct. 7, 1861, in Hassler, *One of Lee's Best Men,* 76–77.

88. Pender to Pender, Dec. 9, 1861, in Hassler, *One of Lee's Best Men,* 108–9.

89. "The Northern and Southern Confederacies," *Nashville Union and American,* July 11, 1861.

90. George B. McClellan's Army of the Potomac (so named on July 26, 1861) was the main Union army in the eastern theater of the war, while the Army of Northern Virginia was the main eastern Confederate army by March 1862. It was led first by Joseph E. Johnston and from June 1, 1862, by his West Point classmate Robert E. Lee, who permanently established the army's famous name.

91. Dabney to Elizabeth Randolph Dabney, Dec. 28, 1860, in *The Life and Letters of Robert Lewis Dabney,* by Thomas Cary Johnson (Richmond, VA: Presbyterian Committee of Publication, 1903), 215.

92. Dabney to mother, Jan. 12, 1861, Dabney Family Papers, VMHC.

93. Dabney to Moses Drury Hoge, Jan. 4, 1861, Dabney Family Papers, VMHC.

94. Robert Dabney, "Address, to the Clergy and Laity," *Central Presbyterian,* Jan. 26, 1861.

95. Dabney to Charles Hodge, Jan. 23, 1861, Box 2, Robert Lewis Dabney Papers, Union Theological Seminary, Richmond, VA.

96. Boyd B. Stutler, *West Virginia in the Civil War* (Charleston, WV: Education Foundation, 1966), vi. See also C. Stuart McGehee, "The Tarnished Thirty-fifth Star," in *Virginia at War, 1861,* ed. William C. Davis and James I. Robertson Jr. (Lexington: University Press of Kentucky, 2005), 149–58.

97. Dabney to Elizabeth Catherine Dabney, Bull's Run, Prince William County, July 19, 1861, Dabney Family Papers, VMHC.

98. Dabney to Dabney, Manassas Junction, July 22, 1861, VMHC.

99. Coulling, *Preston,* 118.

100. John T. L. Preston Diary, Sept. 20, 1861, LC.

101. Elizabeth Preston Allan, *The Life and Letters of Margaret Junkin Preston* (Boston: Houghton Mifflin, 1903), 126.

102. Margaret Preston, "All's Well" (original poem), in John T. L. Preston Diary, Aug. 20, 1861, LC.

103. Coulling, *Preston,* 139.

104. *Fayetteville Observer,* Aug. 22, 1861.

105. William Taylor to Enon Primitive Baptist Church, Aug. 18, 1867, quoted in *Middle Tennessee Society Transformed, 1860–1870: War and Peace in the Upper South,* by Stephen V. Ash (Baton Rouge: Louisiana State University Press, 1988), 76.

106. Electa Dawes to Henry L. Dawes, July 25, 1861, Henry L. Dawes Papers, LC.

107. OR, 2:314–15; William C. Davis, *Battle at Bull Run: A History of the First Major Campaign of the Civil War* (New York: Doubleday, 1977), 76.

108. New York and Pennsylvania were the most populous states in 1860. With a combined population of nearly 6.8 million, a fifth of all Americans lived in these mid-Atlantic states, and almost a third of the military age population that the Union could draw from.

109. Scarborough, *Masters of the Big House,* 317, 324.

110. Herman Hattaway, *General Stephen D. Lee* (Jackson: University Press of Mississippi, 1976), chaps. 2 and 3; Clyde N. Wilson, *Carolina Cavalier: The Life and Mind of James Johnston Pettigrew* (Athens: University of Georgia Press, 1990), 151.

111. Sam Davis Elliott, ed., *Doctor Quintard, Chaplain C.S.A. and Second Bishop of Tennessee: The Memoir and Civil War Diary of Charles Todd Quintard* (Baton Rouge: Louisiana State University Press, 2003), 18n12. Porter returned in Charleston in 1863 as rector of the Church of the Holy Communion. In 1866 he founded the first African American school in Charleston and a year later a school for the sons of impoverished Confederate veterans.

112. Daniel Harvey Hill to Isabella Hill, July 5, 1861, quoted in Bridges, *Lee's Maverick General,* 25.

113. J. Michael Cobb, Edward Hicks, and Wythe Holt, *Battle of Big Bethel: Crucial Clash in Early Civil War Virginia* (El Dorado Hills, CA: Savas Beatie, 2013), 176.

114. Russell K. Brown, *To the Manner Born: The Life of General William H. T. Walker* (Athens: University of Georgia Press, 1994), 82–83.

115. *Augusta Chronicle and Sentinel,* Jan. 11, 1861.

116. Brown, *To the Manner Born,* 89, 91, 97.

117. Brown, *To the Manner Born,* 103.

118. William H. T. Walker to Henry C. Wayne, Feb. 26, 1862, Civil War Collection, HL.

119. James M. McPherson, *Battle Cry of Freedom: The Civil War Era* (New York: Oxford University Press, 1988), 360.

120. Sears, *McClellan,* 110.

121. J. H., *A Prophecy of the Southern Confederacy* (Jefferson County, VA, ca. Dec. 1861), David Lawrence Hopkins Papers, WLU.

122. Nathaniel Cheairs Hughes Jr., *General William J. Hardee: Old Reliable* (Baton Rouge: Louisiana State University Press, 1965), 77; Clement Anselm Evans, ed., *Confederate Military History,* 12 vols. (Atlanta: Confederate Publishing, 1899), 10:305.

123. John Gordon Law, "Diary of J. G. Law," *Southern Historical Society Papers* 12 (1884): 507.

124. Lowell H. Harrison, ed., "A Confederate View of Southern Kentucky, 1861," *Register of the Kentucky Historical Society* 70 (July 1972): 175.

125. Sam Davis Elliott, *Soldier of Tennessee: General Alexander P. Stewart and the Civil War in the West* (Baton Rouge: Louisiana State University Press, 1999), 168–69.

126. Alexander P. Stewart to Catherine Jones, Sept. 26, 1838, in *General A. P. Stewart, His Life and Letters,* by Marshall Wingfield (Memphis: West Tennessee Historical Society, 1954), 26.

127. Elliott, *Soldier of Tennessee,* 15.

128. Allen C. Guelzo, *Lincoln's Emancipation Proclamation: The End of Slavery in America* (New York: Simon & Schuster, 2004), 50–54.

129. Jessie Benton Frémont to Dorothea Lynde Dix, ca. 1862, Folder 4, Box 1, Frémont Family Papers, Bancroft Library, University of California, Berkeley.

130. Guelzo, *Lincoln's Emancipation Proclamation,* 54.

131. Guelzo, *Lincoln's Emancipation Proclamation,* 55.

132. Frémont to Dix, ca. 1862, Folder 4, Box 1, Frémont Family Papers, University of California, Berkeley.

133. Sarah M. Grimke to Sarah Wattles, Dec. 10, 1861, Weld-Grimké Family Papers, UM.

134. D. Laurence Rogers, *Apostles of Equality: The Birneys, the Republicans, and the Civil War* (East Lansing: Michigan State University Press, 2011), chap. 16.

135. Margaret Washington Creel, *A Peculiar People: Slave Religion and Community-Culture among the Gullahs* (New York: New York University Press, 1988), chap. 1.

136. Willie Lee Rose, *Rehearsal for Reconstruction: The Port Royal Experiment* (Indianapolis: Bobbs-Merrill, 1964), 11–15.

137. Rose, *Rehearsal for Reconstruction,* 16.

138. Niven, *Chase,* chap. 16.

139. William Sprague to Salmon P. Chase, Dec. 1, 1861, Item 10, Port Royal Correspondence, Records of Civil War Special Agencies of the Treasury Department, Record Group 366, NA; William H. Reynolds to Chase, Dec. 23, 1861, Item 24, ibid.; Rose, *Rehearsal for Reconstruction,* 19.

140. Clinton, *Tubman,* 152.

141. C. R. Vaughan to George Whipple, Jan. 25, 1862, AMA.

142. Gulielma Breed to Emily Howland, Feb. 20, 1861, Emily Howland Papers, CU.

143. Salmon P. Chase to William S. Rosecrans, Oct. 25, 1862, William Starke Rosecrans Papers, Charles E. Young Research Library, University of California, Los Angeles.

144. Edward A. Miller, *Lincoln's Abolitionist General: The Biography of David Hunter* (Columbia: University of South Carolina Press, 1997), chaps. 3 and 4.

145. Miller, *Lincoln's Abolitionist General,* 104–5.

146. Christopher Memminger speech, *Savannah Morning News,* Feb. 11, 1861.

147. Robert E. Bonner, *Colors and Blood: Flag Passions of the Confederate South* (Princeton, NJ: Princeton University Press, 2002), 100. See also St. George Tucker, "The Southern Cross," *Southern Literary Messenger* 32 (Jan. 1861): 75–76.

148. W. H. Seat, *The Confederate States of America in Prophecy* (Nashville: Southern Methodist Publishing House, 1861).

149. Paul Quigley, *Shifting Grounds: Nationalism and the American South, 1848–1865* (New York: Oxford University Press, 2012), 207.

150. Seat, *Confederate States of America in Prophecy.*

151. Quigley, *Shifting Grounds,* 207.

3. Robert L. Dabney's Apocalypse, 1862

1. J. L. Burrows, *Shiloh: A Sermon* (N.p., ca. 1862), 1.

2. Burrows, *Shiloh*, 6.

3. Burrows, *Shiloh*, 8.

4. Charles A. Heckman to Charles S. Olden, Mar. 15, 1862, in *The History of the Ninth New Jersey Veteran Volunteers: A Record of Its Service from September 13, 1861, to July 12, 1865*, by J. Madison Drake (Elizabeth, NJ: Journal Printing House, 1889), 65–66.

5. Woodward, *Mary Chesnut's Civil War*, 301 (Mar. 10, 1862).

6. William H. Dunham to Henrietta Dunham, Meadow Bluffs, VA, June 3, 1862, William H. Dunham Papers, Box 27, Civil War Miscellaneous Collection, USAHEC. Dunham resigned his commission later that month.

7. *OR*, 11(2):24–37. In addition, McClellan commanded the 1st US Sharpshooter Regiment (composed of four New York and three Michigan companies, and one company each from New Hampshire, Vermont, and Wisconsin) and nine regular regiments (or parts thereof).

8. John H. Matsui, "Political Violence, Violent Politics: Protestant Democrats and Republicans at War in Virginia, 1862," *History* 101:346 (July 2016): 379–95.

9. *OR*, 11(2):483–89.

10. John G. Barrett, *The Civil War in North Carolina* (Chapel Hill: University of North Carolina Press, 1963), chap. 5; Archie K. Davis, *Boy Colonel of the Confederacy: The Life and Times of Henry King Burgwyn, Jr.* (Chapel Hill: University of North Carolina Press, 1985), 176.

11. William Dorsey Pender to Fanny Pender, Camp Barton, Mar. 30, 1862, in Hassler, *One of Lee's Best Men*, 129–30.

12. James G. Leyburn, *The Scotch-Irish: A Social History* (Chapel Hill: University of North Carolina Press, 1962), 200.

13. Stephen L. Longenecker, *Shenandoah Religion: Outsiders and the Mainstream, 1716–1865* (Waco, TX: Baylor University Press, 2002), 25.

14. Charles F. Irons, *The Origins of Proslavery Christianity White and Black Evangelicals in Colonial and Antebellum Virginia* (Chapel Hill: University of North Carolina Press, 2008), 10.

15. Julia Chase Diary, July 12, 1861, in *Winchester Divided: The Civil War Diaries of Julia Chase and Laura Lee*, ed. Michael G. Mahon (Mechanicsburg, PA: Stackpole Books, 2002), 3.

16. Benjamin Brooke Journal, Feb. 3, 1862, HRL.

17. Cecil D. Eby Jr., *"Porte Crayon": The Life of David Hunter Strother* (Chapel Hill: University of North Carolina Press, 1960), 4, 59–60.

18. Sam Coyner quoted in Laura V. Hale, *Four Valiant Years in the Lower Shenandoah Valley, 1861–1865* (Strasburg, VA: Shenandoah, 1968), 120–21.

19. Brooke Journal, Mar. 15, 1862, HRL.

20. Laura Lee Diary, "A History of Our Captivity," Apr. 14, 1862, Earl Gregg Swem Library, College of William and Mary, Williamsburg.

21. John Peyton Clark Diary, Apr. 13 1862, HRL.

22. Brooke Journal, Mar. 15, 1862, HRL.

23. Clark Diary, May 19, 1862, HRL.

24. John R. McKivigan, "The Sectional Division of the Methodist and Baptist Denominations as Measures of Northern Antislavery Sentiment," in *Religion and the Antebellum De-*

bate over Slavery, ed. John R. McKivigan and Mitchell Snay (Athens: University of Georgia Press, 1998), 346; McKivigan, *The War against Proslavery Religion: Abolitionism and the Northern Churches, 1830–1865* (Ithaca, NY: Cornell University Press, 1984), 87.

25. Clark Diary, May 11–12, 1862, HRL.

26. John Mead Gould, *History of the First-Tenth-Twenty-Ninth Maine Regiment: In Service of the United States From May 3, 1861, to June 21, 1866* (Portland, ME: Stephen Berry, 1871), 108.

27. Peter Cozzens, *Shenandoah 1862: Stonewall Jackson's Valley Campaign* (Chapel Hill: University of North Carolina Press, 2008), 368–69.

28. Cozzens, *Shenandoah 1862*, 508.

29. Nathaniel P. Banks to Mary Theodosia Parker Banks, May 28, 1862, Box 5, Nathaniel Prentiss Banks Papers, LC.

30. Nathaniel P. Banks Diary, July 9, 1862, Box 1, Banks Papers, LC.

31. Banks to Banks, Little Washington, July 29, 1862, Box 5, Banks Papers, LC.

32. Banks to Banks, Winchester, June 6, 1862, Box 5, Banks Papers, LC.

33. *Daily Whig*, Feb. 26, 1862.

34. J. B. Jones, *A Rebel War Clerk's Diary at the Confederate States Capital*, 2 vols. (Philadelphia: J. B. Lippincott, 1866), 1:135.

35. Frances Blake Brockenbrough, *A Mother's Parting Words to Her Soldier Boy* (Petersburg, VA: Soldiers' Tract Society, 1862), 4.

36. See *Religious Herald*, Oct. 23, 1862.

37. Melvin Dwinell to *Rome Courier*, Aug. 14, 1862, *Rome Courier*, Aug. 22, 1862.

38. Hill to Isabella Hill, Apr. 24, 1862, quoted in Bridges, *Lee's Maverick General*, 6.

39. Hill to Hill, Apr. 24, 1862, quoted in Bridges, *Lee's Maverick General*, 78–79; John B. Gordon, *Reminiscences of the Civil War* (New York: Charles Scribner's Sons, 1903), 67–68.

40. Johnson, *Life and Letters of Robert Lewis Dabney*, 263.

41. Johnson, *Life and Letters of Robert Lewis Dabney*, 264.

42. Dabney to Margaret Morrison Dabney, "Near Mt. Meridian, Augusta," June 12, 1862, in Johnson, *Life and Letters of Robert Lewis Dabney*, 266.

43. Samuel B. Morrison to Dabney, Mar. 20, 1866, in Johnson, *Life and Letters of Robert Lewis Dabney*, 272.

44. Donald E. Everett, ed., *Chaplain Davis and Hood's Texas Brigade: Being an Expanded Edition of the Rev. Nicholas A. Davis's* The Campaign from Texas to Maryland, with the Battle of Fredericksburg (Baton Rouge: Louisiana State University Press, 1999), 100.

45. Thomas W. Hyde, *Following the Greek Cross; or, Memories of the Sixth Army Corps* (Boston: Houghton Mifflin, 1895), 49.

46. George B. McClellan to Mary Ellen McClellan, July 17, 1862, in *The Civil War Papers of George B. McClellan: Selected Correspondence, 1860–1865*, ed. Stephen W. Sears (New York: Ticknor & Fields, 1989), 363.

47. McClellan to McClellan, July 17, 1862, in Sears, *Civil War Papers of George B. McClellan*, 362.

48. W. T. Leacock to Benjamin F. Butler, Sept. 26, 1862, Benjamin F. Butler Papers, LC.

49. *Knoxville Whig*, Jan. 12, 1861.

50. E. Merton Coulter, *William G. Brownlow: Fighting Parson of the Southern Highlands* (Knoxville: University of Tennessee Press, 1999), 110.

51. William G. Brownlow, *Sketches of the Rise, Progress, and Decline of Secession; with a Narrative of Personal Adventures among the Rebels* (Philadelphia: George W. Childs, 1862), 440.

52. Brownlow, *Speech against the Great Rebellion* (Washington, DC: Scammell and Bros., 1862), in *Southern Unionist Pamphlets and the Civil War*, ed. Jon L. Wakelyn (Columbia: University of Missouri Press, 1999), 114.

53. Goldfield, *America Aflame*, 230–31.

54. Goldfield, *America Aflame*, 231, 233.

55. All but nine of Grant's regiments at Shiloh were of midwestern origin, the rest coming from the Border South (two from Kentucky and the remainder from Missouri). In contrast, eleven of Buell's thirty-five regiments were from Border South (ten from Kentucky) or mid-Atlantic states (one from Pennsylvania).

56. *OR*, 10(2):185–88. Of the 160 volunteer regiments, 28 were from Border South states (Kentucky or Missouri) and 1 was from the mid-Atlantic region (77th Pennsylvania).

57. *OR*, 52(1):26–29. Thirty-nine regiments were from the Upper South (all from Arkansas or Tennessee), twenty-five regiments were from the Deep South, and six were from the Border South (Kentucky or Missouri).

58. *OR*, 10(1):787. Forty-two regiments were from the Upper South (though none from North Carolina or Virginia), forty-three regiments from the Deep South, and four regiments from the Border South state of Missouri.

59. Law, "Diary," 23.

60. Law, "Diary," 23.

61. James Garfield to Lucretia Garfield, Tuscumbia, June 14, 1862, in *Crete and James: Personal Letters of Lucretia and James Garfield*, ed. John Shaw (East Lansing: Michigan State University Press, 1994), 142.

62. Herman Hattaway and Archer Jones, *How the North Won: A Military History of the Civil War* (Urbana: University of Illinois Press, 1983), 214–17.

63. See John H. Matsui, *The First Republican Army: The Army of Virginia and the Radicalization of the Civil War* (Charlottesville: University of Virginia Press, 2016).

64. *OR*, 12(3):581–88.

65. It is important to note that, by not counting these thirteen mid-Atlantic regiments, the Army of Virginia looks significantly more demographically representative of the Republican (and Unionist) population of the United States in 1860 than the Army of the Potomac.

66. Robert K. Krick, *Stonewall Jackson at Cedar Mountain* (Chapel Hill: University of North Carolina Press, 1990), 362–64. Thirty-two regiments were from the Upper South states of North Carolina and Virginia and thirty-one from the Deep South.

67. Robert Gould Shaw to Sarah Blake Sturgis Shaw, Apr. 19, 1862, in *Blue-Eyed Child of Fortune: The Civil War Letters of Colonel Robert Gould Shaw*, ed. Russell Duncan (Athens: University of Georgia Press, 1992), 195.

68. Henry B. Clare to Zachariah Chandler, Aug. 14, 1862, Zachariah Chandler Papers, LC.

69. Shaw to Francis Shaw, Aug. 3, 1862, in Duncan, *Blue-Eyed Child*, 225.

70. Banks to Banks, Culpeper, Aug. 16, 1862, Box 5, Banks Papers, LC. Banks cherished Lincoln's praise: he "never makes any trouble and whether he has a large force or a small force—he knows what his duty is, *and he does it*."

71. Anonymous, "Army of Virginia (Probably [Christopher C.] Augur's Division)," to Kind Jennie, Sulphur Springs, Aug. 18, 1862, Michael Winey Collection, USAHEC.

72. Robert Taggart Diary, Aug. 26, 1862, Robert Taggart Papers, Pennsylvania State Archives, Harrisburg.

73. Rufus Barringer to Mary Anna Jackson, n.d., in *Life and Letters of General Thomas J. Jackson,* by Mary Anna Jackson (New York: Harper & Brothers, 1892), 310.

74. Jackson, *Life and Letters of General Thomas J. Jackson,* 312.

75. Jackson, *Life and Letters of General Thomas J. Jackson,* 314.

76. Jackson, *Life and Letters of General Thomas J. Jackson,* 315.

77. William D. Wilkins,. "My Libby Prison Diary: Aug 12 to Sept 26th 1862," Aug. 12, 1862, William D. Wilkins Papers, LC.

78. Wilkins, "My Libby Prison Diary," Aug. 24, 1862, Wilkins Papers, LC.

79. Wilkins, "My Libby Prison Diary," Aug. 24, 1862, Wilkins Papers, LC.

80. Wilkins, "My Libby Prison Diary," Aug. 31, 1862, Wilkins Papers, LC.

81. George Hyer Brayton Diary, Aug. 17, 1862, Wisconsin Historical Society, Madison.

82. Donald C. Pfanz, *Richard S. Ewell: A Soldier's Life* (Chapel Hill: University of North Carolina Press, 1998), 266; Benjamin S. Ewell, "Jackson and Ewell," *Southern Historical Society Papers* 20 (1892): 29; Peyton H. Hoge, *Moses Drury Hoge: Life and Letters* (Richmond, VA: Presbyterian Committee of Publication, 1899), 167.

83. J. Ross Browne, *Adventures in the Apache Country: A Tour Through Arizona and Sonora, with Notes on the Silver Regions of Nevada* (New York: Harper & Brothers, 1869), 156.

84. Pfanz, *Ewell*, 33.

85. Richard S. Ewell to Rebecca Lowndes Ewell, Nov. 13, 1841, Mar. 2, 1844, Richard Stoddart Ewell Papers, LC; Ewell to Benjamin Stoddert Ewell, Feb. 18, 1844, ibid.

86. Jedediah Hotchkiss to wife, May 31, 1863, Jedediah Hotchkiss Papers, LC; Susan P. Lee, ed., *Memoirs of William Nelson Pendleton, D.D.* (Philadelphia: Lippincott, 1893), 293–94; Pfanz, *Ewell,* 279.

87. John Sumner Wood, *The Virginia Bishop: A Yankee Hero of the Confederacy* (Richmond, VA: Garrett & Massie, 1961), 48.

88. "Journals of Lieut-Col. Stephen Kemble," in *Collections of the New-York Historical Society: For the Year 1883,* vol. 16 (New York, 1883), 91, 96 (Oct. 3, 1776).

89. Robert H. Milroy to Mary Milroy, [Sept.?] 1862, in *Papers of General Robert Huston Milroy,* comp. Margaret B. Paulus, 4 vols. (N.p., 1965), 1:122.

90. Charles Russell speech, Aug. 30, 1862, *Southern Historical Society Papers* 44 (1925): 281.

91. "SDL" Scrapbook III, Jan. 1908, Stephen D. Lee Museum, Columbus, MS, quoted in Hattaway, *Stephen D. Lee,* 162.

92. Benjamin F. Ashenfelter to mother, Camp near New Market, Sept. 12, 1862, Benjamin F. Ashenfelter Papers, Box 1, Harrisburg Civil War Roundtable Collection, USAHEC.

93. Ashenfelter to Father Churchman, Camp near Sharpsburg, Sept. 16, 1862, Ashenfelter Papers, Box 1, Harrisburg Civil War Roundtable Collection, USAHEC.

94. F. B. Carpenter, *Six Months at the White House with Abraham Lincoln* (New York: Hurd and Houghton, 1866), 22.

95. Richard Carwardine, "'A Party Man Who Did Not Believe in Any Man Who Was Not': Abraham Lincoln, the Republican Party, and the Union," in *In the Cause of Liberty: How the*

Civil War Redefined American Ideals, ed. William J. Cooper Jr. and John M. McCardell Jr. (Baton Rouge: Louisiana State University Press, 2009), 60.

96. Hans L. Trefousse, *Thaddeus Stevens: Nineteenth-Century Egalitarian* (Chapel Hill: University of North Carolina Press, 1997), 8, 50.

97. Thaddeus Stevens to Simon Stevens, Lancaster, Sept. 5, 1862, Box 1, Thaddeus Stevens Papers, LC.

98. James J. Gillette to mother, Tenlytown, Sept. 8, 1862, Box 1, James Jenkins Gillette Papers, LC.

99. Henry C. Hall to sister, Fredericksburg, Aug. 10, 1862, Henry C. Hall Papers, DU.

100. James E. Murdock, "Preston in the Rebellion: Company A Seventh W. Va. Infantry," *Preston County Journal*, Sept. 20, 1883.

101. James S. Wadsworth speech, Cooper Union, Oct. 30, 1862, in *James S. Wadsworth of Geneseo: Brevet Major-General, U.S.V.*, by Henry Greenleaf Pearson (New York: Charles Scribner's Sons, 1913), 160.

102. James S. Wadsworth, "Speech of General Wadsworth at Washington, Friday Evening, September 26, 1862," Genesee Valley Collection, Milne Library, State University of New York–Geneseo.

103. Francis R. Walsh, "The *Boston Pilot* Reports the Civil War," *Historical Journal of Massachusetts* 9 (June 1981): 5.

104. *Boston Pilot,* Nov. 1, 1862.

105. Uriah Parmelee to mother, Rockville, Sept. 8, 1862, Samuel Spencer Parmelee and Uriah N. Parmelee Papers, DU.

106. Parmelee to mother, Sept. 8, 1862, Parmelee and Parmelee Papers, DU.

107. John W. Geary to Mary H. Geary, Hagerstown, Sept. 25, 1862, in *A Politician Goes to War: The Civil War Letters of John White Geary*, ed. William A. Blair (University Park: Pennsylvania State University Press, 1995), 56.

108. George T. Chapin to Ella Chapin, Maryland Heights, Oct. 14, 1862, Chapin Family Papers, Indiana Historical Society, Indianapolis.

109. Shaw to Sarah Shaw, Sept. 25, 1862, in Duncan, *Blue-Eyed Child*, 245.

110. Shaw to Shaw, Oct. 5, 1862, in Duncan, *Blue-Eyed Child*, 252.

111. Jay Sexton, *A Nation Forged by Crisis: A New American History* (New York: Basic Books, 2018), 107.

112. Viscount Palmerston to Lord John Russell, Sept. 23, 1862, quoted in *Blue and Gray Diplomacy: A History of Union and Confederate Foreign Relations*, by Howard Jones (Chapel Hill: University of North Carolina Press, 2010), 218.

113. William Taylor, *Cause and Probable Results of the Civil War in America: Facts for the People of Great Britain* (London: Warren Hall, 1862), 5.

114. Taylor, *Cause and Probable Results*, 6.

115. Taylor, *Cause and Probable Results*, 10–11.

116. Taylor, *Cause and Probable Results*, 17.

117. Taylor, *Cause and Probable Results*, 19.

118. Taylor, *Cause and Probable Results*, 22.

119. Taylor, *Cause and Probable Results*, 24.

120. Horn, *Polk*, 270–71.

121. *Pastoral Letter of the Bishops of the Protestant Episcopal Church in the United States of America to the Clergy and Laity of the Same, Friday, October 17, 1862* (New York: Baker & Godwin, 1862).

122. Joseph S. Moore, *Founding Sins: How a Group of Antislavery Radicals Fought to Put Christ into the Constitution* (New York: Oxford University Press, 2016), 120.

123. "Interview with the President," *Reformed Presbyterian and Covenanter* 1:1 (Jan. 1863): 16–18; and 1:2 (Feb. 1863): 48–62; Moore, *Founding Sins*, 120–21.

124. William Henry Walling to sisters, Oct. 25, 1862, William Henry Walling Papers, Box 109, Civil War Miscellaneous Collection, USAHEC.

125. Gerald J. Prokopowicz, *All for the Regiment: The Army of the Ohio, 1861–1862* (Chapel Hill: University of North Carolina Press, 2001), 123.

126. Mead Holmes Jr., *A Soldier of the Cumberland* (Boston: American Tract Society, 1864), 126–27.

127. T. Harry Williams, *Lincoln and His Generals* (New York: Alfred A. Knopf, 1952), 48.

128. *OR*, 16:351; Aide-de-camp to Alexander McCook, June 21, 1862, ibid., ser. 2, 16:44.

129. Daniel Chandler, "5th Indiana Battery," Stones River National Battlefield, Murfreesboro, TN, 27, quoted in Prokopowicz, *All for the Regiment*, 187.

130. John Beatty, *The Citizen-Soldier; or, Memoirs of a Volunteer* (Cincinnati: Wilstach, Baldwin, 1879), 189.

131. Elias Brady to wife, Nov. 24, 1862, Elias Brady Papers, UNC.

132. Narcissa R. Hall to Andrew Johnson, June 27, 1862, in *The Papers of Andrew Johnson*, ed. LeRoy P. Graf and Ralph W. Haskins, 16 vols. (Knoxville: University of Tennessee Press, 1967–2000), 5:509–10.

133. John W. Summerhayes to *Nantucket Weekly Mirror*, Jan. 3, 1863, quoted in *Harvard's Civil War: A History of the Twentieth Massachusetts Volunteer Infantry*, by Richard F. Miller (Hanover, NH: University Press of New England, 2005), 197.

134. James Lee McDonough, *Stones River: Bloody Winter in Tennessee* (Knoxville: University of Tennessee Press, 1980), 115–16.

135. Robert Taylor Scott to Fanny Scott, Dec. 31, 1862, Box 5, Keith Family Papers, VMHC.

136. Carmichael, *Last Generation*, 184.

137. George E. Stephens to "Mr. Editor," Dec. 31, 1862, in *A Voice of Thunder: The Civil War Letters of George E. Stephens*, ed. Donald Yacovone (Urbana: University of Illinois Press, 1997), 216–20.

4. Sojourner Truth's Millennium, 1863

1. *Prophetic Times* 1 (1863), quoted in Sandeen, *Roots of Fundamentalism*, 94.

2. Sandeen, *Roots of Fundamentalism*, 94–95, 81.

3. Charles Hodge, "The Fulfillment of Prophecy," *BRPR* 23 (Jan. 1861).

4. *Prophetic Times* 1 (1863): 13.

5. Sandeen, *Roots of Fundamentalism*, 31; Donald Harman Akenson, *Exporting the Rapture: John Nelson Darby and the Victorian Conquest of North American Evangelicalism* (New York: Oxford University Press, 2018), 330.

6. John Nelson Darby, *The Letters of John Nelson Darby*, 3 vols., 2nd ed. (London, n.d.), 1:351.

7. Darby, *Letters*, 1:354.

8. *Prophetic Times* 1:22.

9. Ira Stoddard to Drusilla Stoddard, Pella, Jan. 9, 1863, Box 3, Stoddard Family Papers, RU.

10. Ira Joy Stoddard to Charlotte Joy Stoddard, ca. 1846, Box 1, Stoddard Family Papers, RU.

11. See Nathan Brown to Stoddard, Dayton, Jan. 17, 1857, Box 3, Stoddard Family Papers, RU.

12. William Dorsey Pender to Fanny Pender, Camp Gregg, Apr. 26, 1863, in Hassler, *One of Lee's Best Men*, 230.

13. Basil Manly Diary, Jan. 18, 1863, 4:56, Manly Family Papers, William Stanley Hoole Special Collections Library, University of Alabama, Tuscaloosa, quoted in *Chaplain to the Confederacy: Basil Manly and Baptist Life in the Old South*, by A. James Fuller (Baton Rouge: Louisiana State University Press, 2000), 302.

14. John F. Marszalek, ed., *The Diary of Miss Emma Holmes* (Baton Rouge: Louisiana State University Press, 1979), 231–32 (Feb. 14, 1863).

15. Henry J. Johnson to Clara Johnson, North Mountain, Jan. 14, 1863, James Schoff Civil War Collection, UM.

16. Johnson to Johnson, Clouds Mills, near Alexandria, June 30, 1862, Schoff Civil War Collection, UM.

17. Johnson to Johnson, Clouds Mills, near Culpeper, Aug. 6, 1862, Schoff Civil War Collection, UM.

18. Johnson to Johnson, Jan. 14, 1863, Schoff Civil War Collection, UM.

19. Nancy Niblack Baxter, *Gallant Fourteenth: The Story of an Indiana Civil War Regiment*, 2nd ed. (Indianapolis: Guild Press of Indiana, 1991), 126.

20. Gary W. Gallagher, *The Union War* (Cambridge: Harvard University Press, 2011), 34.

21. Stephen W. Sears, ed., *On Campaign with the Army of the Potomac: The Civil War Journal of Theodore Ayrault Dodge* (New York: Cooper Square, 2001), 138 (Jan. 2, 1863).

22. Sears, *On Campaign*, 137 (Jan. 1, 1863).

23. John J. Hight, Diary, Apr. 15, 1863, in *History of the Fifty-Eighth Regiment of Indiana Volunteer Infantry* (Princeton, IN: Press of the Clarion, 1895), 273.

24. C. P. Weaver, ed., *Thank God My Regiment an African One: The Civil War Diary of Colonel Nathan W. Daniels* (Baton Rouge: Louisiana State University Press, 1998), 68 (Mar. 29, 1863).

25. Weaver, *Thank God My Regiment an African One*, 135 (Sept. 1, 1863).

26. See David Bell Birney to Gerrit Smith, Headquarters, 3rd Corps, June 9, 1863, Gerrit Smith Papers, E. S. Bird Library, Syracuse University, Syracuse, NY.

27. William Birney to J. Miller McKim, Baltimore, Sept. 11, 1863, Box 10, J. Miller McKim Papers, Samuel J. May Antislavery Collection, CU.

28. Birney to McKim, Baltimore, Aug. 17, 1863, Box 10, McKim Papers, May Antislavery Collection, CU.

29. Birney to McKim, Baltimore, Sept. 28, 1863, Box 10, McKim Papers, May Antislavery Collection, CU.

30. See Sarah Grimké to Sarah Wattles, Perth Amboy, Dec. 10, 1861, Weld-Grimké Family Papers, UM.

31. Elbridge J. Cutler, "Fitzhugh Birney," *Harvard Memorial Biographies*, ed. Thomas Wentworth Higginson, 2 vols. (Cambridge, MA: Sever and Francis, 1866), 2:440.

32. David Bell Birney to Gerrit Smith, "Hd. Qrs. 3d Corps," June 9, 1863, Smith Papers, Bird Library, Syracuse University.

33. Theodore Lyman, Nov. 12, 1864, in *Meade's Headquarters, 1863–1865: Letters of Colonel Theodore Lyman from the Wilderness to Appomattox*, ed. George Agassiz (Boston: Atlantic Monthly Press, 1922), 266.

34. Robert E. Lee to George Washington Custis Lee, Jan. 1861, quoted in *City under Siege: Richmond in the Civil War*, by Mike Wright (Lanham, MD: Rowman and Littlefield, 1995), 287.

35. William Adams, *Christian Patriotism* (New York: Anson D. F. Randolph, 1863), 10.

36. H. Seymour Hall, "Fredericksburg and Chancellorsville," Kansas Military Order of the Loyal Legion of the United States, *War Talks in Kansas* (Kansas City: Franklin Hudson, 1906), 194.

37. Michael C. C. Adams, *Our Masters the Rebels: A Speculation on Union Military Failure in the East, 1861–1865* (Cambridge, MA: Harvard University Press, 1978), 139.

38. Frank Moore, *Anecdotes, Poetry and Incidents of the War: North and South, 1860–1865* (New York: Publication Office, Bible House, 1867), 305.

39. See Christian B. Keller, *Chancellorsville and the Germans: Nativism, Ethnicity, and Civil War Memory* (New York: Fordham University Press, 2007), chap. 2; and Martin Ofele, "German-Americans and the War up to Gettysburg," in *Damn Dutch: Pennsylvania Germans at Gettysburg*, ed. David L. Valuska and Christian B. Keller (Mechanicsburg, PA: Stackpole Books, 2010), 16–43.

40. Joseph Hooker to Edwin M. Stanton, Mar. 20, 1863, Records of the Office of the Secretary of War, Record Group 107, NA.

41. Elijah H. C. Cavins to wife, Apr. 1, 1863, in *The Civil War Letters of Col. Elijah H. C. Cavins, 14th Indiana*, ed. Barbara A. Smith (Owensboro, KY: Cook-McDowell, 1981), 150.

42. Howard, *Autobiography*, 1:348–49.

43. Richard F. Welch, *The Boy General: The Life and Careers of Francis Channing Barlow* (Rutherford, NJ: Fairleigh Dickinson University Press, 2003), 33, 64.

44. Harold Earl Hammond, ed., *Diary of a Union Lady, 1861–1865* (Lincoln: University of Nebraska Press, 2000), 228 (Apr. 8, 1863).

45. Francis Gould Shaw to mother, Mar. 17, 1863, quoted in Buell, *Warrior Generals*, 207.

46. Francis Channing Barlow to Almira Barlow, Mar. 8, 1863, in *"Fear Was Not in Him": The Civil War Letters of Major General Francis C. Barlow, U.S.A.*, ed. Christian G. Samito (New York: Fordham University Press, 2004), 124.

47. Barlow to Barlow, ca. June 1863, quoted in Buell, *Warrior Generals*, 208.

48. See Samito, *"Fear Was Not in Him,"* xxxix.

49. Allan, *Life and Letters of Margaret Junkin Preston*, 163.

50. John Randolph Tucker, *The Southern Church Justified in its Support of the South in the Present War: A Lecture, Delivered before the Young Men's Christian Association of Richmond, on the 21st May, 1863* (Richmond: William H. Clemmitt, 1863), 8.

51. See James Turner Johnson, *Just War Tradition and the Restraint of War: A Moral and Historical Inquiry* (Princeton, NJ: Princeton University Press, 1981), chap. 3; Oliver O'Donovan, *The Just War Revisited* (New York: Cambridge University Press, 2003), chap. 1.

52. Sarah Ann Brock, *Richmond during the War: Four Years of Personal Observation by a Richmond Lady* (New York: G. W. Carleton, 1867), 222, 220.

53. James B. Ramsey, *True Eminence Founded on Holiness: A Discourse Occasioned by the Death of Lieut. Gen. T. J. Jackson* (Lynchburg: Virginian "Water-Power Presses," 1863), 3.

54. Ramsey, *True Eminence*, 10.

55. Ramsey, *True Eminence*, 18.

56. Ramsey, *True Eminence*, 21.

57. See Peter G. Tsouras, *Major General George H. Sharpe and the Creation of American Military Intelligence in the Civil War* (Philadelphia: Casemate, 2018), chap. 3.

58. Oliver O. Howard, "The Eleventh Corps at Chancellorsville," in *Battles and Leaders of the Civil War: Being for the Most Part Contributions by Union and Confederate Officers*, ed. Robert Underwood Johnson and Clarence Clough Buel, 4 vols. (New York: Century, 1884–88), 3:198–99.

59. Howard to Roland B. Howard, May 16, 1863, Oliver Otis Howard Papers, BC.

60. Howard, "Eleventh Corps at Chancellorsville," 202.

61. *San Francisco Chronicle*, undated clipping (ca. 1872), Joseph Hooker Military Papers, HL (emphasis in original).

62. Francis Lieber to Edward Bates, July 23, 1861, Box 23, Francis Lieber Papers, HL.

63. John Fabian Witt, *Lincoln's Code: The Laws of War in American History* (New York: Free Press, 2012), 234.

64. Francis Lieber, "Instructions for the Government of Armies of the United States in the Field," *OR*, 3(3):150, art. 29.

65. Lieber, "Instructions for the Government of Armies."

66. John J. D. Renfroe, *The Battle Is God's: A Sermon Preached before Wilcox's Brigade, Fast Day, the 21st August 1863, near Orange Court-House, Va.* (Richmond, VA: MacFarlane & Ferguson, 1863), 11.

67. Renfroe, *The Battle Is God's*, 25.

68. Milroy speech, Jan. 1, 1863, in Joseph Warren Keifer, *Slavery and Four Years of War: A Political History of Slavery in the United States Together with a Narrative of the Campaigns and Battles of the Civil War in which the Author Took Part, 1861–1865*, 2 vols. (New York: Putnam, 1900), 1:316.

69. "Partial Record of the Secession of the Presbyterian Church of Rensselaer, Jasper County Indiana, 1854–67," in Paulus, *Papers of General Robert Huston Milroy*, 4:84–85.

70. Benjamin F. Kelley to Robert C. Schenck, Jan. 24, 1863, Robert C. Schenck Papers, Rutherford B. Hayes Presidential Center Library, Fremont, OH.

71. Noyalas, *"My Will Is Absolute Law,"* 10–11.

72. Robert H. Milroy to Mary Milroy, July 14, 1862, Robert H. Milroy Collection, Jasper County Public Library, Rensselaer, NY, quoted in Noyalas, *"My Will Is Absolute Law,"* 56.

73. Milroy to Milroy, Aug. 15, 1862, Milroy Collection, Jasper County Public Library, quoted in Noyalas, *"My Will Is Absolute Law,"* 62.

74. Milroy to Milroy, Aug. 15, 1862, in Paulus, *Papers of General Robert Huston Milroy*, 1:236–37.

75. Milroy to Milroy, in Paulus, *Papers of General Robert Huston Milroy*, 1:228.

76. Cornelia Peake McDonald, *A Woman's Civil War: A Diary, with Reminiscences of the War,*

from March 1862, ed. Minrose C. Gwin (Madison: University of Wisconsin Press, 1992), 138, 140.

77. Carl Schurz Diary, July 16, 1862, Box 175, Carl Schurz Papers, LC.

78. Keifer, *Slavery and Four Years of War,* 2:21.

79. Keifer, *Slavery and Four Years of War,* 2:20–21.

80. Nancy Emerson Diary, June 26, 1863, Emerson Family Papers, UVA.

81. *OR,* 27(1):155–68. There were 145 mid-Atlantic, 44 New England, 31 midwestern, and 6 Border South regiments in Meade's army.

82. Henry Ropes to father, June 30, 1863, vol. 1, Civil War Letters of Henry Ropes, 20th Massachusetts Regiment Collection, Boston Public Library.

83. Henry Livermore Abbott to John Codman Ropes, Aug. 7, 1863, in "Reports, Letters, and Papers Appertaining to 20th Mass. Vol. Inf.," 2 vols. (Boston, bound mss., 189?), vol. 1, 20th Massachusetts Regiment Collection, Boston Public Library (emphasis in original).

84. Virginians at the top of the command structure were Lee, Richard S. Ewell, A. P. Hill, J. E. B. Stuart, Jubal Early, Henry Heth, Edward Johnson, George Pickett, and Robert Rodes. Only at brigade level did the Deep South come into its own; nine of thirty-seven infantry brigade commanders were Virginians, although five of six cavalry brigade commanders were from the Old Dominion.

85. *OR,* 27(2):283–91. Eighty-six regiments, or more than half of Lee's infantry force, came from Deep South states. Another seventy-six regiments hailed from the Upper South. A single battalion hailed from the Border South state of Maryland.

86. J. J. Young to Henry King Burgwyn Sr., July 31, 1863, Burgwyn Papers, North Carolina Division of Archives and History, Raleigh; G. P. Collins to Burgwyn, July 3, 1863, Burgwyn Family Papers, UNC.

87. John G. Selby, *Meade: The Price of Command, 1863–1865* (Kent, OH: Kent State University Press, 2018), 15.

88. William Kepler, *History of the Three Months' and Three Years' Service from April 16th, 1861, to June 22d, 1864, of the Fourth Regiment Ohio Volunteer Infantry in the War for the Union* (Huntington, WV: Blue Acorn, 1992), 123–24.

89. Abraham Lincoln to George G. Meade, July 14, 1863, in *The Collected Works of Abraham Lincoln,* ed. Roy W. Basler, 9 vols. (New Brunswick, NJ: Rutgers University Press, 1953), 5:327–28.

90. On this point, see Allen C. Guelzo, *Gettysburg: The Last Invasion* (New York: Alfred A. Knopf, 2013), 224, 322.

91. Lincoln to Howard, July 21, 1863, *The Life and Letters of General George Gordon Meade, Major-General United States Army,* ed. George Gordon Meade, 2 vols. (New York: Charles Scribner's Sons, 1913), 2:138.

92. LaSalle Corbell Pickett, *Pickett and His Men* (Philadelphia: J. B. Lippincott, 1913), 318.

93. Lesley J. Gordon, *General George E. Pickett in Life and Legend* (Chapel Hill: University of North Carolina Press, 1998), 121.

94. Robert E. Lee Jr., *Recollections and Letters of General Robert E. Lee* (New York: Doubleday, Page, 1904), 105–6; Alexander Mendoza, *Confederate Struggle for Command: General James Longstreet and the First Corps in the West* (College Station: Texas A&M University Press, 2008), 28.

95. William R. Aylett to Alice Roane Aylett, June 23, 30, 1863, Aylett Family Papers, VMHC.

96. Aylett to Aylett, July 20, 1863, Aylett Family Papers, VMHC.

97. Aylett to Aylett, July 21, 1863, Aylett Family Papers, VMHC.

98. Carmichael, *Last Generation*, 198.

99. B. W. McDonnald, *Address to Chaplains and Missionaries* (Petersburg, VA: n.p., 1863), 8, 13.

100. Israel F. Silvers Diary, July 29, 1863, Box 1, Israel F. Silvers Family Papers, RU.

101. Silvers Diary, July 31, 1863, Box 1, Silvers Family Papers, RU.

102. Silvers Diary, Aug. 9, 1863, Box 1, Silvers Family Papers.

103. Junkin, *Reverend George Junkin*, 550; Coulling, *Preston*, 134.

104. Mark Grimsley and Todd D. Miller, eds., *The Union Must Stand: The Civil War Diary of John Quincy Adams Campbell, Fifth Iowa Volunteer Infantry* (Knoxville: University of Tennessee Press, 2000), 110 (July 4, 1863).

105. Kate Clifford Larson, *Bound for the Promised Land: Harriet Tubman, Portrait of an American Hero* (New York: Ballantine Books, 2004), 220.

106. Washington, *Sojourner Truth's America*, 306.

107. Thomas W. Higginson to Mary Thatcher Higginson, n.d., in *The Complete Journal and Selected Letters of Thomas Wentworth Higginson*, ed. Christopher Looby (Chicago: University of Chicago Press, 2000), 250.

108. N. G. Collins, "The Prospect—The Speech of Rev. N. G Collins, Chaplain of the 57th Illinois, at Corinth, Miss., on the Day of National Thanksgiving, Aug. 3d, 1863, to the Officers and Men of Col. Bane's Brigade," DU.

109. Faust, *This Republic of Suffering*, 95–96.

110. Jon Pahl, "Shifting Sacrifices: Christians, War, and Peace in America," in *American Christianities: A History of Dominance and Diversity*, eds. Catherine A. Brekus and W. Clark Gilpin (Chapel Hill: University of North Carolina Press, 2011), 450.

111. Daniel, *Conquered*, 148.

112. Andrew J. Daniels to mother, May 4, 1863, in *Civil War Letters*, ed. Steven A. Birchfield (N.p., n.d.).

113. James Brannock to wife, May 19, 1863, Brannock Letters, VMHC.

114. *Religious Herald*, Sept. 3, 1863.

115. Steven Elliott Diary, May 31, 1863, Georgia Department of Archives and History, Morrow, quoted in Daniel, *Conquered*, 153.

116. Daniel, *Conquered*, 153.

117. Leonidas Polk to Stephen Elliott, Aug. 15, 1863, Leonidas Polk Papers, UNC.

118. Benjamin L. Miller, *In God's Presence: Chaplains, Missionaries, and Religious Spaces during the American Civil War* (Lawrence: University Press of Kansas, 2019), 57.

119. Elliott, *Doctor Quintard*, 64, 193–94.

120. Leonidas Polk, General Orders No. 1, Dec. 23, 1863, *OR*, 31(3):857.

121. Aylett to Aylett, July 21, 1863, Aylett Family Papers, VMHC.

122. *OR*, 30(1):40–47. Of Rosecrans's volunteer regiments, 121 were from the Midwest, 16 from the Border South, and 3 from the mid-Atlantic state of Pennsylvania.

123. *OR*, 30(2):11–20. Sixty of Bragg's volunteer infantry regiments were from the Deep South, fifty were from the Upper South, and five were from Kentucky in the Border South.

124. Elliott, *Doctor Quintard*, 70.

125. Robert Watson Diary, Oct. 29, 1863, Chickamauga-Chattanooga National Military Park, Fort Oglethorpe, GA.

126. Donn Piatt and H. V. Boynton, *General George H. Thomas: A Critical Biography* (Cincinnati: Robert Clarke, 1893), 335.

127. Albert R. Greene, "What I Saw of the Quantrill Raid," *Collections of the Kansas State Historical Society*, vol. 13 (Topeka: W. R. Smith, 1915), 447–48.

128. *Washington Republican*, printed in *Lawrence Republican*, July 24, 1862.

129. Angelo M. Crapsey to Frank Silbey, Feb. 7, 1862, quoted in *Pathway to Hell: A Tragedy of the American Civil War*, by Dennis W. Brandt (Bethlehem, PA: Lehigh University Press, 2008), 73.

130. James Lee McDonough and James Pickett Jones, *War So Terrible: Sherman and Atlanta* (New York: W. W. Norton, 1987), 30.

131. Rable, *God's Almost Chosen Peoples*, 99.

132. Congressional Republicans to Anna E. Dickinson, Dec. 1863, Anna E. Dickinson Papers, LC.

133. J. Matthew Gallman, "Anna Dickinson: Abolitionist Orator," in *The Human Tradition in the Civil War and Reconstruction*, ed. Steven E. Woodworth (Wilmington, DE: SR Books, 2000), 93–94.

134. Gallman, "Anna Dickinson," 102.

135. *Addresses of the Hon. W. D. Kelley, Miss Anna E. Dickinson, and Mr. Frederick Douglass, at a mass meeting . . . Philadelphia, July 6, 1863 for the promotion of colored enlistments* (Philadelphia, 1863), LC.

136. Gallman, *America's Joan of Arc*, 33.

137. Frederick Douglass, "Emancipation, Racism, and the Work before Us: An Address Delivered in Philadelphia, Pennsylvania, on 4 December 1863," in *Frederick Douglass Papers*, ser. 1, *Speeches, Debates, and Interviews*, vol. 3, *1855–1863* (New Haven, CT: Yale University Press, 1979), 606–7.

5. George B. McClellan's Apocalypse, 1864

1. *Two Soldiers: The Campaign Diaries of Thomas J. Key C.S.A. and Robert J. Campbell U.S.A.*, ed. Wirt A. Cate (Chapel Hill: University of North Carolina Press, 1938), 19.

2. William H. T. Walker to Mary Townsend Walker, Jan. 1, 1864, W. H. T. Walker Papers, DU.

3. Brown, *To the Manner Born*, 196–97. Cleburne's paper is printed in *OR*, 52(2):586–92.

4. Brown, *To the Manner Born*, 197.

5. Alexander P. Stewart to William H. T. Walker, Jan. 9, 1864, W. H. T. Walker–A. P. Stewart Correspondence, Georgia Historical Society, Savannah.

6. Jefferson Davis to Walker, Jan. 23, 1864, in *OR*, 52(2):596; and Brown, *To the Manner Born*, 201.

7. Walker to Mary T. Walker, Feb. 24, 1864, Walker Papers, DU.

8. Ahlstrom, *Religious History of the American People*, 672.

9. Thomas Cary Johnson, *History of the Southern Presbyterian Church* (New York: Christian Literature, 1894), 426.

10. R. L. Stanton, *The Church and the Rebellion: A Consideration of the Rebellion Against the Government of the United States; and the Agency of the Church, North and South* (New York: Derby & Miller, 1864), 204.

11. James W. Silver, *Confederate Morale and Church Propaganda* (Tuscaloosa: Confederate Publishing, 1957), 101.

12. Stanton, *Church and the Rebellion,* 193–94.

13. Lemuel J. Hoyle to mother, Apr. 25, 1864, Hoyle Papers, UNC. See also Richard S. Webb to mother, Jan. 15, 1864, Webb Family Papers, UNC.

14. James I. Robertson Jr., ed., *The Civil War Letters of General Robert McAllister,* (New Brunswick, NJ: Rutgers University Press, 1965), 405, 400–401.

15. Emil Rosenblatt and Ruth Rosenblatt, eds., *Hard Marching Every Day: The Civil War Letters of Private Wilbur Fisk, 1861–1865* (Lawrence: University Press of Kansas, 1992), 213.

16. John Ripley Adams, *Memorial and Letters of John R. Adams, D.D.* (Cambridge: Cambridge University Press, 1890), 142, 145.

17. W. H. Withington to sister, Dec. 23, 1862, Michigan Historical Collections, Bentley Historical Library, University of Michigan, Ann Arbor.

18. Sears, *Chancellorsville,* 28.

19. Hattaway and Jones, *How the North Won,* 532.

20. Gary W. Gallagher, *Stephen Dodson Ramseur, Lee's Gallant General* (Chapel Hill: University of North Carolina Press, 1985), 20; Howard, *Autobiography,* 1:91–92.

21. Stephen Dodson Ramseur to Ellen Ramseur, Apr. 24–30, 1864, Folder 9, Stephen Dodson Ramseur Papers, UNC.

22. *OR,* 36(1):136–53. Of Meade's volunteer infantry regiments, 122 were from mid-Atlantic states, 33 hailed from New England, 21 were from the midwestern states, and 8 were from Border South states (Delaware, Maryland, and West Virginia). By May 20, eight more heavy artillery regiments—each numbering more than 1,000 effectives—reinforced the army from the Washington defenses.

23. *OR,* 36(3):169. Burnside's corps was far more demographically representative of the postmillenarian alliance of Republicans and southern blacks than Meade's army. Fourteen of thirty-seven IX Corps volunteer regiments were from Republican New England, eight were mid-Atlantic units, seven were from midwestern states, six were black (US Colored Troops) regiments, and two were from Maryland in the Border South.

24. Gordon C. Rhea, *To the North Anna River: Grant and Lee, May 13–25, 1864* (Baton Rouge: Louisiana State University Press, 2000), 386–92. Lee's army by now contained more soldiers from Deep South states than it did in 1863. Ninety-three infantry regiments hailed from the Deep South, while seventy-nine regiments were from the Upper South; none came from Border South states.

25. Steven E. Sodergren, *The Army of the Potomac in the Overland and Petersburg Campaigns* (Baton Rouge: Louisiana State University Press, 2017), 190.

26. The bulk of these reinforcements were the two corps of Benjamin Butler's Army of the James (advancing on Richmond from the east) and a dozen large heavy artillery regiments from the Washington defenses. See William Glenn Robertson, *Back Door to Richmond: The Bermuda Hundred Campaign, April–June 1864* (Baton Rouge: Louisiana State University Press, 1987), 23, 239.

27. Stephen R. Taaffe, *Commanding the Army of the Potomac* (Lawrence: University Press of Kansas, 2006), 156.

28. Earl J. Hess, *In the Trenches at Petersburg: Field Fortifications and Confederate Defeat* (Chapel Hill: University of North Carolina Press, 2009), 45–49.

29. Hess, *In the Trenches at Petersburg*, 87–88.

30. Hess, *In the Trenches at Petersburg*, 97.

31. James E. Murdock, "Preston in the Rebellion: Company A Seventh W. Va. Infantry," *Preston County Journal*, Mar. 20, 1884.

32. Paul M. Higginbotham to Aaron Higginbotham, Aug. 1, 1864, Paul M. Higginbotham Papers, VMHC.

33. Delevan Bates speech, Jan. 1891, in *War Talks of Confederate Veterans*, comp. and ed. George S. Bernard (Petersburg, VA: Fenn & Owen, 1892), 183.

34. William H. Stewart, "The Charge of the Crater," *Southern Historical Society Papers* 25 (1897): 79–80.

35. William H. Stewart, *The Spirit of the South: Orations, Essays, and Lectures* (New York: Neale, 1908), 135.

36. William H. Etheredge, "Another Story of the Crater Battle," *Southern Historical Society Papers* 37 (1909): 205.

37. Stewart, *Spirit of the South*, 135.

38. Henry Van Leuvenigh Bird to unknown, June 30, 1880, Bird Family Papers, VMHC.

39. Frank Kenfield, "Captured by Rebels: A Vermonter at Petersburg, 1864," *Vermont History* 36 (1968): 233.

40. William R. J. Pegram to Jennifer McIntosh, Aug. 1, 1864, Pegram-McIntosh-Johnson Papers, VMHC.

41. Kate Sperry Diary, Apr. 3, 1864, HRL.

42. Julia Chase Diary, Apr. 3, 1864, in Mahon, *Winchester Divided*, 138.

43. David Hunter to Charles G. Halpine, Sept. 20, 1863, Charles G. Halpine Papers, HL.

44. Gutjahr, *Hodge*, 321, 331.

45. Eby, *Virginia Yankee*, 255 (June 12, 1864).

46. Preston Diary, June 12, 1864, in Allan, *Life and Letters of Margaret Junkin Preston*, 189–91.

47. William S. White to Francis McFarland, Lexington, VA, July 6, 1864, Francis McFarland Papers, WLU.

48. Rose Page Pendleton, "The Yankees in Lexington," June 18, 1864, Rose Page Pendleton Journal, WLU.

49. White to McFarland, July 6, 1864, McFarland Papers, WLU.

50. Gutjahr, *Hodge*, 321, 331.

51. Preston Diary, June 13, 1864, in Allan, *Life and Letters of Margaret Junkin Preston*, 192.

52. *OR*, 40(3):223, 37(2):202.

53. George J. Howard to Gertrude Howard, Front Royal, Oct. 11, 1864, in *A War of the People: Vermont Civil War Letters*, ed. Jeffrey D. Marshall (Hanover, NH: University Press of New England, 1999), 264.

54. Howard to Howard, Oct. 11, 1864, in Marshall, *War of the People*, 265–66.

55. Edwin M. Haynes, Civil War Files, Harrisonburg–Rockingham County Historical Soci-

ety, Dayton, VA, quoted in *The Burning: Sheridan in the Shenandoah Valley*, by John L. Heatwole (Charlottesville, VA: Rockbridge, 1998), 93.

56. Louis N. Boudrye, *Historic Records of the Fifth New York Cavalry, First Ira Harris Guard* (Albany, NY: S. R. Gray, 1865), 176.

57. David Silkenat, *Raising the White Flag: How Surrender Defined the American Civil War* (Chapel Hill: University of North Carolina Press, 2019), 181.

58. George A. Bucklin to father, Oct. 5, 1864, John Elliott Private Collection, quoted in Heatwole, *Burning*, 106.

59. Charles Russell Lowell to Josephine Shaw Lowell, Oct. 5, 1864, in *Life and Letters of Charles Russell Lowell*, ed. Edward W. Emerson (Port Washington, NY: Kennikat, 1971), 352–53.

60. Beverly Whittle Diary, Oct. 6, 1864, Beverly K. Whittle Papers, UVA.

61. Joseph Waddell Diary, July 22, 1864, UVA.

62. *Christian Recorder*, Oct. 1, 1864.

63. Laura Lee Diary, Dec. 19, 1864, in Mahon, *Winchester Divided*, 177.

64. *Philadelphia Age*, quoted in *Valley Spirit*, Oct. 19, 1864.

65. *Valley Spirit*, Oct. 26, 1864.

66. Lee, *Memoirs of William Nelson Pendleton*, 414.

67. Tera W. Hunter, *Bound in Wedlock: Slave and Free Black Marriage in the Nineteenth Century* (Cambridge, MA: Belknap Press of Harvard University Press, 2017), 121–35.

68. Lucy Chase to "My Dear Friends," July 1, 1864, in *Dear Ones at Home: Letters from Contraband Camps*, ed. Henry L. Swint (Nashville: Vanderbilt University Press, 1966), 123–24.

69. Office of the Commission of Enrollment, Department of the Gulf to Banks, Feb. 24, 1864, AMA.

70. "Education of the Freedmen in Louisiana," *American Missionary*, Nov. 1864, 258.

71. Emancipation League, *Facts Concerning the Freedmen: Their Capacity and Their Destiny* (Boston: Press of Commercial Printing House, 1863).

72. Bryan Tyson, *The Institution of Slavery in the Southern States, Religiously and Morally Considered in Connection with Our Sectional Troubles* (Washington, DC: H. Polkinhorn, 1863), in *Southern Unionist Pamphlets*, 183.

73. Tyson, *Institution of Slavery*, 171.

74. Tyson, *Institution of Slavery*, 182.

75. Tyson, *Institution of Slavery*, 184.

76. Tyson, *Institution of Slavery*, 190.

77. Tyson, *Institution of Slavery*, 192.

78. John W. Hanson, *Historical Sketch of the Old Sixth Regiment of Massachusetts Volunteers* (Boston: Lee and Shepard, 1866), 161.

79. Hanson, *Historical Sketch of the Old Sixth Regiment*, 170.

80. William G. Kephart to Lewis Tappan, May 9, 1864, AMA.

81. Larson, *Bound for the Promised Land*, 224.

82. Larson, *Bound for the Promised Land*, 226.

83. Gerrit Smith quoted in Larson, *Bound for the Promised Land*, 227.

84. Larson, *Bound for the Promised Land*, 227.

85. Susan V. Greble to Elizabeth Howard, Jan. 30, 1864, Oliver Otis Howard Papers, BC.

86. *Philadelphia Inquirer*, Jan. 29, 1864.

87. McFeely, *Yankee Stepfather,* 212.

88. *OR,* 38(3):638–75. Ninety-nine of Hood's regiments were raised in the Deep South, forty-seven in the Upper South, and eight were from Kentucky or Missouri in the Border South.

89. *OR,* 38(1):89–114. There were 232 midwestern, 27 mid-Atlantic, 4 New England, and 38 Border South regiments (including Kentucky and Tennessee).

90. Daniel, *Conquered,* 156.

91. William J. Hardee to Mary Lewis Hardee, June 5, 1864, quoted in Hughes, *Hardee,* 209.

92. Randall Lee Gibson to Frances Ann Polk, Dec. 26, 1873, Leonidas Polk Papers, UNC.

93. William Harrison Polk to William M. Polk, Oct. 28, 1908, Polk Papers, UNC.

94. Polk to Polk, Oct. 28, 1908, Polk Papers, UNC.

95. Hughes, *Hardee,* 210; Hardee to D. West, June 15, 1864, Gale and Polk Family Papers, UNC.

96. Charles Todd Quintard, *Balm for the Weary and Wounded* (Charleston, SC: Evans & Cogswell, 1864).

97. Hardee to Hardee, June 17, 1864, Polk Papers, UNC.

98. Richard M. McMurry, "Kennesaw Mountain," *Civil War Times Illustrated* 8 (Jan. 1970): 22.

99. David P. Conyngham, *Sherman's March through the South* (New York: Sheldon, 1865), 113.

100. W. Harrison Daniel, *Southern Protestantism in the Confederacy* (Bedford, VA: Print Shop, 1989), 40–41.

101. Edwin Eustace Bryant, *History of the Third Regiment of Wisconsin Veteran Volunteer Infantry, 1861–1865* (Madison, WI: Regimental Veterans Association, 1891), 235.

102. Bryant, *History of the Third Regiment,* 235.

103. William Gilfillan Galvin, ed., *Infantryman Pettit: The Civil War Letters of Corporal Frederick Pettit* (New York: Avon Books, 1991), 78.

104. Galvin, *Infantryman Pettit,* 106.

105. McDonough and Jones, *War So Terrible,* 242–43.

106. McDonough and Jones, *War So Terrible,* 28–29.

107. John W. Geary to Mary Henderson Geary, near Atlanta, July 29, 1864, in Blair, *Politician Goes to War,* 190–91.

108. Geary to Geary, Atlanta, Oct. 18, 1864, in Blair, *Politician Goes to War,* 208.

109. Geary to Geary, Atlanta, Oct. 19, 1864, in Blair, *Politician Goes to War,* 210.

110. Noah Brooks, "Two War-Time Conventions," *Century* 49 (Mar. 1895): 732.

111. Larson, *Bound for the Promised Land,* 226; Painter, *Truth,* 200–3.

112. Martha S. Jones, *All Bound Up Together: The Woman Question in African American Public Culture, 1830–1900* (Chapel Hill: University of North Carolina Press, 2007), 107.

113. Clinton, *Tubman,* 184–86.

114. Washington, *Sojourner Truth's America,* 312.

115. Washington, *Sojourner Truth's America,* 313.

116. Anna Elizabeth Dickinson to Elizabeth Cady Stanton, July 12, 1864, Civil War Collection, HL.

117. Abraham Lincoln memorandum, Aug. 23, 1864, in Basler, *Collected Works of Abraham Lincoln,* 7:514.

118. John Hay Diary, Nov. 11, 1864, in Hay, *Letters of John Hay and Extracts from Diary,* 1:244.

119. Michael Burlingame, *Abraham Lincoln: A Life*, 2 vols. (Baltimore: Johns Hopkins University Press, 2008), 2:675–77.

120. Stephen D. Engle, *Gathering to Save a Nation: Lincoln and the Union's War Governors* (Chapel Hill: University of North Carolina Press, 2016), 328, 344.

121. John Brobst to Mary Englesby, Sept. 27, 1864, in *Well Mary: Civil War Letters of a Wisconsin Volunteer*, ed. Margaret B. Roth (Madison: University of Wisconsin Press, 1969), 92.

122. Fisk to *Green Mountain Freeman*, Oct. 12, 1864, in Rosenblatt and Rosenblatt, *Hard Marching Every Day*, 264–65.

123. Eugene Cole to father, Nov. 22, 1864, Records of the National Labor Relations Board, Record Group 25, NA.

124. Jonathan W. White, *Emancipation, the Union Army, and the Reelection of Abraham Lincoln* (Baton Rouge: Louisiana State University Press, 2014), chap. 4.

125. Ari Kelman, *A Misplaced Massacre: Struggling over the Memory of Sand Creek* (Cambridge, MA: Harvard University Press, 2013), 9–10.

126. Mary E. Kellogg, comp., *Army Life of an Illinois Soldier* (Carbondale: Southern Illinois University Press, 1996), 316.

127. Gary L. Scheel, *Rain, Mud, & Swamps: 31st Missouri Volunteer Infantry Regiment Marching through the South during the Civil War with General William T. Sherman* (Pacific, MO: Gary L. Scheel, 1998).

128. William T. Sherman, *Memoirs of General W. T. Sherman* (New York: Library of America, 1990), 652.

129. Steven E. Woodworth, *Nothing but Victory: The Army of the Tennessee, 1861–1865* (New York: Alfred A. Knopf, 2005), 589–90.

130. Woodworth, *Nothing but Victory*, 591.

131. Geary to Geary, near Savannah, Dec. 1864, in Blair, *Politician Goes to War*, 217.

132. Geary to Geary, Loudoun Heights, Oct. 15, 1862, in Blair, *Politician Goes to War*, 62.

133. Geary to Geary, near Savannah, Dec. 1864, in Blair, *Politician Goes to War*, 217.

134. Elihu Burritt, *Peace Papers for the People* (London: Charles Gilpin, 1851), 40–41.

135. Victoria E. Ott, *Confederate Daughters: Coming of Age during the Civil War* (Carbondale: Southern Illinois University Press, 2008), 1.

136. Miers, *When the World Ended*, 3 (Dec. 31, 1864).

137. Miers, *When the World Ended*, 3 (Dec. 31, 1864).

138. Charles Todd Quintard Diary, Dec. 21, 1864, in Elliott, *Doctor Quintard*, 204.

6. Oliver O. Howard's Millennium, 1865

1. Burlingame, *Lincoln*, 2:752.

2. Jones, *Rebel War Clerk's Diary*, 2:408 (Feb. 3, 1865).

3. *Lynchburg Virginian*, Feb. 7, 1865.

4. Richard E. Beringer, Herman Hattaway, Archer Jones, and William N. Still Jr., *Why the South Lost the Civil War* (Athens: University of Georgia Press, 1986), 353.

5. Miers, *When the World Ended*, 5 (Jan. 1, 1864).

6. See Joseph LeConte, *'Ware Sherman: A Journal of Three Months' Personal Experience in the*

Last Days of the Confederacy (Baton Rouge: Louisiana State University Press, 1999), 1–81; and William Dallam Ames, ed., *The Autobiography of Joseph LeConte* (New York: D. Appleton, 1903), chap. 8.

7. LeConte,*'Ware Sherman*, 1 (Dec. 9, 1864).

8. LeConte,*'Ware Sherman*, 91 (Feb. 17, 1865).

9. Lemuel Moss, *Annals of the United States Christian Commission* (Philadelphia: J. B. Lippincott, 1868), 216–17, 256.

10. Margaret Junkin Preston, "Hymn to the National Flag," *Richmond Sentinel*, Jan. 17, 1865.

11. *Savannah Morning News*, Apr. 23, 28, 1863.

12. Margaret J. Preston, *Beechenbrook: A Rhyme of the War* (Richmond: J. W. Randolph, 1865), 64.

13. Mary Anna Jackson to Preston, Cottage Home, June 6, 1866, Margaret Junkin Preston Papers, UNC.

14. Alice Fahs, *The Imagined Civil War: Popular Literature of the North and South, 1861–1865* (Chapel Hill: University of North Carolina Press, 2001), 145.

15. Wright, *City under Siege*, 214.

16. Richard Lancelot Maury Diary, Mar. 23, 1865, VMHC.

17. John S. Wise, *The End of an Era* (Boston: Houghton, Mifflin, 1901), 434.

18. Wright, *City under Siege*, 260.

19. McClellan to Elizabeth B. McClellan, Nov. 11, 1864, George B. McClellan Papers, LC.

20. McClellan reached the rank of major general at the age of thirty-five. The original Napoleon was eight *years* younger when he reached similar rank during the French Revolution.

21. McClellan to S. L. M. Barlow, Nov. 28, 1864, S. L. M. Barlow Papers, HL.

22. Sears, *McClellan*, 388.

23. Mary Ellen McClellan to Randolph Marcy, Feb. 9, 1865, McClellan Papers, LC.

24. McClellan to Barlow, Apr. 15, 1865, Barlow Papers, HL.

25. Ronald C. White, *Lincoln's Greatest Speech: The Second Inaugural* (New York: Simon & Schuster, 2002), 145.

26. Clinton, *Tubman*, 186.

27. Clinton, *Tubman*, 187–88.

28. Clinton, *Tubman*, 189.

29. Miers, *When the World Ended*, 67–68 (Feb. 26, 1865).

30. Miers, *When the World Ended*, 40 (Feb. 17, 1865).

31. Miers, *When the World Ended*, 41 (Feb. 17, 1865).

32. Miers, *When the World Ended*, 43 (Feb. 18, 1865).

33. Miers, *When the World Ended*, 44 (Feb. 18, 1865).

34. Miers, *When the World Ended*, 50 (Feb. 18, 1865).

35. Miers, *When the World Ended*, 44–45 (Feb. 18, 1865).

36. Miers, *When the World Ended*, 46 (Feb. 18, 1865).

37. Miers, *When the World Ended*, 4 (Dec. 31, 1864).

38. Miers, *When the World Ended*, 52 (Feb. 17, 1865).

39. Miers, *When the World Ended*, 68 (Feb. 26, 1865).

40. Miers, *When the World Ended*, 53 (Feb. 19, 1865).

41. Miers, *When the World Ended*, 56 (Feb. 20, 1865).

42. Williamson Murray and Wayne Wei-siang Hsieh, *A Savage War: A Military History of the Civil War* (Princeton, NJ: Princeton University Press, 2016), 499–501.

43. Elizabeth R. Varon, *Armies of Deliverance: A New History of the Civil War* (New York: Oxford University Press, 2019), 400.

44. Elizabeth R. Varon, *Appomattox: Victory, Defeat, and Freedom at the End of the Civil War* (New York: Oxford University Press, 2014), 42.

45. Emory M. Thomas, *Robert E. Lee: A Biography* (New York: W. W. Norton, 1995), 360.

46. Preston Diary, Apr. 10, 1865, in Allan, *Life and Letters of Margaret Junkin Preston*, 207–8.

47. David Silkenat, *Driven from Home: North Carolina's Refugee Crisis* (Athens: University Press of Georgia, 2016), 166.

48. Bessie Cain Diary, Apr. 16, 1865, John Bailey Lancaster Papers, UNC.

49. Mary Bayard Clarke, "General Sherman in Raleigh," *Old Guard* 4 (Apr. 1866): 226.

50. Oscar Osburn Winther, ed., *With Sherman to the Sea: The Civil War Letters, Diaries, and Reminiscences of Theodore F. Upson* (Bloomington: Indiana University Press, 1958), 166–67.

51. Woodworth, *Nothing but Victory*, 636.

52. Winther, *With Sherman to the Sea*, 167.

53. John W. Geary to Mary Henderson Geary, Raleigh, Apr. 23, 1865, in Blair, *Politician Goes to War*, 241.

54. Geary to Geary, Raleigh, Apr. 19, 1865, in Blair, *Politician Goes to War*, 239.

55. Miers, *When the World Ended*, 90 (Apr. 20[?], 1865).

56. Preston Diary, June 13, 1864, in Allan, *Life and Letters of Margaret Junkin Preston*, 192.

57. Miers, *When the World Ended*, 91 (Apr. 21[?], 1865).

58. Miers, *When the World Ended*, 93 (Apr. 21[?], 1865).

59. Lillie B. Chace to Anna Dickinson, Apr. 23, 1865, Anna E. Dickinson Papers, LC.

60. See Harold Holzer, *Lincoln at Cooper Union: The Speech That Made Abraham Lincoln President* (New York: Simon & Schuster, 2006).

61. Gallman, *America's Joan of Arc*, 43.

62. Showalter, *Civil Wars of Julia Ward Howe*, 173.

63. Showalter, *Civil Wars of Julia Ward Howe*, 166.

64. Miers, *When the World Ended*, 95 (Apr. 23, 1865).

65. Miers, *When the World Ended*, 95–96 (Apr. 23, 1865).

66. Virginia Ingraham Burr, ed., *The Secret Eye: The Journal of Ella Gertrude Clanton Thomas, 1848–1889* (Chapel Hill: University of North Carolina Press, 1990), 252–54 (Jan. 3, 1865).

67. Stephanie McCurry, *Women's War: Fighting and Surviving the American Civil War* (Cambridge, MA: Belknap Press of Harvard University Press, 2019), 147.

68. *New York Herald*, May 9, 1865.

69. Miers, *When the World Ended*, 113–16 (July 5, 1865).

70. Nathaniel Cheairs Hughes Jr. and Timothy Johnson, eds., *A Fighter from Way Back: The Mexican War Diary of Lt. Daniel Harvey Hill* (Kent, OH: Kent State University Press, 2002), 137 (Oct. 17, 1847).

71. McFeely, *Yankee Stepfather*, 57.

72. McFeely, *Yankee Stepfather*, 62–63.

73. William T. Sherman to Howard, May 17, 1865, Oliver Otis Howard Papers, BC.

74. McFeely, *Yankee Stepfather*, 10–11.

75. Francis C. Barlow to Howard, Brookline, July 24, 1865, Howard Papers, BC.

76. E. Knowlton to W. P. Fessenden, May 20, 1865, William Pitt Fessenden Papers, LC.

77. Dabney to "Chief of the Freedmen's Bureau, Washington," Sept. 12, 1865, Dabney Family Papers, UVA.

Epilogue: Edmund Ruffin's Apocalypse, June 1865

1. Edmund Ruffin Diary, June 18 [*sic*], 1865, Edmund Ruffin Papers, LC.

2. Eric H. Walther, *The Fire-Eaters* (Baton Rouge: Louisiana State University Press, 1992), 229–30.

3. Hill quoted in Bridges, *Lee's Maverick General*, 273.

4. Coulling, *Preston*, 153; Gaines M. Foster, *Ghosts of the Confederacy: Defeat, the Lost Cause, and the Emergence of the New South, 1865–1913* (New York: Oxford University Press, 1987), 50.

5. Preston, "Hero's Daughter," *Land We Love* 1 (Oct. 1866): 404; Preston, "Regulus," ibid., 409.

6. Kent T. Dollar, *Soldiers of the Cross: Confederate Soldier-Christians and the Impact of War on Their Faith* (Macon, GA: Mercer University Press, 2005), 183.

7. Giles B. Cooke Diary, Jan. 17, 24, Oct. 9, 1864, Giles Buckner Cooke Papers, VMHC.

8. Dollar, *Soldiers of the Cross*, 215.

9. Robert E. Lee to Giles B. Cooke, Apr. 1866, Cooke Papers, VMHC.

10. William H. Montgomery, *Under Their Own Vine and Fig Tree: The African-American Church in the South, 1865–1900* (Baton Rouge: Louisiana State University Press, 1990), chap. 3.

11. Carmichael, *Last Generation*, 220.

12. See Drew Gilpin Faust, *Mothers of Invention: Women of the Slaveholding South in the American Civil War* (Chapel Hill: University of North Carolina Press, 1996), 242.

13. Diane Miller Sommerville, *Rape and Race in the Nineteenth-Century South* (Chapel Hill: University of North Carolina Press, 2004), 144–45. Almost half of those convicted were transported out of the state, not executed.

14. Eugen Weber, *Apocalypses: Prophecies, Cults, and Millennial Beliefs through the Ages* (Cambridge, MA: Harvard University Press, 1999), 181.

15. Dabney, *Defence of Virginia*, 355.

16. Dabney, *Defence of Virginia*, 5.

17. Joseph LeConte to Emma LeConte, Newton, July 21, 1866, LeConte and Furman Family Papers, UNC.

18. Ames, *Autobiography of Joseph LeConte*, 238.

19. *Equal Suffrage: An Address from the Colored Citizens of Norfolk, Va., to the People of the United States* (1865), in *Proceedings of the Black National and State Conventions*, eds. Philip S. Foner and George E. Walker, 2 vols. (Philadelphia: Temple University Press, 1979–80), 1:83–89.

20. Blair, *Politician Goes to War*, 243.

21. *The Two Platforms* (Clymer campaign poster), ca. Aug. 1866, Wikimedia Commons, uploaded Jan. 29, 2008, https://commons.wikimedia.org/wiki/File:Racistcampaignposter1.jpg (accessed Aug. 1, 2019). See also Forrest G. Wood, *Black Scare: The Racist Response to Emancipation and Reconstruction* (Berkeley: University of California Press, 1970), 79.

22. W. E. B. Du Bois, "Of the Dawn of Freedom," in *The Souls of Black Folk: Essays and Sketches* (Chicago: A. C. McClurg, 1903), 40.

23. McFeely, *Yankee Stepfather*, 2.

24. McFeely, *Yankee Stepfather*, 128.

25. Rayford W. Logan, *Howard University: The First Hundred Years, 1861–1967* (New York: New York University Press, 1969), 12–13.

26. Logan, *Howard University*, 15.

27. McFeely, *Yankee Stepfather*, 28.

28. Elizabeth Keckley, *Behind the Scenes; or, Thirty Years a Slave, and Four Years in the White House* (New York: G. W. Carleton, 1868), 316.

29. Clinton, *Tubman*, 193.

30. Clinton, *Tubman*, 191.

31. Washington, *Sojourner Truth's America*, 358.

32. *San Francisco Chronicle*, undated clipping (ca. 1872), Joseph Hooker Military Papers, HL.

33. Sarah E. Gardner, *Blood and Irony: Southern White Women's Narratives of the Civil War, 1861–1937* (Chapel Hill: University of North Carolina Press, 2004), 96.

34. Margaret J. Preston, "Personal Reminiscences of Stonewall Jackson," *Century* 32 (Oct. 1886): 936.

35. Klein, *Preston*, 53.

36. Margaret J. Preston, "Stonewall Jackson's Grave," in *War Lyrics and Songs of the South* (London: Spottiswoode, 1866), 2.

37. Julia Ward Howe to Francis Lieber, July 31 [ca. 1846], Box 1, Julia Ward Howe Papers, LC.

38. Julia Ward Howe, "Optimism and Pessimism as Efficient Social Forces," ca. 1898, Box 4, Howe Papers, LC; "Julia Ward Howe: Considered by Europeans as the Foremost Woman in America," *Evening Argus*, Oct. 13, 1898, 6.

39. Julia Ward Howe, "Optimism and Pessimism as Efficient Social Forces," Box 4, Howe Papers, LC.

40. Julia Ward Howe, "Optimism and Pessimism as Efficient Social Forces," Box 4, Howe Papers, LC.

41. Howe to Lieber, July 31 [ca. 1846], Box 1, Howe Papers, LC.

42. Rev. J. E. Jackson, Solomon S. Bruce, and Grace Slaughter to Howe, Chicago, ca. May 1910, Box 1, Howe Papers, LC.

43. Julia Ward Howe, sermon on the continuity of divine providence, n.d., Box 5, Howe Papers, LC.

44. Julia Ward Howe, sermon, Box 5, Howe Papers, LC.

45. See James A. Rogers, *Richard Furman: Life and Legacy* (Macon, GA: Mercer University Press, 1985).

46. Gallman, *America's Joan of Arc*, 89–91, 128–30, 144–46, 206–7.

47. Charles Reagan Wilson, "Religion and the American Civil War in Comparative Perspective," in *Religion and the American Civil War*, ed. Randall M. Miller, Harry S. Stout, and Charles Reagan Wilson (New York: Oxford University Press, 1998), 402.

48. Wilbur Zelinsky, *Nation into State: The Shifting Symbolic Foundations of American Nationalism* (Chapel Hill: University of North Carolina Press, 1988), 235.

49. Wilson, "Religion and the American Civil War," 403.

50. Molly Oshatz, *Slavery and Sin: The Fight against Slavery and the Rise of Liberal Protestantism* (New York: Oxford University Press, 2012), 115.

51. John Morton Blum, *The Republican Roosevelt,* 2nd ed. (Cambridge, MA: Harvard University Press, 1977), 1–2.

52. Arthur S. Link, "Woodrow Wilson: The American as Southerner," *Journal of Southern History* 36:1 (Feb. 1970): 3–17.

53. John Milton Cooper Jr., *The Warrior and the Priest: Woodrow Wilson and Theodore Roosevelt* (Cambridge, MA: Belknap Press of Harvard University Press, 1983).

54. W. Fitzhugh Brundage, "Race, Memory, and Masculinity: Black Veterans Recall the Civil War," in *The War Was You and Me: Civilians in the American Civil War,* ed. Joan E. Cashin (Princeton, NJ: Princeton University Press, 2002), 148.

55. "General Pope's Letter," *Georgia Weekly Opinion,* Sept. 3, 1867, 4.

56. Jon Pahl, "Shifting Sacrifices: Christians, War, and Peace in America," in Brekus and Gilpin, *American Christianities,* 450. As George Rable argued, "the Confederacy never surrendered beyond the mere laying down of arms." See *But There Was No Peace: The Role of Violence in the Politics of Reconstruction* (Athens: University of Georgia Press, 1984), 188.

Bibliography

PRIMARY SOURCES—MANUSCRIPTS

Boston Public Library

20th Massachusetts Regiment Collection

George J. Mitchell Department of Special Collections and Archives, Hawthorne-Longfellow Library, Bowdoin College, Brunswick, ME

Joshua L. Chamberlain Papers
Oliver Otis Howard Papers

Chicago Historical Museum

Anonymous Civil War Diary
Nathaniel Prentiss Banks Papers
William Butler Papers
Salmon P. Chase Papers
James L. Converse Papers
Zebina Eastman Papers
Charles F. Gunther Papers
Henry Wager Halleck Papers
George B. McClellan Papers
Irvin McDowell Collection
John Pope Papers
James Clay Rice Papers
George David Ruggles Papers
Franz Sigel Papers

Kroch Library, Cornell University, Ithaca, NY

Emily Howland Papers

Samuel J. May Antislavery Collection

David M. Rubinstein Library, Duke University, Durham, NC

H. G. Ayer Diary

Nathaniel Prentiss Banks Papers

Henry Besancon Diaries

Anna B. Campbell Papers

N. G. Collins Speech

Hubert A. C. Dilger Papers

Joseph Sherman Diltz Correspondence

Peter C. Earnhardt Diary

Findley Family Correspondence

John Mead Gould Papers

Griswold Family Papers

Henry C. Hall Papers

Constant C. Hanks Letters

Alexander Holmes Papers

Lane Family Papers

Francis Lieber Pamphlet

Nina Cornelia Mitchell Papers

Stephen Osgood Papers

Yelverton Peyton Page Papers

Samuel Spencer Parmelee and Uriah N. Parmelee Papers

William T. Pippey Papers

William Young Ripley Papers

Lauramann Howe Russell Papers

Helen L. and Mary Virginia Shell Papers

Horace Smith Papers

Walter Wallace Smith Papers

Darius Starr Papers

Stetson Family Papers

Jeremiah Stuart Letters

Cabell Tavenner Papers

Harriet Waldron Papers

W. H. T. Walker Papers

Shadeck-Fackenthal Library, Franklin and Marshall College, Lancaster, PA

Reynolds Family Papers

Stewart Bell Jr. Archives, Handley Regional Library, Winchester, VA

Benjamin Brooke Journal
John Peyton Clark Diary
Louisa Morrow Crawford Papers
Kate Sperry Diary

Harvard University Archives, Pusey Library, Harvard University, Cambridge, MA

Records of the Harvard Class of 1854

Houghton Library, Harvard University, Cambridge, MA

Robert Gould Shaw Papers

Huntington Library, San Marino, CA

S. L. M. Barlow Papers
Civil War Collection
Charles G. Halpine Papers
Joseph Hooker Military Papers
Francis Lieber Papers

Indiana Historical Society, Indianapolis

John Barnard Letters
Thomas H. Benton Letters
Sylvester C. Bishop Papers
John A. Blackwell Letters
Chapin Family Papers
George Henry Chapman Diaries
Solomon Simpson Hamrick Papers
Samuel V. List Collection
McLaughlin-Jordan Family Papers
Solomon Meredith Papers
Robert H. Milroy Letter

William Roby Moore Reminiscences
19th Indiana Infantry Regiment Records
7th Indiana Infantry Regiment Records
Turpin Family Papers
George Wagner Documents
Amos C. Weaver Letters
Worthington B. Williams Family Papers

Library of Congress, Washington, DC

Nathaniel Prentiss Banks Papers
Benjamin F. Butler Papers
Zachariah Chandler Papers
Lydia Maria Child Papers
Henry L. Dawes Papers
Anna E. Dickinson Papers
Richard Stoddart Ewell Papers
William Pitt Fessenden Papers
James Jenkins Gillette Papers
Jedediah Hotchkiss Papers
Julia Ward Howe Papers
George B. McClellan Papers
John T. L. Preston Diary
Edmund Ruffin Papers
Carl Schurz Papers
Thaddeus Stevens Papers
William D. Wilkins Papers

National Archives, Washington, DC

Record Group 25, Records of the National Labor Relations Board
Record Group 107, Records of the Office of the Secretary of War
Record Group 366, Records of Civil War Special Agencies of the Treasury Department

Pennsylvania State Archives, Harrisburg

Robert Taggart Papers

Special Collections, Alexander Library, Rutgers University, New Brunswick, NJ

Israel F. Silvers Family Papers
Stoddard Family Papers

Milne Library, State University of New York–Geneseo

Genesee Valley Collection

E. S. Bird Library, Syracuse University, Syracuse, NY

Gerrit Smith Papers

Amistad Research Center, Tulane University, New Orleans

American Missionary Association Archives

US Army Heritage and Education Center, Carlisle, PA

John W. Ames Papers
David Bell Birney Papers
Crook-Kennon Papers
Edmund D. Halsey Papers
John D. Vautier Papers

Civil War Miscellaneous Collection
Amos S. Abbott Papers
Matthias M. Bechter Papers
Allen L. Bevan Papers
John H. Bevan Papers
Joseph E. Blake Papers
Gideon B. "Kit" Blasland Diary
John H. Boyer Letters
Charles Brandegee Letters
Julius Broadbent Papers
James Carman Papers
James S. Colwell Papers
Samuel Lee Conde Correspondence
Leander E. Davis Papers
William H. Dunham Papers

Robert E. Erwin Letters
Graham Family Papers
Luther B. Mesnard Reminiscences
Curtis C. Pollock Papers
James B. Post Papers
Albert Rake Papers
James Ralph Papers
Frederick Ranger Papers
Charles H. Roundy Memoirs
William M. Sayre Papers
James Randolph Simpson Papers
Timothy F. Vedder Papers
Charles Henry Veil Memoirs
William Henry Walling Papers
Samuel Waters Diary
Francis E. Wheaton Letter

Civil War Times Illustrated Collection
John E. Armstrong Reminiscence
John Henry Burrill Letters
Charles E. Gardner Papers
Henry Gerrish Memoirs
Jacob Heffelfinger Diary
Charles C. Perkins Papers
Jonathan P. Stowe Papers
Silas D. Wesson Papers

Harrisburg Civil War Roundtable Collection
Benjamin F. Ashenfelter Papers
John I. and Leo W. Faller Correspondence
Henry Flick Memoir
Luther C. Furst Papers
Lewis Leigh Collection
Benjamin Roher Papers

Pardee-Robison Collection
Ario Pardee Jr. Letters
Calvin Pardee Letters
Bell Robison Letters
Jane Robison Letters

Pennsylvania "Save the Flags" Civil War Collection
Bates Alexander Memoirs
Charles Becker Papers
Andrew J. Elliott Diaries
Thomas Goldsborough Letters
Thomas F. McCoy Papers
Adoniram J. Warner Memoir

Murray J. Smith Collection
Walter A. Eames Papers

Wiley Sword Collection
Thomas H. Benton Letters
Fletcher Webster Letters

Michael Winey Collection
Anonymous Letter, August 18, 1862

Cadbury Library, University of Birmingham, Birmingham, UK

Church Missionary Society Archive

Bancroft Library, University of California, Berkeley

Frémont Family Papers

Charles E. Young Research Library, University of California, Los Angeles

William Starke Rosecrans Papers

Bentley Historical Library, University of Michigan, Ann Arbor

Michigan Historical Collections

William L. Clements Library, University of Michigan, Ann Arbor

Birney Family Papers
James S. Schoff Civil War Collection
Weld-Grimké Family Papers

Southern Historical Collection, Louis Wilson Library, University of North Carolina, Chapel Hill

Elias Brady Papers
Burgwyn Family Papers
Gale and Polk Family Papers
D. H. Hill Papers
John Bailey Lancaster Papers
LeConte and Furman Family Papers
William Nelson Pendleton Papers
Leonidas Polk Papers
Margaret Junkin Preston Papers
Stephen Dodson Ramseur Papers
Webb Family Papers

South Caroliniana Library, University of South Carolina, Columbia

Mary Boykin Chesnut Journal

Albert and Shirley Small Special Collections Library, University of Virginia, Charlottesville

Lawrence O'Bryan Branch Papers
John Eston Cooke Papers
Dabney Family Papers
Emerson Family Papers
Julia Ward Howe Papers
Student and Alumni Papers
Charles Tenney Letters
Virginia Political Correspondence
Joseph Waddell Diary
George William White Papers
Beverly K. Whittle Papers

Virginia Museum of History and Culture, Richmond

James D. Albright Diary
Aylett Family Papers
Charles Edward Bates Papers
Bird Family Papers
Brannock Letters
J. Thompson Brown Papers

Cooke Family Papers
Giles Buckner Cooke Papers
Dabney Family Papers
Paul M. Higginbotham Papers
Keith Family Papers
Richard Lancelot Maury Diary
Meade Family Papers
Pegram-McIntosh-Johnson Papers

Special Collections, James G. Leyburn Library, Washington and Lee University, Lexington, VA

James K. Edmondson Correspondence, Rockbridge Historical Society Manuscripts
Daniel Harvey Hill Papers
David Lawrence Hopkins Papers
John Newton Lyle, "Stonewall Jackson's Guard, the Washington College Company"
Cornelia Peake McDonald Diary
Francis McFarland Papers
Elisha Frank Paxton Papers
Rose Page Pendleton Journal
J. D. H. Ross Papers
Jane Isabella Watt White Papers

Wisconsin Historical Society, Madison

George Hyer Brayton Diary

PRIMARY SOURCES—PUBLISHED

Adams, John Ripley. *Memorial and Letters of John R. Adams, D.D.* Cambridge: Cambridge University Press, 1890.

Agassiz, George, ed. *Meade's Headquarters, 1863–1865: Letters of Colonel Theodore Lyman from the Wilderness to Appomattox.* Boston: Atlantic Monthly Press, 1922.

Alexander, Edward Porter. *Military Memoirs of a Confederate: A Critical Narrative.* New York: Charles Scribner's Sons, 1907.

Allan, Elizabeth Preston. *The Life and Letters of Margaret Junkin Preston.* Boston: Houghton Mifflin, 1903.

Ames, William Dallam, ed. *The Autobiography of Joseph LeConte.* New York: D. Appleton, 1903.

Auer, J. Jeffrey, ed. *Antislavery and Disunion, 1858–1861: Studies in the Rhetoric of Compromise and Conflict.* New York: Harper & Row, 1963.

Basler, Roy W., ed. *The Collected Works of Abraham Lincoln.* 9 vols. New Brunswick, NJ: Rutgers University Press, 1953.

Beatty, John. *The Citizen-Soldier; or, Memoirs of a Volunteer.* Cincinnati: Wilstach, Baldwin, 1879.

Beecher, Henry Ward. *Fast Day Sermons; or, The Pulpit on the State of the Country.* New York: Rudd & Carleton, 1861.

———. *Patriotic Addresses in America and England, 1855–1886.* Edited by John R. Howard. Boston: Pilgrim, 1887.

Beecher, Lyman. *A Plea for the West,* 2nd ed. Cincinnati: Truman & Smith, 1835.

Bernard, George S., comp. and ed. *War Talks of Confederate Veterans.* Petersburg, VA: Fenn & Owen, 1892.

Birchfield, Steven A., ed. *Civil War Letters.* N.p., n.d.

Blair, William Alan, ed. *A Politician Goes to War: The Civil War Letters of John White Geary.* University Park: Pennsylvania State University Press, 1995.

Brock, Peter, ed. *Liberty and Conscience: A Documentary History of the Experiences of Conscientious Objectors in American through the Civil War.* New York: Oxford University Press, 2002.

Brock, Sarah Ann. *Richmond during the War: Four Years of Personal Observation by a Richmond Lady.* New York: G. W. Carleton, 1867.

Brockenbrough, Frances Blake. *A Mother's Parting Words to Her Soldier Boy.* Petersburg, VA: Soldiers' Tract Society, 1862.

Browne, J. Ross. *Adventures in the Apache Country: A Tour Through Arizona and Sonora, with Notes on the Silver Regions of Nevada.* New York: Harper & Brothers, 1869.

Brownlow, William G. *Sketches of the Rise, Progress, and Decline of Secession; with a Narrative of Personal Adventures among the Rebels.* Philadelphia: George W. Childs, 1862.

Burr, Virginia Ingraham, ed. *The Secret Eye: The Journal of Ella Gertrude Clanton Thomas, 1848–1889.* Chapel Hill: University of North Carolina Press, 1990.

Burritt, Elihu. *Peace Papers for the People.* London: Charles Gilpin, 1851.

Burrows, J. L. *Shiloh: A Sermon.* N.p., ca. 1862.

Butler, Benjamin F. *Autobiography and Personal Reminiscences of Major-General Benjamin F. Butler.* Boston: A. M. Thayer, 1892.

Carpenter, F. B. *Six Months at the White House with Abraham Lincoln.* New York: Hurd and Houghton, 1866.

Cate, Wirt A., ed. *Two Soldiers: The Campaign Diaries of Thomas J. Key C.S.A. and Robert J. Campbell U.S.A.* Chapel Hill: University of North Carolina Press, 1938.

Cherry, Conrad, ed. *God's New Israel: Religious Interpretations of American Destiny.* Rev. ed. Chapel Hill: University of North Carolina Press, 1998.

Chesebrough, David B., ed. *"God Ordained This War": Sermons on the Sectional Crisis, 1830–1865.* Columbia: University of South Carolina Press, 1991.

Conyngham, David P. *Sherman's March through the South.* New York: Sheldon, 1865.

Crabtree, Beth, and James Patton, eds. *Journal of a Secesh Lady: The Diary of Catherine Ann Devereux Edmondston, 1860–1866.* Raleigh: North Carolina Department of Archives and History, 1979.

Crawford, Samuel Wylie. *The Genesis of the Civil War: The Story of Sumter, 1860–1861.* New York: Charles L. Webster, 1887.

Crummell, Alexander. *The Future of Africa: Being Addresses, Sermons, Etc., Etc., Delivered in the Republic of Liberia.* New York: Charles Scribner, 1862.

Curran, Robert Emmett, ed. *John Dooley's Civil War: An Irish American's Journey in the First Virginia Infantry Regiment.* Knoxville: University of Tennessee Press, 2012.

Cutrer, Thomas W., and T. Michael Parrish, eds. *Brothers in Gray: The Civil War Letters of the Pierson Family.* Baton Rouge: Louisiana State University Press, 1997.

Dabney, Robert L. *A Defence of Virginia, in Recent and Pending Contests Against the Sectional Party.* New York: E. J. Hale, 1867.

Darby, John Nelson. *The Letters of John Nelson Darby.* 3 vols. 2nd ed. London, n.d.

Dawes, Rufus R. *Service with the Sixth Wisconsin Volunteers.* Marietta, OH: E. R. Alderman & Sons, 1890.

Dicey, Edward. *Spectator of America.* Edited by Herbert Mitgang. Chicago: Quadrangle Books, 1971. First published 1863 as *Six Months in the Federal States*, 2 vols., by Macmillan (London).

Doubleday, Abner. *Reminiscences of Forts Sumter and Moultrie in 1860–'61.* New York: Harper & Brothers, 1876.

Duncan, Russell, ed. *Blue-Eyed Child of Fortune: The Civil War Letters of Colonel Robert Gould Shaw.* Athens: University of Georgia Press, 1992.

Eby, Cecil D., Jr., ed. *A Virginia Yankee in the Civil War: The Diaries of David Hunter Strother.* Chapel Hill: University of North Carolina Press, 1961.

Elliott, Sam Davis, ed. *Doctor Quintard, Chaplain C.S.A. and Second Bishop of Tennessee: The Memoir and Civil War Diary of Charles Todd Quintard.* Baton Rouge: Louisiana State University Press, 2003.

Emerson, Edward W, ed. *Life and Letters of Charles Russell Lowell.* Port Washington, NY: Kennikat, 1971.

Everett, Donald E., ed. *Chaplain Davis and Hood's Texas Brigade: Being an Expanded Edition of the Reverend Nicholas A. Davis's* The Campaign from Texas to Maryland, with The Battle of Fredericksburg. Baton Rouge: Louisiana State University Press, 1999. Davis, *Campaign from Texas to Maryland,* originally published 1863 by Office of the Presbyterian Committee of Publication of the Confederate States (Richmond).

Fast Day Sermons; or, The Pulpit on the State of the Country. New York: Rudd & Carleton, 1861.

Foner, Philip S., and George E. Walker, eds. *Proceedings of the Black National and State Conventions.* 2 vols. Philadelphia: Temple University Press, 1979–80.

Gaff, Alan D., and Donald H. Gaff, eds. *A Corporal's Story: Civil War Recollections of the Twelfth Massachusetts.* Norman: University of Oklahoma Press, 2014.

Galvin, William Gilfillan, ed. *Infantryman Pettit: The Civil War Letters of Corporal Frederick Pettit*. New York: Avon Books, 1991.

Gordon, John B. *Reminiscences of the Civil War*. New York: Charles Scribner's Sons, 1903.

Graf, LeRoy P., and Ralph W. Haskins, eds. *The Papers of Andrew Johnson*. 16 vols. Knoxville: University of Tennessee Press, 1967–2000.

Grimsley, Mark, and Todd D. Miller, eds. *The Union Must Stand: The Civil War Diary of John Quincy Adams Campbell, Fifth Iowa Volunteer Infantry*. Knoxville: University of Tennessee Press, 2000.

Gwin, Minrose C., ed. *A Woman's Civil War: A Diary, with Reminiscences of the War, from March 1862*. Madison: University of Wisconsin Press, 1992.

Hammond, Harold Earl, ed. *Diary of a Union Lady, 1861–1865*. Lincoln: University of Nebraska Press, 2000.

Hassler, William W., ed. *One of Lee's Best Men: The Civil War Letters of General William Dorsey Pender*. Chapel Hill: University of North Carolina Press, 1999.

Hay, Clara S., comp. *Letters of John Hay and Extracts from Diary*. 3 vols. Washington, DC, 1908.

Helper, Hinton Rowan. *The Impending Crisis of the South: How to Meet It*. New York: Burdick Brothers, 1857.

Hight, John J. *History of the Fifty-Eighth Regiment of Indiana Volunteer Infantry*. Princeton, IN: Press of the Clarion, 1895.

Hill, Daniel Harvey. *A Consideration of the Sermon on the Mount*. Philadelphia: William S. and Alfred Martien, 1858.

Holmes, Mead, Jr. *A Soldier of the Cumberland*. Boston: American Tract Society, 1864.

Howard, Oliver Otis. *Autobiography of Oliver Otis Howard: Major General, United States Army*. 2 vols. New York: Baker & Taylor, 1907.

Howe, Julia Ward. "The Battle Hymn of the Republic." *Atlantic Monthly* 9:52 (February 1862).

———. *Reminiscences, 1819–1899*. Boston: Houghton Mifflin, 1900.

Hughes, Nathaniel Cheairs, Jr., and Timothy Johnson, eds. *A Fighter from Way Back: The Mexican War Diary of Lt. Daniel Harvey Hill*. Kent, OH: Kent State University Press, 2002.

Jackson, Mary Anna. *Life and Letters of General Thomas J. Jackson*. New York: Harper & Brothers, 1892.

Johnson, Robert Underwood, and Clarence Clough Buel, eds. *Battles and Leaders of the Civil War: Being for the Most Part Contributions by Union and Confederate Officers*. 4 vols. New York: Century, 1884–88.

Jones, J. B. *A Rebel War Clerk's Diary at the Confederate States Capital*. 2 vols. Philadelphia: J. B. Lippincott, 1866.

Keckley, Elizabeth. *Behind the Scenes; or, Thirty Years a Slave, and Four Years in the White House*. New York: G. W. Carleton, 1868.

Keifer, Joseph Warren. *Slavery and Four Years of War: A Political History of Slavery in the United States Together with a Narrative of the Campaigns and Battles of the Civil War in which the Author Took Part, 1861–1865.* 2 vols. New York: Putnam, 1900.

Kellogg, Mary E., comp. *Army Life of an Illinois Soldier.* Carbondale: Southern Illinois University Press, 1996.

Kelso, John R. *Bloody Engagements: John R. Kelso's Civil War.* Edited by Christopher Grasso. New Haven, CT: Yale University Press, 2017.

Kohl, Lawrence Frederick, ed. *Irish Green and Union Blue: The Civil War Letters of Peter Welsh, Color Sergeant.* New York: Fordham University Press, 1986.

LeConte, Joseph. *'Ware Sherman: A Journal of Three Months' Personal Experience in the Last Days of the Confederacy.* Baton Rouge: Louisiana State University Press, 1999.

Lee, Robert E., Jr. *Recollections and Letters of General Robert E. Lee.* New York: Doubleday, Page, 1904.

Lee, Susan P., ed. *Memoirs of William Nelson Pendleton, D.D.* Philadelphia: Lippincott, 1893.

Levine, Robert S., ed. *Martin R. Delany: A Documentary Reader.* Chapel Hill: University of North Carolina Press, 2003.

Looby, Christopher, ed. *The Complete Journal and Selected Letters of Thomas Wentworth Higginson.* Chicago: University of Chicago Press, 2000.

Mahon, Michael G., ed. *Winchester Divided: The Civil War Diaries of Julia Chase and Laura Lee.* Mechanicsburg, PA: Stackpole Books, 2002.

Marshall, Jeffrey D., ed. *A War of the People: Vermont Civil War Letters.* Hanover, NH: University Press of New England, 1999.

Marszalek, John, ed. *The Diary of Miss Emma Holmes, 1861–1866.* Baton Rouge: Louisiana State University Press, 1979.

McCardle, Linda S., ed. *A Just and Holy Cause? The Civil War Letters of Marcus Bethune Ely and Martha Frances Ely.* Mercer, GA: Mercer University Press, 2016.

McCaslin, Richard B., ed. *A Soldier's Letters to Charming Nellie: The Correspondence of Joseph B. Polley, Hood's Texas Brigade.* Knoxville: University of Tennessee Press, 2007.

McDonnald, B. W. *Address to Chaplains and Missionaries.* Petersburg, VA: n.p., 1863.

Messent, Peter, and Steve Courtney, eds. *The Civil War Letters of Joseph Hopkins Twichell: A Chaplain's Story.* Athens: University of Georgia Press, 2006.

Minnigerode, Charles. *"He That Believeth Shall Not Make Haste": A Sermon Preached on the First of January, 1865, in St. Paul's Church, Richmond.* Richmond: Charles H. Wynne, 1865.

Miers, Earl Schenck, ed. *When the World Ended: The Diary of Emma LeConte.* New York: Oxford University Press, 1957.

Moore, Frank. *Anecdotes, Poetry and Incidents of the War: North and South, 1860–1865.* New York: Publication Office, Bible House, 1867.

Paulus, Margaret B., comp. *Papers of General Robert Huston Milroy.* 4 vols. N.p., 1965.

Peabody, Elizabeth. *Chronological History of the United States, Arranged with Plates on Bem's Principle.* New York: Sheldon, Blakeman, 1856.

Pierce, Edward L., ed. *Memoir and Letters of Charles Sumner*, 4 vols. Boston: Roberts Brothers, 1877–93.

Preston, Margaret J. *Beechenbrook: A Rhyme of the War*. Richmond: J. W. Randolph, 1865.

———. *War Lyrics and Songs of the South*. London: Spottiswoode, 1866.

Ramsey, James B. *True Eminence Founded on Holiness: A Discourse Occasioned by the Death of Lieut. Gen. T. J. Jackson*. Lynchburg: Virginian "Water-Power Presses," 1863.

Renfroe, John J. D. *The Battle Is God's: A Sermon Preached before Wilcox's Brigade, Fast Day, the 21st August 1863, near Orange Court-House, Va*. Richmond, VA: MacFarlane & Ferguson, 1863.

Roberts, Timothy Mason, ed. *"This Infernal War": The Civil War Letters of William and Jane Standard*. Kent, OH: Kent State University Press, 2018.

Robertson, James I., Jr, ed. *The Civil War Letters of General Robert McAllister*. New Brunswick, NJ: Rutgers University Press, 1965.

Rosenblatt, Emil, and Ruth Rosenblatt, eds. *Hard Marching Every Day: The Civil War Letters of Private Wilbur Fisk, 1861–1865*. Lawrence: University Press of Kansas, 1992.

Roth, Margaret B., ed. *Well Mary: Civil War Letters of a Wisconsin Volunteer*. Madison: University of Wisconsin Press, 1969.

Ruffin, Edmund. *Anticipations of the Future, to Serve as Lessons for the Present Time*. Richmond: J. W. Randolph, 1860.

Samito, Christian G., ed. *"Fear Was Not in Him": The Civil War Letters of General Francis C. Barlow*. New York: Fordham University Press, 2004.

Sears, Stephen W., ed. *The Civil War Papers of George B. McClellan: Selected Correspondence, 1860–1865*. New York: Ticknor & Fields, 1989.

———, ed. *On Campaign with the Army of the Potomac: The Civil War Journal of Theodore Ayrault Dodge*. New York: Cooper Square, 2001.

Seat, W. H. *The Confederate States of America in Prophecy*. Nashville: Southern Methodist Publishing, 1861.

Shaw, John, ed. *Crete and James: Personal Letters of Lucretia and James Garfield*. East Lansing: Michigan State University Press, 1994.

Sherman, William T. *Memoirs of General W. T. Sherman*. New York: Library of America, 1990.

Simms, William Gilmore. *A City Laid Waste: The Capture, Sack, and Destruction of the City of Columbia*. Edited by David Aiken. Columbia: University of South Carolina Press, 2005.

Smith, Barbara A., ed. *The Civil War Letters of Col. Elijah H. C. Cavins, 14th Indiana*. Owensboro, KY: Cook-McDowell, 1981.

Stanton, R. L. *The Church and the Rebellion: A Consideration of the Rebellion against the Government of the United States; and the Agency of the Church, North and South, in Relation Thereto*. New York: Derby and Miller, 1864.

Stewart, William H. *The Spirit of the South: Orations, Essays, and Lectures*. New York: Neale, 1908.

Stiles, Joseph C. *Modern Reform Examined; or, The Union of North and South on the Subject of Slavery*. Philadelphia: J. B. Lippincott, 1857.

———. *National Rectitude the Only True Basis of National Prosperity: An Appeal to the Confederate States*. Petersburg, VA: Evangelical Tract Society, 1863.

Summers, Festus P., ed. *A Borderland Confederate*. Pittsburgh: University of Pittsburgh Press, 1962.

Swint, Henry L., ed. *Dear Ones at Home: Letters from Contraband Camps*. Nashville, TN: Vanderbilt University Press, 1966.

Taylor, William. *Cause and Probable Results of the Civil War in America: Facts for the People of Great Britain*. London: Warren Hall, 1862.

Thornwell, James Henley. *The State of the Country: An Article Republished from the Southern Presbyterian Review*. Jackson, MS: E. Barksdale, 1861.

Toney, Marcus B. *The Privations of a Private: Campaigning with the First Tennessee, C.S.A., and Life Thereafter*. Tuscaloosa: University of Alabama Press, 2005.

Tucker, John Randolph. *The Southern Church Justified in its Support of the South in the Present War: A Lecture, Delivered before the Young Men's Christian Association, of Richmond, on the 21st May, 1863*. Richmond: William H. Clemmitt, 1863.

US War Department. *The War of the Rebellion: A Compilation of the Official Records of the Union and Confederate Armies*. 129 vols. Washington, DC: Government Printing Office, 1880–1901.

Wakelyn, Jon L., ed. *Southern Unionist Pamphlets and the Civil War*. Columbia: University of Missouri Press, 1999.

Washington, Margaret, ed. *Narrative of Sojourner Truth*. New York: Vintage, 1994.

Weaver, C. P., ed. *Thank God My Regiment an African One: The Civil War Diary of Colonel Nathan W. Daniels*. Baton Rouge: Louisiana State University Press, 1998.

Weiner, Marli F., ed. *Heritage of Woe: The Civil War Diary of Grace Brown Elmore, 1861–1868*. Athens: University of Georgia Press, 1997.

Whitman, Walt. *Specimen Days in America*. London: Walter Scott, 1887.

Wilberforce, Samuel. *A History of the Protestant Episcopal Church in America*. London: James Burns, 1844.

Williams, Edward B., ed. *Rebel Brothers: The Civil War Letters of the Truehearts*. College Station: Texas A&M University Press, 1995.

Winther, Oscar Osburn, ed. *With Sherman to the Sea: The Civil War Letters, Diaries, and Reminiscences of Theodore F. Upson*. Bloomington: Indiana University Press, 1958.

Wise, John S. *The End of an Era*. Boston: Houghton Mifflin, 1901.

Woodward, C. Vann, ed. *Mary Chesnut's Civil War*. New Haven, CT: Yale University Press, 1981.

Yacovone, Donald, ed. *A Voice of Thunder: The Civil War Letters of George E. Stephens*. Urbana: University of Illinois Press, 1997.

Aamodt, Terrie Dopp. *Righteous Armies, Holy Cause: Apocalyptic Imagery and the Civil War.* Mercer, GA: Mercer University Press, 2002.

Abbott, Richard H. *The Republican Party and the South, 1855–1877: The First Southern Strategy.* Chapel Hill: University of North Carolina Press, 1986.

Abruzzo, Margaret. *Polemical Pain: Slavery, Cruelty and the Rise of Humanitarianism.* Baltimore: Johns Hopkins University Press, 2011.

Adams, Michael C. C. *Living Hell: The Dark Side of the Civil War.* Cambridge, MA: Harvard University Press, 2014.

———. *Our Masters the Rebels: A Speculation on Union Military Failure in the East, 1861–1865.* Cambridge, MA: Harvard University Press, 1978.

Ahlstrom, Sydney E. *A Religious History of the American People.* 2nd ed. New Haven, CT: Yale University Press, 2004.

Aho, James Alfred. *Religious Mythology and the Art of War: Comparative Religious Symbolisms of Military Violence.* Westport, CT: Greenwood, 1981.

Akenson, Donald Harman. *Exporting the Rapture: John Nelson Darby and the Victorian Conquest of North American Evangelicalism.* New York: Oxford University Press, 2018.

Allmendinger, David F., Jr. *Ruffin: Family and Reform in the Old South.* New York: Oxford University Press, 1989.

Ambrose, Stephen E. *Upton and the Army.* Baton Rouge: Louisiana State University Press, 1964.

Anbinder, Tyler G. *Nativism and Slavery: The Northern Know Nothings and the Politics of the 1850s.* New York: Oxford University Press, 1992.

Andrew, Rod, Jr. *Long Gray Lines: The Southern Military School Tradition, 1839–1915.* Chapel Hill: University of North Carolina Press, 2001.

———. *Wade Hampton: Confederate Warrior to Southern Redeemer.* Chapel Hill: University of North Carolina Press, 2008.

Applegate, Debby. *The Most Famous Man in America: The Biography of Henry Ward Beecher.* New York: Doubleday, 2006.

Arielli, Nir. *From Byron to bin Laden: A History of Foreign War Volunteers.* Cambridge, MA: Harvard University Press, 2018.

Armitage, David. *Civil Wars: A History in Ideas.* New York: Knopf, 2017.

Armstrong, Warren B. *For Courageous Fighting and Confident Dying: Union Chaplains in the Civil War.* Lawrence: University Press of Kansas, 1998.

Armstrong, William H. *A Friend to God's Poor: Edward Parmelee Smith.* Athens: University of Georgia Press, 1993.

———. *Major McKinley: William McKinley and the Civil War.* Kent, OH: Kent State University Press, 2000.

———. *Warrior in Two Camps: Ely S. Parker, Union General and Seneca Chief.* Syracuse, NY: Syracuse University Press, 1978.

Army, Thomas F., Jr. *Engineering Victory: How Technology Won the Civil War*. Baltimore: Johns Hopkins University Press, 2016.

Ash, Stephen V. *Middle Tennessee Society Transformed, 1860–1870: War and Peace in the Upper South*. Baton Rouge: Louisiana State University Press, 1988.

———. *Rebel Richmond: Life and Death in the Confederate Capital*. Chapel Hill: University of North Carolina Press, 2019.

———. *When the Yankees Came: Conflict and Chaos in the Occupied South, 1861–1865*. Chapel Hill: University of North Carolina Press, 1995.

Astor, Aaron. *Rebels on the Border: Civil War, Emancipation, and the Reconstruction of Kentucky and Missouri*. Baton Rouge: Louisiana State University Press, 2015.

Atchison, Ray M. "The Land We Love: A Southern Post-Bellum Magazine of Agricultural, Literary, and Military History." *North Carolina Historical Review* 37 (October 1960): 506–15.

Ayers, Edward L. *In the Presence of Mine Enemies: The Civil War in the Heart of America, 1859–1864*. New York: W. W. Norton, 2003.

———. *The Thin Light of Freedom: The Civil War and Emancipation in the Heart of America*. New York: W. W. Norton, 2017.

Bailey, David T. *Shadow on the Church: Southwestern Evangelical Religion and the Issue of Slavery, 1783–1860*. Ithaca, NY: Cornell University Press, 1985.

Baker, Jean H. *Affairs of Party: The Political Culture of Northern Democrats in the Mid-Nineteenth Century*. Ithaca, NY: Cornell University Press, 1983.

———. *Mary Todd Lincoln: A Biography*. New York: W. W. Norton, 1987.

Balmer, Randall, and Lauren F. Winner. *Protestantism in America*. New York: Columbia University Press, 2002.

Barefoot, Daniel W. *General Robert F. Hoke: Lee's Modest Warrior*. Winston-Salem, NC: John F. Blair, 1996.

Barkun, Michael. *Crucible of the Millennium: The Burned-Over District of New York in the 1840s*. Syracuse, NY: Syracuse University Press, 1986.

Barney, William L. *The Making of a Confederate: Walter Lenoir's Civil War*. New York: Oxford University Press, 2007.

Barrett, John G. *The Civil War in North Carolina*. Chapel Hill: University of North Carolina Press, 1963.

Bartholomees, J. Boone, Jr. *Buff Facings and Gilt Buttons: Staff and Headquarters Operations in the Army of Northern Virginia, 1861–1865*. Columbia: University of South Carolina Press, 1998.

Barton, Michael L., and Larry M. Logue, eds. *The Civil War Soldier: A Historical Reader*. New York: New York University Press, 2002.

Baxter, Nancy Niblack. *Gallant Fourteenth: The Story of an Indiana Civil War Regiment*. 2nd ed. Indianapolis: Guild Press of Indiana, 1991.

Bay, Mia. *The White Image in the Black Mind: African-American Ideas about White People, 1830–1925*. New York: Oxford University Press, 2000.

Baym, Nina. "The Ann Sisters: Elizabeth Peabody's Millennial Historicism." *American Literary History* 3:1 (Spring 1991): 29–30.

Bean, W. G. *The Liberty Hall Volunteers: Stonewall's College Boys*. Charlottesville: University Press of Virginia, 1964.

———. *Stonewall's Man: Sandie Pendleton*. Chapel Hill: University of North Carolina Press, 1959.

Beilein, Joseph M. *Bushwhackers: Guerrilla Warfare, Manhood, and the Household in Civil War Missouri*. Kent, OH: Kent State University Press, 2016.

Bellows, Barbara. *Two Charlestonians at War: The Civil War Odysseys of a Lowcountry Aristocrat and a Black Abolitionist*. Baton Rouge: Louisiana State University Press, 2018.

Bergeron, Paul H. *Andrew Johnson's Civil War and Reconstruction*. Knoxville: University of Tennessee Press, 2011.

Beringer, Richard E., Herman Hattaway, Archer Jones, and William N. Still Jr. *Why the South Lost the Civil War*. Athens: University of Georgia Press, 1986.

Berkin, Carol. *Civil War Wives: The Lives and Times of Angelina Grimke Weld, Varina Howell Davis, and Julia Dent Grant*. New York: Alfred A. Knopf, 2009.

Berlin, Ira. *Many Thousands Gone: The First Two Centuries of Slavery in North America*. Cambridge, MA: Belknap Press of Harvard University Press, 1998.

Bernath, Michael T. *Confederate Minds: The Struggle for Intellectual Independence in the Civil War South*. Chapel Hill: University of North Carolina Press, 2010.

Berry, Stephen W., II. *All That Makes a Man: Love and Ambition in the Civil War South*. New York: Oxford University Press, 2003.

Bertelson, David. *The Lazy South*. New York: Oxford University Press, 1967.

Best, Geoffrey. *Humanity in Warfare*. New York: Columbia University Press, 1980.

Binnington, Ian. *Confederate Visions: Nationalism, Symbolism, and the Imagined South in the Civil War*. Charlottesville: University of Virginia Press, 2013.

Blackett, R. J. M. *The Captive's Quest for Freedom: Fugitive Slaves, the 1850 Fugitive Slave Law, and the Politics of Slavery*. New York: Cambridge University Press, 2018.

Blair, William A. *With Malice toward Some: Treason and Loyalty in the Civil War Era*. Chapel Hill: University of North Carolina Press, 2014.

Bledsoe, Andrew S. *Citizen-Officers: The Union and Confederate Volunteer Junior Officer Corps in the American Civil War*. Baton Rouge: Louisiana State University Press, 2015.

Bledsoe, Andrew S., and Andrew F. Lang, eds. *Upon the Fields of Battle: Essays on the Military History of America's Civil War*. Baton Rouge: Louisiana State University Press, 2018.

Blight, David W. *Frederick Douglass: Prophet of Freedom*. New York: Simon & Schuster, 2018.

———. *Frederick Douglass' Civil War: Keeping Faith in Jubilee*. Rev. ed. Baton Rouge: Louisiana State University Press, 1991.

———. *Race and Reunion: The Civil War in American Memory.* Cambridge, MA: Belknap Press of Harvard University Press, 2001.

Blin, Arnaud. *War and Religion: Europe and the Mediterranean from the First through the Twenty-First Centuries.* Berkeley: University of California Press, 2019.

Blum, Edward J. "'The First Secessionist Was Satan': Secession and the Politics of Hell in Civil War America." *Civil War History* 90:3 (September 2014): 234–69.

———. *Reforging the White Republic: Race, Religion, and American Nationalism, 1865–1898.* Baton Rouge: Louisiana State University Press, 2005.

Blum, Edward J., and W. Scott Poole, eds. *Vale of Tears: New Essays on Religion and Reconstruction.* Macon: Mercer University Press, 2005.

Blum, John Morton. *The Republican Roosevelt.* 2nd ed. Cambridge, MA: Harvard University Press, 1977.

Blyden, Nemata Amelia Ibitayo. *African Americans and Africa: A New History.* New Haven, CT: Yale University Press, 2019.

Bobrick, Benson. *Master of War: The Life of General George H. Thomas.* New York: Simon & Schuster, 2009.

Bogue, Allan G. *The Congressman's Civil War.* New York: Cambridge University Press, 1989.

———. *The Earnest Men: Republicans of the Civil War Senate.* Ithaca, NY: Cornell University Press, 1981.

Boman, Dennis K. *Lincoln and Citizens' Rights in Civil War Missouri: Balancing Freedom and Security.* Baton Rouge: Louisiana State University Press, 2011.

Bonan, Gordon B. *The Edge of Mosby's Sword: The Life of Confederate Colonel William Henry Chapman.* Carbondale: Southern Illinois University Press, 2009.

Bonner, Robert E. *Colors and Blood: Flag Passions of the Confederate South.* Princeton, NJ: Princeton University Press, 2002.

———. *Mastering America: Southern Slaveholders and the Crisis of American Nationhood.* New York: Cambridge University Press, 2009.

Boritt, Gabor S., ed. *Jefferson Davis's Generals.* New York: Oxford University Press, 1999.

———, ed. *Lincoln, the War President: The Gettysburg Lectures.* New York: Oxford University Press, 1992.

———, ed. *Lincoln's Generals.* New York: Oxford University Press, 1994.

———, ed. *Why the Confederacy Lost.* New York: Oxford University Press, 1992.

Boudrye, Louis N. *Historic Records of the Fifth New York Cavalry, First Ira Harris Guard.* Albany, NY: S. R. Gray, 1865.

Bowman, Matthew. *Christian: The Politics of a Word in America.* Cambridge, MA: Harvard University Press, 2018.

Boyer, Paul. *When Time Shall Be No More: Prophecy Belief in Modern American Culture.* Cambridge, MA: Belknap Press of Harvard University Press, 1992.

Boylan, Anne M. *Sunday School: The Formation of an American Institution, 1790–1880.* New Haven, CT: Yale University Press, 1988.

Bradley, George C., and Richard L. Dahlen. *From Conciliation to Conquest: The Sack of Athens and the Court-Martial of Colonel John B. Turchin*. Tuscaloosa: University of Alabama Press, 2006.

Brady, Lisa M. *War upon the Land: Military Strategy and the Transformation of Southern Landscapes during the American Civil War*. Athens: University of Georgia Press, 2012.

Brandt, Dennis W. *Pathway to Hell: A Tragedy of the American Civil War*. Bethlehem, PA: Lehigh University Press, 2008.

Brasher, Glenn David. *The Peninsula Campaign and the Necessity of Emancipation: African Americans and the Fight for Freedom*. Chapel Hill: University of North Carolina Press, 2012.

Breen, Patrick H. *The Land Shall Be Deluged in Blood: A New History of the Nat Turner Revolt*. New York: Oxford University Press, 2015.

Brekus, Catherine A., and W. Clark Gilpin, eds. *American Christianities: A History of Dominance and Diversity*. Chapel Hill: University of North Carolina Press, 2011.

Bridges, Hal. *Lee's Maverick General: Daniel Harvey Hill*. New York: McGraw-Hill, 1961.

Brinsfield, John W., Jr. *Summon Only the Brave! Commanders, Soldiers, and Chaplains at Gettysburg*. Macon, GA: Mercer University Press, 2016.

Brodrecht, Grant. *Our Country: Northern Evangelicals and the Union during the Civil War Era*. New York: Fordham University Press, 2018.

Broomall, James J. *Private Confederacies: The Emotional Worlds of Southern Men as Citizens and Soldiers*. Chapel Hill: University of North Carolina Press, 2019.

Brophy, Alfred L. *University, Court, and Slave: Pro-Slavery Thought in Southern Colleges and the Coming of the Civil War*. New York: Oxford University Press, 2016.

Brown, Richard D. *Self-Evident Truths: Contesting Equal Rights from the Revolution to the Civil War*. New Haven, CT: Yale University Press, 2017.

Brown, Russell K. *To the Manner Born: The Life of General William H. T. Walker*. Athens: University of Georgia Press, 1994.

Brown, Thomas J. *Civil War Monuments and the Militarization of America*. Chapel Hill: University of North Carolina Press, 2019.

Browning, Judkin. *Shifting Loyalties: The Union Occupation of Eastern North Carolina*. Chapel Hill: University of North Carolina Press, 2011.

Bruce, Susannah Ural. *The Harp and the Eagle: Irish-American Volunteers and the Union Army, 1861–1865*. New York: New York University Press, 2006.

Brundage, W. Fitzhugh. *Civilizing Torture: An American Tradition*. Cambridge, MA: Belknap Press of Harvard University Press, 2018.

Bryan, Jimmy L., Jr., ed. *The Martial Imagination: Cultural Aspects of American Warfare*. College Station: Texas A&M University Press, 2013.

Bryant, Edwin Eustace. *History of the Third Regiment of Wisconsin Veteran Volunteer Infantry, 1861–1865*. Madison, WI: Regimental Veterans Association, 1891.

Budiansky, Stephen. *Oliver Wendell Holmes: A Life in War, Law, and Ideas*. New York: W. W. Norton, 2019.

Buell, Thomas B. *The Warrior Generals: Combat Leadership in the Civil War*. New York: Crown, 1997.

Bundy, Carol. *The Nature of Sacrifice: A Biography of Charles Russell Lowell Jr., 1835–64*. New York: Farrar, Straus, and Giroux, 2005.

Burk, Kathleen. *The Lion and the Eagle: The Interaction of the British and American Empires, 1783–1972*. New York: Bloomsbury, 2019.

Burlingame, Michael. *Abraham Lincoln: A Life*. 2 vols. Baltimore: Johns Hopkins University Press, 2008.

Burton, Orville Vernon. *The Age of Lincoln*. New York: Hill and Wang, 2007.

Burton, Orville Vernon, Jerald Podair, and Jennifer Weber, eds. *The Struggle for Equality: Essays on Sectional Conflict, the Civil War, and the Long Reconstruction*. Charlottesville: University of Virginia Press, 2011.

Bushman, Richard L. *From Puritan to Yankee: Character and the Social Order in Connecticut, 1690–1765*. Cambridge, MA: Harvard University Press, 1967.

Calhoon, Robert M. *Evangelicals and Conservatives in the Early South, 1740–1861*. Columbia: University of South Carolina Press, 1988.

Cameron, Christopher. *Black Freethinkers: A History of African American Secularism*. Evanston, IL: Northwestern University Press, 2019.

Campbell, Duncan Andrew. *Unlikely Allies: Britain, America, and the Victorian Origins of the Special Relationship*. New York: Hambledon Continuum, 2007.

Campbell, Jacqueline Glass. *When Sherman Marched North from the Sea: Resistance on the Confederate Home Front*. Chapel Hill: University of North Carolina Press, 2003.

Campbell, James T. *Middle Passages: African American Journeys to Africa, 1787–2005*. New York: Penguin, 2006.

———. *Songs of Zion: The African Methodist Church in the United States and South Africa*. New York: Oxford University Press, 1995.

Carlson, John D., and Jonathan H. Ebel, eds. *From Jeremiad to Jihad: Religion, Violence, and America*. Berkeley: University of California Press, 2012.

Carmichael, Peter S. *The Last Generation: Young Virginians in Peace, War, and Reunion*. Chapel Hill: University of North Carolina Press, 2005.

———. *Lee's Young Artillerist: William R. J. Pegram*. Charlottesville: University Press of Virginia, 1995.

———. *The War for the Common Soldier: How Men Thought, Fought, and Survived in Civil War Armies*. Chapel Hill: University of North Carolina Press, 2018.

Carpenter, John A. *Sword and Olive Branch: Oliver Otis Howard*. Pittsburgh: University of Pittsburgh Press, 1964.

Carwardine, Richard J. *Evangelicals and Politics in Antebellum America*. New Haven, CT: Yale University Press, 1993.

———. *Lincoln*. Harlow, UK: Pearson Longman, 2003.

Case, Jay Riley. *An Unpredictable Gospel: American Evangelicals and World Christianity, 1812–1920*. New York: Oxford University Press, 2012.

Cashin, Joan E. *First Lady of the Confederacy: Varina Davis's Civil War.* Cambridge, MA: Belknap Press of Harvard University Press, 2006.

———. *War Stuff: The Struggle for Human and Environmental Resources in the American Civil War.* New York: Cambridge University Press, 2018.

———, ed. *The War Was You and Me: Civilians in the American Civil War.* Princeton, NJ: Princeton University Press, 2002.

Cathey, M. Todd. *Combat Chaplain: The Life and Civil War Experiences of Rev. James H. McNeilly, Army of Tennessee.* Macon, GA: Mercer University Press, 2017.

Cilella, Salvatore G., Jr. *Upton's Regulars: The 121st New York Infantry in the Civil War.* Lawrence: University Press of Kansas, 2009.

Clampitt, Bradley R. *The Confederate Heartland: Military and Civilian Morale in the Western Confederacy.* Baton Rouge: Louisiana State University Press, 2011.

Clark, J. P. *Preparing for War: The Emergence of the Modern U.S. Army, 1815–1917.* Cambridge, MA: Harvard University Press, 2017.

Cleaves, Freeman. *Meade of Gettysburg.* Norman: University of Oklahoma Press, 1960.

Clinton, Catherine. *Fanny Kemble's Civil Wars.* New York: Simon & Schuster, 2000.

———. *Harriet Tubman: The Road to Freedom.* New York: Little, Brown, 2004.

———. *Stepdaughters of History: Southern Women and the American Civil War.* Baton Rouge: Louisiana State University Press, 2016.

Clinton, Catherine, and Nina Silber, eds. *Battle Scars: Gender and Sexuality in the American Civil War.* New York: Oxford University Press, 2006.

———, eds. *Divided Houses: Gender and the Civil War.* New York: Oxford University Press, 1992.

Cobb, J. Michael, Edward Hicks, and Wythe Holt. *Battle of Big Bethel: Crucial Clash in Early Civil War Virginia.* El Dorado Hills, CA: Savas Beatie, 2013.

Coffey, John. *Exodus and Liberation: Deliverance Politics from John Calvin to Martin Luther King Jr.* New York: Oxford University Press, 2014.

Connelly, Donald B. *John M. Schofield and the Politics of Generalship.* Chapel Hill: University of North Carolina Press, 2006.

Connelly, Thomas Lawrence, and Archer Jones. *The Politics of Command: Factions and Ideas in Confederate Strategy.* Baton Rouge: Louisiana State University Press, 1973.

Conyngham, David Power. *Soldiers of the Cross, the Authoritative Text: The Heroism of Catholic Chaplains in the American Civil War.* Edited by David J. Endres and William B. Kurtz. Notre Dame, IN: University of Notre Dame Press, 2019.

Cook, Robert J. *Civil War Memories: Contesting the Past in the United States since 1865.* Baltimore: Johns Hopkins University Press, 2017.

———. *Civil War Senator: William Pitt Fessenden and the Fight to Save the American Republic.* Baton Rouge: Louisiana State University Press, 2011.

Cooling, Benjamin Franklin. *Forts Henry and Donelson: Key to the Confederate Heartland.* Knoxville: University of Tennessee Press, 1987.

Cooper, John Milton, Jr. *The Warrior and the Priest: Woodrow Wilson and Theodore Roosevelt*. Cambridge, MA: Belknap Press of Harvard University Press, 1983.

Cooper, William J., Jr. *Jefferson Davis, American*. New York: Alfred A. Knopf, 2000.

———. *We Have the War Upon Us: The Onset of the Civil War, November 1860–April 1861*. New York: Alfred A. Knopf, 2012.

Cooper, William J., Jr., and John M. McCardell Jr., eds. *In the Cause of Liberty: How the Civil War Redefined American Ideals*. Baton Rouge: Louisiana State University Press, 2009.

Coulling, Mary Price. *Margaret Junkin Preston: A Biography*. Winston-Salem, NC: John F. Blair, 1993.

Coulter, E. Merton. *William G. Brownlow: Fighting Parson of the Southern Highlands*. Knoxville: University of Tennessee Press, 1999.

Couper, William. *One Hundred Years at V.M.I.* 4 vols. Richmond, VA: Garrett and Massie, 1939.

Cowdrey, Albert E. *This Land, This South: An Environmental History*. Rev. ed. Lexington: University Press of Kentucky, 1996.

Cox, R. David. *The Religious Life of Robert E Lee*. Grand Rapids, MI: Eerdmans, 2017.

Cozzens, Peter. *Shenandoah 1862: Stonewall Jackson's Valley Campaign*. Chapel Hill: University of North Carolina Press, 2008.

Creel, Margaret Washington. *A Peculiar People: Slave Religion and Community-Culture among the Gullahs*. New York: New York University Press, 1988.

Crofts, Daniel W. *Old Southampton: Politics and Society in a Virginia County, 1834–1869*. Charlottesville: University Press of Virginia, 1992.

———. *Reluctant Confederates: Upper South Unionists in the Secession Crisis*. Chapel Hill: University of North Carolina Press, 1989.

Cross, Whitney R. *The Burned-Over District: The Social and Intellectual History of Enthusiastic Religion in Western New York, 1800–1850*. Ithaca, NY: Cornell University Press, 1950.

Crowther, Edward R. *Southern Evangelicals and the Coming of the Civil War*. Lewiston, NY: Edwin Mellen, 2000.

Cutrer, Thomas W. *Theater of a Separate War: The Civil War West of the Mississippi River, 1861–1865*. Chapel Hill: University of North Carolina Press, 2017.

Daly, John Patrick. *When Slavery Was Called Freedom: Evangelicalism, Proslavery, and the Causes of the Civil War*. Lexington: University Press of Kentucky, 2002.

Daniel, Larry J. *Conquered: Why the Army of Tennessee Failed*. Chapel Hill: University of North Carolina Press, 2019.

———. *Days of Glory: The Army of the Cumberland, 1861–1865*. Baton Rouge: Louisiana State University Press, 2004.

———. *Soldiering in the Army of Tennessee: A Portrait of Life in a Confederate Army*. Chapel Hill: University of North Carolina Press, 1991.

Daniel, Larry J., and Lynn N. Bock. *Island No. 10: Struggle for the Mississippi Valley.* Tuscaloosa: University of Alabama Press, 1996.

Daniel, W. Harrison. *Southern Protestantism in the Confederacy.* Bedford, VA: Print Shop, 1989.

Darsey, James. *The Prophetic Tradition and Radical Rhetoric in America.* New York: New York University Press, 1997.

Davis, Archie K. *Boy Colonel of the Confederacy: The Life and Times of Henry King Burgwyn, Jr.* Chapel Hill: University of North Carolina Press, 1985.

Davis, David Brion. *Inhuman Bondage: The Rise and Fall of Slavery in the New World.* New York: Oxford University Press, 2006.

Davis, William C. *Battle at Bull Run: A History of the First Major Campaign of the Civil War.* New York: Doubleday, 1977.

———. *Breckinridge: Statesman, Soldier, Symbol.* Baton Rouge: Louisiana State University Press, 1974.

———. *"A Government of Their Own": The Making of the Confederacy.* New York: Free Press, 1994.

———. *Inventing Loreta Velazquez: Confederate Soldier Impersonator, Media Celebrity, and Con Artist.* Carbondale: Southern Illinois University Press, 2016.

———. *Lincoln's Men: How President Lincoln Became Father to an Army and a Nation.* New York: Simon & Schuster, 1999.

Davis, William C., and James I. Robertson Jr., eds. *Virginia at War, 1861.* Lexington: University Press of Kentucky, 2005.

Dean, Adam Wesley. *An Agrarian Republic: Farming, Antislavery Politics, and Nature Parks in the Civil War Era.* Chapel Hill: University of North Carolina Press, 2015.

Dean, Eric T., Jr. *Shook Over Hell: Post-Traumatic Stress, Vietnam, and the Civil War.* Cambridge, MA: Harvard University Press, 1997.

DeCaro, Louis A., Jr. *"Fire from the Midst of You": A Religious Life of John Brown.* New York: New York University Press, 2002.

Delbanco, Andrew, et al. *The Abolitionist Imagination.* Cambridge, MA: Harvard University Press, 2012.

———. *The War before the War: Fugitive Slaves and the Struggle for America's Soul from the Revolution to the Civil War.* New York: Penguin, 2018.

Dell, Christopher. *Lincoln and the War Democrats: The Grand Erosion of Conservative Tradition.* Rutherford, NJ: Associated Universities Press, 1975.

Desjardin, Thomas A. *Stand Firm Ye Boys from Maine: The 20th Maine and the Gettysburg Campaign.* New York: Oxford University Press, 1995.

Dew, Charles B. *Apostles of Disunion: Southern Secession Commissioners and the Causes of the Civil War.* Charlottesville: University Press of Virginia, 2001.

Diemer, Andrew K. *The Politics of Black Citizenship: Free African Americans in the Mid-Atlantic Borderland, 1817–1863.* Athens: University of Georgia Press, 2016.

Dilbeck, D. H. *Frederick Douglass: America's Prophet*. Chapel Hill: University of North Carolina Press, 2018.

———. *A More Civil War: How the Union Waged a Just War*. Chapel Hill: University of North Carolina Press, 2016.

Dochuk, Darren. *Anointed with Oil: How Christianity and Crude Made Modern America*. New York: Basic Books, 2019.

Dollar, Kent T. *Soldiers of the Cross: Confederate Soldier-Christians and the Impact of War on Their Faith*. Mercer, GA: Mercer University Press, 2005.

Donald, David Herbert. *Charles Sumner and the Coming of the Civil War*. New York: Alfred A. Knopf, 1960.

———. *Lincoln*. New York: Simon & Schuster, 1995.

Dorn, T. Felder. *Challenges on the Emmaus Road: Episcopal Bishops Confront Slavery, Civil War, and Emancipation*. Columbia: University of South Carolina Press, 2013.

Downs, Gregory P. *After Appomattox: Military Occupation and the Ends of War*. Cambridge, MA: Harvard University Press, 2015.

———. *Declarations of Dependence: The Long Reconstruction of Popular Politics in the South, 1861–1908*. Chapel Hill: University of North Carolina Press, 2011.

Doyle, Don H. *The Cause of All Nations: An International History of the American Civil War*. New York: Basic Books, 2017.

Drake, J. Madison. *The History of the Ninth New Jersey Veteran Volunteers: A Record of Its Service from September 13, 1861, to July 12, 1865*. Elizabeth, NJ: Journal Printing House, 1889.

Duberman, Martin. *Charles Francis Adams, 1807–1886*. Boston: Houghton Mifflin, 1961.

Du Bois, W. E. B. *The Souls of Black Folk: Essays and Sketches*. Chicago: A. C. McClurg, 1903.

Duncan, Richard R. *Beleaguered Winchester: A Virginia Community at War, 1861–1865*. Baton Rouge: Louisiana State University Press, 2007.

Dunn, Durwood. *The Civil War in Southern Appalachian Methodism*. Knoxville: University of Tennessee Press, 2013.

Eby, Cecil D., Jr. *"Porte Crayon": The Life of David Hunter Strother*. Chapel Hill: University of North Carolina Press, 1960.

Efford, Alison Clark. *German Immigrants, Race, and Citizenship in the Civil War Era*. New York: Cambridge University Press, 2013.

Egerton, Douglas R. *Thunder at the Gates: The Black Civil War Regiments That Redeemed America*. New York: Basic Books, 2016.

Eichhorn, Niels. *Liberty and Slavery: European Separatists, Southern Secession, and the American Civil War*. Baton Rouge: Louisiana State University Press, 2019.

Elder, Robert. *The Sacred Mirror: Evangelicalism, Honor, and Identity in the Deep South, 1790–1860*. Chapel Hill: University of North Carolina Press, 2016.

Elliott, Mark. *Color-Blind Justice: Albion Tourgee and the Quest for Racial Equality from the Civil War to* Plessy v. Ferguson. New York: Oxford University Press, 2006.

Elliott, Sam Davis. *Isham G. Harris of Tennessee: Confederate Governor and United States Senator.* Baton Rouge: Louisiana State University Press, 2010.

———. *Soldier of Tennessee: General Alexander P. Stewart and the Civil War in the West.* Baton Rouge: Louisiana State University Press, 1999.

Engle, Stephen D. *Don Carlos Buell: Most Promising of All.* Chapel Hill: University of North Carolina Press, 1999.

———. *Gathering to Save a Nation: Lincoln and the Union's War Governors.* Chapel Hill: University of North Carolina Press, 2016.

———. *Yankee Dutchman: The Life of Franz Sigel.* Fayetteville: University of Arkansas Press, 1993.

Engs, Robert F., and Randall M. Miller, eds. *The Birth of the Grand Old Party: The Republicans' First Generation.* Philadelphia: University of Pennsylvania Press, 2002.

Erie, Stephen P. *Rainbow's End: Irish-Americans and the Dilemmas of Urban Machine Politics, 1840–1985.* Berkeley: University of California Press, 1988.

Ernest, John. *Liberation Historiography: African American Writers and the Challenge of History.* Chapel Hill: University of North Carolina Press, 2004.

Escott, Paul D. *After Secession: Jefferson Davis and the Failure of Confederate Nationalism.* Baton Rouge: Louisiana State University Press, 1978.

———. *Lincoln's Dilemma: Blair, Sumner, and the Republican Struggle over Racism and Equality in the Civil War Era.* Charlottesville: University of Virginia Press, 2014.

———. *"What Shall We Do with the Negro?": Lincoln, White Racism, and Civil War America.* Charlottesville: University of Virginia Press, 2009.

Evans, Clement Anselm, ed. *Confederate Military History.* 12 vols. Atlanta: Confederate Publishing, 1899.

Eyal, Yonatan. *The Young America Movement and the Transformation of the Democratic Party, 1828–1861.* New York: Cambridge University Press, 2007.

Fagan, Benjamin. *The Black Newspaper and the Chosen Nation.* Athens: University of Georgia Press, 2016.

Fahs, Alice. *The Imagined Civil War: Popular Literature of the North and South, 1861–1865.* Chapel Hill: University of North Carolina Press, 2001.

Fahs, Alice, and Joan Waugh, eds. *The Memory of the Civil War in American Culture.* Chapel Hill: University of North Carolina Press, 2004.

Farmer, James O., Jr. *The Metaphysical Confederacy: James Henley Thornwell and the Synthesis of Southern Values.* Macon, GA: Mercer University Press, 1986.

Farrelly, Maura Jane. *Anti-Catholicism in America, 1620–1860.* New York: Cambridge University Press, 2018.

Faulkner, Carol. *Lucretia Mott's Heresy: Abolition and Women's Rights in Nineteenth-Century America.* Philadelphia: University of Pennsylvania Press, 2011.

Faust, Drew Gilpin. "Christian Soldiers: The Meaning of Revivalism in the Confederate Army." *Journal of Southern History* 53:1 (February 1987): 63–90.

———. *Mothers of Invention: Women of the Slaveholding South in the American Civil War.* Chapel Hill: University of North Carolina Press, 1996.

———. *This Republic of Suffering: Death and the American Civil War.* New York: Knopf, 2008.

Fellman, Michael. *In the Name of God and Country: Reconsidering Terrorism in American History.* New Haven, CT: Yale University Press, 2010.

Fenton, Elizabeth. *Religious Liberties: Anti-Catholicism and Liberal Democracy in Nineteenth-Century U.S. Literature and Culture.* New York: Oxford University Press, 2011.

Finkelman, Paul, and Donald R. Kennon, eds. *Congress and the People's Contest: The Conduct of the Civil War.* Athens: Ohio University Press, 2018.

Fisher, Noel C. *War at Every Door: Partisan Politics and Guerrilla Violence in East Tennessee, 1860–1869.* Chapel Hill: University of North Carolina Press, 1997.

Fitzgerald, Frances. *The Evangelicals: The Struggle to Shape America.* New York: Simon & Schuster, 2017.

Fitzpatrick, David J. *Emory Upton: Misunderstood Reformer.* Norman: University of Oklahoma Press, 2017.

Fleche, Andre M. *The Revolution of 1861: The American Civil War in the Age of Nationalist Conflict.* Chapel Hill: University of North Carolina Press, 2012.

Fleming, Thomas. *A Disease in the Public Mind: A New Understanding of Why We Fought the Civil War.* New York: Da Capo, 2013.

Foner, Eric. *The Fiery Trial: Abraham Lincoln and American Slavery.* New York: W. W. Norton, 2010.

———. *Free Soil, Free Labor, Free Men: The Ideology of the Republican Party before the Civil War.* New York: New York: Oxford University Press, 1995.

———. *Politics and Ideology in the Age of the Civil War.* New York: Oxford University Press, 1980.

Foote, Lorien. *The Gentlemen and the Roughs: Manhood, Honor, and Violence in the Union Army.* New York: New York University Press, 2010.

———. *Seeking the One Great Remedy: Francis George Shaw and Nineteenth-Century Reform.* Athens: Ohio University Press, 2003.

Foote, Lorien, and Kanisorn Wongsrichanalai, eds. *So Conceived and So Dedicated: Intellectual Life in the Civil War–Era North.* New York: Fordham University Press, 2015.

Ford, Lacy K. *Deliver Us from Evil: The Slavery Question in the Old South.* New York: Oxford University Press, 2009.

Foreman, Amanda. *A World on Fire: Britain's Crucial Role in the American Civil War.* New York: Random House, 2010.

Foster, Gaines M. *Ghosts of the Confederacy: Defeat, the Lost Cause, and the Emergence of the New South, 1865–1913.* New York: Oxford University Press, 1987.

Fountain, Daniel L. *Slavery, Civil War, and Salvation: African American Slaves and Christianity, 1830–1870.* Baton Rouge: Louisiana State University Press, 2010.

Fox-Genovese, Elizabeth, and Eugene D. Genovese. *The Mind of the Master Class: History and Faith in the Southern Slaveholders' Worldview*. New York: Cambridge University Press, 2005.

———. *Slavery in White and Black: Class and Race in the Southern Slaveholders' New World Order*. New York: Cambridge University Press, 2008.

Frank, Lisa Tendrich. *The Civilian War: Confederate Women and Union Soldiers during Sherman's March*. Baton Rouge: Louisiana State University Press, 2015.

Fredrickson, George M. *Big Enough to Be Inconsistent: Abraham Lincoln Confronts Slavery and Race*. Cambridge, MA: Harvard University Press, 2008.

———. *The Black Image in the White Mind: The Debate on Afro-American Character and Destiny, 1817–1914*. New York: Harper & Row, 1971.

———. *The Inner Civil War: Northern Intellectuals and the Crisis of the Union*. New York: Harper & Row, 1965.

Freehling, William W. *The Road to Disunion*. 2 vols. New York: Oxford University Press, 1991–2007.

———. *The South vs. the South: How Anti-Confederate Southerners Shaped the Course of the Civil War*. New York: Oxford University Press, 2001.

Freeman, Joanne B. *The Field of Blood: Violence in Congress and the Road to Civil War*. New York: Farrar, Straus, and Giroux, 2018.

Fritz, Karen E. *Voices in the Storm: Confederate Rhetoric, 1861–1865*. Denton: University of North Texas Press, 1999.

Fuller, A. James. *Chaplain to the Confederacy: Basil Manly and Baptist Life in the Old South*. Baton Rouge: Louisiana State University Press, 2000.

———. *Oliver P. Morton and the Politics of the Civil War and Reconstruction*. Kent, OH: Kent State University Press, 2017.

Fullerton, Dan C. *Armies in Gray: The Organizational History of the Confederate States Army in the Civil War*. Baton Rouge: Louisiana State University Press, 2017.

Gallagher, Gary W. *Becoming Confederates: Paths to a New National Loyalty*. Athens: University of Georgia Press, 2013.

———, ed. *The Richmond Campaign of 1862: The Peninsula and the Seven Days*. Chapel Hill: University of North Carolina Press, 2000.

———, ed. *The Shenandoah Valley Campaign of 1864*. Chapel Hill: University of North Carolina Press, 2006.

———. *Stephen Dodson Ramseur, Lee's Gallant General*. Chapel Hill: University of North Carolina Press, 1985.

———. *The Union War*. Cambridge, MA: Harvard University Press, 2011.

———, ed. *The Wilderness Campaign*. Chapel Hill: University of North Carolina Press, 1997.

Gallagher, Gary W., and Elizabeth R. Varon, eds. *New Perspectives on the Union War*. New York: Fordham University Press, 2019.

Gallman, J. Matthew. *America's Joan of Arc: The Life of Anna Elizabeth Dickinson*. New York: Oxford University Press, 2006.

———. *Defining Duty in the Civil War: Personal Choice, Popular Culture, and the Union Home Front*. Chapel Hill: University of North Carolina Press, 2015.

———. *Receiving Erin's Children: Philadelphia, Liverpool, and the Irish Famine Migration, 1845–1855*. Chapel Hill: University of North Carolina Press, 2000.

Gamble, Richard M. *A Fiery Gospel: The Battle Hymn of the Republic and the Road to Righteous War*. Ithaca, NY: Cornell University Press, 2019.

Gardner, Eric. *Black Print Unbound: The Christian Recorder, African American Literature, and Periodical Culture*. New York: Oxford University Press, 2015.

Gardner, Sarah E. *Blood and Irony: Southern White Women's Narratives of the Civil War, 1861–1937*. Chapel Hill: University of North Carolina Press, 2004.

Gedge, Karin E. *Without Benefit of Clergy: Women and the Pastoral Relationship in Nineteenth-Century American Culture*. New York: Oxford University Press, 2003.

Geiger, Mark W. *Financial Fraud and Guerrilla Violence in Missouri's Civil War, 1861–1865*. New Haven, CT: Yale University Press, 2010.

Genovese, Eugene D. *A Consuming Fire: The Fall of the Confederacy in the Mind of the White Christian South*. Athens: University of Georgia Press, 1998.

———. *Roll, Jordan, Roll: The World the Slaves Made*. New York: Pantheon Books, 1974.

Gerard, Philip. *The Last Battleground: The Civil War Comes to North Carolina*. Chapel Hill: University of North Carolina Press, 2019.

Gienapp, William E. *The Origins of the Republican Party, 1852–1856*. New York: Oxford University Press, 1987.

Giesberg, Judith. *Army at Home: Women and the Civil War on the Northern Home Front*. Chapel Hill: University of North Carolina Press, 2009.

Giesberg, Judith, and Randall M. Miller, eds. *Women and the American Civil War: North-South Counterpoints*. Kent, OH: Kent State University Press, 2018.

Gillette, William. *Jersey Blue: Civil War Politics in New Jersey, 1854–1865*. New Brunswick, NJ: Rutgers University Press, 1995.

Ginzberg, Lori D. *Women and the Work of Benevolence: Morality, Politics, and Class in the Nineteenth-Century United States*. New Haven, CT: Yale University Press, 1990.

Gjerde, Jon. *Catholicism and the Shaping of Nineteenth Century America*. New York: Cambridge University Press, 2012.

———. *The Mind of the West: Ethnocultural Evolution in the Rural Middle West, 1830–1917*. Chapel Hill: University of North Carolina Press, 1997.

Glatthaar, Joseph T. *Forged in Battle: The Civil War Alliance of Black Soldiers and White Officers*. New York: Free Press, 1990.

———. *General Lee's Army: From Victory to Collapse*. New York: Free Press, 2008.

———. *The March to the Sea and Beyond: Sherman's Troops in the Savannah and Carolinas Campaigns*. New York: New York University Press, 1985.

———. "A Tale of Two Armies: The Confederate Army of Northern Virginia and the Union Army of the Potomac and Their Cultures." *Journal of the Civil War Era* 6:3 (September 2016): 315–46.

Glover, Lorri. *Southern Sons: Becoming Men in the New Nation*. Baltimore: Johns Hopkins University Press, 2007.

Glymph, Thavolia. *The Women's Fight: The Civil War Battles for Home, Freedom, and Nation*. Chapel Hill: University of North Carolina Press, 2020.

Go, Julian. *Patterns of Empire: The British and American Empires, 1688 to the Present*. New York: Cambridge University Press, 2011.

Goen, C. C. *Broken Churches, Broken Nation: Denominational Schisms and the Coming of the American Civil War*. Mercer, GA: Mercer University Press, 1985.

Goldfield, David. *America Aflame: How the Civil War Created a Nation*. New York: Bloomsbury, 2011.

Gordon, Lesley J. *A Broken Regiment: The 16th Connecticut's Civil War*. Baton Rouge: Louisiana State University Press, 2014.

———. *General George E. Pickett in Life and Legend*. Chapel Hill: University of North Carolina Press, 1998.

Gorski, Philip. *American Covenant: A History of Civil Religion from the Puritans to the Present*. Princeton, NJ: Princeton University Press, 2017.

Gould, Edward Kalloch, ed. *Major-General Hiram G. Berry: His Career as a Contractor, Bank President, Politician, and Major-General of Volunteers in the Civil War, Together with His War Correspondence, Embracing the Period from Bull Run to Chancellorsville*. Rockland, ME: Press of the Courier-Gazette, 1899.

Gould, John Mead. *History of the First-Tenth-Twenty-Ninth Maine Regiment: In Service of the United States From May 3, 1861, to June 21, 1866*. Portland, ME: Stephen Berry, 1871.

Graber, Samuel. *Twice-Divided Nation: National Memory, Transatlantic News, and American Literature in the Civil War Era*. Charlottesville: University of Virginia Press, 2019.

Grandin, Greg. *The End of the Myth: From the Frontier to the Border Wall in the Mind of America*. New York: Metropolitan Books, 2019.

Grasso, Christopher. *Skepticism and American Faith: From the Revolution to the Civil War*. New York: Oxford University Press, 2018.

Green, Jennifer R. *Military Education and the Emerging Middle Class in the Old South*. New York: Cambridge University Press, 2008.

Green, Michael S. *Freedom, Union, and Power: Lincoln and His Party during the Civil War*. New York: Fordham University Press, 2004.

Green, Steven K. *Inventing a Christian America: The Myth of the Religious Founding*. New York: Oxford University Press, 2015.

Gribben, Crawford. *Evangelical Millennialism in the Trans-Atlantic World, 1500–2000*. New York: Palgrave Macmillan, 2011.

Grimsley, Mark. *The Hard Hand of War: Union Military Policy toward Southern Civilians, 1861–1865*. New York: Cambridge University Press, 1995.

Grow, Michael J. *"Liberty to the Downtrodden": Thomas L. Kane, Romantic Reformer*. New Haven, CT: Yale University Press, 2009.

Guelzo, Allen C. *Abraham Lincoln: Redeemer President*. Wm. B. Eerdmans, 1999.

———. *Fateful Lightning: A New History of the Civil War and Reconstruction*. New York: Oxford University Press, 2012.

———. *Gettysburg: The Last Invasion*. New York: Alfred A. Knopf, 2013.

———. *Lincoln's Emancipation Proclamation: The End of Slavery in America*. New York: Simon & Schuster, 2004.

Guterl, Matthew Pratt. *American Mediterranean: Southern Slaveholders in the Age of Emancipation*. Cambridge, MA: Harvard University Press, 2008.

Gutjahr, Paul C. *Charles Hodge: Guardian of American Orthodoxy*. New York: Oxford University Press, 2011.

Guyatt, Nicholas. *Providence and the Invention of the United States, 1607–1876*. New York: Cambridge University Press, 2007.

Hager, Christopher. *I Remain Yours: Common Lives in Civil War Letters*. Cambridge, MA: Harvard University Press, 2018.

Hahn, Steven. *A Nation under Our Feet: Black Political Struggles in the Rural South from Slavery to the Great Migration*. Cambridge, MA: Belknap Press of Harvard University Press, 2003.

———. *A Nation without Borders: The United States and Its World in an Age of Civil Wars, 1830–1910*. New York: Viking, 2016.

Hale, Laura V. *Four Valiant Years in the Lower Shenandoah Valley, 1861–1865*. Strasburg, VA: Shenandoah, 1968.

Harari, Yuval Noah. *The Ultimate Experience: Battlefield Revelations and the Making of Modern War Culture, 1450–2000*. New York: Palgrave Macmillan, 2008.

Harlow, Luke E. *Religion, Race, and the Making of Confederate Kentucky, 1830–1880*. New York: Cambridge University Press, 2014.

Harp, Gillis J. *Protestants and American Conservatism: A Short History*. New York: Oxford University Press, 2019.

Harper, Matthew. *The End of Days: African American Religion and Politics in the Age of Emancipation*. Baton Rouge: Louisiana State University Press, 2016.

Harrold, Stanley. *The Abolitionists and the South, 1831–1861*. Lexington: University Press of Kentucky, 1995.

———. *American Abolitionism: Its Direct Political Impact from Colonial Times into Reconstruction*. Charlottesville: University of Virginia Press, 2019.

———. *Lincoln and the Abolitionists*. Carbondale: Southern Illinois University Press, 2018.

———. *Subversives: Antislavery Community in Washington, D.C., 1828–1865*. Baton Rouge: Louisiana State University Press, 2003.

Hassler, Warren W. *Commanders of the Army of the Potomac*. Baton Rouge: Louisiana State University Press, 1962.

———. *General George B. McClellan: Shield of the Union*. Baton Rouge: Louisiana State University Press, 1957.

Hassler, William Woods. *Colonel John Pelham: Lee's Boy Artillerist*. Chapel Hill: University of North Carolina Press, 1960.

Hassner, Ron E. *Religion on the Battlefield*. Ithaca, NY: Cornell University Press, 2016.

Hastings, Adrian. *The Construction of Nationhood: Ethnicity, Religion, and Nationalism*. New York: Cambridge University Press, 1997.

Hattaway, Herman. *General Stephen D. Lee*. Jackson: University Press of Mississippi, 1976.

Hattaway, Herman, and Archer Jones. *How the North Won: A Military History of the Civil War*. Urbana: University of Illinois Press, 1983.

Hearn, Chester G. *Lincoln, the Cabinet, and the Generals*. Baton Rouge: Louisiana State University Press, 2010.

———. *When the Devil Came Down to Dixie: Ben Butler in New Orleans*. Baton Rouge: Louisiana State University Press, 1997.

Heatwole, John L. *The Burning: Sheridan in the Shenandoah Valley*. Charlottesville, VA: Rockbridge, 1998.

Hebblethwaite, Brian. *The Christian Hope*. Rev. ed. New York: Oxford University Press, 2010.

Hebert, Walter H. *Fighting Joe Hooker*. Indianapolis: Bobbs-Merrill, 1944.

Hedrick, Joan D. *Harriet Beecher Stowe: A Life*. New York: Oxford University Press, 1994.

Heidler, David S. *Pulling the Temple Down: The Fire-Eaters and the Destruction of the Union*. Mechanicsburg, PA: Stackpole Books, 1994.

Henry, Stuart C. *Unvanquished Puritan: A Portrait of Lyman Beecher*. Grand Rapids, MI: Wm. B. Eerdmans, 1973.

Hernon, Joseph M., Jr. *Celts, Catholics, and Copperheads: Ireland Views the American Civil War*. Columbus: Ohio State University Press, 1968.

Herrera, Ricardo A. *For Liberty and the Republic: The American Citizen as Soldier, 1775–1861*. New York: New York University Press, 2015.

Herring, George C. *From Colony to Superpower: U.S. Foreign Relations since 1776*. New York: Oxford University Press, 2008.

Hess, Earl J. *Braxton Bragg: The Most Hated Man of the Confederacy*. Chapel Hill: University of North Carolina Press, 2016.

———. *In the Trenches at Petersburg: Field Fortifications and Confederate Defeat*. Chapel Hill: University of North Carolina Press, 2009.

———. *Lee's Tar Heels: The Pettigrew-Kirkland-McRae Brigade*. Chapel Hill: University of North Carolina Press, 2002.

———. *Liberty, Virtue, and Progress: Northerners and Their War for the Union*. New York: New York University Press, 1988.

Hettle, Wallace. "The Minister, the Martyr, and the Maxim: Robert Lewis Dabney and Stonewall Jackson Biography." *Civil War History* 49 (December 2003): 353–69.

———. *The Peculiar Democracy: Southern Democrats in Peace and Civil War*. Athens: University of Georgia Press, 2001.

Higginson, Thomas Wentworth, ed. *Harvard Memorial Biographies*. 2 vols. Cambridge, MA: Sever and Francis, 1866.

Hinton, Richard J. *John Brown and His Men*. New York: Arno, 1968.

Hobson, Christopher Z. *The Mount of Vision: African American Prophetic Tradition, 1800–1950*. New York: Oxford University Press, 2012.

Hodes, Martha. *Mourning Lincoln*. New Haven, CT: Yale University Press, 2015.

Hoge, Peyton H. *Moses Drury Hoge: Life and Letters*. Richmond, VA: Presbyterian Committee of Publication, 1899.

Holifield, E. Brooks. *The Gentlemen Theologians: American Theology in Southern Culture, 1795–1860*. Durham, NC: Duke University Press, 1978.

———. *Theology in America: Christian Thought from the Age of the Puritans to the Civil War*. New Haven, CT: Yale University Press, 2003.

Holm, April E. *A Kingdom Divided: Evangelicals, Loyalty, and Sectionalism in the Civil War Era*. Baton Rouge: Louisiana State University Press, 2017.

Holt, Michael F. *The Election of 1860: A Campaign Fraught with Consequences*. Lawrence: University Press of Kansas, 2017.

———. *The Rise and Fall of the American Whig Party: Jacksonian Politics and the Onset of the Civil War*. New York: Oxford University Press, 1999.

Holzer, Harold. *Lincoln at Cooper Union: The Speech That Made Abraham Lincoln President*. New York: Simon & Schuster, 2006.

Honeck, Mischa. *We Are the Revolutionists: German-Speaking Immigrants and American Abolitionists after 1848*. Athens: University of Georgia Press, 2011.

Hopkins, A. G. *American Empire: A Global History*. Princeton, NJ: Princeton University Press, 2018.

Horn, Huston. *Leonidas Polk: Warrior Bishop of the Confederacy*. Lawrence: University Press of Kansas, 2019.

Howard, Victor B. *Religion and the Radical Republican Movement, 1860–1870*. Lexington: University Press of Kentucky, 1990.

Hsieh, Wayne Wei-siang. *West Pointers and the Civil War: The Old Army in War and Peace*. Chapel Hill: University of North Carolina Press, 2009.

Hughes, Nathaniel Cheairs, Jr. *General William J. Hardee: Old Reliable*. Baton Rouge: Louisiana State University Press, 1965.

Humez, Jean M. *Harriet Tubman: The Life and the Life Stories*. Madison: University of Wisconsin Press, 2003.

Humphreys, Margaret. *Marrow of Tragedy: The Health Crisis of the American Civil War*. Baltimore: Johns Hopkins University Press, 2013.

Hunter, James Davison. *To Change the World: The Irony, Tragedy, and Possibility of Christianity in the Late Modern World*. New York: Oxford University Press, 2010.

Hunter, Tera W. *Bound in Wedlock: Slave and Free Black Marriage in the Nineteenth Century*. Cambridge, MA: Belknap Press of Harvard University Press, 2017.

———. *To 'Joy My Freedom: Southern Black Women's Lives and Labors after the Civil War*. Cambridge, MA: Harvard University Press, 1997.

Huston, James L. *The American and British Debate over Equality, 1775–1920*. Baton Rouge: Louisiana State University Press, 2017.

Hutchinson, Mark, and John Wolffe. *A Short History of Global Evangelicalism*. New York: Cambridge University Press, 2012.

Hutchison, William R., and Hartmut Lehmann, eds. *Many Are Chosen: Divine Election and Western Nationalism*. Minneapolis: Fortress, 1994.

Hyde, Thomas W. *Following the Greek Cross; or, Memories of the Sixth Army Corps*. Boston: Houghton Mifflin, 1895.

Inscoe, John C. *Race, War, and Remembrance in the Appalachian South*. Lexington: University Press of Kentucky, 2008.

Irons, Charles F. *The Origins of Proslavery Christianity: White and Black Evangelicals in Colonial and Antebellum Virginia*. Chapel Hill: University of North Carolina Press, 2008.

Isenberg, Nancy. *White Trash: The 400-Year Untold History of Class in America*. New York: Viking, 2016.

Jackson, Holly. *American Radicals: How Nineteenth-Century Protest Shaped the Nation*. New York: Crown, 2019.

Jackson, Kellie Carter. *Force and Freedom: Black Abolitionists and the Politics of Violence*. Philadelphia: University of Pennsylvania Press, 2019.

Jackson, William J. *New Jerseyans in the Civil War: For Union and Liberty*. New Brunswick, NJ: Rutgers University Press, 2000.

Janney, Caroline, ed. *Remembering the Civil War: Reunion and the Limits of Reconciliation*. Chapel Hill: University of North Carolina Press, 2013.

Jenkins, Sally, and John Stauffer. *The State of Jones*. New York: Doubleday, 2009.

Jimerson, Randall C. *The Private Civil War: Popular Thought during the Sectional Conflict*. Baton Rouge: Louisiana State University Press, 1988.

Johnson, James Turner. *Just War Tradition and the Restraint of War: A Moral and Historical Inquiry*. Princeton, NJ: Princeton University Press, 1981.

Johnson, Paul E. *A Shopkeeper's Millennium: Society and Revivals in Rochester, New York, 1815–1837*. New York: Hill and Wang, 1978.

Johnson, Paul E., and Sean Wilentz. *The Kingdom of Matthias: A Story of Sex and Salvation in 19th-Century America*. New York: Oxford University Press, 1994.

Johnson, Sylvester A. *African American Religions, 1500–2000: Colonialism, Democracy, and Freedom*. New York: Cambridge University Press, 2015.

Johnson, Thomas Cary. *History of the Southern Presbyterian Church*. New York: Christian Literature, 1894.

———. *The Life and Letters of Robert Lewis Dabney*. Richmond, VA: Presbyterian Committee of Publication, 1903.

Jones, Howard. *Blue and Gray Diplomacy: A History of Union and Confederate Foreign Relations.* Chapel Hill: University of North Carolina Press, 2010.

Jones, Martha S. *All Bound Up Together: The Woman Question in African American Public Culture, 1830–1900.* Chapel Hill: University of North Carolina Press, 2007.

———. *Birthright Citizens: A History of Race and Rights in Antebellum America.* New York: Cambridge University Press, 2018.

Jones, Terry L. *Lee's Tigers: The Louisiana Infantry in the Army of Northern Virginia.* Rev. ed. Baton Rouge: Louisiana State University Press, 2017.

Jordan, Brian Matthew. *Marching Home: Union Veterans and Their Unending Civil War.* New York: Liveright, 2014.

Jordan, Ryan B. *Slavery and the Meetinghouse: The Quakers and the Abolitionist Dilemma, 1820–1865.* Bloomington: Indiana University Press, 2007.

Joyce, Barry. *The First U.S. History Textbooks: Constructing and Disseminating the American Tale in the Nineteenth Century.* Lanham, MD: Lexington Books, 2015.

Junkin, D. X. *The Reverend George Junkin, D.D., L.L.D.: A Historical Biography.* Philadelphia: J. B. Lippincott, 1871.

Kalyvas, Stathis N. *The Logic of Violence in Civil War.* New York: Cambridge University Press, 2006.

Kantrowitz, Stephen. *More Than Freedom: Fighting for Black Citizenship in a White Republic, 1829–1889.* New York: Penguin, 2012.

Karp, Matthew. *This Vast Southern Empire: Slaveholders at the Helm of American Foreign Policy.* Cambridge, MA: Harvard University Press, 2016.

Kaveny, Cathleen. *Prophecy without Contempt: Religious Discourse in the Public Square.* Cambridge, MA: Harvard University Press, 2016.

Keating, Ryan W. *Shades of Green: Irish Regiments, American Soldiers, and Local Communities in the Civil War Era.* New York: Fordham University Press, 2017.

Keith, LeeAnna. *When It Was Grand: The Radical Republican History of the Civil War.* New York: Hill and Wang, 2020.

Keller, Christian B. *Chancellorsville and the Germans: Nativism, Ethnicity, and Civil War Memory.* New York: Fordham University Press, 2007.

Kelman, Ari. *A Misplaced Massacre: Struggling over the Memory of Sand Creek.* Cambridge, MA: Harvard University Press, 2013.

Kepler, William. *History of the Three Months' and Three Years' Service from April 16th, 1861, to June 22d, 1864, of the Fourth Regiment Ohio Volunteer Infantry in the War for the Union.* Huntington, WV: Blue Acorn, 1992.

Kiper, Richard L. *Major General John Alexander McClernand: Politician in Uniform.* Kent, OH: Kent State University Press, 1999.

Kirshner, Ralph. *The Class of 1861: Custer, Ames, and Their Classmates after West Point.* Carbondale: Southern Illinois University Press, 1999.

Klein, Maury. *Edward Porter Alexander.* Athens: University of Georgia Press, 1971.

Klein, Stacey Jean. *Margaret Jean Preston, Poet of the Confederacy: A Literary Life.* Columbia: University of South Carolina Press, 2007.

Kloppenberg, James T. *Toward Democracy: The Struggle for Self-Rule in European and American Thought.* New York: Oxford University Press, 2016.

Kornblith, Gary J., and Carol Lasser. *Elusive Utopia: The Struggle for Racial Equality in Oberlin, Ohio.* Baton Rouge: Louisiana State University Press, 2018.

Kreiser, Lawrence A., Jr. *Defeating Lee: A History of the Second Corps Army of the Potomac.* Bloomington: Indiana University Press, 2011.

Krick, Robert K. *Stonewall Jackson at Cedar Mountain.* Chapel Hill: University of North Carolina Press, 1990.

Kuklick, Bruce. *A Political History of the USA: One Nation under God.* New York: Palgrave Macmillan, 2009.

Kurtz, William B. *Excommunicated from the Union: How the Civil War Created a Separate Catholic America.* New York: Fordham University Press, 2016.

Kytle, Ethan J. *Romantic Reformers and the Antislavery Struggle in the Civil War Era.* New York: Cambridge University Press, 2014.

Kytle, Ethan J., and Blain Roberts. *Denmark Vesey's Garden: Slavery and Memory in the Cradle of the Confederacy.* New York: New Press, 2018.

Lamb, Blaine. *The Extraordinary Life of Charles Pomeroy Stone: Soldier, Surveyor, Pasha, Engineer.* Yardley, PA: Westholme, 2016.

Landes, Richard. *Heaven on Earth: The Varieties of the Millennial Experience.* New York: Oxford University Press, 2011.

Landis, Michael Todd. *Northern Men with Southern Loyalties: The Democratic Party and the Sectional Crisis.* Ithaca, NY: Cornell University Press, 2014.

Lang, Andrew F. *In the Wake of War: Military Occupation, Emancipation, and Civil War America.* Baton Rouge: Louisiana State University Press, 2017.

Lantzer, Jason. *Rebel Bulldog: The Story of One Family, Two States, and the Civil War.* Indianapolis: Indiana Historical Society Press, 2017.

Larson, Kate Clifford. *Bound for the Promised Land: Harriet Tubman, Portrait of an American Hero.* New York: Ballantine Books, 2004.

Lash, Jeffrey N. *A Politician Turned General: The Civil War Career of Stephen Augustus Hurlbut.* Kent, OH: Kent State University Press, 2003.

Laughlin-Schultz, Bonnie. *The Tie That Bound Us: The Women of John Brown's Family and the Legacy of Radical Abolitionism.* Ithaca, NY: Cornell University Press, 2013.

Lause, Mark A. *Young America: Land, Labor, and the Republican Community.* Urbana: University of Illinois Press, 2005.

Lawson, Melinda. *Patriot Fires: Forging a New American Nationalism in the Civil War North.* Lawrence: University Press of Kansas, 2002.

Lee, Wayne E. *Barbarians and Brothers: Anglo-American Warfare, 1500–1865.* New York: Oxford University Press, 2011.

Leonard, Elizabeth D. *Yankee Women: Gender Battles in the Civil War.* New York: W. W. Norton, 1994.

Levin, Kevin M. *Remembering the Crater: War as Murder.* Lexington: University of Kentucky Press, 2012.

———. *Searching for Black Confederates: The Civil War's Most Persistent Myth.* Chapel Hill: University of North Carolina Press, 2019.

Levine, Bruce. *The Fall of the House of Dixie: The Civil War and the Social Revolution That Transformed the South.* New York: Random House, 2013.

Leyburn, James G. *The Scotch-Irish: A Social History.* Chapel Hill: University of North Carolina Press, 1962.

Logan, Rayford W. *Howard University: The First Hundred Years, 1867–1967.* New York: New York University Press, 1969.

Longacre, Edward G. *The Commanders of Chancellorsville: The Gentleman versus the Rogue.* Nashville, TN: Rutledge Hill, 2005.

Longenecker, Stephen L. *Shenandoah Religion: Outsiders and the Mainstream, 1716–1865.* Waco, TX: Baylor University Press, 2002.

Losson, Christopher. *Tennessee's Forgotten Warriors: Frank Cheatham and His Confederate Division.* Knoxville: University of Tennessee Press, 1989.

Loughery, John. *Dagger John: Archbishop John Hughes and the Making of Irish America.* Ithaca, NY: Cornell University Press, 2018.

Loveland, Anne C. *Southern Evangelicals and the Social Order, 1800–1860.* Baton Rouge: Louisiana State University Press, 1980.

Lowe, Richard G. *Republicans and Reconstruction in Virginia, 1856–70.* Charlottesville: University Press of Virginia, 1991.

Luke, Bob, and John David Smith. *Soldiering for Freedom: How the Union Army Recruited, Trained, and Deployed the U.S. Colored Troops.* Baltimore: Johns Hopkins University Press, 2014.

Lum, Kathryn Gin. *Damned Nation: Hell in America from the Revolution to Reconstruction.* New York: Oxford University Press, 2014.

Lynerd, Benjamin T. *Republican Theology: The Civil Religion of American Evangelicals.* New York: Oxford University Press, 2014.

Lynn, John A., II. *Another Kind of War: The Nature and History of Terrorism.* New Haven, CT: Yale University Press, 2019.

Lynn, Joshua A. *Preserving the White Man's Republic: Jacksonian Democracy, Race, and the Transformation of American Conservatism.* Charlottesville: University of Virginia Press, 2019.

Mackowski, Chris, and Kristopher D. White, eds. *Turning Points of the American Civil War.* Carbondale: Southern Illinois University Press, 2018.

Maddex, Jack P., Jr. "Proslavery Millennialism: Social Eschatology in Antebellum Southern Calvinism." *American Quarterly* 31:1 (Spring 1979): 46–62.

Mahoney, Timothy R. *From Hometown to Battlefield in the Civil War Era: Middle Class Life in Midwest America*. New York: Cambridge University Press, 2016.

Maizlish, Stephen E. *A Strife of Tongues: The Compromise of 1850 and the Ideological Foundations of the American Civil War*. Charlottesville: University of Virginia Press, 2016.

Manning, Chandra. *Troubled Refuge: Struggling for Freedom in the Civil War*. New York: Alfred A. Knopf, 2016.

———. *What This Cruel War Was Over: Soldiers, Slavery, and the Civil War*. New York: Alfred A. Knopf, 2007.

Marvel, William. *Burnside*. Chapel Hill: University of North Carolina Press, 1991.

———. *Lincoln's Autocrat: The Life of Edwin Stanton*. Chapel Hill: University of North Carolina Press, 2015.

———. *Lincoln's Mercenaries: Economic Motivation among Union Soldiers during the Civil War*. Baton Rouge: Louisiana State University Press, 2018.

Marx, Anthony W. *Faith in Nation: Exclusionary Origins of Nationalism*. New York: Oxford University Press, 2003.

Maryniak, Benedict R., and John Wesley Brinsfield, Jr., eds. *The Spirit Divided: Memoirs of Civil War Chaplains*. Macon, GA: Mercer University Press, 2007.

Mason, Matthew. *Apostle of Union: A Political Biography of Edward Everett*. Chapel Hill: University of North Carolina Press, 2016.

Mason, Matthew, Katheryn P. Viens, and Conrad Edick Wright, eds. *Massachusetts and the Civil War: The Commonwealth and National Disunion*. Amherst: University of Massachusetts Press, 2015.

Masur, Kate. *An Example for All the Land: Emancipation and the Struggle over Equality in Washington, D.C.* Chapel Hill: University of North Carolina Press, 2010.

Masur, Louis P. *Lincoln's Last Speech: Wartime Reconstruction and the Crisis of Reunion*. New York: Oxford University Press, 2015.

Mathews, Donald G. *Religion in the Old South*. Chicago: University of Chicago Press, 1977.

Mathisen, Erik. *The Loyal Republic: Traitors, Slaves, and the Remaking of Citizenship in Civil War America*. Chapel Hill: University of North Carolina Press, 2018.

Matsui, John H. *The First Republican Army*. Charlottesville: University of Virginia Press, 2016.

Mauldin, Erin Stewart. *Unredeemed Land: An Environmental History of Civil War and Emancipation in the Cotton South*. New York: Oxford University Press, 2018.

McArthur, Judith N., and Orville Vernon Burton. *"A Gentleman and an Officer": A Military and Social History of James B. Griffin's Civil War*. New York: Oxford University Press, 1996.

McBride, Mary Gorton, and Ann M. McLaurin. *Randall Lee Gibson of Louisiana: Confederate General and New South Reformer*. Baton Rouge: Louisiana State University Press, 2007.

McCurry, Stephanie. *Confederate Reckoning: Power and Politics in the Civil War South.* Cambridge, MA: Harvard University Press, 2010.

———. *Masters of Small Worlds: Yeoman Households, Gender Relations, and the Political Culture of the Antebellum South Carolina Low Country.* New York: Oxford University Press, 1995.

———. *Women's War: Fighting and Surviving the American Civil War.* Cambridge, MA: Belknap Press of Harvard University Press, 2019.

McDonnell, Lawrence T. *Performing Disunion: The Coming of the Civil War in Charleston, South Carolina.* New York: Cambridge University Press, 2018.

McDonough, James Lee. *Shiloh: In Hell before Night.* Knoxville: University of Tennessee Press, 1977.

———. *Stones River: Bloody Winter in Tennessee.* Knoxville: University of Tennessee Press, 1980.

———. *William Tecumseh Sherman: In the Service of My Country.* New York: W. W. Norton, 2016.

McDonough, James Lee, and James Pickett Jones. *War So Terrible: Sherman and Atlanta.* New York: W. W. Norton, 1987.

McFeely, William S. *Yankee Stepfather: General O. O. Howard and the Freedmen.* New Haven, CT: Yale University Press, 1968.

McGreevy, John T. *Catholicism and American Freedom: A History.* New York: W. W. Norton, 2003.

McKenzie, Robert Tracy. *Lincolnites and Reels: A Divided Town in the American Civil War.* New York: Oxford University Press, 2006.

McKinney, Francis F. *Education in Violence: The Life of George H. Thomas and the History of the Army of the Cumberland.* Detroit: Wayne State University Press, 1961.

McKivigan, John R. *The War against Proslavery Religion: Abolitionism and the Northern Churches, 1830–1865.* Ithaca, NY: Cornell University Press, 1984.

McKivigan, John R., and Mitchell Snay, eds. *Religion and the Antebellum Debate over Slavery.* Athens: University of Georgia Press, 1998.

McKnight, Brian D., and Barton A. Myers, eds. *The Guerrilla Hunters: Irregular Conflicts during the Civil War.* Baton Rouge: Louisiana State University Press, 2017.

McLoughlin, William G. *Revivals, Awakenings, and Reform: An Essay on Religion and Social Change in America, 1607–1977.* Chicago: University of Chicago Press, 1978.

McMillen, Sally G. *To Raise Up the South: Sunday Schools in Black and White Churches, 1865–1915.* Baton Rouge: Louisiana State University Press, 2001.

McMurry, Richard M. *Two Great Rebel Armies: An Essay in Confederate Military History.* Chapel Hill: University of North Carolina Press, 1989.

McPherson, James M. *Battle Cry of Freedom: The Civil War Era.* New York: Oxford University Press, 1988.

———. *Crossroads of Freedom: Antietam, the Battle That Changed the Course of the Civil War.* New York: Oxford University Press, 2002.

———. *Embattled Rebel: Jefferson Davis as Commander in Chief.* New York: Penguin, 2014.

———. *For Cause and Comrades.* New York: Oxford University Press, 1996.

———. *War on the Waters: The Union and Confederate Navies, 1861–1865.* Chapel Hill: University of North Carolina Press, 2012.

———. *The War That Forged a Nation: Why the Civil War Still Matters.* New York: Oxford University Press, 2015.

———. *What They Fought For, 1861–1865.* Baton Rouge: Louisiana State University Press, 1994.

McPherson, James M., and William J. Cooper Jr., eds. *Writing the Civil War: The Quest to Understand.* Columbia: University of South Carolina Press, 1998.

McWhiney, Grady, ed. *Grant, Lee, Lincoln, and the Radicals: Essays on Civil War Leadership.* Evanston, IL: Northwestern University Press, 1964.

McWhiney, Grady, and Perry D. Jamieson. *Attack and Die: Civil War Military Tactics and the Southern Heritage.* Tuscaloosa: University of Alabama Press, 1982.

McWhirter, Christian. *Battle Hymns: The Power and Popularity of Music in the Civil War.* Chapel Hill: University of North Carolina Press, 2012.

Meade, George Gordon, ed. *The Life and Letters of General George Gordon Meade, Major-General United States Army.* 2 vols. New York: Charles Scribner's Sons, 1913.

Mellott, David W., and Mark A. Snell. *The Seventh West Virginia Infantry: An Embattled Union Regiment from the Civil War's Most Divided State.* Lawrence: University Press of Kansas, 2019.

Melton, Brian C. *Sherman's Forgotten General: Henry W. Slocum.* Columbia: University of Missouri Press, 2007.

Mendez, James G. *A Great Sacrifice: Northern Black Soldiers, Their Families, and the Experience of Civil War.* New York: Fordham University Press, 2019.

Mendoza, Alexander. *Confederate Struggle for Command: General James Longstreet and the First Corps in the West.* College Station: Texas A&M University Press, 2008.

Merchant, Holt. *South Carolina Fire-Eater: The Life of Laurence Massillon Keitt, 1824–1864.* Columbia: University of South Carolina Press, 2014.

Merritt, Keri Leigh. *Masterless Men: Poor Whites and Slavery in the Antebellum South.* New York: Cambridge University Press, 2017.

Miller, Benjamin L. *In God's Presence: Chaplains, Missionaries, and Religious Space during the American Civil War.* Lawrence: University Press of Kansas, 2019.

Miller, Edward A. *Lincoln's Abolitionist General: The Biography of David Hunter.* Columbia: University of South Carolina Press, 1997.

Miller, Randall M., Harry S. Stout, and Charles Reagan Wilson, eds. *Religion and the American Civil War.* New York: Oxford University Press, 1998.

Miller, Richard F. *Harvard's Civil War: A History of the Twentieth Massachusetts Volunteer Infantry.* Hanover, NH: University Press of New England, 2005.

Miller, Robert J. *Both Prayed to the Same God: Religion and Faith in the American Civil War.* Lanham, MD: Lexington Books, 2007.

Mitchell, Mary Niall. *Raising Freedom's Child: Black Children and Visions of the Future after Slavery.* New York: New York University Press, 2008.

Mitchell, Reid. *Civil War Soldiers.* New York: Viking, 1988.

———. *The Vacant Chair: The Northern Soldier Leaves Home.* New York: Oxford University Press, 1995.

Montgomery, William H. *Under Their Own Vine and Fig Tree: The African-American Church in the South, 1865–1900.* Baton Rouge: Louisiana State University Press, 1990.

Moody, Wesley. *Demon of the Lost Cause: Sherman and Civil War History.* Columbia: University of Missouri Press, 2011.

Moore, Christopher C. *Apostle of the Lost Cause: J. William Jones, Baptists, and the Development of Confederate Memory.* Knoxville: University of Tennessee Press, 2019.

Moore, Joseph S. *Founding Sins: How a Group of Antislavery Radicals Fought to Put Christ into the Constitution.* New York: Oxford University Press, 2016.

Moorhead, James H. *American Apocalypse: Yankee Protestants and the Civil War, 1860–1869.* New Haven, CT: Yale University Press, 1978.

———. "The Erosion of Postmillennialism in American Religious Thought, 1865–1925." *Church History* 53:1 (March 1984): 61–77.

Morone, James A. *Hellfire Nation: The Politics of Sin in American History.* New Haven, CT: Yale University Press, 2003.

Morris, J. Brent. *Oberlin, Hotbed of Abolitionism: College, Community, and the Fight for Freedom and Equality in Antebellum America.* Chapel Hill: University of North Carolina Press, 2014.

Moses, Wilson Jeremiah. *Alexander Crummell: A Study of Civilization and Discontent.* New York: Oxford University Press, 1989.

———. *The Golden Age of Black Nationalism, 1850–1925.* Rev. ed. New York: Oxford University Press, 1988.

Moss, Lemuel. *Annals of the United States Christian Commission.* Philadelphia: J. B. Lippincott, 1868.

Muhlenfeld, Elisabeth. *Mary Boykin Chesnut: A Biography.* Baton Rouge: Louisiana State University Press, 1981.

Mullen, Lincoln A. *The Chance of Salvation: A History of Conversion in America.* Cambridge, MA: Harvard University Press, 2017.

Mullin, Robert Bruce. *Episcopal Vision/American Reality: High Church Theology and Social Thought in Evangelical America.* New Haven, CT: Yale University Press, 1986.

Murray, Williamson, and Wayne Wei-siang Hsieh. *A Savage War: A Military History of the Civil War.* Princeton, NJ: Princeton University Press, 2016.

Myers, Barton A. *Rebels against the Confederacy: North Carolina's Unionists.* New York: Cambridge University Press, 2014.

Nabors, Forrest A. *From Oligarchy to Republicanism: The Great Task of Reconstruction.* Columbia: University of Missouri Press, 2017.

Nagel, Paul C. *The Lees of Virginia: Seven Generations of an American Family*. 2nd ed. New York: Oxford University Press, 2007.

Neely, Mark E. *The Civil War and the Limits of Destruction*. Cambridge, MA: Harvard University Press, 2007.

———. *The Fate of Liberty: Abraham Lincoln and Civil Liberties*. New York: Oxford University Press, 1991.

———. *The Last Best Hope of Earth: Abraham Lincoln and the Promise of America*. Cambridge, MA: Harvard University Press, 1995.

———. *Lincoln and the Democrats: The Politics of Opposition in the Civil War*. New York: Cambridge University Press, 2017.

———. *The Union Divided: Party Conflict in the Civil War North*. Cambridge, MA: Harvard University Press, 2002.

Neiman, Susan. *Learning from the Germans: Race and the Memory of Evil*. New York: Farrar, Straus, and Giroux, 2019.

Nelson, Megan Kate. *Ruin Nation: Destruction and the American Civil War*. Athens: University of Georgia Press, 2012.

Nelson, Scott Reynolds, and Carol Sheriff. *A People at War: Civilians and Soldiers in America's Civil War, 1854–1877*. New York: Oxford University Press, 2007.

Newport, Kenneth G. C. *Apocalypse and Millennium: Studies in Biblical Eisegesis*. New York: Cambridge University Press, 2000.

Newton, Steven H. *Joseph E. Johnston and the Defense of Richmond*. Lawrence: University Press of Kansas, 1998.

Nichols, Edward J. *Toward Gettysburg: A Biography of General John F. Reynolds*. University Park: Pennsylvania State University Press, 1958.

Nichols-Belt, Traci. *Onward Southern Soldiers: Religion and the Army of Tennessee in the Civil War*. Charleston, SC: History Press, 2011.

Niven, John. *Salmon P. Chase: A Biography*. New York: Oxford University Press, 1995.

Noe, Kenneth W. *Reluctant Rebels: The Confederates Who Joined the Army after 1861*. Chapel Hill: University of North Carolina Press, 2010.

Noe, Kenneth W., and Shannon H. Wilson, eds. *The Civil War in Appalachia: Collected Essays*. Knoxville: University of Tennessee Press, 1997.

Nolan, Cathal J. *The Allure of Battle: A History of How Wars Have Been Won and Lost*. New York: Oxford University Press, 2017.

Noll, Mark A. *America's God: From Jonathan Edwards to Abraham Lincoln*. New York: Oxford University Press, 2002.

———. *The Civil War as a Theological Crisis*. Chapel Hill: University of North Carolina Press, 2006.

Noyalas, Jonathan A. *"My Will Is Absolute Law": A Biography of Union General Robert H. Milroy*. Jefferson, NC: McFarland, 2006.

Oakes, James. *Freedom National: The Destruction of Slavery in the United States, 1861–1865*. New York: W. W. Norton, 2013.

————. *The Ruling Race: A History of American Slaveholders.* New York: Alfred A. Knopf, 1982.

————. *The Scorpion's Sting: Antislavery and the Coming of the Civil War.* New York: W. W. Norton, 2014.

Oates, Stephen B. *A Woman of Valor: Clara Barton and the Civil War.* New York: Free Press, 1994.

O'Connor, Peter. *American Sectionalism in the British Mind, 1832–1863.* Baton Rouge: Louisiana State University Press, 2017.

O'Donovan, Oliver. *The Just War Revisited.* New York: Cambridge University Press, 2003.

O'Harrow, Robert, Jr. *The Quartermaster: Montgomery C. Meigs, Lincoln's General, Master Builder of the Union Army.* New York: Simon & Schuster, 2016.

O'Leary, Stephen D. *Arguing the Apocalypse: A Theory of Millennial Rhetoric.* New York: Oxford University Press, 1994.

Oshatz, Molly. *Slavery and Sin: The Fight against Slavery and the Rise of Liberal Protestantism.* New York: Oxford University Press, 2012.

Osterhammel, Jürgen. *The Transformation of the World: A Global History of the Nineteenth Century.* Princeton, NJ: Princeton University Press, 2014.

Ott, Victoria E. *Confederate Daughters: Coming of Age during the Civil War.* Carbondale: Southern Illinois University Press, 2008.

Owens, Harry P., and James J. Cooke, eds. *The Old South in the Crucible of War.* Jackson: University Press of Mississippi, 1983.

Oxx, Katie. *The Nativism Movement in America: Religious Conflict in the Nineteenth Century.* New York: Routledge, 2013.

Pagels, Elaine. *Revelations: Visions, Prophecy, and Politics in the Book of Revelation.* New York: Viking, 2012.

Painter, Nell Irvin. *Sojourner Truth: A Life, a Symbol.* New York: W. W. Norton, 1996.

Parkinson, Robert G. *The Common Cause: Creating Race and Nation in the American Revolution.* Chapel Hill: University of North Carolina Press for the Omohundro Institute of Early American History and Culture, 2016.

Parks, Joseph H. *General Leonidas Polk, C.S.A.: The Fighting Bishop.* Baton Rouge: Louisiana State University Press, 1962.

Parrish, T. Michael. *Richard Taylor: Soldier Price of Dixie.* Chapel Hill: University of North Carolina Press, 1992.

Parsons, Elaine Frantz. *Ku Klux: The Birth of the Klan during Reconstruction.* Chapel Hill: University of North Carolina Press, 2016.

Peterson, Carla L. *Black Gotham: A Family History of African Americans in Nineteenth-Century New York City.* New Haven, CT: Yale University Press, 2011.

Peterson, Mark. *The City-State of Boston: The Rise and Fall of an Atlantic Power, 1630–1865.* Princeton, NJ: Princeton University Press, 2019.

Pfanz, Donald C. *Richard S. Ewell: A Soldier's Life.* Chapel Hill: University of North Carolina Press, 1998.

Phillips, Christopher. *The Rivers Ran Backward: The Civil War and the Remaking of the American Middle Border.* New York: Oxford University Press, 2016.

Phillips, Clifton Jackson. *Protestant America and the Pagan World: The First Half Century of the American Board of Commissioners for Foreign Missions, 1810–1860.* Cambridge, MA: Harvard University Press, 1969.

Phillips, Jason. *Diehard Rebels: The Confederate Culture of Invincibility.* Athens: University of Georgia Press, 2007.

———. *Looming Civil War: How Nineteenth-Century Americans Imagined the Future.* New York: Oxford University Press, 2018.

Phillips, Kevin. *The Cousins' Wars: Religion, Politics, and the Triumph of Anglo-America.* New York: Basic Books, 1999.

Phipps, Sheila R. *Genteel Rebel: The Life of Mary Greenhow Lee.* Baton Rouge: Louisiana State University Press, 2004.

Piatt, Donn, and H. V. Boynton. *General George H. Thomas: A Critical Biography.* Cincinnati: Robert Clarke, 1893.

Pickett, LaSalle Corbell. *Pickett and His Men.* Philadelphia: J. B. Lippincott, 1913.

Pietsch, B. M. *Dispensational Modernism.* New York: Oxford University Press, 2015.

Piston, William Garrett. *Lee's Tarnished Lieutenant: James Longstreet and His Place in Southern History.* Athens: University of Georgia Press, 1987.

Polk, William M. *Leonidas Polk: Bishop and General.* 2 vols. New York: Longmans, Green, 1893.

Poole, W. Scott. *Satan in America: The Devil We Know.* Lanham, MD: Rowman & Littlefield, 2009.

Postel, Charles. *Equality: An American Dilemma, 1866–1896.* New York: Farrar, Straus, and Giroux, 2019.

Power, J. Tracy. *Lee's Miserables: Life in the Army of Northern Virginia from the Wilderness to Appomattox.* Chapel Hill: University of North Carolina Press, 1998.

Preston, Andrew. *Sword of the Spirit, Shield of Faith: Religion in American War and Diplomacy.* New York: Alfred A. Knopf, 2012.

Prokopowicz, Gerald J. *All for the Regiment: The Army of the Ohio, 1861–1862.* Chapel Hill: University of North Carolina Press, 2001.

Quigley, Paul, ed. *The Civil War and the Transformation of American Citizenship.* Baton Rouge: Louisiana State University Press, 2018.

———. *Shifting Grounds: Nationalism and the American South, 1848–1865.* New York: Oxford University Press, 2012.

Rable, George C. *But There Was No Peace: The Role of Violence in the Politics of Reconstruction.* Athens: University of Georgia Press, 1984.

———. *Civil Wars: Women and the Crisis of Southern Nationalism.* Urbana: University of Illinois Press, 1989.

———. *The Confederate Republic: A Revolution against Politics.* Chapel Hill: University of North Carolina Press, 1994.

————. *Damn Yankees! Demonization and Defiance in the Confederate South*. Baton Rouge: Louisiana State University Press, 2015.

————. *Fredericksburg! Fredericksburg!* Chapel Hill: University of North Carolina Press, 2002.

————. *God's Almost Chosen Peoples: A Religious History of the American Civil War*. Chapel Hill: University of North Carolina Press, 2010.

Rafuse, Ethan S. *McClellan's War: The Failure of Moderation in the Struggle for the Union*. Bloomington: Indiana University Press, 2005.

Ramage, James A. *Gray Ghost: The Life of Col. John Singleton Mosby*. Lexington: University Press of Kentucky, 1999.

Rankin, David C. *Diary of a Christian Soldier: Rufus Kinsley and the Civil War*. New York: Cambridge University Press, 2003.

Raus, Edmund J., Jr. *Banners South: A Northern Community at War*. Kent, OH: Kent State University Press, 2005.

Reimers, David M. *White Protestantism and the Negro*. New York: Oxford University Press, 1965.

Reynolds, David S. *John Brown, Abolitionist: The Man Who Killed Slavery, Sparked the Civil War, and Seeded Civil Rights*. New York: Alfred A. Knopf, 2005.

————. *Mightier Than the Sword: Uncle Tom's Cabin and the Battle for America*. New York: W. W. Norton, 2011.

Rhea, Gordon C. *The Battle of the Wilderness: May 5–6, 1864*. Baton Rouge: Louisiana State University Press, 1994.

————. *The Battles for Spotsylvania Court House and the Road to Yellow Tavern, May 7–12, 1864*. Baton Rouge: Louisiana State University Press, 1997.

————. *Cold Harbor: Grant and Lee, May 26–June 3, 1864*. Baton Rouge: Louisiana State University Press, 2002.

————. *To the North Anna River: Grant and Lee, May 13–25, 1864*. Baton Rouge: Louisiana State University Press, 2000.

Richards, Leonard L. *The Slave Power: The Free North and Southern Domination, 1780–1860*. Baton Rouge: Louisiana State University Press, 2000.

Richardson, Heather Cox. *To Make Men Free: A History of the Republican Party*. New York: Basic Books, 2014.

Richardson, Joe M. *Christian Reconstruction: The American Missionary Association and Southern Blacks, 1861–1890*. Athens: University of Georgia Press, 1986.

Roberts, Giselle. *The Confederate Belle*. Columbia: University of Missouri Press, 2003.

Roberts, Rita. *Evangelicalism and the Politics of Reform in Northern Black Thought, 1776–1863*. Baton Rouge: Louisiana State University Press, 2010.

Robertson, James I., Jr. *The Stonewall Brigade*. Baton Rouge: Louisiana State University Press, 1963.

————. *Stonewall Jackson: The Man, the Soldier, the Legend*. New York: Macmillan, 1997.

Robertson, Stacey M. *Hearts Beating for Liberty: Women Abolitionists in the Old Northwest.* Chapel Hill: University of North Carolina Press, 2010.

Robertson, William Glenn. *Back Door to Richmond: The Bermuda Hundred Campaign, April–June 1864.* Baton Rouge: Louisiana State University Press, 1987.

Robins, Glenn. *The Bishop of the Old South: The Ministry and Civil War Legacy of Leonidas Polk.* Macon, GA: Mercer University Press, 2006.

Rogers, D. Laurence. *Apostles of Equality: The Birneys, the Republicans, and the Civil War.* East Lansing: Michigan State University Press, 2011.

Rogers, James A. *Richard Furman: Life and Legacy.* Macon, GA: Mercer University Press, 1985.

Roland, Charles P. *Albert Sidney Johnston, Soldier of Three Republics.* 2nd ed. Lexington: University Press of Kentucky, 2001.

Rolfs, David. *No Peace for the Wicked: Northern Protestant Soldiers and the American Civil War.* Knoxville: University of Tennessee Press, 2009.

Romero, Sidney J. *Religion in the Rebel Ranks.* Lanham, MD: University Press of America, 1983.

Ronda, Bruce A. *Elizabeth Palmer Peabody: A Reformer on Her Own Terms.* Cambridge, MA: Harvard University Press, 1999.

Rose, Anne C. *Victorian America and the Civil War.* New York: Cambridge University Press, 1994.

Rose, Willie Lee. *Rehearsal for Reconstruction: The Port Royal Experiment.* Indianapolis: Bobbs-Merrill, 1964.

Roth, Randolph. *American Homicide.* Cambridge, MA: Belknap Press of Harvard University Press, 2009.

Rowland, Thomas J. *George B. McClellan and Civil War History: In the Shadow of Grant and Sherman.* Kent, OH: Kent State University Press, 1998.

Rubin, Anne Sarah. *A Shattered Nation: The Rise and Fall of the Confederacy, 1861–1868.* Chapel Hill: University of North Carolina Press, 2005.

———. *Through the Heart of Dixie: Sherman's March and American Memory.* Chapel Hill: University of North Carolina Press, 2014.

Rugemer, Edward Bartlett. *The Problem of Emancipation: The Caribbean Roots of the American Civil War.* Baton Rouge: Louisiana State University Press, 2008.

Ruminski, Jarret. *The Limits of Loyalty: Ordinary People in Civil War Mississippi.* Jackson: University Press of Mississippi, 2017.

Ryrie, Alec. *Protestants: The Faith That Made the Modern World.* New York: Viking, 2017.

Saillant, John, ed. *Afro-Virginian History and Culture.* New York: Garland, 1999.

Salyer, Lucy E. *Under the Starry Flag: How a Band of Irish Americans Joined the Fenian Revolt and Sparked a Crisis over Citizenship.* Cambridge, MA: Harvard University Press, 2018.

Samito, Christian G. *Becoming American under Fire: Irish Americans, African Americans, and the Politics of Citizenship during the Civil War Era.* Ithaca, NY: Cornell University Press, 2009.

Sandeen, Ernest R. *The Roots of Fundamentalism: British and American Millenarianism, 1800–1930*. Chicago: University of Chicago Press, 1970.

Sands, Kathleen M. *America's Religious Wars: The Embattled Heart of Our Public Life*. New Haven, CT: Yale University Press, 2019.

Scarborough, William Kauffman. *Masters of the Big House: Elite Slaveholders of the Mid-Nineteenth-Century South*. Baton Rouge: Louisiana State University Press, 2003.

Schaff, Morris. *The Spirit of Old West Point, 1858–1862*. Boston: Houghton Mifflin, 1907.

Schantz, Mark S. *Awaiting the Heavenly Country: The Civil War and America's Culture of Death*. Ithaca, NY: Cornell University Press, 2008.

Scheel, Gary L. *Rain, Mud, & Swamps: 31st Missouri Volunteer Infantry Regiment Marching through the South during the Civil War with General William T. Sherman*. Pacific, MO: Gary L. Scheel, 1998.

Schweiger, Beth Barton. *The Gospel Working Up: Progress and the Pulpit in Nineteenth-Century Virginia*. New York: Oxford University Press, 2000.

Schweiger, Beth Barton, and Donald G. Mathews, eds. *Religion in the American South: Protestants and Others in History and Culture*. Chapel Hill: University of North Carolina Press, 2003.

Scott, Sean A. *A Visitation of God: Northern Civilians Interpret the Civil War*. New York: Oxford University Press, 2011.

Sears, Stephen W. *Chancellorsville*. Boston: Houghton Mifflin, 1996.

———. *Controversies and Commanders: Dispatches from the Army of the Potomac*. Boston: Houghton Mifflin, 1999.

———. *George B. McClellan: The Young Napoleon*. New York: Ticknor & Fields, 1988.

———. *Landscape Turned Red: The Battle of Antietam*. New York: Ticknor & Fields, 1983.

———. *Lincoln's Lieutenants: The High Command of the Army of the Potomac*. New York: Simon & Schuster, 2017.

———. *To the Gates of Richmond: The Peninsula Campaign*. New York: Ticknor & Fields, 1992.

Sedgwick, John. *Blood Moon: An American Epic of War and Splendor in the Cherokee Nation*. New York: Simon & Schuster, 2018.

Selby, John G. *Meade: The Price of Command, 1863–1865*. Kent, OH: Kent State University Press, 2018.

Sernett, Milton C. *Harriet Tubman: Myth, Memory, and History*. Durham, NC: Duke University Press, 2007.

———. *North Star Country: Upstate New York and the Crusade for African American Freedom*. Syracuse, NY: Syracuse University Press, 2002.

Sexton, Jay. *A Nation Forged by Crisis: A New American History*. New York: Basic Books, 2018.

Shalev, Eran. *American Zion: The Old Testament as a Political Text from the Revolution to the Civil War*. New Haven, CT: Yale University Press, 2013.

Shattuck, Gardiner, Jr. *A Shield and Hiding Place: The Religious Life of the Civil War Armies*. Macon, GA: Mercer University Press, 1985.

Shea, William M. *The Lion and the Lamb: Evangelicals and Catholics in America*. New York: Oxford University Press, 2004.

Sheehan-Dean, Aaron. *The Calculus of Violence: How Americans Fought the Civil War*. Cambridge, MA: Harvard University Press, 2018.

———. *Why Confederates Fought: Family and Nation in Civil War Virginia*. Chapel Hill: University of North Carolina Press, 2007.

Showalter, Elaine. *The Civil Wars of Julia Ward Howe: A Biography*. New York: Simon & Schuster, 2016.

Siddali, Silvana R. *From Property to Person: Slavery and the Confiscation Acts, 1861–1862*. Baton Rouge: Louisiana State University Press, 2005.

Silber, Nina. *Daughters of the Union: Northern Women Fight the Civil War*. Cambridge, MA: Harvard University Press, 2005.

Silbey, Joel H. *The American Political Nation, 1838–1893*. Stanford, CA: Stanford University Press, 1991.

———. *A Respectable Minority: The Democratic Party in the Civil War Era*. New York: W. W. Norton, 1977.

Silkenat, David. *Driven from Home: North Carolina's Civil War Refugee Crisis*. Athens: University of Georgia Press, 2016.

———. *Moments of Despair: Suicide, Divorce, and Debt in Civil War Era North Carolina*. Chapel Hill: University of North Carolina Press, 2011.

———. *Raising the White Flag: How Surrender Defined the American Civil War*. Chapel Hill: University of North Carolina Press, 2019.

Silver, James W. *Confederate Morale and Church Propaganda*. Tuscaloosa: Confederate Publishing, 1957.

Simpson, Craig M. *A Good Southerner: The Life of Henry A. Wise of Virginia*. Chapel Hill: University of North Carolina Press, 1985.

Simpson, James. *Permanent Revolution: The Reformation and the Illiberal Roots of Liberalism*. Cambridge, MA: Belknap Press of Harvard University Press, 2019.

Sinha, Manisha. *The Counterrevolution of Slavery: Politics and Ideology in Antebellum South Carolina*. Chapel Hill: University of North Carolina Press, 2000.

Skelton, William B. *An American Profession of Arms: The Army Officer Corps, 1784–1861*. Lawrence: University Press of Kansas, 1993.

Slotkin, Richard. *The Long Road to Antietam: How the Civil War Became a Revolution*. New York: Liveright, 2012.

———. *No Quarter: The Battle of the Crater, 1864*. New York: Random House, 2009.

Smith, Adam I. P. *The Stormy Present: Conservatism and the Problem of Slavery in Northern Politics, 1846–1865*. Chapel Hill: University of North Carolina Press, 2017.

Smith, H. Shelton. *In His Image, But . . . : Racism in Southern Religion, 1780–1910*. Durham, NC: Duke University Press, 1972.

Smith, Michael Thomas. *The Enemy Within: Fears of Corruption in the Civil War North.* Charlottesville: University of Virginia Press, 2011.

Smith, Ted A. *The New Measures: A Theological History of Democratic Practice.* New York: Cambridge University Press, 2007.

———. *Weird John Brown: Divine Violence and the Limits of Ethics.* Stanford, CA: Stanford University Press, 2015.

Snay, Mitchell. *Gospel of Disunion: Religion and Separatism in the Antebellum South.* New York: Cambridge University Press, 1993.

Sodergren, Steven E. *The Army of the Potomac in the Overland and Petersburg Campaigns: Union Soldiers and Trench Warfare, 1864–1865.* Baton Rouge: Louisiana State University Press, 2017.

Sommerville, Diane Miller. *Rape and Race in the Nineteenth-Century South.* Chapel Hill: University of North Carolina Press, 2004.

Spurgeon, Ian Michael. *Man of Douglas, Man of Lincoln: The Political Odyssey of James Henry Lane.* Columbia: University of Missouri Press, 2008.

Stahr, Walter. *Seward: Lincoln's Indispensable Man.* New York: Simon and Schuster, 2012.

Stanley, Matthew J. *The Loyal West: Civil War and Reunion in Middle America.* Urbana: University of Illinois Press, 2017.

Startup, Kenneth Moore. *The Root of All Evil: The Protestant Clergy and the Economic Mind of the Old South.* Athens: University of Georgia Press, 1997.

Stauffer, John, and Benjamin Soskis. *The Battle Hymn of the Republic: A Biography of the Song That Marches On.* New York: Oxford University Press, 2013.

———. *The Black Hearts of Men: Radical Abolitionists and the Transformation of Race.* Cambridge, MA: Harvard University Press, 2002.

Stephan, Scott. *Redeeming the Southern Family: Evangelical Women and Domestic Devotion in the Antebellum South.* Athens: University of Georgia Press, 2008.

Steplyk, Jonathan M. *Fighting Means Killing: Civil War Soldiers and the Nature of Combat.* Lawrence: University Press of Kansas, 2018.

Stith, Matthew M. *Extreme Civil War: Guerrilla Warfare, Environment, and Race on the Trans-Mississippi Frontier.* Baton Rouge: Louisiana State University Press, 2016.

Stout, Harry S. *American Aristocrats: A Family, a Fortune, and the Making of American Capitalism.* New York: Basic Books, 2017.

———. *Upon the Altar of the Nation: A Moral History of the Civil War.* New York: Viking, 2006.

Stowe, Steven M. *Keep the Days: Reading the Civil War Diaries of Southern Women.* Chapel Hill: University of North Carolina Press, 2018.

Stowell, Daniel W. *Rebuilding Zion: The Religious Reconstruction of the South, 1863–1877.* New York: Oxford University Press, 1998.

Strathern, Alan. *Unearthly Powers: Religious and Political Change in World History.* New York: Cambridge University Press, 2019.

Strausbaugh, John. *City of Sedition: The History of New York City during the Civil War.* New York: Twelve, 2016.

Stutler, Boyd B. *West Virginia in the Civil War.* Charleston, WV: Education Foundation, 1966.

Swanberg, W. A. *Sickles the Incredible.* New York: Charles Scribner's Sons, 1956.

Symonds, Craig L. *Stonewall of the West: Patrick Cleburne and the Civil War.* Lawrence: University Press of Kansas, 1997.

Syrett, John. *The Civil War Confiscation Acts: Failing to Reconstruct the South.* New York: Fordham University Press, 2005.

Taaffe, Stephen R. *Commanding the Army of the Potomac.* Lawrence: University Press of Kansas, 2006.

Tap, Bruce. *Over Lincoln's Shoulder: The Committee on the Conduct of the War.* Lawrence: University of Kansas Press, 1998.

Tarter, Brent. *Daydreams and Nightmares: A Virginia Family Faces Secession and War.* Charlottesville: University of Virginia Press, 2015.

Taylor, Amy Murrell. *The Divided Family in Civil War America.* Chapel Hill: University of North Carolina Press, 2005.

———. *Embattled Freedom: Journeys through the Civil War's Slave Refugee Camps.* Chapel Hill: University of North Carolina Press, 2018.

Teters, Kristopher. *Practical Liberators: Union Officers in the Western Theater during the Civil War.* Chapel Hill: University of North Carolina Press, 2018.

Thomas, Emory M. *Bold Dragoon: The Life of J. E. B. Stuart.* New York: Harper & Row, 1986.

———. *The Confederate Nation, 1861–1865.* New York: Harper & Row, 1979.

———. *Robert E. Lee: A Biography.* New York: W. W. Norton, 1995.

Thomson, David. "Oliver Otis Howard: Reassessing the Legacy of the 'Christian General.'" *American Nineteenth Century History* 10:3 (2009): 273–98.

Thornton, J. Mills, III. *Politics and Power in a Slave Society: Alabama, 1800–1860.* Baton Rouge: Louisiana State University Press, 1978.

Tomek, Beverly C. *Colonization and Its Discontents: Emancipation, Emigration, and Antislavery in Antebellum Pennsylvania.* New York: New York University Press, 2011.

Townsend, Mary Bobbitt. *Yankee Warhorse: A Biography of Major General Peter Osterhaus.* Columbia: University of Missouri Press, 2010.

Traylor, Richard C. *Born of Water and Spirit: The Baptist Impulse in Kentucky, 1776–1860.* Knoxville: University of Tennessee Press, 2015.

Trefousse, Hans L. *Carl Schurz: A Biography.* Knoxville: University of Tennessee Press, 1982.

———. *Thaddeus Stevens: Nineteenth-Century Egalitarian.* Chapel Hill: University of North Carolina Press, 1997.

Trulock, Alice Rains. *In the Hands of Providence: Joshua L. Chamberlain and the American Civil War.* Chapel Hill: University of North Carolina Press, 1992.

Tsouras, Peter G. *Major General George H. Sharpe and the Creation of American Military Intelligence in the Civil War.* Philadelphia: Casemate, 2018.

Tuchinsky, Adam-Max. *Horace Greeley's* New York Tribune: *Civil War–Era Socialism and the Crisis of Free Labor.* Ithaca, NY: Cornell University Press, 2009.

Tucker, Philip Thomas. *The Confederacy's Fighting Chaplain: Father John B. Bannon.* Tuscaloosa: University of Alabama Press, 1992.

Tucker, Spencer C. *Brigadier General John D. Imboden: Confederate Commander in the Shenandoah.* Lexington: University Press of Kentucky, 2003.

Tunnell, Ted. *Edge of the Sword: The Ordeal of Carpetbagger Marshall H. Twitchell in the Civil War and Reconstruction.* Baton Rouge: Louisiana State University Press, 2001.

Ural, Susannah J., ed. *Civil War Citizens: Race, Ethnicity, and Identity in America's Bloodiest Conflict.* New York: New York University Press, 2010.

———. *Hood's Texas Brigade: The Soldiers and Families of the Confederacy's Most Celebrated Unit.* Baton Rouge: Louisiana State University Press, 2017.

Ussishkin, Daniel. *Morale: A Modern British History.* New York: Oxford University Press, 2017.

Valuska, David L., and Christian B. Keller. *Damn Dutch: Pennsylvania Germans at Gettysburg.* Mechanicsburg, PA: Stackpole Books, 2004.

Varon, Elizabeth R. *Appomattox: Victory, Defeat, and Freedom at the End of the Civil War.* New York: Oxford University Press, 2014.

———. *Armies of Deliverance: A New History of the Civil War.* New York: Oxford University Press, 2019.

———. *Disunion! The Coming of the American Civil War, 1789–1859.* Chapel Hill: University of North Carolina Press, 2008.

Volkman, Lucas P. *Houses Divided: Evangelical Schisms and the Crisis of the Union in Missouri.* New York: Oxford University Press, 2018.

Vondung, Klaus. *The Apocalypse in Germany.* Translated by Stephen D. Ricks. Columbia: University of Missouri Press, 2000.

Von Frank, Albert J. *The Trials of Anthony Burns: Freedom and Slavery in Emerson's Boston.* Cambridge, MA: Harvard University Press, 1998.

Waldman, Steven. *Sacred Liberty: America's Long, Bloody, and Ongoing Struggle for Religious Freedom.* New York: Harper One, 2019.

Wallenstein, Peter, and Bertram Wyatt-Brown, eds. *Virginia's Civil War.* Charlottesville: University of Virginia Press, 2005.

Walters, Ronald G. *American Reformers, 1815–1860.* Rev. ed. New York: Hill and Wang, 1997.

Walther, Eric H. *The Fire-Eaters.* Baton Rouge: Louisiana State University Press, 1992.

Warshauer, Matthew. *Connecticut in the American Civil War: Slavery, Sacrifice, and Survival.* Middletown, CT: Wesleyan University Press, 2011.

Washington, Margaret. *Sojourner Truth's America.* Urbana: University of Illinois Press, 2009.

Waugh, John C. *Surviving the Confederacy: Rebellion, Ruin, and Recovery—Roger and Sara Pryor during the Civil War.* New York: Harcourt, 2002.

Weber, Eugen. *Apocalypses: Prophecies, Cults, and Millennial Beliefs through the Ages.* Cambridge, MA: Harvard University Press, 1999.

Weber, Jennifer L. *Copperheads: The Rise and Fall of Lincoln's Opponents in the North.* New York: Oxford University Press, 2006.

Weber, Max. *The Protestant Ethic and the Spirit of Capitalism.* Translated and edited by Stephen Kalberg. Rev. ed. New York: Routledge, 2012.

Weitz, Eric D. *A World Divided: The Global Struggle for Human Rights in the Age of Nation-States.* Princeton, NJ: Princeton University Press, 2019.

Welch, Richard F. *The Boy General: The Life and Careers of Francis Channing Barlow.* Rutherford, NJ: Fairleigh Dickinson University Press, 2003.

Wells, Jonathan Daniel. *The Origins of the Southern Middle Class, 1800–1861.* Chapel Hill: University of North Carolina Press, 2004.

———. *Women Writers and Journalists in the Nineteenth-Century South.* New York: Cambridge University Press, 2011.

Wert, Jeffry D. *Civil War Barons: The Tycoons, Entrepreneurs, Inventors, and Visionaries Who Forged Victory and Shaped a Nation.* New York: Da Capo, 2018.

———. *A Glorious Army: Robert E. Lee's Triumph, 1862–1863.* New York: Simon & Schuster, 2011.

Wesley, Timothy L. *The Politics of Faith during the Civil War.* Baton Rouge: Louisiana State University Press, 2013.

White, Jonathan W. *Emancipation, the Union Army, and the Reelection of Abraham Lincoln.* Baton Rouge: Louisiana State University Press, 2014.

———. *Midnight in America: Darkness, Sleep, and Dreams during the Civil War.* Chapel Hill: University of North Carolina Press, 2017.

White, Richard. *The Republic for Which It Stands: The United States during Reconstruction and the Gilded Age, 1865–1896.* New York: Oxford University Press, 2017.

White, Ronald C. *Lincoln's Greatest Speech: The Second Inaugural.* New York: Simon & Schuster, 2002.

Whites, LeeAnn, and Alecia P. Long, eds. *Occupied Women: Gender, Military Occupation, and the American Civil War.* Baton Rouge: Louisiana State University Press, 2009.

Wiley, Bell Irvin. *The Life of Billy Yank: The Common Soldier of the Union.* Baton Rouge: Louisiana State University Press, 1952.

Williams, David. *I Freed Myself: African American Self-Emancipation in the Civil War Era.* New York: Cambridge University Press, 2014.

Williams, T. Harry. *Lincoln and His Generals.* New York: Alfred A. Knopf, 1952.

Williamson, Arthur H. *Apocalypse Then: Prophecy and the Making of the Modern World.* Westport, CT: Praeger, 2008.

Wills, Brian Steel. *Confederate General William Dorsey Pender: The Hope of Glory.* Baton Rouge: Louisiana State University Press, 2013.

———. *George Henry Thomas: As True as Steel.* Lawrence: University Press of Kansas, 2012.

———. *Inglorious Passages: Noncombat Deaths in the American Civil War.* Lawrence: University Press of Kansas, 2017.

Wills, Gregory A. *Democratic Religion: Freedom, Authority, and Church Discipline in the Baptist South, 1785–1900.* New York: Oxford University Press, 2003.

Wilson, Charles Reagan. *Baptized in Blood: The Religion of the Lost Cause, 1865–1920.* 2nd ed. Athens: University of Georgia Press, 2009.

Wilson, Clyde Norman. *Carolina Cavalier: The Life and Mind of James Johnston Pettigrew.* Athens: University of Georgia Press, 1990.

Wingfield, Marshall. *General A. P. Stewart, His Life and Letters.* Memphis: West Tennessee Historical Society, 1954.

Winship, Michael P. *Hot Protestants: A History of Puritanism in England and America.* New Haven, CT: Yale University Press, 2018.

Witt, John Fabian. *Lincoln's Code: The Laws of War in American History.* New York: Free Press, 2012.

Wongsrichanalai, Kanisorn. *Northern Character: College-Educated New Englanders, Honor, Nationalism, and Leadership in the Civil War Era.* New York: Fordham University Press, 2016.

Wood, Forrest G. *Black Scare: The Racist Response to Emancipation and Reconstruction.* Berkeley: University of California Press, 1970.

Wood, John Sumner. *The Virginia Bishop: A Yankee Hero of the Confederacy.* Richmond, VA: Garrett & Massie, 1961.

Woodward, Colin Edward. *Marching Masters: Slavery, Race, and the Confederate Army during the Civil War.* Charlottesville: University of Virginia Press, 2014.

Woodworth, Steven E., ed. *The Human Tradition in the Civil War and Reconstruction.* Wilmington, DE: SR Books, 2000.

———. *No Band of Brothers: Problems in the Rebel High Command.* Columbia: University of Missouri Press, 1999.

———. *Nothing but Victory: The Army of the Tennessee, 1861–1865.* New York: Alfred A. Knopf, 2005.

———. *While God Is Marching On: The Religious World of Civil War Soldiers.* Lawrence: University Press of Kansas, 2001.

Work, David. *Lincoln's Political Generals.* Urbana: University of Illinois Press, 2009.

Wright, Ben, and Zachary W. Dresser, eds. *Apocalypse and the Millennium in the American Civil War Era.* Baton Rouge: Louisiana State University Press, 2013.

Wright, Daniel S. *"The First of Causes to Our Sex": The Female Moral Reform Movement in the Antebellum Northeast, 1834–1848.* New York: Routledge, 2006.

Wright, Mike. *City under Siege: Richmond in the Civil War.* Lanham, MD: Rowman and Littlefield, 1995.

Wyatt-Brown, Bertram. *The Shaping of Southern Culture: Honor, Grace, and War, 1760s–1880s.* Chapel Hill: University of North Carolina Press, 2001.

———. *Southern Honor: Ethics and Behavior in the Old South.* New York: Oxford University Press, 1982.

———. *A Warring Nation: Honor, Race, and Humiliation in America and Abroad.* Charlottesville: University of Virginia Press, 2014.

———. *Yankee Saints and Southern Sinners.* Baton Rouge: Louisiana State University Press, 1985.

Wyeth, John Allan. *That Devil Forrest: Life of General Nathan Bedford Forrest.* Edited by Albert Castel. Baton Rouge: Louisiana State University Press, 1989.

Wylie, Paul R. *The Irish General: Thomas Francis Meagher.* Norman: University of Oklahoma Press, 2007.

Wynstra, Robert J. *At the Forefront of Lee's Invasion: Retribution, Plunder, and Clashing Cultures on Richard S. Ewell's Road to Gettysburg.* Kent, OH: Kent State University Press, 2018.

Young, Ralph. *Dissent: The History of an American Idea.* New York: New York University Press, 2015.

Zamoyski, Adam. *Holy Madness: Romantics, Patriots, and Revolutionaries, 1770–1871.* New York: Viking, 1999.

Zelinsky, Wilbur. *Nation into State: The Shifting Symbolic Foundations of American Nationalism.* Chapel Hill: University of North Carolina Press, 1988.

SECONDARY SOURCES—THESES AND DISSERTATIONS

Case, Timothy Allen. "'Living in the Confluence of Two Eternities': The Impact of Politicized Religion in Richmond, Virginia, 1845–1914." MA thesis, San Jose State University, 2015.

Croskery, Robert H. "Religious Rebels: The Religious Views and Motivations of Confederate Generals." Ph.D. diss., University of Western Ontario, 2012.

Lynn, Joshua A. "Preserving the White Man's Republic: The Democratic Party and the Transformation of American Conservatism, 1847–1860." Ph.D. diss., University of North Carolina at Chapel Hill, 2015.

Index